growing
artists

teaching art to young children

Joan Bouza Koster
Broome Community College

Delmar Publishers

 an International Thomson Publishing company

Albany • Bonn • Boston • Cincinnati • Detroit • London • Madrid
Melbourne • Mexico City • New York • Pacific Grove • Paris • San Francisco
Singapore • Tokyo • Toronto • Washington

NOTICE TO THE READER

Cover design: Eva Ruutopõld

Delmar Staff
Senior Editor: Jay S. Whitney
Associate Editor: Erin J. O'Connor Traylor
Project Editor: Timothy Coleman

Production Coordinator: Sandra Woods
Art and Design Coordinator: Timothy Conners
Editorial Assistant: Glenna Stanfield

COPYRIGHT © 1997
By Delmar Publishers
a division of International Thomson Publishing Inc.

The ITP logo is a trademark under license

Printed in the United States of America.

For more information, contact:

Delmar Publishers
3 Columbia Circle, Box 15015
Albany, New York 12212-5015

International Thomson Publishing Europe
Berkshire House
168–173 High Holborn
London WC1V 7AA
England

Thomas Nelson Australia
102 Dodds Street
South Melbourne, 3205
Victoria, Australia

Nelson Canada
1120 Birchmont Road
Scarborough, Ontario
Canada M1K 5G4

International Thomson Editores
Campos Eliseos 385, Piso 7
Col Polanco
11560 Mexico D F Mexico

International Thomson Publishing GmbH
Konigswinterer Strasse 418
53227 Bonn
Germany

International Thomson Publishing Asia
221 Henderson Road
#05-10 Henderson Building
Singapore 0315

International Thomson Publishing—Japan
Hirakawacho Kyowa Building, 3F
2-2-1 Hirakawacho
Chiyoda-ku, Tokyo 102
Japan

1 2 3 4 5 6 7 8 9 10 XXX 02 01 00 99 98 97 96

Library of Congress Cataloging-in-Publication Data

Koster, Joan Bouza.
    Growing artists : art for young children   /   Joan Bouza Koster.
       p.   cm.
    ISBN 0-8273-7544-1
    1. Art—Study and teaching (Early childhood)   I. Title.
LB1139.5.A78K67   1996
372.5'044—dc20

96–17237
CIP

Contents

~~~~~~

Preface

~~~~~~

Nothing ever becomes real till it is experienced.

JOHN KEATS (LETTER TO HIS CHILDREN, FEBRUARY, 1819)

TO WHOM IS THIS BOOK ADDRESSED?

This is a book about art and young children. It is an outgrowth of a concern for the direction early childhood art education will take as we head into the twenty-first century. It speaks first and foremost to the students who are now preparing to work with young children. They, more than anyone, will most directly influence the young artists of our future. But it is also addressed to anyone, whether parent, teacher, or caregiver, who has ever given a child a crayon and said, "Draw me a picture"—and then wondered at the result.

WHAT IS THE PURPOSE OF THIS BOOK?

There have been many thoughtful educators who have considered the meaning and importance of child art, and many theories and approaches to early childhood art education have been suggested. This book offers a synthesis of workable ideas from which the practicing educator can develop a style and method of working with art. A good program will foster the growth of children physically, mentally, socially, and cognitively, and will allow them to exercise their inherent creativity.

To help the inexperienced practitioner, the book suggests ways to deliver rich and varied open-ended art explorations and aesthetically challenging activities in the context of a multicultural society. Both thematic and project approaches are presented in a format appropriate for young children. The use of the computer as an art tool is encouraged as a way to start children on the path of computer literacy. Developmentally appropriate cooperative art activities are recommended. Finally, the role of assessment and the presentation of art projects in an early childhood art program is considered and a plan of action suggested.

This book provides a resource of ideas, methods, and suggested practices which will provide a springboard for readers to design their own curriculum. As such this book goes beyond the presentation of isolated "projects"; instead it provides child-tested traditional and innovative art experiences in such a way that inexperienced teachers can use them as a resource and model while creating their own repertoire of activities. More experienced early childhood educators may expand their current art offerings and integrate them more fully into the total educational program they offer.

WHAT IS THE THEORETICAL APPROACH OF THIS BOOK?

The approach taken in this book is based on over 25 years of working with and observing children and adults of all ages as they have grown successfully through art. It presents the unique viewpoint of a practicing educator and professional artist who has taught in the early childhood classroom, the elementary art room, and at the college level. It is grounded in a developmental theory of child art which includes the recent research and thought of Howard Gardner (1991) and Anna Kindler and Bernard Darras (1994). It broadens the role of art in early childhood education, drawing on the use of art as a means of expressing children's experiences, as exemplified in the Reggio Emilia preprimary programs (Edwards, Gandini, and Forman, 1992). Art is also linked with early literacy development (Olson, 1992; Cecil and Lauritzen, 1995) in a way that makes sense in the varied educational environments where young artists are found: child care, home care, preschool, kindergarten, and early primary.

It also represents the author's firmly held belief that of all the experiences an adult can provide a child, the most important is the relationship between that child and that caring adult. Art provides a perfect context in which to initiate deep and thoughtful dialogues with children. However, art is an intensely personal experience, and one about which every adult has a deep-seated feeling of great confidence, of mediocrity, or of incompetence. How teachers relate to young artists directly reflects their beliefs about themselves as artists. Throughout this book there are thought-provoking questions, intellectual challenges, and affirming activities that are designed to help readers become more attuned to their artistic heritage, philosophy, and experiences. This foundation will provide the necessary preparation to successfully guide young children as they create their artistic personas.

WHAT IS THE PLAN OF THIS BOOK?

The Chapter

Each chapter in this book focuses on a theme relevant to early childhood art. The information is presented in the form of answers to questions that students new to this field might have. Within each chapter there are many special features.

Young Artists at Work. Short vignettes, based on the observations of real children in real situations, provide vivid pictures of the kind of child art interactions most new teachers can expect to find in their rooms.

Art Words. Interspersed throughout the book are relevant art words and their definitions or examples of how to use them.

 Teacher Tips. These are brief practical ideas that may prove helpful to teachers who are just starting out.

 Teacher-to-Parent. Sample letters to parents are included in many chapters to provide examples of the ways teachers should reach out to the parents of the children they teach.

 Special Needs. These are suggestions for adapting art activities to make them accessible to all children.

Music Boxes. These offer many lively songs and chants to accompany art activities.

Quotations. Interspersed throughout the book are carefully chosen quotations taken from a wide variety of sources. These are designed to provoke, to inspire, and to give a feel for the wide range of thought concerning the topic of early childhood art. The quotes provide a representative survey of the researchers, educators, philosophers, and writers who have been involved with children and their art, both in the past and in the present.

Further Reading. The books listed in this section are briefly annotated. They have been specifically selected either to expand on the ideas and concepts presented in the chapter or to further personal artistic and creative development. Readers are encouraged to read as many of these books as possible if they wish to become well grounded in the field and to learn more about themselves as artists. Instructors may choose to use these books as supplements to the text or as recommended reading.

Art Focus Sections. In these sections a particular art medium is discussed in detail and activities appropriate for different ages of children are modeled. Each section includes a list of materials needed, how to introduce the activity, what to say during the activity, and how to conclude.

Studio Pages. Each chapter ends with a series of Studio Pages. These pages contain activities designed to help readers think further about the information presented in the chapter. Use additional sheets of paper when necessary.

Instructor's Manual. If the book is being used as a text for a course preparing college students to teach young children, class uses for the Studio Pages, including many cooperative learning activities, will be found in the accompanying instructor's manual, available by ordering ISBN 082737545X.

Appendices. Appendix A: Teacher Resources provides a list of sources for the special supplies, computer software, art prints and artifacts, and recipes mentioned in the text. Appendix B: Children's Literature on Art is a bibliography of over 300 children's books about art, each annotated with suggested uses and cross-referenced by topic. Appendix C: Teacher References is an annotated listing of books that will provide further information about art for the teacher of young children.

WHAT DO THE TERMS MEAN?

Young Artist

For the purposes of this book the term *young artist* (or *child*) is used to refer to children 18 months to eight years old. This age range is based on the mode of delivery for art education in our society. Most children eight and under are in settings such as kindergarten, primary programs, preschool, child care, nursery school, play groups, or at home, where art activities take a wide range of directions depending on the training and knowledge of the adult in charge.

In addition, these years also form an artistically and conceptually unified whole, because it is during this span that children develop their first graphic symbol system through art. Children in the midst of this process need a nourishing environment in which to create art.

Educational Settings

Programs for young children meet in many different locations, ranging from private homes and church basements to public and private school buildings. For simplicity the term *classroom* refers to the inside area used by the children and outdoor area has been used to refer to any contiguous outside play area. Adaptations are included for activities in the home as are suggestions about when to use the outdoor area.

Guiding Adults

Throughout the text the term *guiding adult* is used interchangeably with teacher, parent, aide, and caregiver. The role of the adult in art is to be a guide—someone who selects and prepares the supplies, maps out the possible routes, provides encouragement along the way, takes time for side trips, and celebrates each milepost the child reaches.

Acknowledgments

Writing a book takes a tremendous amount of love and effort. I could not possibly have succeeded without the help of my family, co-workers, and friends. The constant support and encouragement of my husband, Harold, who patiently listened to my ideas for years and has always said, "You should write the book," helped me keep going no matter how tired I was. Nor could it have come about without the love and sacrifice of my children, Matthew and Laurel, who have provided me with the joy of watching them grow from helpless infants to active teens. They have shouldered extra chores, understood why I missed their sports events, and made room in our busy home for "Mom's book." I also want to thank my parents for teaching me that anything is possible if you believe in yourself.

Michael Schafer was the first to suggest that I share my expertise in art with future teachers at the college level. Darlene Gumaer, Sandy Moran, Jeanne Rose, and Ann Scalzo, together representing over 40 years of experience with young children in a wide variety of educational settings, provided invaluable feedback on the practicality and readablity of this book. Michael Scalzo, of the Endicott Teachers Resource Center, took precious time to review the computer sections and to teach me the intimate details of surfing the Internet. Barbara Nilsen, Chair of the Early Childhood Education Department at Broome Community College, also took time from writing her own book to review my work and provided needed encouragement throughout the intense writing process. Susan McCormick and Elizabeth Manvell provided both support and understanding.

I wish to thank the Broome County Kidstuff program and the Maine Endwell School District for allowing me to spend many hours visiting their early childhood programs and photographing the children. I also appreciate the time Sal Paredez, of the Handicapped Children's Association of Broome County, spent sharing with me the early childhood program they offer.

I wish to give special thanks to Mary Jane Walker, who openly welcomed me into her classroom for many hours over the past year, allowing me to interrupt her program, set up activities, and photograph with abandon. She also contacted parents and obtained the necessary permissions from many families.

I also appreciate the kindness of my fellow teachers Carol Sienko and Ken Rozek, who helped collect samples of children's artwork and allowed photography in their rooms.

The photographs in this book represent the work of many people. I would like to personally thank the following parents and children for helping with the photography: The Doyle family, Allison Breidinger, Edgar Bugoyou, Erica Robinson, and David Tseng. Phil Rose provided invaluable assistance with the developing and printing.

I want to thank Jay S. Whitney, Senior Editor at Delmar Publishers, for providing the inspiration to create this book and for listening to my calls for help. My thanks also go to all the members of my publishing team who have seen this work through to completion.

For the last two years the children in my primary classroom have lived my book with me. They have followed the process, experienced the highs and the lows, watched me struggle, and shared my successes. For these children writing a book has become a very real thing. That alone has made this whole process worthwhile.

I must also thank all the thousands of children I have taught in the last 26 years, each of whom in their own special way helped me become a better teacher of art.

Lastly, the thoughtful and detailed advice of the following reviewers was invaluable:

Kristin G. Congdon,
University of Central Florida,
Orlando, Florida

Claudia Cornett,
Wittenberg University,
Springfield, Ohio

Jill Englebright Fox,
Virginia Commonwealth University,
Richmond, Virginia

Eilene Glasgow,
Pacific Lutheran University,
Tacoma, Washington

Jann James,
Oglethorpe University,
Duluth, Georgia

Michael Marsh,
DeAnza College,
Cupertino, California

Ann Schmidt,
Champlain College,
Burlington, Vermont

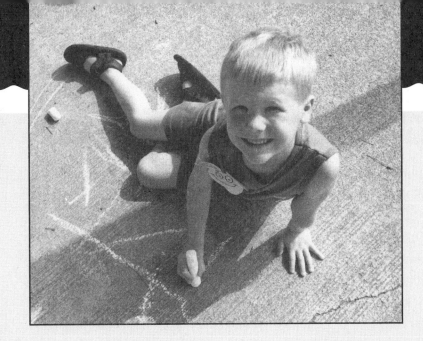

Growing Young Artists

Philosophy and Goals

> " *Every day everywhere in the world, young children make a fist around a pencil or crayon, or drag their fingers in earth or frosty windows, to scribble.* "
>
> •
>
> SYLVIA FEIN (1993, P. XII)

Questions addressed in this chapter:

Who are the young artists?

Why should art be taught to young children?

What are the components of a thoughtful art program for young children?

What direction do current research and educational theory provide?

What should the guiding principles be?

What does a thoughtful art program look like?

SUMMARY: The Thoughtful Art Program

FURTHER READING

ART FOCUS: Getting Ready for Art

Young Artists at Work

Maria, age one, pulls her finger through a drop of spilled cereal and then licks her finger.

Steve, age two, amuses himself during his bath by decorating the tub with handfuls of bubbly white soap foam.

Lorna, age four, splashes through a puddle and then with careful deliberation makes a pattern of wet footprints on the pavement. With every step she looks back to see her "trail."

Paul, age six, spends a busy day at the beach building sand mountains and decorating them with broken shells and beach pebbles. Other children join in his fun, and watch excitedly as the surf slowly creeps up and then finally washes each mountain away.

WHO ARE THE YOUNG ARTISTS?

Each of these children is a young artist, investigating elements of visual art—line, shape, color, texture, form, and pattern. They are making the same artistic discoveries and decisions that all of us have made in our own lives. In doing so they are repeating a process that has gone on as long as people have inhabited the earth. Like the circles, swirls, and lines on the walls of the caves and cliffs that were the canvasses of the earliest men and women, the chiseled carvings on temple walls at Tikal, the stone-smoothed satin black pot of a Pueblo potter, and the flowing line of the Chinese calligrapher, the art of young children expresses their personal and cultural history. Their art reflects who they are at that moment in time.

Children between the ages of one and eight are busy discovering the nature of their world. They are not consciously artists in the way an adult is. They do not stop and say, "Now I am creating a piece of art." They are not creating a product—they are involved in a process!

They are at play. They enjoy manipulating the many materials that they find around them and expressing their creative power to change a piece of their world. They are communicating their feelings and what they have learned. As they learn, they grow and develop.

They gain control over their large and small muscles. Their skill in handling different materials improves. They expand their repertoire of lines and shapes and patterns. They repeat their successes over and over. They learn to use symbols that have meaning not just to themselves, but to the others around them. By the time these young artists reach the age of eight, they already know a great deal about the world of artistic expression.

But these growing artists are also still very young. They do not yet have skillful control over all their materials. They make messes. They cry if they spill paint on their shoes. Young children have short attention spans and are infinitely curious. They get distracted by a noise and run off, leaving their paintbrush in the middle of their picture. They do not always do things in an orderly sequence. Sometimes they glue their paper to the table. Sometimes they drop clay on the floor and unintentionally step on it in trying to pick it up. Anyone working with these children soon learns that great patience is needed.

But most important, each child is unique. As young as they are, they each bring to the art experience their own personalities as well as their family and cultural heritage. Some are timid. Others are bold. Some have used many art materials and others have used none. One child may have been taught not to get dirty and will not touch finger-paint, while another revels in being as messy as possible and smears paint up to the elbows. They grow at their own pace, but through sensitive planning of art experiences, each child can find personal joy and growth through art.

Developmentally Appropriate Practice: DAP

> A developmentally appropriate curriculum for young children is planned to be appropriate for the age span of the children within the group and is implemented with attention to the different needs, interests, and developmental levels of those individual children.
>
> NATIONAL ASSOCIATION FOR THE EDUCATION OF YOUNG CHILDREN (NAEYC) (1986, P. 6)

Developmentally appropriate practice (DAP) is based on the belief that there are universal, predictable sequences of physical, emotional, social, and cognitive growth. Within these sequences each child follows a unique pattern influenced by personality, learning style, and family background. As proposed by the National Association for the Education of Young Children (NAEYC) and representing the research and experience of many educators, appropriate learning activities should match the children's developing abilities. DAP activities are designed to match the children's ability levels so that they will meet with success while facing challenges that are within their capabilities.

DAP directs us to ask ourselves two questions when selecting art activities for young children.

1. Is this art activity suitable for children of this age?
2. Is this art activity suitable for this particular child?

Within the age range of one-and-a-half through eight, children vary tremendously. A child of 18 months will react to art explorations very differently from an eight-year-old. Age categories can provide a useful way of understanding how children will generally behave. At the same time, however, children mature at different rates and even within an age group there may be marked differences in the way children approach art. The age divisions used in this text follow those of the NAEYC (1986). They are intended to provide general guidelines from which appropriate art activities may be selected.

Guidelines For Selecting Appropriate Art Activities

Children in these age groupings *usually* exhibit these typical characteristics.

Toddler. Throughout the text *toddler* is used to refer to children from 18 months to three years who may exhibit these characteristics:

- Need to explore with all their senses and may still put objects in mouth
- Have limited self-regulatory skills and require close supervision
- Engage in parallel play
- Show developing control over large muscles in the arm

- Have short attention spans, usually less than 10 minutes, and need simple materials to explore
- Need to repeat actions over and over
- Say names of objects and understand more words than they can say

Appropriate art activities for toddlers. Appropriate art activities for toddlers allow them to manipulate and explore art materials without pressure to produce a product. Art materials should be simple and direct, with few instructions required. They should be safe if ingested. Explorations must be closely supervised with active adult participation.

Three-year-olds. Most children of this age display these characteristics:

- Show increasing self-control and can work side by side in small groups
- Usually will not put inappropriate items in mouth
- Show developing control over wrists, hands, and fingers
- Have an increasing attention span and can work independently for 10 minutes or more at a time

Appropriate art activities for three-year-olds. Three-year-olds may be offered more varied materials that require finer muscle control. Representation of actual objects should not be expected and process must be valued over product. Children of this age can be encouraged to use art materials in self-initiated, creative, and expressive ways. Adult supervision is still required, but the teacher may move away at times and allow children to work independently.

Four- and five-year-olds. Most children in this age range show the following behaviors:

- Show developing control over wrists and hands and exhibit a more mature grip on drawing tools
- Can concentrate for a period of time, 30 minutes or more, on a self-selected art activity
- Can work together in small groups of three to six on common projects and are able to share supplies
- May dictate or write stories with invented spelling
- Can follow a three-step direction
- Can classify objects and make predictions
- Can use words to describe the qualities of objects—color, size, and shape—and can begin to sort them by those qualities

Appropriate art activities for four- and five-year-olds. Children of this age can participate in a wide range of self-selected individual and group explorations, using a variety of art media. They are ready for aesthetic and art appreciation activities as well. As they develop graphic symbols they can begin to use art to express their ideas and learning in other curriculum areas. Children can be expected to work on their own and manage their own materials with occasional adult supervision.

Six-, seven- and eight-year-olds. Most children in this age range show the following behaviors:

- Hold drawing tools with a mature grip
- Can concentrate for an hour or more on a self-selected art activity, and can return to an ongoing art project over a period of several days
- Initiate, participate, and assume roles in cooperative group art activities
- May write stories, inspired by or illustrated with their art work, with the majority using conventional spelling by the end of the eighth year

- Understand that objects can share one or more qualities and can use this knowledge to make predictions and comparisons, and to draw conclusions.

Appropriate art activities for six- to eight-year-olds. Primary age children continue to need many opportunities to participate in self-selected art explorations using a wide variety of art media. They can also begin to be introduced to art activities that require specialized skills and sequencing behavior such as papier-mâché, weaving, and pottery making. Children can be expected to use acquired skills and knowledge to respond to experiences and to demonstrate what they have learned in other curriculum areas. As they develop a greater understanding of time, the earth, and its peoples, they can be introduced to the social and historical context of a wide variety of art forms. In the primary years children can also be expected to take more personal responsibility for initiating, organizing, and carrying out individual and cooperative art activities.

WHY SHOULD ART BE TAUGHT TO YOUNG CHILDREN?

Their art is important not so much for the finished product but for the mediation it provides between their inner and outer worlds.

GEORGE SZEKELY (1991, P. 3)

Art Is Everywhere

We need to teach art to young children because it is an integral part of our lives. Visual art is often approached by adults as a pleasant pastime—something to do when the work of the day is over, objects to see in a museum on a Sunday outing, or an activity done by a few individuals for personal pleasure or fame. But if we truly understand

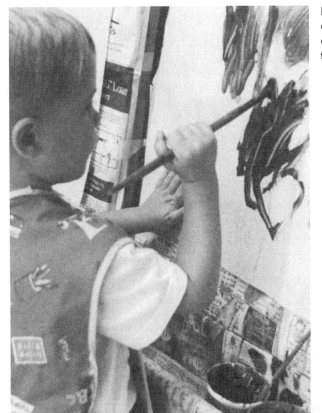

FIGURE 1–1 Art is more than painting at the easel. Through art, children gain skills and develop concepts that increase their ability to function in their environment.

what visual art is, we will suddenly discover how deeply it affects us. It is so much a part of our lives that we can only recognize its existence by imagining its absence. Envision our homes and clothing without patterns, textures, and colors, our books without illustrations, advertisements without photographs, and our homes, furniture, and cars without form. Visual art is the manipulation of the visual and spatial elements of line, texture, color, pattern, shape, and form. Its purpose can be decorative—as in the interior design of a home; communicative—as in an illustration or advertisement; or aesthetically and spiritually expressive—as in a painting of a beautiful sunset.

In the same way, art is a part of every activity we offer children. It is there in the box of blocks we give them to use. It is in the picture book we read to them, or when we ask the child to select the red ball or the blue one. The colors, textures, and forms of the toys we purchase, the pictures we choose to hang on the walls, and the patterns on our floors all form the artistic environment of the child. Art surrounds us constantly. We can choose to ignore it, or we can select activities for children with an awareness of the role art plays in our lives.

Art Is a Child's First Language

Children need opportunities to create art because it is essential to the growth of their minds. Young children do not separate art from their other daily activities. Experimenting with a blue crayon is as compelling as trying to climb up the stairs, and yet, art is different. It provides a record of that experiment and the inner workings that created it.

Art is the first written language. It reflects how children's minds are groping with and forming a concept of the world long before they can put their constructs into words. The world is touched and tasted and observed. Lines, colors, patterns, and textures are explored as they discover what happens when they smear the paste, put black paint over white, or smash their fist into the clay. It is through this exploration of materials and environment that the child artist begins to develop graphic symbols with which to represent his thoughts.

Art Helps Children Grow

Through art, children gain skills and develop concepts which increase their self-confidence and ability to function in their environment.

Physically. Art helps children develop physically by (1) improving the ability to control large and small muscles and (2) by refining hand-eye coordination.

Providing a wide range of materials and tools helps young artists improve their ability to control their large and small muscles. Soft, pliable play doughs and clays improve finger strength. Using brushes at an easel develops control of the arm and wrist. Large and small muscles are exercised and challenged through the manipulation of materials and tools when children stack blocks or pick up tiny beads. Cutting a shape from paper or placing a leaf in a dab of glue requires the eye and hand to work together. Kinesthetic activities such as imagining one's body as clay which can be made into different shapes helps the child relate physical movement and concepts.

Emotionally. Art helps children develop emotionally by encouraging more self-confidence. Providing a wide range of open-ended, developmentally appropriate art activities allows young children to be successful, to feel pride in their work, and become more self-confident.

Art helps children develop emotionally by teaching them to express feelings in a socially acceptable way. Youngsters who know that the adults around them are caring and accepting of their explorations become more open in expressing their feelings through their art. They discover that their art can communicate meaning to others and can bring positive attention to themselves.

Children who feel angry or sad or happy will be encouraged in such an environment to show these feelings in their paintings and drawings. Children who act out in inappropriate ways such as pinching or hitting learn to redirect these activities to a lump of clay. Creating art can help children deal with the stress and violence of our society.

Children also learn to see themselves as capable and trusted when they successfully manipulate complex and dangerous tools such as scissors.

Perceptually. Art helps children develop perceptually by using their senses to develop concepts about the nature of objects, actions, and events. Children learn through their senses. Arnheim (1969) has shown that visual perception is really "visual thinking," a cognitive process that takes images and gives them meaning. Teachers need to provide experiences that are sensually rich and varied, and which require children to use their perceptual abilities in many different ways. Observational and visual perception skills are heightened as children use their senses to study the patterns, colors, textures, and shapes found in nature and in the artwork of others.

Art also enhances perceptive skills by teaching spatial concepts. Art activities allow the child to play with and use spatial concepts such as big/small, long/thin, and top/bottom, as well as the visual and tactile constructs of color, shape, pattern, form, and placement in space.

Socially. Art helps children develop socially by teaching them to (1) take turns and to share materials with others, and (2) to make choices in personal behavior. When children share art supplies and work spaces, they learn to consider the needs of others and learn to choose behavior that contributes to the harmony of the group.

Art provides opportunities for children to work together with others to reach a common goal. Art often requires children to work with others to accomplish a project, or to produce a single, unified piece of art. In doing so they learn to consider the ideas and artistic expression of others. Sharing space and supplies, laughter and tears, and working on group projects with other young artists helps children learn to cooperate and empathize with others.

Cognitively. Art helps children grow cognitively by practicing numeration skills. Art supplies invite counting, sorting, and classifying. Through questioning, children can become aware of the number concepts they use in their artwork. They can count the number of flowers they have drawn or how many blue lines they have made. They can graph the shapes in their collages and sort the leftover paper scraps by color.

Art also provides children with practice in developing skill in planning and sequencing. Well designed art activities require children to make their own decisions and to order their behavior to accomplish a goal. In doing so they learn they must put the glue on the paper first before attaching the piece of yarn. They must dip the brush in the water to clean the paint off it. They must find a pair of scissors if they want to cut out a shape. When they are done, they must put their materials in the proper place so they will be ready to use again.

Art provides children with experience in (1) identifying how properties change, and (2) discovering examples of cause and effect. Handling art materials allows children to explore the properties of different substances—sticky glue, damp clay, shifting sand. Art activities and materials allow the child to observe changes in the physical properties of art supplies, such as drying glue, paint, and clay. Cause and effect is discovered when a child pushes a finger through a piece of play dough and makes a hole in it, or when a painted shape is pressed on a piece of paper and creates a print. Through discussion and questioning, teachers can help children formulate concepts about these changes.

Children's cognitive abilities are enhanced through art when they (1) learn ways to describe and discuss art materials, processes, art forms, and works of art; (2) observe and describe the objects in their environment using art and language; and (3) relate spoken language and graphic symbols. Providing opportunities for children to verbalize about their artwork, and helping them develop a vocabulary for doing so, allows children to develop the relationship between word and picture as a means of communication. Children learn new words to describe what they are doing as they explore new media.

Children share their artwork in a variety of ways, some nonverbally, some through sound effects, others with intricate oral explanations and stories. The receptive adult who understands that this is an important part of language development—the prewriting stage—will provide many opportunities for the interrelation of art and language. For example, when inspired by the characters, settings, and events depicted in their art, children can make up and tell stories orally, or invent new ways of writing them down as they discover the meaning of symbols.

Finally, children develop cognitively by developing a graphic symbol system to record their inner and outer observations. When children are asked to make artwork as a response to an experience, they are being asked to record their ideas and thoughts in a graphic mode. Between the ages of two and eight, children acquire the ability to make symbols and learn that these symbols can communicate to others. Responsive activities, such as making a painting about a visit to the zoo and then talking or writing about it, help them use this developing symbol system and refine the nature of their communication.

Creative problem-solving skills. The unstructured quality of art media allows children to experiment with these familiar materials in new ways. They can use their own ideas and their own power to initiate and to cause change, and to produce original actions and combinations. Paint that drips, paste that does not hold, block towers that fall down, and all the other small difficulties that art materials present challenge children to find their own solutions to problems.

WHAT ARE THE COMPONENTS OF A THOUGHTFUL ART PROGRAM FOR YOUNG CHILDREN?

An art program for young children is made up of four parts that interlink to form a whole: goals, environment, delivery, and activities. They answer the corresponding questions: why, where, how, and which. Careful consideration must be given to each area in order to design the best possible art program.

Goals

Goals are the long-term changes in behavior that the activity are meant to foster in children. They are *why* the activities are selected. These are not something that will happen after one activity or even two. Children need many opportunities in which to learn and to practice. Self-confidence, for example, comes after many successful experiences. A runner does not try out for the Olympics after winning her very first race, but only after years of learning skills and techniques and after many grueling hours of practice.

Young Artists at Work

Eighteen-month-old Olga sits in her play chair at a low table. With her mother beside her, she makes bright red marks across the paper with a thick crayon grasped tightly in the fist of her hand.

Two-year-old Adam punches and pats a ball of play dough. After a while he pokes his finger all the way through it. He holds the hole to his eye and says, "I can see you!"

Three-year-old Sarah carefully spreads white glue on her white paper. Then she spreads some more. She cautiously touches the wet glue and then looks at her fingers. Satisfied, she takes a small piece of colored paper and pats it down in the glue. Glue oozes out and spreads down the paper. "I'm done!" she says happily.

Four-year-old Kendall cuts a piece of blue paper into long rectangular strips. Then he carefully tapes the strips end to end. "I'm making a train," he says. Then he runs around the room, trailing the paper behind him and chugging like a train.

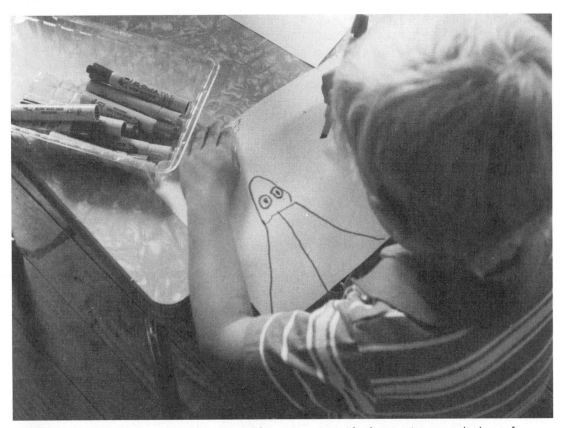

FIGURE 1–2 The well-planned art program provides young artists with adequate time to work, plenty of space, real art materials, and a nurturing environment.

Environment

The environment is everything that surrounds children when they create art. It is *where* the child works and learns. It is the room and any other space used for art—hallways, play areas, and the outdoors. It is how orderly the supplies are and how appropriately sized the furniture is. It is the arrangement of the work space and the other children in it. How this environment is planned and used will determine how much the child can concentrate on learning about and creating art.

Delivery

This is *how* the activities are presented—how the materials are chosen and prepared, what the teachers do and say, and how they respond to the needs and actions of the children. How art activities are offered to young children is as important as which ones are being presented. Teachers need to be aware of how their teaching style, their method of interacting with the children, and what they say all affect how much the children will learn and grow.

Activities

These provide the content—the concepts, tools, media, and techniques—that will foster the children's growth as identified in the goals. They are *what* teachers will use to reach their goals.

Art activities should be carefully selected in order to foster the most encompassing growth. Childhood passes quickly. Art activities, as engrossing as they are, will only occupy a small part of the total day of an active young child and it is best not to waste time on activities that do not help the child learn and grow.

WHAT DIRECTION DO CURRENT RESEARCH AND EDUCATIONAL THEORY PROVIDE?

> Art must be acknowledged as basic to individual development and, therefore, be taught effectively beginning in the early years.
>
> Lila Laskey & Rose Mukerji (1980, p. 2)

Building a Philosophical Base for Art Education

Young children do not have a set goal in mind as they begin to create with art materials, any more than they start the day with the goal of learning 10 new words. They are caught up in the process of doing and making, responding to and playing with the stimuli around them, such as the way paint drips, the way clay stretches and bends, and the way another child tears paper into little bits.

Adults, on the other hand, see the children growing and developing through the art activities they have designed. They see the changes in behavior that come with increasing experience with art materials—from the first tentative brush strokes of the two-year-old to the colorful lines and symbols of the mature eight-year-old. But it is also necessary that children grow in ways that will make them more successful in their interactions with the world.

FIGURE 1-3 "The school bus is flying over the house." Marker—Nick, age 5

The nature of an early childhood art program is determined by a philosophy of child art—the set of beliefs about how young children learn about and through art. For the last 60 years, under the influence of Thomas Dewey (1934), Rhonda Kellogg (1969), Viktor Lowenfeld and W. Lambert Brittain (1987), and others, art has held a central place in the education of children. Visits to most preschools, childcare centers, and primary school programs will find children drawing and painting, and cutting and pasting. However, what the children are actually making as they draw, paint, cut, and paste will vary widely depending on what the adults in charge believe young children are capable of doing, what they think is the correct way to teach them, and how they interpret what child art represents.

To strengthen our philosophy we need to examine contemporary viewpoints, research, and approaches to art in the education and growth of the young. These ideas will help us redefine what art is and should be, and provide direction in the creation of a successful and meaningful art program for children.

Multiple Intelligences: MI Theory

> The degree to which a child's drawing is fully cognitive appears to go far beyond what most adults are yet able to comprehend or are willing to acknowledge.
>
> JANET L. OLSON (1992, P. 38-39)

Based on cognitive research, Howard Gardner (1983, 1991) has proposed that there are seven intellectual capabilities or **intelligences**. These intelligences represent biological and psychological potentials within each individual. Each of us has capabilities in each intelligence with special strengths in one or more of them. Gardner has identified seven intelligences.

1. **Linguistic**: The ability to manipulate the symbols of language
2. **Logical-Mathematical**: The ability to manipulate numerical patterns and concepts
3. **Spatial**: The ability to visualize the configuration of objects in space
4. **Musical**: The ability to manipulate rhythm and sound
5. **Bodily-Kinesthetic**: The ability to use the body to solve problems or to make things
6. **Interpersonal**: The ability to understand and work with others
7. **Intrapersonal**: The ability to understand oneself

Traditional educational practice has focused on strengths in the logical-mathematical and linguistic intelligences. Gardner believes early childhood education for preschoolers and primary age children should be broad-based and rich with materials that enable children to use the range of intelligences. Art as a learning and symbolic tool is particularly valued because it embraces intelligences often overlooked in the traditional educational system.

Gardner's descriptions of these different intelligences give more value to the intellectual skills involved in areas other than language and mathematical reasoning. They provide a framework upon which teachers can build a more educationally balanced program—one that better meets the needs of children with talents in different intelligences. A program that values the varied potentials of the children will have more personalized activities (Gardner, 1995).

Not every activity will engage all the intelligences, but when activities are chosen that incorporate many of the intelligences, children can learn in whatever way best fits their intellectual strengths. In this book, Gardner's intelligences have been interrelated with the physical, social, emotional, perceptual, and cognitive growth areas in order to create models of such balanced art activities.

Artist As Teacher/Teacher As Artist

In addition, in what is characterized as an apprentice-master relationship, Gardner (1991) believes it is of great value for children to be able to watch older peers or competent adults play and work in these areas so they will better understand how the materials can be used and what skills are needed.

Art is best taught by someone who is sensitive to the visual elements in art and the environment and who is comfortable creating with these elements. When adults who work with young children lack experience or confidence in art, they have difficulty fully exploring all facets of art with their children. Gardner advocates that art must be taught by people who have a "...deep knowledge of how to *think* in an artistic medium" (1993, p. 142).

One of the keys to the integration of art at the Reggio Emilia preprimary program is the inclusion of an art educator in each school (Edwards et al., 1992). It is possible for others to bring this same level of artistic mastery to children. Professional artists who can model artistic processes and competencies need to be integrated into art programs. Teachers need to explore their own artistic natures and abilities as well. One of the goals of this book is to help those who work with young children and their art become more aware of and comfortable with their artistic natures, so that they can offer the most meaningful art program possible.

Art, Literacy, and Integrated Learning

Building on the strong relationship between drawing as graphic symbol and the pre-literacy activities of young children, several educators have put forward integrated learning programs in which art and other curriculum areas are combined. Child art,

FIGURE 1–4 Art is a child's first written language.

instead of being viewed as a unique entity unto itself, is seen as an important part of children's developing ability to perceive their environment and express what they have absorbed in a graphic form.

Art and writing. Olson (1992) finds that children learn writing skills in the same way that written language has developed from pictograph to phonetic script. Drawing on the work of Vygotsky (1978), Olson identifies children's drawings as "first order symbols" that represent objects or actions. She proposes that children be encouraged to draw visual narratives and then engage in dialogues about them.

In this cognitive view of art in general and drawing in particular, visual symbols are seen as intricately tied to verbal ones. Olson provides methods by which learners can be identified as visual or verbal in terms of preferred learning styles. She then offers ways to use this information, combined with art, to improve the children's writing. In order to reach all learners, Olson proposes a joining of art and language instruction.

Viewing art as the beginning of writing has tremendous implications for early art education. If art is equivalent to writing, then preliterate children can use their art to record and "read" experiences and ideas. This moves art from the "make and take" table to the forefront of the entire curriculum. Art can be used to record what happened in a science experiment, to make a notation of the pattern in a musical piece, or to compose a story.

Art and knowing: Integrating the curriculum. Some educators feel that creating art in response to a stimulus not only records learning but enriches it multifold. Edwards et al. (1992), New (1990), and Seefeldt (1995), writing in response to observations made at the Reggio Emilia Preprimary Schools in Italy, feel that children's drawings and the quality of cognitive growth they can stimulate have been underestimated in the United States. They feel that visual art needs to be taken much more seriously as a way for children to express what they have learned in all subject areas.

In the Reggio Emilia program, children's art is used as one method of recording observations, ideas, and memories of experiences in which the children have participated. It provides a way to record what they have learned through thematic or child-initiated projects based on the children's interests. Unlike in the United States, where artwork is usually sent home at the end of each day, in Reggio Emilia, children are asked to return to their artwork, to reconsider, to discuss and to critique, to rework, or to repeat their responsive art activities.

FIGURE 1–5 "I'm writing just like you." Marker—Matthew, age 2½

Thematic teaching and the project approach. In a similar vein, Katz and Chard (1991) propose a curriculum based on thematic teaching units in which learning is organized around a theme developed from the interests of the children. Art, rather than being a separate part of the curriculum, is then used throughout the other subject areas as another way children can explore ideas and communicate about the project or theme. Art is used as a communication tool through which children can express concepts and analyze what they have learned.

Integrating art means rethinking the use of the traditional art project where each day a "new " art experience is offered. It means seeing art as more than a way for children to amuse themselves in creating an interesting product. It means approaching art as a way children can interact and communicate about their interests and learning. The total educational program must be carefully planned so that art activities are connected to all areas of learning. Chapter 5 presents a variety of ways to use thematic teaching and curriculum connections in order to accomplish this.

Culture and Visual Perception: The Importance of Environment

McFee and Degge (1981) have pointed out the importance of culture in determining what kind of art children are expected to produce. Analyzing the cross-cultural studies of children's art done by anthropologists, as well as research by psychologists on how children learn to perceive visual elements, they argue that all studies of children's art must consider the cultural environment in which it is created. In a culture such as the United States', in which words are valued over images, beliefs about child art will reflect that value system. The emphasis on using art as another form of language is indicative of this.

All children's art is influenced by the amount and kind of visual stimulation to which they have been exposed, their exposure or lack of exposure to the artwork and symbols of others, and the style of art which they have encountered. In cultures in which verbal learning is stressed, child art often shows less attention to visual detail and exhibits more stereotypical symbols. McFee and Degge argue that activities that foster the growth of visual perception skills are vital; they enable children to express their thoughts more clearly with meaningful images. This is best done by including multi-sensory explorations of the child's environment. Children who have seen, touched, and cared for a rabbit will draw much more detailed and meaningful pictures of a rabbit than children who have only heard a rabbit described.

Creativity and Children

> Every human child is creative, for children's minds develop not just by learning new facts, but also by coming to have ideas which they simply could not have had before.
>
> MARGARET BODEN (1990, p. 37)

Creativity is a confusing term. There is no generally accepted definition. Different ways that creativity has been defined include inventing something new or seeing something in an unusual way. Torrance (1970) defined creativity as being able to see a problem, form ideas about it, and then communicate the results. When children manipulate and explore art materials they are creating something new and unique; in doing so they are being creative. As will be illustrated in chapter 7, creativity is not something that can be taught, but something that must be nurtured.

Creativity is nourished by providing open-ended activities that allow children to experiment with a wide variety of materials. Art activities should provide challenges and the opportunity for children to solve their own problems. As described in chapter 7, there are many parts to the creative process and each of them is vital to the child's learning. Knowledge, motivation, skill development, and the time to immerse oneself in an activity are essential to solving problems. It is the process through which the child turns random marks into graphic symbols. But children's creativity will flourish or wither depending upon the activities offered the child. The goal should be to create an environment in which creativity can flourish.

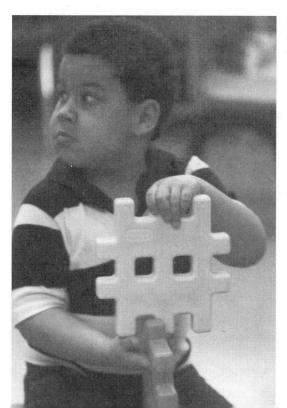

FIGURE 1–6 Creativity is nourished by open-ended activities that provide children with challenges and opportunities to solve their own problems.

Discipline-Based Art Education: DBAE

In the 1980s, the John Paul Getty Center for Education in the Arts (Eisner, 1983) proposed a new curriculum for art education which recommended decreasing emphasis on the making of art and an increase in teaching related to art history, aesthetics, and art criticism. The proposal emphasized talking and verbal learning and relegated hands-on art making to a small part of the art program.

This drew strong response from many researchers in the field (Gardner, 1990a; London, 1991; McWinnie, 1992), who pointed out that it is important for children's cognitive growth to have many opportunities to explore graphic symbol creation through art production. In the arts, being able to produce symbols precedes being able to comprehend them and children must be allowed many hands-on experiences (Winner, Blank, Massey, and Gardner, 1983).

Although the DBAE proposal is not directed specifically toward early childhood art education, it does point out that an art program based entirely on making things does not help children develop a sense of the place of art in their lives and does not prepare them to respond to the art of others. As educators we need to introduce self-reflection about art and examples of adult art into early childhood programs, not as a replacement for hands-on art, but as way of increasing children's visual perceptual abilities and aesthetic sense (Mesrobian, 1992; Wolf, 1984).

National Art Education Association (NAEA) Developmentally Appropriate Practices

The National Art Education Association has incorporated both the recommendations of the NAEYC and the positive aspects of DBAE in their guidelines for early childhood art education. Colbert and Taunton (1992), writing for the NAEA, recommend the following criteria.

1. Children need many opportunities to create art.
2. Children need many opportunities to look at and talk about art.
3. Children need to become aware of art in their everyday lives.

In designing art programs for children, educators are urged to consider the following aspects.

Curriculum. The art program should foster children's cognitive, social, physical, emotional, and perceptual growth. Developmentally appropriate activities should be based on the children's interests, needs, and abilities. Creativity is nurtured through activities that have no predetermined end product. There is a balance between creating art, perceptual activities, and responsive activities that fosters physical, cognitive, and affective growth.

Art Materials. Materials must be safe, easily manipulated, and must allow for experimentation. They are organized so that children can independently choose and return supplies. Art materials and art reproductions reflect the diversity of their culture.

Integration. Art and other curriculum areas are interrelated. Art enhances learning in other subjects and activities in other curriculum areas extend learning in art.

Display. Children should participate in choosing and creating displays. Art should be hung at the children's height to invite children to observe and interact with it.

Responding to Art. Children observe and respond to their own work, the work of their peers, and work created by many other people, in many different times and places.

Anti-Bias and Multicultural Education

Derman-Sparks and the A.B.C. Task Force (1989) suggest ways that art activities can help children accept racial and cultural differences and reject stereotypes. They recommend that art activities should involve using art materials in many colors, and opportunities should be provided to experience art created by people from diverse backgrounds. Through seeing, touching, and talking about a wide variety of art forms selected both from their own culture and from different cultures, children learn that art reflects the ideas and feelings of other people, and increases the children's stores of visual images in a variety of styles. Educators should provide access to the art of others through field trips, guest artists, prints, and artifacts; they should also initiate discussion about these works.

WHAT SHOULD THE GUIDING PRINCIPLES BE?

The viewpoints that have been presented here are based on careful and thoughtful observation of real children and their art. All of them give high value to children's artwork and the associated cognitive growth that art creation fosters. The important elements of each can be incorporated into the following guiding principles that can be used to create a successful art program.

An art program for young children should:

1. Help the child grow—physically, emotionally, socially, perceptually, and cognitively
2. Educate the whole child through activities involving all the multiple intelligences
3. Be taught by someone who can think artistically
4. Integrate art into the curriculum
5. Utilize art as a way children can express what they know
6. Provide perceptual, sensory, and kinesthetic experiences
7. Encourage self-reflection and responding to the art of others
8. Introduce children to rich visual experiences from a wide range of artistic heritages
9. Provide an environment in which the creative process can flourish

WHAT DOES A THOUGHTFUL ART PROGRAM LOOK LIKE?

A classroom for young children often looks for all the world like an artist's studio. The products that come out are children's products, but the process that goes on is the artist's process. The rich availability of easels, paints, brushes, paper, clay, and collage materials helps young children live like artists.

JAMES L. HYMES (1989, P. 81)

These goals, delivered with consideration of how and in what environment children learn successfully, can be the basis for a wonderful program for children. The following is a description of one day of an integrated art program in a preschool setting that services about 15 three- to five-year-olds for half a day.

In this example art is inseparable from the total program. There is no art corner or art project of the day. A wide variety of art materials is available in many places in the room. There is the traditional easel, as well as tables for gluing projects, places to draw and cut, art materials for book making, blocks for building, and a computer art program to try. There is a place to work with modeling materials. Children move to these areas when they have something to express or want to explore. They know where the supplies are located and are confident that they will be there when they need them.

Young Artists at Work

Art is integrated into the curriculum through thematic teaching.

It is a warm spring day, and sunlight streams through the windows of the large bright room. Photographs of fish and sea creatures decorate one wall. Children's books about the sea are on display on the bookshelf. The teacher has already read several books about the sea to the children, and talked to the children about experiences they have had during visits to the beach. Seashells, starfish, fishnets, floats, and other sea-related objects are placed around the room. It is easy to tell that the theme of the week is "Under the Sea."

Children develop socially by working on a group project.

In the center of the room an aide and several children ages three and four are hard at work painting a refrigerator box in which round windows and two doors have been cut. They are using yellow poster paint and large house paintbrushes. Newspapers cover the floor. One child is painting broad strokes of color across the box while the other presses the brush down again and again making rectangular stamp marks in one small section. In the background a tape of the Beatles' classic "Yellow Submarine" can be heard.

The teacher enthusiastically responds to the artistic elements in the child's work with positive feedback.

While the painters work away on the submarine, other children are playing at the water table experimenting with a variety of objects in different sizes, colors, and shapes which either sink or float. At an easel a four-year-old has filled his paper with waving lines using mixtures of blue, green, and yellow paint. The teacher stops to help the painter at the easel remove his smock. "Look at all the blue-greens and turquoises you have made," she tells him, pointing to examples of those colors.

Art activities are open-ended. Children choose to use the art supplies in their own way.

At a round table three children have taken cardboard paper towel tubes from the supply shelf and are decorating them with paper, yarn, glue, and crayons. One child asks the teacher to attach a piece of blue cellophane to the end of his "scope." A second child puts her tube up to her nose. "I'm a swordfish. This is my sword. I have a beautiful sword," she tells another girl. A three-year-old is exploring what happens when he glues a piece of yarn on the tube

Young Artists at Work (continued)

and then pulls it off. In another corner two boys are engaged in noisy, animated play with the trucks and blocks. At the computer a four-year-old is making a multi-colored line travel a wiggly path over the screen.

Visual images from diverse sources enrich the children's experience.

At the game table two children are matching pictures. The cards have been made from prints of paintings, sculptures, and crafts from many cultures that illustrate subjects about the sea. These have been cut out of museum catalogs, glued to card stock, and laminated. On the wall behind them is a poster-size print of one of the artworks. One child finds a card that matches the poster and walks over and compares the two pictures. "They're the same, but this one is littler," he notes, holding the picture card up to the print.

Visitors provide real experiences that lead to integrated learning.

Suddenly everyone stops working. A special visitor has arrived! A father of one of the children brings in two plastic buckets, and all the children circle round. In the tubs are saltwater creatures borrowed from the pet store where he works. The children gather about to study a sea urchin, an anemone, and a sea snake. One child looks at the sea urchin through his cellophane covered tube. "It changes color," he states with wonder. He shares his tube with the others so they can see the change too.

Art and language activities are unified.

When the visitor leaves, some children head off to a table where crayons, markers, and stapled paper booklets are set out. "I'm writing a story about a sea snake and an 'anoome,'" says one five-year-old girl. She draws a long wiggly line on one page. "Here he is very sad." Then she draws a purple circle. "This is his friend, the 'anoome.' Now he is happy!" When she finishes her book, she "reads" it to her teacher, inventing a long detailed story to go with her pictures. "You made your anemone the same color as the one Sam's father brought to show us," the teacher says. The girl beams with pride and skips off to read her book to her friend.

Children explore sensory experiences.

A three-year-old has settled in with a lump of play dough. He rolls out a long "worm." "Look—I can make it wiggle like a sea snake," he says, as he twists and turns

Young Artists at Work (continued)

the play dough. Some children take cardboard tubes to decorate. They want to put cellophane on theirs so they can have their own "scopes." Several other children have taken colored paper, markers, and scissors. They talk quietly together as they invent new sea creatures.

"Mine has tentacles like the sea urchin."

"I'm going to give mine a big mouth and teeth," says another. They cut out their creatures and take them to the teacher.

Children initiate and choose what they want displayed.

"Put a string on them and hang them up so they can swim in our sea," says one. The teacher hangs their creatures from clips suspended from the ceiling. They join other paper sea creatures, made by other children, that are already afloat on the air currents.

Meanwhile several other children have moved into the submarine. They are busy arranging blankets and pillows.

"I think it is softer this way," says Peter. Sam lies down and tries it out. He curls up and sucks his thumb.

"I think we should have a yellow blanket in the yellow submarine," says Sue, bringing in a piece of yellow cloth from the dress-up box. Other children look in through the portholes and make faces at their friends.

Kinesthetic movement grows out of the children's dramatic play and provides a smooth transition to story time.

"We will be the fish swimming around the submarine!" they tell them. The teacher observes the children's play and puts on Saint-Saens' *The Swan*. The music matches the children's actions as they move around the box inventing fish sounds and motions. The teacher joins the dancers, and invites the children in the box to come out and swim in the sea with them. Sue swirls the yellow cloth behind her. "This is my tail," she sings.

"Story time!" says the teacher. "Let's swim to the rug." The dancing children and those working about the room move to the rug and settle around the teacher who reads the story *The Rainbow Fish* by Marcus Pfister. The children lie back and look at their floating sea creatures.

"We need a rainbow fish," says one boy.

Young Artists at Work (continued)

| Children have made plans and look forward to the next day. | "Let's make lots of rainbow fish tomorrow," joins in another.

"I will find some shiny rainbow paper for you," says the teacher. Full of excitement about the next day, the children help put away the materials they have used and then get ready to leave. |

Science, language, and art activities are integrated. The water-table activity is both art and science. The children are not just exploring the objects' physical properties, but also their visual and tactile qualities. Their observations of the living sea life are expressed through the story that is drawn, the clay snake that is modeled, and the sea creature mobiles. Examples of multicultural fine art are used for card matching activities instead of stereotypical sea pictures. This increases the visual discrimination skills of the children, and at the same time they are introduced to richer visual images through the art of others.

Activities are open-ended and developmentally appropriate. Cardboard tubes have been put out for the children to use, but they have not been told what they might make from them. The three-year-old's exploration is just as valid as the more theme-related projects of the older children. The children who are painting the box yellow are exploring the effects of a different kind of brush.

FIGURE 1–7 "The rainbow fish is in trouble. His friend will save him." Crayon and watercolor—Ben, age 5½

Two children decided they wanted their paper fish to swim, so they started the idea of hanging them from the ceiling. Other children can now join in their project if they wish, but they are not required to do so. It is not expected that their sea creatures will resemble any real fish. Will it make a difference how many sea creatures are hung up by the end of the week or what they end up looking like?

Every child is not expected to participate in theme activities or produce a project. The children in the block corner and at the computer are pursuing their own interests of the moment. It does not matter if they do not have a sea-related art project to take home or show their parents that day. The teacher, the parents, and the children know that learning has been taking place.

The children are not rushed in their work. There is enough time for the children to do several activities. The children have learned that story time is a time for breaking off their activities and coming together as a group. It provides closure to the day. The teacher draws on the current interests of the children by asking them to move like fish to the rug for story time. This is an effective and gentle transition. After the story is ended and the illustrations in the book shared, there will be time for cleaning up and putting away any materials that are still out.

It all seems so effortless. There is a rhythm and flow to a well-planned program that creates the sense that this is what will happen if the children are just told to have fun with a lot of interesting materials. Nothing could be further from the truth.

Behind that successful program is superb planning and knowledge about how children think, learn, and respond to stimuli in their environment. There are guiding adults who know what to say about art production, how to say it, and when it is best left unsaid. They know when to interact and when to wait and watch. They are confident that they will not be judged on the art products of the children, but on their growth. Such teachers are also continually learning and growing along with their young artists from the first contact to the last. They are constantly improving the program they offer, assessing each activity, and noting how the children show growth in relation to the goals they have set for them. It is a program of their own creation, both meaningful and thoughtful.

SUMMARY: THE THOUGHTFUL ART PROGRAM

> When we think of art for children, we too often think of media and product first and only then the child. We need to be sensitive to the child first—sensitive to growth and development, aware of the child's needs.
>
> BEV BOS (1978, P. 4)

The stage has now been set for developing a rich and meaningful art program for children. Children are natural artists, in the sense that they play creatively with the elements of art that they find in their surroundings. But those surroundings must be provided, and they are determined by a philosophy of what child art is and what it means. We need to consider why children should do certain art activities, which ones should be selected, how they should be delivered and what environment is most conducive to their performance.

This chapter has closely examined the why: philosophy and principles. The following chapters will consider the how: how the delivery of art activities affects what children learn as well as how the way the child learns affects what activities will be

FIGURE 1–8 "I painted lots of animals." Tempera painting—Vicky, age 6

successful; the where: the environment in which child artists will work; and the what: the appropriate selection and efficient delivery of art concepts and skills. These ideas and suggestions will help guide the formation of a thoughtful art program for children.

It is the educator's role to nurture the artist within every young child. Although the focus will always be on guiding the artistic development of the child, in doing so the artist within the adult will also be rekindled. Adults and children must become part of the artistic continuum that stretches from our distant human past into the future. To guide young children as they grow through art is a deeply rewarding experience.

FURTHER READING

> Art, like language and religion, is a cultivator of human experience, basic to development.
> JUNE KING MCFEE (1961, P. 10)

The books listed below illustrate the place of child art in human experience.

Bredekamp, S. (Ed.). (1987). *Developmentally appropriate practice in early childhood programs serving children from birth through age 8*. Washington, DC: NAEYC.
This book outlines clearly and concisely what consitutes a developmentally appropriate curriculum for young children.

Fein, S. (1993). *First drawings: Genesis of visual thinking*. Pleasant Hill, CA: Exelrod Press.

Sylvia Fein presents a beautifully illustrated and elegant comparison between the art of our prehistoric past and the first symbols developed by children.

Gardner, H. (1983). *Frames of mind*. New York: Basic Books.

Gardner, H. (1993). *Multiple intelligences: The theory in practice*. New York: Basic Books. These books present Howard Gardner's theory of multiple intellegences and how it applies to educating children.

Olson, J. L. (1992). *Envisioning writing*. Portsmouth, NH: Heinemann. Janet Olson demonstrates the interrelationship between art and writing and details ways to use art to improve writing and writing to enhance art.

Paulsen, G. (1991). *The monument*. New York: Dell. This novel introduces a lonely girl and an eccentric artist. Hired to construct a monument to the town's war dead, the artist inspires the young girl while teaching the town the meaning of art. Although marketed as a young adult book, the book has meaning for all ages.

Art Focus

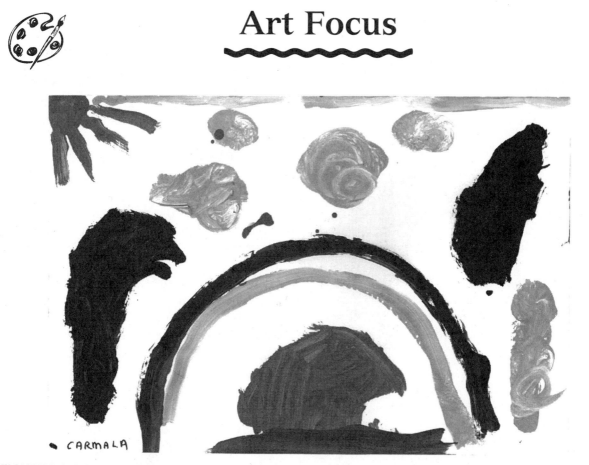

FIGURE 1–9 "It's a pretty day and the sun is shining." Tempera painting—Carmala, age 4½

GETTING READY FOR ART

The philosophical framework discussed in this chapter presents many factors that must be considered when designing an art program for young children. There are many "idea" books on the market, which offer all kinds of art projects to do and recipes to try. It is the teacher's role to carefully select from these, and modify them, in order to create an integrated art program that will work with a unique group of children in a particular educational setting.

This Art Focus provides a framework for the selection and organization of art activities in a meaningful art program.

Selecting Art Activities

It is not enough to have wonderful intentions. The art activities and how they are delivered will ultimately determine the children's art experience. Every activity must be carefully designed to meet the needs of each child, to fit the philosophy of artistic growth, and to achieve the learning goals of the total program.

There are hundreds of books on the market describing all kinds of "artsy" projects, such as cutting out a preprinted bunny picture, coloring it, and gluing on a cotton tail. Many of these projects sound like fun and often result in pleasant experiences. Most of them, however, will not encourage the emotional, social, physical, aesthetic, perceptual, linguistic, and cognitive growth of a well-designed art experience. Nor will they provide for an integrated and reflective art program.

Some of them, unfortunately, will even work against the goals of the art program. A child who cannot stay in the lines does not feel successful after scribbling over a coloring book picture. Children who are told, step by step, how to put together precut pieces to make a reindeer, have not learned to solve a problem creatively on their own. Worse, they have learned that they are not trusted to make their own choices about how to use the art materials.

Well-planned art activities should fit the following criteria.

They are open-ended. An open-ended activity is one in which there are many possible ways the child can approach his artwork, and in which the child is responsible for making his own artistic decisions. Although children may be influenced by their experiences or by the cultural images around them, they need to be able to incorporate these elements in their own unique way. In an open-ended art activity, the teacher has no preset idea about what the end product will look like. The children choose from the available materials, tools, and techniques, and then decide how they will use them. It is the children who determine what the end result will be and what will be done with any products that might result.

There is adequate time to explore and experiment. Young children cannot be rushed. Children who feel pressured to finish in a certain amount of time become frustrated, often to the point of crying. Sufficient time must be planned to allow the child to explore and experiment until satisfied. If it is necessary to end an activity, the teacher needs to provide a stimulus that will move the children away from their exploration in a gentle and orderly way. Some projects may require multiple-day access to materials so children can return to their work to add complexity and a sense of closure.

There is an ample supply of high-quality, basic art materials, stimulating to the senses, that children can work with in a creative and safe way. Children need real art supplies and tools—paint, paper, drawing materials, good brushes, scissors that work, and more. Many times because of limited funding, children's art activities have been reduced to creating with the junk of our society. Although there is a place for found and recycled materials in an art program, constant exposure to activities that use such things as paper plates, egg cartons, and packaging materials, which are not the basic materials of the adult artist, trivializes art in the minds of children and their parents.

Art materials need to be varied and must appeal to the senses. For example, paper should be available in different sizes and shapes, and in different colors and textures. Many different sizes of brushes and many colors of paint and crayons and markers should be present. Young artists need clays to mold, materials to build things, and a computer to draw on. Supplies do need to be plentiful. Young children use a lot of paper, glue, and paint!

They also need to be hazard-free. Children's safety is important above all else. The detailed information about art hazards in chapter 6 will assist in the selection of the safest art materials for young artists.

Activities should invite repetition. Skill development requires that children do similar activities over and over. Basic art materials need to be available at all times, so children may repeat activities in which they have enjoyed success. Children who are allowed and encouraged to experiment with art materials on their own, in a stress-free environment, and on a regular basis, will be willing to take the risks required to find new and creative ways to solve problems.

Activities should grow out of the children's interests and needs. Art creation is intrinsically motivating. It is often enough to put out the supplies and let the children explore them. Drawing, painting, collage, and modeling materials are always popular and should be offered on a regular basis, because they allow children at all skill levels to pursue their own interests. Other more specific types of activities should grow out of an experience that has created interest in the children. For example, after a trip to a construction site, an assortment of wood scraps can be laid out for the children to glue into sculptures. If the children need more experience cutting with scissors or working cooperatively, offer open-ended activities that emphasize these skills.

Organizing Successful Art Activities

Basic art supplies. An excellent art program for children from 18 months to eight years can be run with the following basic supplies:

Brushes: An assortment of different sizes including short and long handles, round and flat, house-painting brushes, and foam brushes

Chalk: Blackboard and sidewalk in white and colors

Craft paper: A large roll in basic brown or a color, for murals (24" or 36" in width by 100' or more in length)

Crayons: Both thick and regular size in assorted colors, including various skin tones

Finger paint: Commercial fingerpaint in a range of bright colors such as yellow, red, and blue as well as brown and black

Non-hardening modeling clay

Paper: Large sheets (12″ × 18″ and 18″ × 24″) of assorted papers—colored construction, manila, newsprint, white drawing

Play dough: Commercial (Play Doh) or home-made

School paste

Scissors: Child-sized, blunt-tipped

Tempera paint (liquid): Basic colors—white, red, yellow, blue, black, and brown (Optional: green, violet, orange, gold, and silver)

Waterbased broad-tipped markers

White glue: 4-oz. bottles

Yarn: Assorted colors, thicknesses, and textures

Supplementary supplies. These basic materials can be supplemented with found materials and special supplies. It is important, however, to make sure that these do not become the focus of the art activity, but rather add to the basic media of drawing, painting, collage, construction, modeling, printmaking, and so on. Instead of saying to the child, "Make something out of this egg carton," it is better to say, "How can you use this interesting texture from the top of the egg carton in your collage?"

Examples of supplementary materials include such things as buttons, cardboard pieces, cellophane, cloth, feathers, felt, spools, and wood pieces. Many more suggestions are offered in the Art Focus sections throughout this text.

Food-related supplies. Over the years many food items have found their way into art activities for young children. This has become a very controversial issue in early childhood education. Although it is easy to say that such items should never be used, in actual practice educators vary greatly in how they define foods. Chapter 6 presents both sides of this debate. Throughout the book, whenever food items are mentioned that might be used in art activities they have been marked with an asterisk* (for example: rice*). After reading chapter 6, each educator must con-sider the implications of using such food items in artwork and decide whether he or she feels this particular item is appropriate or not.

Basic Preparation. Although each art medium has its own specific setup requirements, the following general guidelines apply to most art activities.

1. Allow plenty of space for each child to work. The younger the child, the more space is required.

2. Protect any surface or clothing that might be damaged by the material in use. Make sure the protective covering is clearly different from any supplies being used. It is not necessary to cover surfaces that are easily washed.

3. Provide a sufficient amount of supplies so that no more than two children have to share the same resource at a time. Certain supplies, such as scissors, should not be shared as they can be dangerous when passed from child to child.

4. Have plenty of cleanup supplies on hand for the children and adults to use.

5. Activities that make the hands messy should be set up very close to a water supply.

6. Define areas in which certain materials must be kept. This can be done by such things as color coding the tables, hanging signs or symbols, placing tape on the floor, or teaching simple rules such as "clean hands only" on the rug, at the computer, or in the book corner.

Using the Art Focus Sections

In the next Art Focus section, a way to plan and organize open-ended art activities is presented. In succeeding sections, specific ways to present and use the basic art media are described using the same activity plan format. These are intended to illustrate the kinds of activities that match the philosphical framework and educational goals discussed in this chapter. They are designed to provide a model for beginning practitioners who have limited experience with young children and their art, and are full of helpful hints and suggestions that will prove of use to anyone who is teaching art to young children.

Studio Page *1*

MY PHILOSOPHY

All of the following have been suggested as important parts of early childhood art education.
- Think carefully about each item and then rank them by how important you feel each one is.
- Write a number in front of each, with 1 being the highest rank and 9 being the lowest.
- Based on your ranking, write a statement that summarizes your personal philosophy of early childhood art education.

❑ Developmental appropriateness
❑ Enhancing the multiple intelligences
❑ Teacher models artistic thinking
❑ Early linguistic development
❑ Perceptual, sensory, and kinesthetic experiences
❑ Multicultural art experiences
❑ Curriculum integration
❑ Responding to the art of others
❑ Nurturing creativity

MY PHILOSOPHY

My personal philosophy of early childhood art education is…

_____

_____

_____

_____

_____

_____

_____

_____

_____

_____

_____

_____

_____

_____

_____

_____

_____

_____

_____

_____

_____

_____

_____

_____

_____

_____

_____

_____

_____

_____

Studio Page 3

PHILOSOPHY IN ACTION

Read each description of the following early childhood art experiences and determine what principles are being addressed.

Scene 1: Two children are building with blocks. In a corner a child is busy painting at an easel.
Principles:

_____

Scene 2: On a table the teacher has put out a variety of paper shapes, glue, and scissors.
Principles:

_____

Scene 3: A child has found a beautiful stone. The teacher says, "How does your stone feel?"
Principles:

_____

Scene 4: Two children are painting a box together.
Principles:

_____

Scene 5: It is the third time that Mike's block tower has collapsed and he is very frustrated. The teacher says, "Why don't you play with the play dough now?"
Principles:

_____

Scene 6: At the easel the teacher has put brushes of many different sizes.
Principles:

_____

Scene 7: The teacher hangs a print of an African mask at child eye level.
Principles:

_____

Scene 8: A potter visits the class and shows the children how she makes a clay pot.
Principles:

_____

HOW TO HAVE A SUCCESSFUL OBSERVATION

Observing children involved in art activities is an invaluable way to learn how children react to various kinds of art experiences. As an observer you are free of the pressure of performing and can devote your attention to the small details that busy, overworked caregivers often miss.

The following checklist will help you and the participants in the program you are visiting have a pleasant and rewarding experience.

Before the Visit

❏ 1. Call for an appointment and get permission to visit.
❏ 2. Write down the names of the people you speak to on the phone and those of the teachers whose children you will be observing.
❏ 3. If you intend to use a camera or camcorder, make sure you have all the necessary permissions. Parents must sign a release form that allows their children to be photographed. Some schools may already have these on file.
❏ 4. Prepare a form on which to record your observations.

On the Day of the Visit

❏ 1. Arrive on time and introduce yourself to the teachers. If possible have them introduce you to the children. If asked, give a simple explanation for your visit, such as, "My name is _____. I can't wait to see what you are doing today."
❏ 2. Observe and record carefully. Do not bother the teachers. They are there to work with the children, not you.
❏ 3. When it is time for you to leave, do not disturb the children or the teachers.

After the Observation

❏ 1. As soon as possible, review your notes and add any special details you remember. Some people find it helpful to make an audiotape recording while the experience is still fresh in their minds.
❏ 2. Write a note of thanks to everyone with whom you had contact. A special handmade card for the children is always welcome.

Studio Page 5

FIRST OBSERVATION: ART AND THE CHILD

The purpose of this observation is to observe young children in a typical learning situation. The observation will focus on the artistic behavior of the children in a group educational situation. This observation may be done in an organized school or a child care setting that services children between the ages of one and eight. The observation should last 40 minutes to an hour.

Date of Observation: _____   Length of Observation: _____

Ages of Children: _____   Group Size: _____

Observation

1. What activities are the children involved in?

   _____

   _____

   _____

   _____

2. What are the adults doing?

   _____

   _____

   _____

   _____

3. How are art activities made available to the children?

   _____

   _____

   _____

   _____

4. What is the range of participation children showed in the art activities? (Examples: Tried once then left; engaged in nonverbal or verbal interaction with children and/or adults; worked alone; length of time at activity.)

   _____

   _____

   _____

   _____

Studio Page 6

ANALYSIS: ART AND THE CHILD

Based on your observation, write a response to these questions:

1. How do the activities of the children relate to the areas of artistic growth discussed in this chapter?

_____
_____
_____
_____
_____
_____
_____
_____

2. Which artistic goals for children were being met and which ones were not? Why?

_____
_____
_____
_____
_____
_____
_____
_____
_____

3. What do you think is the philosophy of early childhood art education of the teachers in this program?

_____
_____
_____
_____
_____
_____
_____
_____

2

66 *The very language one speaks conditions the style and structure of thought and experience.* 99

•

JEROME BRUNER (1979, P. 16)

The Artist Inside

Seeing Oneself as an Artist and Educator

Questions addressed in this chapter:

What is the teacher's role in early childhood art?

How does the teacher's behavior affect young artists?

How should teachers respond to young artists nonverbally?

How should teachers respond to young artists verbally?

How should teachers respond to problems?

How does teaching style affect program delivery?

SUMMARY: Delivering the Thoughtful Art Program

FURTHER READING

ART FOCUS: Planning for Art

Young Artists at Work

It was a cold day in February and a small group of four-year-olds was happily cutting and pasting paper shapes. A visitor who was helping for the day walked over to the table and admired the children's collages. She picked up a piece of paper and absentmindedly cut out a heart. "Can I have it?" one little girl asked.

"Sure," replied the visitor. Smugly the girl pasted it in the center of her paper.

"Make me one!" "Make me one!" came an instant chorus.

"Here, I'll show you how," said the visitor, and she patiently showed them how to fold the paper and cut half a heart shape. But when the children tried it, their hearts did not look like the visitor's; they were jagged and misshapen. One boy crumpled his up in disgust. Another child tried to tear the original "perfect" heart off the first girl's paper. While the visitor tried to quiet the aggressor, the last child at the table began to cry.

Hearing the commotion, the teacher came over to the table. "I don't know how you do this all day," said the visitor, "The children are so demanding. They want their hearts to be perfect."

"I want their hearts to be perfect too, full of joy and hope, but I want their artwork to be their own—each unique and different," replied the teacher. "That's why I don't provide models and patterns."

WHAT IS THE TEACHER'S ROLE IN EARLY CHILDHOOD ART?

Good teaching requires most of all a thoughtful, caring teacher committed to the lives of students.

WILLIAM AYRES (1995, P. 25)

Young artists need many things to be successful. They need safe, exciting art supplies, comfortable surroundings, ample space, and time to explore. Most of all they need a teacher who will enable them to be successful. The teacher is the most important ingredient in allowing children to develop their artistic natures. The teacher is like a gardener, providing the "fertile ground"—the enriched environment—that gives a child a start in thinking and in working as an artist. As the child grows in skill and confidence, enthusiasm and encouragement—the "nutrients" provided by the teacher—allow the child's creativity to flower.

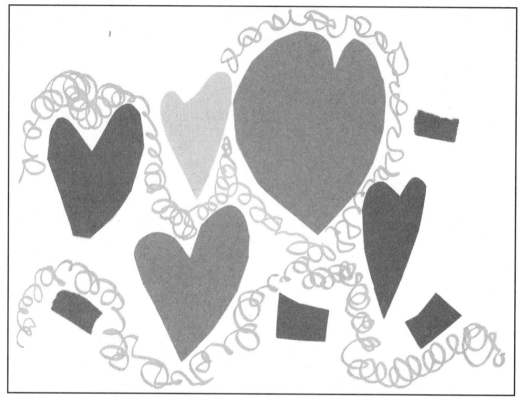

FIGURE 2–1 "Hearts Collage." Cut paper—Susan, age 5

Factors Affecting How Teachers Teach

What are the factors that determine a teaching approach? First and foremost is how teachers view themselves as artists. They must feel comfortable with art exploration before they can lead children's explorations. They must also understand the creative process and have a broad, rich definition of art. In order to increase their ability to guide young artists' growth, they must understand their own art history.

Each of us has had a different experience of art. For some the word conjures up happy images of fingerpainting in kindergarten. For others it revives the memory of a drawing praised by a teacher. Unfortunately, for many adults in our society the idea of producing art makes them feel incompetent. "I'm not good at art." "I can't draw a straight line." "A child can draw better than I can." These are common statements of adults who have not had a chance to develop their own artistic self-confidence, or who suffered through a poorly taught or highly directed art program.

Teachers need to discover our own artistic natures, no matter how we view our artistic abilities, so that we will be able to model enthusiasm, enjoyment, and competency in art for our young students, and thereby facilitate their artistic growth. By understanding the artistic process we will be better equipped to understand how young children feel as they explore the world of art. Lay-Dopyera and Dopyera (1992, p. 19–20) present research proving that children show more constructive behavior and relationships when their teacher is warm, friendly, and actively and positively involved in their activities.

How to see oneself as an artist. We are all artists. Art is not limited to the production of a visual product, although that may often be the result. Art is the process of manipulating the visual elements of line, shape, color, pattern, form, and texture. When we choose the colors of our clothing, the style of our hair, or the furnishing of our homes, we are making artistic decisions that are no different from the ones we make when drawing with crayons on paper.

The artist is constantly picking and choosing from the materials available, responding to the effect that is produced when making the next decision. Young children, just like adults, need time and freedom to explore art materials so that they can experience making their own artistic decisions. Activities need to be planned so that children are encouraged and enabled to make as many decisions as possible in each exploration. The activities for children in this book will provide models of open-ended lessons that allow children to make their own such decisions. They are best taught by a teacher who provides guidance but knows when to step back and let the children explore on their own.

Personal "art history." Art is not produced in a vacuum. Art begins as a manipulation of the basic visual elements of line, shape, color, pattern, form, and texture, but once these elements become recognizable as a piece of art to the artists or those around them, they become part of the artists' memories and part of their beliefs about themselves as artistic people. How people feel about themselves as artists is based upon judgments they have made about their abilities based on past experiences.

In the same way, how children feel about themselves is intricately tied to how they judge their own success and how they perceive the response of others. Very young children are often unconcerned about the finished product of their art explorations. For them it is the process itself through which they express themselves. As children grow older, they begin to show pride in their ability to manipulate art materials, the graphic symbols they invent, and the artwork they produce. Teachers need to value all aspects of artistic production. How the teacher responds to the child as an artist, both verbally and nonverbally, is just as important as providing exciting activities for the children to do.

There are many ways to respond to children's art explorations. This is a skill that develops with practice. It helps to keep one's own art memories fresh, whether happy or frustrating, while creating memories for the children.

How we view our creative nature. Every person has the ability to create something new. People use the creative process daily whether they are aware of it or not. Any time they have to do something unfamiliar or change a habit, such as when child-proofing a room or figuring out how to get to work when the car breaks down, they are using the process. Children are busy learning about a new world and their place in it by following the creative process. Unlike adults, young children do not have a large repertoire of habitual responses to draw on, and so they exhibit high levels of creativity in all areas of learning.

Adults need to provide time, space, and activities to allow children to pursue the creative process. They also need to be prepared for the unique actions and products that may result. Sometimes adults can learn a great deal from young children about how art media can be used! Teachers need to maintain high levels of personal creativity so that they can react and change in response to the uniqueness of the young children with whom they work. No one can plan activities that will work well with all children in every situation. Educators need to rely on their own inherent creative abilities to adapt what they learn and to fit their goals to the reality in which they find themselves.

How we define art. In every culture, people are taught what art is or is not. In some cultures creative work is viewed differently from our own. An African mask maker takes a piece of wood and waits for the spirit to guide his hands in the shaping of the mask. He has not created a piece of art, but has been a tool in the creation of a spiritual item that will be used in ceremony and then discarded. By his definition the mask is not art, and he is not an artist. But removed from the culture that made it and hung on the wall of a museum, that same mask becomes art to be studied, judged, and honored.

In this society people do not always agree on what is art. Their definitions of art are based on what they have been taught by their parents and teachers, on what they have experienced in museums and in literature about art, and on what they are exposed to from the mass culture, such as what they see on TV and in popular magazines.

Children will acquire their definition of art from the materials to which they are exposed. They need to know that there is more to art than crayons on paper. Their experience will only be as rich as the teacher's definitions and knowledge of art. Teachers need to learn as much as possible about the art of the world. Many activities in this book provide examples of related art forms from a wide variety of times, cultures, and people, as well as ways to present them to young children. Other activities expand the definition of art beyond the bounds of the newspaper-covered table. These will provide the beginnings of an expanded view of art.

HOW DOES THE TEACHER'S BEHAVIOR AFFECT YOUNG ARTISTS?

> Children must know that they, the ideas they have, and the art they produce will be accepted and respected.
>
> CAROL SEEFELDT (1995, p. 41)

Children want to be like the adults they admire. They pretend they are grown-ups—a doctor making a sick doll better, a firefighter putting out a fire in a block building, a mom or a dad cooking dinner on the play stove. Most children are not often exposed to adults creating and talking about art. Adults doing art are rarely depicted on TV or in children's books. Art for many young children is something children do at child care or school. Children play with play dough, not adults; children paint at the easel, not adults. Many adults feel art is a childlike activity and of peripheral value to society, because they lacked artistic models. It is not enough for teachers to provide wonderful art experiences to children—they must also model artistic behavior.

How to Be an Artistic Role Model

The teacher can model artistic behavior by exhibiting the following qualities:

Self-confidence. Teachers must model artistic self-confidence. Would a teacher say to a child, "I'm not a very good reader," or "I can't write the letter 'A' very well," and then expect the child to want to be a good reader or to make a well-formed "A"? But many adults do not hesitate to tell children that they think themselves poor artists, or that they cannot even draw a straight line. It is easy for the child to think that if this important adult who can read so well and knows so much cannot create art, then it must be very hard to be good at art.

If teachers are not self-confident artists then they need to think about why this might be so. What art experiences convinced them that they could not do art? What do they need to do to increase their self-confidence? Sometimes just becoming aware of the source of their artistic discomfort—a thoughtless comment by a teacher, a rejected

FIGURE 2–2 "Me." Crayon—Laurel, age 4

piece of work, being laughed at by a friend—is enough to change our view of our artistic potential. Taking a drawing course, a painting workshop, or reading about and studying the nature of creativity can change our view of our artistic nature and help us avoid self-deprecating remarks.

Fairness. Adults often say to children, "You're such a better artist than I," even though they would never say to one child that her art was better than her friend's. Putting themselves down in this way does not build up the confidence of children, but instead introduces the element of comparative value. The child thinks, "How can mine be better than the teacher's? Can some art be better than others?" Comparing the value of one person's artwork with another's is like comparing apples and oranges. There should be no "better" or "best" artwork in an early childhood setting, for either children or adults.

Enthusiasm. How the guiding adults feel about art will be mirrored by the children. If teachers are fearful and tentative about a project, the children will react with hesitation. If teachers dislike the feel of a certain material, the children will sense this and show discomfort. Use of art media or activities which are personally disliked should be avoided. It is important to be able to express enthusiasm for doing art. Words full of warmth and joy should be used, such as:

"I can't wait to share this painting with you!"

"Look at all the bright colors!"

"Oooo, this play dough feels so smooth!"

Appearance. Personal appearance is a way of showing how people value art and to attract attention to artistic elements and concepts. Dressing in shades of blue when studying the color blue, or wearing a wool sweater when talking about fiber art can provide a catalyst for discussion. Appreciation of artwork from other cultures can be shown by wearing African prints, Guatemalan ikat weavings, Indian embroidery, Native American jewelry, and so forth on a regular basis.

Participation. It is important for children to see that adults also use art materials, and that they are not hesitant to touch and play with them. But teachers must be careful to model process and not product. There is a difference between showing children that adults enjoy doing art and providing them with a set model to copy.

When children are just beginning to explore or work with a material, they are unsure of what to do and most vulnerable to trying to imitate what someone else is doing. At this point it is extremely important to not overwhelm them with adult-level artwork.

Modeling process. Sit with a group of children involved in an art activity. Handle the materials while the children begin to explore and use them. Start an artwork after the children have begun, but only do a few things to it. For example, if the children are making collages, glue one or two simple shapes to the paper. If they are painting, paint a line or two. If using play dough, knead and manipulate it, but do not make anything.

Sitting beside children and doing our own artwork can be a warm and comforting experience similar to reading a book together. In joining in the children's art activities, however, it is important not to make something that is well beyond their ability to create. For example, rolling perfect balls of clay while working with two-year-olds and many three-year-olds instantly causes those children to become frustrated. They do not have the fine motor control to roll the clay between their palms, and their efforts to copy the adult's perfect ball will be fruitless. This leads children to beg, "Make me one," which stops the children's exploratory process and causes them to become dissatisfied with their own efforts. Watch the kinds of motions the children are making and use similar or just slightly more advanced motions than theirs. For example, cutting out simple shapes with straight cuts models a skill that is within the ability of many three- and four-year-olds, but cutting out a perfect heart or shape of a rabbit does not. Many four- and five-year-olds who are developing symbols of their own are particularly disconcerted by watching an adult they admire draw versions of the same thing they are drawing. Adults should always let children begin first and then draw something completely different.

When adults produce a finished work, it can also overwhelm young artists. An adult can work faster, and be far neater and more controlled. It is not necessary to finish the artwork. It is easy to become involved in the children's work or be called away so that there is no need to finish. If reminded by the children to finish, the teacher may say, "I will work on it later, when I am not so busy. I need time to do my best." Later the teachers can share their finished work in the same way the children share theirs.

Modeling technique (demonstrate). If an activity calls for a simple pattern or method that the children must follow in order to explore the medium, show just that piece of the process while verbally explaining. For example, if the children will be doing sponge prints say, "Dip the sponge in the paint and press on the paper," while doing so. Do this once or twice, but do not continue to produce a finished product. In this book the word *demonstrate* is used to indicate such simple modeling.

If children are involved in an activity and ask how to do something, or become frustrated because they lack a particular technique, it needs to be explained or demonstrated for them. If it is within the child's ability, suggest a different approach or ask a leading question. For example, if children complain that the paint keeps dripping down their paper, show them how to wipe their paintbrush on the side of the container. If, when using scissors, the children's paper keeps bending and they become frustrated, suggest that they move to a new place to start cutting. A child who is struggling to glue a piece of yarn on paper might be asked, "What is another way you can put glue on the paper?"

New techniques must be within the skill range of the child, and the child must be really interested in learning them. It is helpful to ask, "Do you need help? You look frustrated. Would you like me to show you a way to stop the paint from dripping?" Children learn best when the technique that is being taught is delivered at just the right time—when the children need it to solve a problem of their own creation.

It takes a high degree of observational skill to be aware of the technical needs of a group of children all actively involved in art processes. With more experience it becomes easier to know which children are ready for a new technique and when they need it. In many cases, a simple pairing of two children of slightly different ages and/or skill levels may be the best way to increase the skill level of a child without direct adult interference.

The line between needed intervention and being directive is a fine one. Teachers do not want to miss the "teachable moment" nor interfere with the children's solving their own problems. This is the art of fine teaching. Teachers must be in tune with their children, understanding their past experiences, sensitivities, and desires. It is not easy. Children are always "...dangerously on the brink between presence that they want and repression that they don't want" (Malaguzzi in Edwards et. al. 1993, p. 58).

HOW SHOULD TEACHERS RESPOND TO YOUNG ARTISTS NONVERBALLY?

To use words but rarely is to be natural.

LAO TZU XXIII: 51

Body Language

We speak with more than words. Our whole body communicates our meaning. How close we stand, how we move our arms, and the expression on our faces tell children how we feel about them and their art. It is important that our nonverbal behavior match what we are saying to children.

Faces are a mirror of our feelings. Smiling at a child is telling that child that we are pleased with him or her and that we like what he or she is doing. Frowns and cold stares distance us from the child and show disapproval. Teachers need to be aware of the messages they are sending. If a teacher says to a child, "You used the glue in an interesting way," but frowns at the same time because the glue is dripping on the floor, the words have no meaning. It is better to react honestly. If the dripping glue is deeply disturbing, deal with the problem first before commenting on the artwork. The teacher might say, "Let's put your collage over here and wipe up all the glue; then I can look at your collage."

How we move and gesture are also strong expressions of our feelings. It is important to remain at the children's level by sitting or stooping when interacting with them as they participate in the art process. Using expansive arm motions can signal enthusiasm or inclusion. More subtly, hand signals and American Sign Language can be used

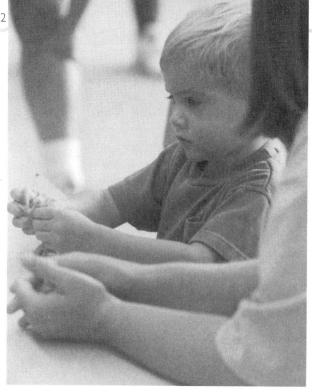

FIGURE 2–3 Sitting beside children and using art materials can be a warm comforting experience.

to introduce the children to other ways of communicating, while at the same time providing a quick and nonintrusive way to signal a child without disturbing the other children. A simple "thumbs up" sign, for example, can communicate to a child who is wiping up some paint drips that she is doing something that is appreciated.

Sharing Emotions

No matter how hard we try to cover up our emotions, children seem to sense how we are feeling. It is often better to be open about how we feel. It is hard to shrug off the frustration of a car that would not start that morning or the anger left from sharp words with a friend. Art can provide a way to express such feelings. Share with the children the source of the feeling and then say, for example, "That car is so frustrating, I'm going to make a painting of it and show how it is all broken," or "I am going to draw a whole bunch of angry lines on my paper and get rid of some of this angry feeling." Showing the children that adults use art as a release for emotions lets children know that people of all ages use art for emotional release.

Active Listening

Active listening is one of the most important ways a teacher or caregiver can respond to a child and should be one of the first responses when children share information about their artwork. Especially with new children, it is extremely important to listen before responding verbally, in order to learn more about the artists' intent before deciding what to say to them. We also need to listen to the children we know well to show that we care about what they are saying. Active listening consists of the following components.

Waiting. Do not always respond instantly and verbally to everything a child says. Establish eye contact and wait for the child to speak. This will also provide time to formulate a thoughtful verbal response if the child does not offer a comment.

Looking. Maintain eye contact with the children while they are talking. Remain at the child's eye level if possible.

Responding. Respond with value-free grunts, head nods, appropriate facial expressions, and "hums" as the child talks.

HOW SHOULD TEACHERS RESPOND TO YOUNG ARTISTS VERBALLY?

> The teacher's ways of talking, responding, and acting will reflect both her interest in the child and her belief that the content of the learning experience should be in tune with what is meaningful, important, and pleasurable to young children.
>
> BARBARA BIBER (1984, p. 73)

Words are powerful. They can transform a humdrum experience into an exhilarating one or destroy a special moment in a second. What adults say to young artists can have a profound effect on how they view art for the rest of their lives. Many adults can trace the origin of their feeling of artistic incompetence to a thoughtless comment by a caring adult. Guiding adults need to take care in offering comments to children. We should not just speak off the top of our heads or repeat the words spoken to us when we were children. What teachers say and how they respond to the children is one of the most significant parts of the educational process, and it takes practice to choose words wisely and sparingly.

Research indicates that the younger the child, the more important it is to deliver on a one-to-one basis rather than in a large group situation (Lay-Dopyera and Dopyera,

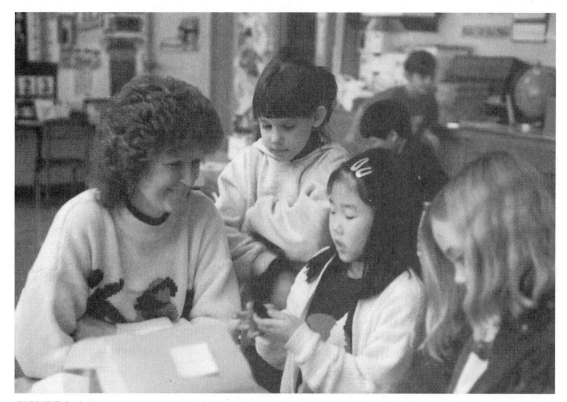

FIGURE 2–4 How teachers respond to young children will affect how children see themselves as artists.

1992). Art activities provide significant moments for personal dialogue between a child and a caring adult. This relationship is an important one. Both short-term and long-term studies find that when there are many warm, positive interactions between adults and young children, there is a beneficial effect on social and emotional development.

In addition, by choosing words thoughtfully we not only help children feel good about themselves, but expand their thought processes and make the art experience more meaningful to them as well.

The Problem with Praise

Probably one of the most common responses to children's art work is unconditional and false praise. "Good work!" "Great painting!", and "Nice picture!" are said quickly to the child as the teacher scoops up the drippy painting or hustles the child off to the next activity. The intent is to give encouragement and indicate to children that they have successfully used the art medium. However, studies indicate that consistent overuse of such praise actually diminishes the behavior being complimented (Brandt, 1995, p. 14). Said over and over, the words become empty and meaningless. How can every picture be great or wonderful? The children come to believe that the teachers are not really looking at their work. In addition, unconditional praise does not help children think more deeply about their work or make the experience more educational for them.

Teachers often unintentionally use words that are value-laden and judgmental. "That's a pretty picture," "What a beautiful painting!", and "Oh, that's lovely! You made a great project!" are frequently said by well-meaning adults who are afraid of hurting a child's feelings. But not every piece of artwork done by a child is beautiful, pretty, or lovely, and such words introduce the contrasting idea that there must also be child artwork that is ugly or unpleasant, and that adults would not praise. If teachers, in an attempt to be fair, apply such words to all child art, the terms become more meaningless unconditional praise and convey no information to the children about how they really perceive their work.

When teachers say, "I like it!" or "I like the way you _____, " they are also making judgments and expressing their personal values. Besides being overused, such terms open the door to more deleterious results. Many adults prefer realistic artwork that is neat and orderly. They are more likely to respond positively to a painting of a house flanked by two trees and overlooked by a smiling sun, than to a dripping paper covered in thick swirls of olive-green paint. Expressing adult personal taste in young children's art can lead to some children believing they are better at art and others feeling like failures. As many art teachers who work with adults have noted (Edwards, 1979; Cameron, 1992), a large number of people have poor artistic self-images because as very young children a piece of their artwork was disliked or compared unfavorably to another's work by a significant adult in their life.

In addition, Marshall (1995, p. 26) and Kohn (cited in Brandt, 1995, p. 16) warn that by focusing the children's attention on whether or not their behavior is likable, they learn that they must perform to please the teacher rather than to successfully accomplish the learning task. The child's joy in self-expression through the art media is then replaced with the child's conscious effort to produce something likable.

Unfortunately, this sort of praise naturally flows from most adults' lips. Arguments can be made that in some sense adults do want children to behave in pleasing ways; telling them we like something may increase the likelihood that they will repeat the action. However, creative art is based on the expansion of new behaviors rather than repetition of limited actions. Consider what meaningful information a child receives when a teacher says something such as, "I like the way you used green paint today." Does the teacher really want the child to repeat the same use of green paint in every painting, or is there some better way to respond to this child's work?

Positive Feedback

Positive feedback tells children precisely what they did well. Instead of saying "Great painting!", the thoughtful teacher says, "I noticed you wiped your brush on the edge of the paint container so the paint didn't drip." Positive feedback is best used to let children know when they have used a technique well or behaved in a way that will give them further success at the activity.

In order to respond specifically teachers need to have a clear idea in their minds what techniques and behaviors are appropriate and possible for the child and then must carefully observe the child at work. Positive feedback enhances children's feelings of self-confidence—it provides information on what they have done well and it communicates to them that adults are personally interested enough in their art activities to observe specific things they have done.

Even though positive feedback seems more like a wordy description than praise, when it is delivered with the same facial expression and same warm enthusiastic tone of voice that we would use for "Great job!", it is received by the child as praise for being successful in a very specific way.

Positive feedback can take several forms, each appropriate in different situations. With practice this kind of response can become a natural way of talking to children about their art in daily interactions.

Providing positive feedback through descriptive statements. A descriptive statement can be used to make a children aware of their behavior, of how they solved a problem, or to increase their understanding of art concepts. Such descriptive statements show children that teachers value their individuality, because careful observation is necessary to provide a meaningful description. Often at the same activity the teacher may give each child a different comment.

Describing behavior. These kinds of statements refer to how the child is working either with others or with the materials. They are the easiest statements to formulate and can serve as a good entrance into a conversation with children about their work.

If children are working with a material, comment on how they manipulated it, for example:

> "I noticed that you rolled the clay into a long snake."
> "You moved the (computer) mouse in a circular way to make those curved lines."

When children work well with others describe their behavior.

> "I see that you are sharing your glue with your partner."
> "I noticed you gave a piece of your shiny paper to Mike when he couldn't find another one."
> "I see that you and Anna have decided who will go first at the computer in a fair way."

Statements can also refer to the amount of effort children have put into an activity.

"You spent a great deal of time working with Allan on your dinosaur project."

"This clay piece represents a tremendous effort on your part."

"You spent almost a whole hour getting the shape just the way you wanted."

Describing artistic decisions. Verbalizing the steps children have taken to solve a problem or summarizing their solutions are important ways to make children aware of how they worked through a process.

If the child has struggled to find a solution to a problem, describe the specific steps taken.

"I noticed that you tried several ways to attach the tubes together. First you tried gluing them and then you tried bending them. Now you have pushed one inside the other and they are holding together well."

In responding to a finished piece of work we might summarize what choices the child has made. Artistic decision statements often contain the following phrases: you tried, you found, you discovered, you chose. For example:

"You have chosen to use three different colors of paper in your collage today."

"I noticed you found a way to attach that unusually shaped button to your puppet for its nose."

Describing art concepts. Descriptive statements can increase children's vocabulary, further their understanding of the art elements they have used, and make them aware of the sensory qualities of their artwork. This is different from teachers trying to describe what the artwork seems to depict to them. A superficial description of the subject of the picture does not extend the child's learning and puts the emphasis on product rather than process. Everyone who works with children and art should be familiar with the art elements that are found in most artworks. Chapter 8 provides a detailed description of these elements and also of the sensory qualities of art, which should form the basis of this kind of verbal description.

Using art concepts as the basis of descriptions allows higher level responses to toddlers' scribbles and explorations, for example:

"Look at all the swirling lines you have made!"

"I see many different colors in your painting."

"Your play-dough pancake feels so smooth!"

"Look at the way the wet paint sparkles!"

These same responses can be used even if the child's subject matter seems to be obvious. (See following section, "Interpretive Statements.") If a comment on the subject matter seems appropriate, focus on the art elements that the child used to express that subject, for example:

"I see you have used many different sizes of rectangles to make your house."

"You used many round yellow shapes to make your flowers."

Art Words

Descriptive Art Words

Lines

Straight, curved, wiggly, zig zag, jagged, crisscross

Shapes

Square, rectangular, round, triangular, irregular, oval

Colors

Bright colors: red, orange, yellow, green, blue

Dull colors: gray, olive green, deep brown

Neutral colors: white, beige, gray, tan, brown

Pastel colors: pink, coral, sky blue, lavender, pale green

Intense colors: magenta, purple, fuschia, red-orange, turquoise

Textures

Soft, hard, bumpy, rough, jagged, smooth, wet, sticky

Forms

Spheres, cubes, pyramids

Contrasts

Light/dark, big/small, top/bottom, front/back, round/square, bright/dull, intense/soft, hard/soft, rough/smooth, patterned/plain, thick/thin, straight/curved

Patterns

Plaid, polka dot, stripe, floral, all over, border, checkered

---

Paraphrasing. To paraphrase, teachers repeat what the child has just said in their own words. This is an excellent way to show children that the teacher has been listening to them, for example:

> Child: "I made lots of green lines."
> Teacher: "Yes, you did make many green lines."

Interpretive statements. When teachers respond to a child's artwork on an interpretive level, they model for the child the way art communicates to other people. We can refer to a personal sensation or a visual memory by saying, for example, "The yellows in your picture make me feel warm inside," or "The rectangles in your collage remind me of all the colorful windows in the apartment across the street." The expression of emotions, however, must be done with care. A banal, "Your picture makes me feel happy," does not communicate a depth of feeling nor explain to the child the source of that response. Instead, tie positive emotional responses to the art elements in the work, for example: "I feel so peaceful when I look at the blues in your print."

Negative emotional responses must be dealt with differently. We must be careful when responding with the powerful emotions of sadness and anger. We do not want to overwhelm the child with our own negative feelings which can be received as criticism, and yet, we still want to allow the child to express these emotions.

In the case of negative emotions it is better to put into words what the child is expressing for herself rather than how it makes us feel. In order to do this successfully it is important to know how the child is feeling and why, and then tie that feeling into the art elements the child has chosen to use.

For example:

> **"You used lots of jagged lines to express your anger at being knocked over by your friend."**
> **"The dark colors you used show how sad you are that your dog ran away."**

Interpretive responses based on feelings and memories must be genuine, unique, and thoughtful. They are easily overused and can become as meaningless as "That's lovely," or "Good work." Not every yellow painting should make us feel warm or happy. Teachers' personal interpretive responses to children's artwork should arise spontaneously as part of their interaction with a particular child. They should be carefully phrased so that the interpretation is not imposed on the child, but clearly expresses a personal response. Instead of saying, "Boy, what an angry (happy, sad) picture you made today!" use words that indicate a personal response, such as: "I feel," and "I remember," "I am reminded."

Hall and Duffy (cited in Noyce and Christie, 1988, p. 46) found that when teachers initiated conversations with children by making a statement about their personal feelings or experiences, children gave less stilted, longer, and more spontaneous replies. Used appropriately, such responses can create a wonderful depth of communication between the child and adult.

Teachers interpret child art when they assume that they know what the subject of a piece is, as when they respond, before listening to the child's description: "It looks like you painted your family today," or "That must be a picture of your dog." If the child is still at the scribbling stage, attributing a subject has no meaning for the child and serves only to satisfy an adult desire to find reality in all art, instead of appreciating the way the child has used the artistic elements. A better response is to describe the lines, shapes, colors, and other aesthetic elements of the artwork.

Even when children are beginning to develop symbols that somewhat represent reality, it is difficult for adults to identify the intended subjects with accuracy. A misidentified subject can cause a child to react with anger or disappointment, because children often assume that adults know everything. Although a bold child may reply to the teacher's mistaken, "Oh, you drew your house today," with "Can't you see I made the school?", many children react silently and wonder what was wrong with their artwork that this adult could not understand what they were trying to express. It is easy to avoid this difficulty if we take the time to wait for the child to explain her work or ask questions that will elicit a description from the child.

However, children like to test adults. With a "Guess what I made?", they challenge us to find their meaning. Even in this situation, it is still better to resort to simple description of media and artistic elements than to risk misidentification and emotional hurt. For example, if the child has made a painting that might show a house, say: "I see you have made a painting using many different colored shapes." Follow this immediately with an open-ended question that will elicit a further description from the child.

TEACHING TIP

Using Positive Feedback

Typical examples of unconditional praise:	*Positive feedback:*
Good glue job!	I noticed you put the glue on the back of your shapes and then attached them to your paper!
Nice collage!	I see you used straight cuts with your scissors to make your shapes!
Good clean-up!	I saw you pick up all the papers and put them in the right containers!
Super print!	You made this pattern by pressing the sponge down on your paper over and over!

Typical examples of judgmental statements:	*Positive feedback:*
Beautiful painting!	The golds and yellows in your painting make me feel as warm as sunshine.
Lovely work!	The lines in your picture swirl in and out like a maze.

Typical examples of imposing statements:	*Positive feedback:*
That's an angry picture!	I see you used lots of black and red and green to show your anger about the accident.
What a happy painting!	Your painting reminds me of a walk I took in my grandmother's garden.
It looks like your mother.	I see you used many interesting patterns and shapes in this picture. Is there a story to go with it?

Engaging in Artistic Dialogue

Questioning or making a leading statement is one way to learn directly from the artists what their intent was in an artwork. Questions can also be used to further the child's understanding of art process, to help children reflect on the consequences of their actions, and to assess what the child has learned from the art activity. By encouraging children to verbalize about their artwork, we also help them develop language skills and clarify their thought processes. Questions must be phrased very carefully so that they are not intrusive, allow many possible responses from the child, and make the child feel comfortable talking about art.

Creating a responsive atmosphere. Before we can expect a child to freely respond to our questions we must create an atmosphere in which the child feels safe expressing her thoughts and feelings. There are four ways to do this.

First, by providing plenty of opportunities for children to look at art (by displaying art prints and art books), and by talking about artwork regularly, an atmosphere of verbalizing about art becomes a natural part of the child's experience (see chapter 9). If children are used to asking questions about someone else's artwork, they will be more comfortable answering questions about their own work.

Second, by expressing our comments about children's artwork in the form of positive feedback, we provide a model of how children can describe their own art.

Third, the style of delivery in asking a question is extremely important. Questions need to be asked in a tone of voice that contains enthusiastic curiosity. Voices need to be soft. Eyes need to make contact, and once the child begins to respond we need to practice active listening.

Finally, questions need to be asked at the right moment. Not every piece of artwork needs to be explained by a child. Choose carefully the moment to elicit a verbal response. If the child has just finished a painting and is eager to join some friends in the block area, do not try to engage the child in a deep conversation about the artwork. At this moment a simple descriptive form of positive feedback will suffice. If a child has been working a long time on a clay sculpture and has stopped for a moment to get another piece of clay, this may provide an opportunity for a discussion about the work.

Take care not to overwhelm the child with a long string of questions. The children should not feel that they are being grilled. If they must constantly answer questions or explain their art they may become resentful and avoid art activities. Use a question to begin a *conversation*. Continue the conversation only if the child is interested in doing so, and formulate responses based on the direction the child's answer takes.

Phrasing questions. Learning how to phrase questions directed to children takes practice. Although when confronted with a dripping puddle of blue and purple paint, or a much-handled piece of play dough, our initial reaction many be one of "What is it?" or "What is that supposed to be?", such an intrusive and insulting question must be avoided. Not all child art is intended to be something. Much of a child's initial work with a medium will consist of exploration and experiments with the materials and tools, and have no end result in mind. This kind of question is limiting in that it puts all the focus on the product and places children in the position of having to give an answer they think will please the questioner.

To learn more about the artist's thoughts, phrase questions in such a way that the child can give a wide range of answers. Alternatives to "What is it?" ask children to reflect on their artwork in much deeper ways. They allow children to respond with descriptive statements that go beyond subject matter and include thoughts about art processes and artistic decision making. Such questions can take several forms.

Art element questions. Questions can focus the children's attention on the art elements in their work:

> "I noticed you used many different pieces of cloth on your puppet. Do any of them have an interesting texture?"
> "What kinds of lines did you make with the crayons?"

Process questions. The child can be asked to explain the process she used:

> "You used three different sizes of brushes today. Which lines did you make with the big one?"

"How did you make the play dough so bumpy?"

Explaining decisions. Artistic decisions can be explained:

"Where on your collage did you decide to put those interesting pebbles you found?"
"Which fingers did you use to make your fingerpainting?"
"How did you make this color?"

Exploring relationships. Questions can be used to focus the children's attention on what they might do next and to see relationships between their behavior and the results. Kamii and Devries (1993, p. 27) have postulated four types of questions that help children learn about how objects and events are related.

1. Predicting:
   "What do you think will happen when you press your fingers into the clay?"
   "What do you think might happen if you mixed these two colors of play dough together?"
2. Creating an Effect:
   "Can you make different kinds of lines with your paintbrush?"
   "What do you think you could do if I gave you these pieces of yarn for your collage?"
3. Connecting Events:
   "How did you make all these rectangular shapes?"
   "How did you make this color brown?"
4. Finding the Cause:
   "Why don't the pebbles fall off your collage now?"

Integrating art. Questions can also be used to extend the child's learning in art to other curriculum areas:

Science: "What are the different kinds of leaves you used in your collage?"
Math: "How many balls of clay have you made so far?"
Language: "What kind of voice does your puppet have?"

Assessing knowledge. Through gentle questioning we can assess what the child knows:

"Which object in your collage is rough (smooth, round, biggest...)?"
"What colors did you use in your painting today?"

Eliciting stories. The relationship between a child's thought processes and the artwork produced is an important one. Many educators advocate using children's art as a springboard for the development of early literacy skills (Cecil & Lauritzen, 1995; Olson 1994). The Reggio Emilia program (Edwards et al., 1992), for example, uses art as a way for preliterate children to document what they know or have learned.

Many teachers commonly ask children to dictate a title or story to go with their art-work. However, before diving into asking all children to provide a detailed explanation of their art, it is important to consider the child's purpose in creating each particular piece of art and what might be the best way to record or recognize the child's verbalizations about it.

Explorations. When children are first becoming familiar with an art medium, regardless of their age, their focus is not on expressing any deep thoughts. Instead they are just playing, experimenting, and learning to control the tools and materials. For example, a child handling a pair of scissors for the first time is going to be more interested in how to make them open and close, and how to hold them straight and make them cut, than in trying to make a particular shape. It would be inappropriate to ask this child to invent a title for the resulting "project" or to make up a story about it. Instead the child might be asked what he or she learned about using scissors.

One way to use art explorations to build literacy is to create a "work log" for the child. After selected explorations or when the child requests, record the child's description of what was learned about that particular medium. The log could be illustrated with photographs of the child using the material and/or samples of the child's explorations. The child should be actively involved in deciding what goes in the log, in illustrating the cover and pages, and in giving the log a title such as *Martha's First Book of Cutting* or *Kira's Color Mixing Experiments*.

Skill development or practice activities. Once children have developed some control over an art material, they may repeat, with small variations, artistic elements that they have learned to make successfully. A child, for example, might make a series of easel paintings that feature houses, or a group of collages that are made from cut-and-glued rectangles.

To provide an early literacy experience using practice activities, save the child's work instead of sending home the finished projects each day. A large piece of folded paper labeled with the child's name can serve as a portfolio. (See chapter 12 for more information about using portfolios.) When several pieces in the same medium have been collected, take some time to sit with the child and talk about each piece using positive feedback and leading questions. Then offer to help the child make a book of her artwork if she wishes. Glue the artwork on a colored paper background, punch holes and tie with yarn, or staple the pages together. Have the child think of a title for her art book, such as *My House Paintings* or *Lots of Rectangles*.

Reactive activities. Reactive activities done in response to an experience are intended to express the children's thoughts about what they have done, and are, therefore, an appropriate place to elicit a description from children. For example, if after a visit to the supermarket, several children have chosen to make collages using pieces of food packaging or have drawn pictures of the stacks of food, invite them to share their artwork and talk about what they remember about the trip. The children's discussion can be recorded on audio- or videotape, or written on a separate piece of paper to accompany the artwork.

Taking dictation. What is the best way to write down a child's comments? Many teachers write the child's dictation about their artwork directly on their pictures. In a busy preschool program or child care facility, this is often the quickest and easiest method to capture the words of many children in a short time. Many children do not seem to mind this. However, there are some children who are deeply disturbed by having someone else write on their paper. Most artists do not have someone else's writing across their artwork. Always ask permission before writing anything, including the child's name, on the front of an artwork and respect the children's right to write their own name or words if they wish, even if they are not yet able to do so precisely. Better yet, write on the back of the piece or on a separate piece of paper. One idea is to write the children's names ahead of time on self-stick labels which can then be stuck to the back of artwork as needed. Mounting the artwork on a colored paper background provides a space for title and name in the border. If artwork is being made into a book, the child's description can be written on the page opposite the artwork.

It is not always necessary to write down a child's words at the time the artwork is done. Saving the work until another day when there is a quiet moment to give the child undivided attention and really listening to what the child is saying can make the art-language experience much more meaningful for both the child and the teacher. This same conferencing procedure will be practiced in the writing process in later years.

TEACHER TO PARENT

Sample Letter to Parents: Responding to Their Child's Art

Parents also need to know how to respond to their child's art. Send home a letter that offers suggestions of ways they can talk to their child about the artwork.

Dear Parent,

It is a special occasion when your child brings home a piece of art. Each child's artwork is unique, a special part of him or her. Please take a moment to share the art with your child.

Children have many purposes in creating art. Perhaps today was a chance to explore what happened when blue and yellow mixed together. Or maybe your child practiced using scissors and glue and discovered a new way to make shapes.

To our adult eyes we may see only some mixed-up colors or odd sticky shapes. Do not ask "What is it?". It may not be important to your child that the art be something. Do not guess what it might be. You might be wrong.

Instead ask how it was done: You will help your child use words to describe what was learned.

Ask if there is a story to go with it. You will learn much more about the artist's imagination and assist in language development.

Describe what you see in the artwork—the lines, the colors, the shapes, the textures, and the patterns—and ask your child to do the same. You will help your child build vocabulary.

Share a memory of a piece of art you created or have seen. You will be teaching your child that art has been created by many people.

After sharing a piece of art, hang it in a special place for the family to see, such as on a door or a refrigerator. When a new artwork comes home, remove the old one and store it away. Someday your child will enjoy looking at his or her art and remembering that special moment.

Your child's teacher,

FIGURE 2–5 "Caitlin and I like to play with all these toys." Marker and crayon—Brittany, age 5

HOW SHOULD TEACHERS RESPOND TO PROBLEMS?

> Spending time in the art area talking to children is one of the best ways to show them that you value their work.
>
> DIANE TRISTER DODGE AND LAURA J. COLKER (1992, P. 80)

As children participate in art activities, a variety of difficulties can arise. Some of these are the result of the previous art experiences children bring with them. If a program is designed around open-ended activities that draw on the children's interests, and if the teachers show children that they value their artwork through thoughtful conversation, many of these problems will slowly disappear on their own.

Others are due to the variety of ways art materials respond to young children's manipulation. In responding to these problems it is important to keep in mind that children do not develop skills when an adult does the work for them nor do they develop self-confidence in their own abilities if their project is "improved" by a teacher.

Giving Encouragement

There will always be some children who hold back from participating in art activities. They may be afraid to take risks because they have had a bad experience with that material previously or are uncertain what to do. This fear must be respected. It is important to try to find out why they are afraid and then provide the needed assurance. Children may have been scolded for getting dirty, for drawing on the wall, or may have been made to copy art projects too difficult for them.

Never force a child to participate in an art activity. Allow children to watch others working. If they seem interested, offer to stay nearby and invite them to investigate the activity. Be subtle and positive. Offer materials to use and then slowly withdraw.

Children have different tolerance levels for messiness. Some dive into sticky and gooey materials with glee; others hold back. Allow children to explore the material on their own terms. Like adults, each child will like some art materials better than others.

If a child indicates a fear of getting clothes dirty, provide a smock to wear and discuss with the child's parents that young children do get art materials on their clothes sometimes. Suggest that parents should dress their child in simple, easy-to-wash clothing. A note should be sent to all parents asking them to dress their children in clothing appropriate for doing art. (See chapter 5, "Art Focus: Painting" for more detail on appropriate dress.)

Providing Comfort

Children cannot produce art if they are upset or worried. Teachers need to create a calm, accepting atmosphere that allows children to feel free to experiment and explore. This can be done by modeling an accepting attitude when interacting with children and their art. For example, if one child criticizes another's art by saying it is stupid or ugly, respond immediately with a statement appropriate to the incident, such as in the example that follow:

Start by making a positive statement about the artwork in question, such as, "Michelle has used many different textures in her collage." This provides assurance and comfort to the injured child.

Make it clear that the comment made was hurtful and unacceptable and that all art is acceptable. For example: "It is hurtful to say that about someone's art. Everybody makes their artwork the way they want."

Providing Direction

If a child is misusing an art tool or supply or struggling with a technique, intervene as subtly as possible. A quiet restatement of the directions, repetition of the safety rules, or a quick demonstration is usually sufficient when given directly to the child.

Building Self-Confidence

It is surprising that even very young children often exhibit a lack of confidence in being able to create art. It does not take much to make a child afraid to create art openly. When a child uses art materials, a product of some kind results, and even if the child is just exploring, in some sense that product is an extension of the child. An unkind word, an accident, a well-meaning attempt to make the product better, or the presence of a model that is beyond the ability of the child to copy can all diminish artistic confidence.

When children say, "Make it for me," there has been some interference in their natural desire to explore and play with art materials. These children need reassurance that their art is acceptable as they choose to make it. This can be done by eliminating patterns and models to copy, and by maintaining a "hands off" policy. An adult should never work on or "fix" a child's art.

If children insist they cannot create art, provide assurance by affirming that difference is valued. For example: "Each artist creates in her own way. Look at all the different ways the other children have used the paint (crayons, paper, boxes…)." Then ask a leading question:

"Can you invent a new way to...?"
"What would happen if...?"
"Have you tried...?"

HOW DOES TEACHING STYLE AFFECT PROGRAM DELIVERY?

Precut or patterned activities teach children that their own work is not valuable because it's never as tidy or realistic as the patterns.

SYDNEY GUREWITZ CLEMENS (1991, P. 9)

The Teacher as Facilitator

Children have been creating art on their own long before there were organized methods for the teaching of "art." Scratching lines in the dirt with a stick, building sand castles, and making footprint patterns in the snow are all highly creative child-initiated art activities. In educational situations, however, the creation of art reflects the interrelationship of the child with the purposes of the teacher.

Providing open-ended activities. An open-ended activity is one in which there are many possible ways the children can approach their artwork, and in which they are responsible for making their own artistic decisions. While children may be influenced by their experiences and/or the cultural images around them, they need to be able to incorporate these elements in their own unique way. In an open-ended activity, the teacher has

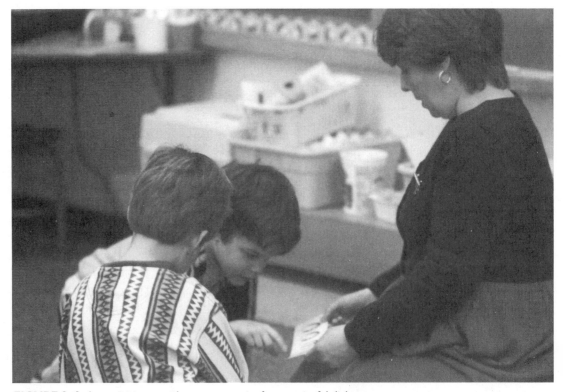

FIGURE 2–6 Art activities provide an opportunity for meaningful dialogue.

no preset idea about what the end product will look like. The children choose from the available materials, tools, and techniques, and then decide how they will use them. It is the children who determine the end result.

Demonstrating confidence. Teachers who provide open-ended art activities demonstrate a high level of confidence. They do not worry about what the product will look like or how it will be judged. They are more interested in the process the child goes through than in the product that may or may not result. These teachers are highly creative in setting up environments that are safe and interesting for curious artists to explore, and in providing experiences that inspire the children to produce art.

Providing a context. The teacher, as a facilitator, may sometimes provide a context for the art activity. The art exploration that is offered may relate to an experience that the children have shared, such as a book that has been read, or a field trip they have taken. The teacher may offer a special selection of materials for the children to investigate, or may model the use of certain materials. In doing so, the teacher must avoid adhering to a preconceived notion about how the activity should progress or what the results will be, and must be willing to follow the interests of the children even when they do not relate to the context the teacher has provided.

TEACHER TIP

Qualities of a Facilitating Teacher

1. The teacher displays many examples of artwork in the room, but does not present them as models for the children to copy.
2. The teacher provides a choice of materials.
3. The teacher allows children to use the materials as they wish.
4. The teacher does not require that the artwork look a certain way.
5. The teacher provides the children with ample time.

The Teacher as Director

Book after book, article after article, has railed against the prevailing practices in so many early childhood programs: giving children precut pieces to assemble, hanging up teacher-made models so the children can "see" how it is done, tracing hands to make turkeys, using paper plates to make lion faces, and giving children preprinted pictures to color, and perhaps, cut out and make into bag puppets.

There are many reasons why these practices have been so hard to eliminate.

It's safe. Many educators lack confidence in their own art abilities. They feel safe putting together a packaged product and feel they can teach the children how to do this. These teachers need to learn more about their own artistic abilities, by doing activities such as those on the following Studio Pages.

It pleases parents. These educators do not understand child art and are unsure of their goals, so they cannot explain the nature of child art to the parents. They think parents want to see "recognizable" art products. These teachers need to analyze their goals, study the nature of child art, and develop a program for educating parents. (See chapter 12 for guidance.)

It's harmless fun. Children who have experienced these kinds of pseudo-art projects are the ones who say they cannot draw or want the teacher to do it for them. It is not harmless. It takes away children's initiative and artistic self-confidence.

It's traditional. There is a place for tradition in classrooms, but it must have educational meaning. Easels are traditional in early childhood programs. They provide a wonderful, open-ended painting experience for preschoolers. Gluing eyes on precut pumpkins is not an educational experience. It is restricting and uncreative. It is a tradition children can do without.

It's convenient. Early childhood educators are overworked, have limited time, and too many children to service. It is easy to grab a commercial pattern for the "art table." This is perhaps a major underlying reason for the prevalence of precut and patterned projects.

To have a truly rich program in any of the curriculum areas takes thoughtful consideration and time. However, educators who hold strong beliefs about what child art should be will never compromise this belief, regardless of the time it takes.

TEACHER TIP

Aspects of an Overly Directive Approach

1. A model made by an adult or "competent" child is displayed by the teacher to show the children how their projects should look.
2. The teacher gives children only prepared materials such as precut shapes and/or counted-out pieces.
3. The teacher does not allow children to add any other materials to their projects.
4. The teacher gives the children adult-made or commercial stencils to trace, or pictures to color.
5. Children complain that they cannot do art. They want the teacher to do their projects for them.
6. The teacher limits the amount of time the children can work on their projects.
7. The teacher fixes, finishes, or changes a child's project so it "looks right."

SUMMARY: DELIVERING THE THOUGHTFUL ART PROGRAM

Our creations are in the first place, ourselves.

OZENFANT (MOGELON, 1969, P. 88)

Adults working with children and art need to be aware of themselves and what they bring to the interaction. How the teacher chooses to present art activities can result in self-confident, creative children or in frustrated, uninterested ones. If the teacher does not feel comfortable with an art material, the children will acquire this discomfort. If the teacher limits the children's choices or experiences, the children will rebel or withdraw. If the teacher provides teacher-made patterns, the children will be frustrated and feel that they cannot be successful in art.

The following list summarizes the information teachers need to know about themselves in order to understand and develop their skill as nurturers of young artists.

FIGURE 2–7 "My teacher." Crayon—David, age 3

1. We are artists when we make artistic decisions.
2. Our beliefs about ourselves as artists come from our past experiences.
3. Everyone uses the creative process to solve problems and explore ideas.
4. Our personal definition of art grows out of our past experiences with art.

It is not just children who need to grow. Teaachers and nurturing adults who work with young children need to examine their artistic past and plan their future. Whether teachers are starting out or have been working with children for years, they always need to be changing. Every group of children is different. Every activity will have a life of its own. There will be new art forms, new ways of working, and exciting new media. Traditional media may be found hazardous and fade from use. We will not always say the right thing at the right time. Our philosophy of art education will become more refined. Our definition of art will grow more inclusive. We will have successes and we will face failure.

There is no room for guilt. We must learn from our experiences, listen to others, and be willing to take risks. With thought and care, we will create the best possible art program for young artists.

FURTHER READING

> Learning in young children is the result of interaction between the child's thoughts and experiences with materials, ideas, and people.
>
> NAEYC (1986, p. 4)

These books will continue your growth as a creative and an artistic teacher.

Bos, B. (1978). *Don't move the muffin tins.* Roseville, CA: Turn-the-Page Press.
  This simple book describes a well-designed preschool art program based on open-ended explorations. There are many good suggestions and clearly described activities. However, a few may not meet current safety standards.

Cohen, E. P. and Gainer, R. S. [1976] (1995). *Art: Another language for learning.* Portsmouth, NH: Heinemann.
  Beautifully written vignettes of children and their art are skillfully combined with models of exemplary art teaching.

Edwards, B. (1979). *Drawing on the right side of the brain.* Los Angeles, CA: J. P. Tarcher.
  This book is a series of drawing lessons designed to increase visual perception and to create an understanding of the drawing process. The exercises are an excellent way for adults to increase their self-confidence in art.

Art Focus

PLANNING FOR ART

> Lay plans for the accomplishment of the difficult before it becomes difficult; make something big by starting with it when it is small.
>
> LAO TZU LXIII:149

Art is a complex discipline involving many skills and processes. There are many influences on teacher's decisions about what art activities they ultimately provide to their students. We have already seen how philosophy, goals, and teacher behavior affect the children's art program. Whether a curriculum is planned around themes, projects, learning centers, or play areas, the individual components are the activities—the specific things the children and the educator will be doing. It is important to plan these activities carefully, as a means of ensuring that nothing is forgotten, and as a way of providing a measure against which we can assess our delivery.

Activities need to be planned around the specific factors that will affect the dynamics of a particular group of children. The plans need to answer the following questions: who, why, where, when, what, and how? By planning answers to

FIGURE 2–8 When surrounded by active young children, it is important to have plans in place.

each of these questions ahead of time, teachers are better prepared to guide the art activities they offer the children. In this Art Focus section, each of these components is explained. In later Art Focus sections, specific activities using the basic art media are presented using this same structure.

Who? Group Composition

Every group of children is unique. The following characteristics must be considered when making plans:

What is the age and number of children? The age and number of students will affect the amount of time, space, and supervision for which the teacher must plan. Planning an activity with four one-year-olds will require very different decisions than designing a program for 20 five-year-olds. If the children are of mixed ages, will all of them be able to work with the same amount of supervision and be successful?

What are the children's previous experiences with art? The less familiar children are with an art medium, the more exploration they need. If the children are competent with a material, then more responsive activities can be planned. If a group contains children of various ages, developmental phases, and experience with media, carefully selected open-ended art activities will allow children to work comfortably at their own developmental levels.

Are there children with special needs? Check that each activity will be able to be accomplished by individual children. Do the activities need adaptation so that a child with special needs can have success? Select art activities that can be done by a wide range of children, and modify the materials, tools, and setup as necessary. (See chapter 11 for suggested ways to modify art activities.)

When? Time Frame

Consider the amount of time that will be available for the children to actually work on their art activities. Make sure there will be sufficient time to complete an activity whether on the same day or over a period of days. Will there be enough time for wet projects to dry? Be sure to allow time for sharing, discussing, and mounting finished work as well.

Why? Objectives

An *objective* is a statement describing a behavior that can be accomplished within the time frame of the activity. This is different from a **goal**, which is a statement of the kind of growth in the children's behavior that would be expected over a period of time and after many explorations.

Each objective is ultimately related to one of the growth areas. However, it is important to remember that growth in any of these areas is dependent on repetition and practice. The one experience provided in the activity must be repeated many times in other activities in order to foster meaningful growth. For example, the objective that the child will practice cutting paper with a scissors relates to the physical growth of the small muscles of the hand. It would not be expected that after one opportunity a child would be expert with a scissors or would have fully developed the small hand muscles.

Objectives are usually written using words that describe *observable* and *measurable* behaviors, specific to the activity. An example of an objective for a cutting activity might be: "The child will practice using a scissors to independently cut out a variety of shapes." Well-written objectives immediately focus our attention on the behaviors we need to facilitate so that the child will be successful. A good activity will have objectives from most or all of the growth areas. The following sample objectives show how objectives relate to the growth areas discussed in chapter 1.

Sample objectives and related growth areas.

1. In this activity the child will develop *emotionally* by:
   - Using a scissors independently
   - Painting how it felt when he petted the rabbit
2. In this activity the child will develop *socially* by:
   - Sharing a box of markers with another child without disagreement
   - Working inside a designated space on the mural
3. In this activity the child will develop *physically* by:
   - Cutting a variety of shapes out of paper without adult aid
   - Applying glue to paper and attaching small objects so that they are well fastened
4. In this activity the child will develop *cognitively* by:
   - Using the color names for the paint
   - Answering questions about an art print
   - Observing and describing what happened when two colors are mixed together.

Where? Setup

Teachers need to consider where the children will be working. How should the furniture be arranged? Where should the supplies be located? What changes will have to be made so that this activity will run smoothly?

What? Materials

The materials and preparation required for an activity often influence whether teachers decide to offer the activity. It is important to list the supplies needed for each activity. This will quickly indicate what items are on hand, and what has to be found or bought. It is often possible, with a little creativity, to make substitutions, but the key to success is to keep the materials basic and safe. The more the children can handle the supplies on their own, without constant supervision, the more they will grow artistically.

Beware of activities that have a long list of required materials, and ones that involve a great deal of preparation such as cutting certain sizes, sorting objects, or gluing pieces together. None of this is necessary for a great art activity and may, in fact, reflect an overly directed one.

In the long run the most essential consideration is the creative possibilities inherent in the materials and tools. Some materials allow more exploration than others. For example, the soft flexibility of play dough has made it one of the most popular modeling materials for young children. Precut bear shapes, on the other hand, have only a few possible ways to be used by the children.

Use the following material checklist for judging the materials used in an activity.

Materials Checklist

1. This material allows children to explore independently.
2. This material can be used many times and in many ways by the children.
3. This material is pleasant and easy to use.
4. This material is safe for the children who will use it.
5. This material does not require excessive preparation or cleanup.

How? Procedure

Once an activity is selected it is necessary to plan how to organize it. Decide how to introduce the materials and procedures to the children.

The transition into the activity. The transition should be designed to get the children interested and at the same time let them know where and how to use the materials. The type of transition will depend on the age of the children and their previous experiences. There are many examples of transitions in the Art Focus sections in the following chapters.

What to do. This is the step-by-step procedure that describes what the teacher and children will be doing.

What to say. Teachers need to consider carefully the kinds of questions to ask, vocabulary to use, and responses to give to the young artists at work.

The transition out of the activity. At the end of the activity, provide the children with closure. This can be a statement that summarizes what the children have been doing, or a question that makes them reflect on their learning. There should then be a procedure for how the child will put away the supplies and finished work. This should be followed by a smooth transition to the next activity.

If the children do not know what to do next, use their interests to draw attention to another area. An example of a closing statement might be: "You had a grand time drawing all those lines! Put your drawing in your cubby and then maybe you would like to play with the line puzzle on the game table."

What are the teacher's personal objectives?

In every plan, teachers need to establish their own goals for self-improvement. The teacher can put a box of crayons on a table and let the children draw. It happens every day! But a truly inspiring teacher can take a simple activity and, through thoughtful actions and words, increase the children's artistic growth multifold.

Educators need to aim high. At the same time there is so much to think and do when surrounded by active young children, that very few activities are perfectly delivered. Choose one area to concentrate on improving during each activity. It could be how to respond to the children's art, the way to ask questions, or how well the supplies are arranged. Teachers need to study the way children respond to their behavior or classroom setup. They are the best indicators of success.

What Has the Teacher Learned?

After presenting an activity to a group of young children, take a moment for quiet reflection. Assess whether or not the activity went the way it was planned. Try to isolate the particular factors that made the activity successful or unsuccessful.

- Were the materials properly presented?

ACTIVITY PLAN FORMAT

ACTIVITY:

Who?	Group composition age(s): Group size:
When?	Time frame:
Why?	Objectives: In this activity the child will develop…
Where?	Setup:
What?	Materials:
How?	Procedure: Transition in: What to do: What to say: Transition out:

Personal objective:

What I have learned:

FIGURE 2–9 Activity plan format

- Did the children become excited about the activity?
- What made the children visibly satisfied?
- Was there a terrible mess to clean up?
- Ask what could be improved or changed to make the activity more appropriate for these children.
- Record these observations on the activity plan. These brief notes will help tremendously the next time a similar activity is planned.

Writing an Activity Plan

Figure 2–9 provides an activity plan format that summarizes the above information. This or a similar form can be used whenever a new activity is being considered. The outline provides all the basic information needed to create successful activities. See figure 2–10 for a sample activity plan.

SAMPLE ACTIVITY PLAN: A Painting Exploration

Who?   **Group composition age(s):** Three- and four-year-olds
            Group size: 2 or 3 at a time

When?   **Time frame:** 3-hour session

Why?   **Objectives:**

In this activity children will develop...

1. Emotionally, by being trusted to mix paint
2. Socially, by playing a group game and then working alongside others and taking turns mixing paints
3. Physically, by filling scoops, by mixing paint with spoons, and by manipulating a variety of paintbrushes in different thicknesses of paint
4. Cognitively, by comparing the textures of different paints, by making predictions, and by using words to describe colors, shapes, and textures

Where?   **Setup:**
Transition on rug. Painting at easel or table.

What?   **Materials:**
Containers of tempera paint in a variety of colors
Labeled containers of different materials to add to paint: sand, salt, soap flakes
Small scoops, brushes, and paper at the easel or on newspaper-covered table

How?   **Procedure:**
Transition in:
Large group:(on rug) Play "Texture Search" game: Name a texture; each child has to find something with that texture and touch it. Have children take turns naming textures they find.

What to do:
1. Ask: "What is the texture of paint?"
   "How could we change the texture of paint?"
   "What do you think would happen if you added these things to the paint?"
   "Would you like to add one and see what happens?"
2. Demonstrate how to add one of the materials to the paint. Tell children that they can add any of the materials to their paint when they come to the painting place.
3. As children come to paint, supervise them as they add materials to the color of their choice and then use it in their paintings.

What to say:
Descriptive: "You are using the large brush."   "You used the textured paint to _____"
Questioning: "Which paint did you like using better?"   "Which paint was hard to spread?"

Transition out:
Say: "You had fun painting with the different textured paint. You can add a different texture the next time you paint. Let's put your painting over here to dry. What would you like to do now? I see your friend Ann is having fun with the blocks."

Personal objective:
I will work on improving my "wait" time. I need to allow the children more time to work before I start talking to them. I will watch for the child to pause before interacting, so that I do not interrupt the creative process.

What I have learned:
I need to find a better place to set up the paint and texture additions so the children can independently add textures whenever they wish.

FIGURE 2–10 Sample activity plan

Studio Page 7

SELF-EXPLORATION: WHAT SHOULD I DRAW?

Use crayons to draw the first thing that comes into your head. When you are finished, answer these questions.

What was the first color you chose?

_____

Where did you place the first thing on your paper?

_____

Did your ideas change as you worked?

_____

How did you know when you were finished?

_____

What artistic decisions did you make?

_____

How is your art like a child's? How is it different?

_____

Studio Page *8*

SELF-EXPLORATION: MY FIRST ART EXPERIENCE

What is the earliest art experience you remember?

_____

_____

_____

What did you do?

_____

_____

_____

Where and when was it?

_____

_____

_____

What materials did you use?

_____

_____

_____

Who was there with you? What did they say?

_____

_____

_____

Did anyone comment on your work?

_____

_____

_____

What emotions did you feel?

_____

_____

_____

Studio Page 9

MY PERSONAL TIME LINE OF ART

Fill in all the art experiences you remember, at about the age you experienced them. You can include such things as art courses you have taken, museums you visited, a specific artwork you made, an art book you read, an art movie you have seen, a comment made by a teacher or parent about your art, and so forth.

AGE	EXPERIENCE
Birth to age 5	
5 to 10 years	
10 to 15 years	
15 to 20 years	
20 to 30 years	
20 to 30 years	
30 to 40 years	
40 to 50 years	
50+ years	

WHAT DOES MY TIME LINE TELL ME?

Study your time line and ask yourself these questions:

1. Do you remember more experiences from your early childhood or more from your later years?

2. How many are happy memories?

3. Do any memories make you feel uncomfortable?

4. Do you remember any of the adults who participated in creating these memories?

5. How will these memories affect the way you will approach young children and their art?

Studio Page 10

SELF-EXPLORATION: WHAT'S IN A NAME?

In this box, write your name in as many different ways as possible. When the paper is full or you run out of ideas, make a list of all the ways they are different in terms such as color, size, and thickness.

How many different ways did you invent?

_____

How many look similar to your signature?

_____

How many look different?

_____

How did you use your creativity to invent new ways to write your name?

_____

_____

_____

_____

_____

_____

_____

SELF-EXPLORATION ACTIVITY: DEFINING ART

Close your eyes and picture a piece of artwork you have seen in a book, museum, home, or store. Look at it carefully.

What colors and shapes do you see?

_____

_____

_____

_____

What art media is it made with?

_____

_____

_____

_____

Where did you see it?

_____

_____

_____

Who made it?

_____

_____

_____

Why is it a piece of art?

_____

_____

_____

Where did you acquire the ability to define art?

_____

_____

_____

_____

Studio Page 12

SELF-EXPLORATION: WHAT DO I BELIEVE A TEACHER IS?

1. On a piece of paper, draw a picture of a teacher teaching a class. Draw the picture any way you like. It can be detailed or simple, realistic or symbolic.

2. When you are finished, study your picture and answer these questions:

    Is the teacher a man or a woman?

    _____

    What is the teacher doing?

    _____

    Is the teacher a director or facilitator?

    _____

    Do you know who the teacher is?

    _____

    What age are the children?

    _____

    What are the children doing?

    _____

    How is the room arranged?

    _____

3. What kind of person do you think a teacher should be?

    _____

    _____

    _____

    _____

    _____

    _____

    _____

    _____

    _____

    _____

    _____

How Young Artists Grow

Children's Artistic Development

❝ *The teacher who knows the difference between adult and child world views is likely to communicate and educate more successfully than one not so prepared.* ❞

•

DAVID ELKIND (1974, P. 134)

Questions addressed in this chapter:

When does art begin?

Why is drawing important for young children?

How do the very young draw?

What is known about the artistic development of children?

What social and cultural factors affect artistic development?

What do child art development models tell educators?

SUMMARY: The Child Artist

FURTHER READING

ART FOCUS: Exploring Drawing

Young Artists at Work

Andy picks up a crayon and grasps it tightly in his fist. He slowly approaches the large white paper before him. Arm held stiffly, he rubs the crayon on the paper. Lifting the crayon, he looks at the smudge he has left behind. With his other hand he touches it, rubs it, and looks at his fingers. The mark is still there. He bends over and sniffs it with his nose. Cautiously, Andy looks up. Is this all right? Can he do this? But no one is stopping him. He returns to the paper. With broad strokes, Andy makes his first true marks on the world. Broad sweeps of color up and down, back and forth. Again and again, on paper after paper, at the beginning of his second year of life, he draws…

WHEN DOES ART BEGIN?

Just as the first sounds that babies make are the same around the world, children's first scribbles are also the same.

ELAINE PEAR COHEN AND RUTH STRAUS GAINER (1995, P. 28)

It begins with the line—a line that reflects the physical control of the child over his body. The one-year-old is at the beginning of a long and complex process, which in the eighth year of life, will end with a mastery of line that is remarkably expressive and controlled. Toddlers do not know that this is where their explorations with line will lead; they only know the moment—this pleasurable and exciting moment in which they have used a tool and produced a result.

All of us were once infants, unable to move on our own. Step by step, we learned to crawl and then to walk. At first we walked unsteadily, clasping a guiding hand. Soon we could take baby steps on our own, and in no time at all we could run, and run we did!

In the same way each child grows as an artist. Although no newborn is an artist by reason of birth or genetic heritage, inside every infant is the potential to grow into an artist. When the time is right, the children start their artistic journey, tentatively making small marks upon the world. These marks enlarge and change from wavy scribbles, to enclosed shapes, to symbols that encompass the child's experience. This pattern of artistic growth repeats itself in every young child, everywhere in the world. Each child goes through visible stages of artistic growth, reflecting the increasing muscular control and rapid cognitive growth of the very young. This development does not proceed alone, but accompanies simultaneous growth in language and reasoning. By viewing artistic growth as a developmental process, one that every human being has gone through, guiding adults will be better able to respond to the artistic growth of the young children in their care.

WHY IS DRAWING IMPORTANT FOR YOUNG CHILDREN?

Drawing is only one of many art forms, and yet it plays an overwhelmingly important role in the definition and analysis of children's art. Why is drawing more important than painting, modeling, construction, and designing? An artist would say drawing is the manipulation of lines to create a visual effect. At its simplest, drawing can be done with a finger in the dust or on a frosty window pane. The tools used for drawing are little more than the extensions of the finger—a stick in the dirt, a pencil, a pen. Drawing is where the toddler's art exploration begins, and where the adult achieves mastery and recognition as an artist. In our culture, which shows less respect than it should for other art forms and artistic abilities, we fully expect that self-proclaimed "artists" can draw well.

But drawing is more than an art form. Drawing is also intimately linked to linguistic growth. The earliest written languages were drawings of pictographs. Children's drawings are the beginning of their writing. Artistic growth also reflects the cognitive growth that is necessary for them to become writers. When we place a drawing tool in a child's hand, we are also handing them a writing tool. Drawing is important, because it is a tool with which to think and communicate. As the United States Department of Education states, "Children who are encouraged to draw and 'scribble' stories at an early age will later learn to compose more easily, more effectively, and with greater confidence than children who do not have this encouragement" (1986, p. 14).

HOW DO THE VERY YOUNG DRAW?

Toddlers between the ages of one and three need many opportunities to draw. They need to hold in their hands a tool that marks and pull and push it over a variety of surfaces. At

FIGURE 3–I "Mommy yelling." Marker—Laurel, age 4

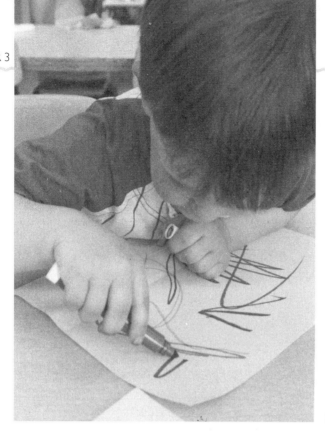

FIGURE 3–2 Art begins with a scribble.

first their movements will be aimless, and they will use paper by the mile. But in spurts and in sputters, children begin to repeat and vary the marks they have made previously. During this period, toddlers become comfortable with the drawing tools and refine their control over the direction and type of line they can produce. Physical growth of their bodies is reflected in how they hold the drawing tool and in the direction of the lines they make.

Physical Growth and Drawing

Much of the artwork produced by toddlers is determined by their physical development.

One-year-olds. Children develop from the head down and from the center of the body out (Cherry et al.,1989, p. 53). At the age of one, arm movement is undifferentiated. Children grasp the crayon or pencil tightly in their fists and make whole arm movements, up and down, back and forth. They can also lift and drop their arms, stabbing and punching the paper with much gusto and verbal expression. This period has been called by some researchers that of the "random or uncontrolled scribble," (Lowenfeld and Brittain, 1987). Watching the child at work, it does seem at times that the scribble has a mind of its own, careening off the edges of the paper and onto the table or floor. But there is also thoughtful deliberation. Watch the child at work, pausing in mid-line, expressing delight. The arm and hand may not yet be under control, but a mind is growing there!

Two-year-olds. Between the ages of one and two, toddlers begin to have control over their elbows. This allows them to create new marks. Sweeping arcs are created as children move the lower arm independently. Lines now have curved edges. They loop and swirl across the paper exuberantly. Children may also become conscious of the act of drawing as separate from other activities, verbalizing their desire to draw and curiously watching others draw and write.

Three-year-olds. With continued physical maturation, children develop control over their wrists. Now they can control the line that issues from their drawing tools. They can start and stop at will, and lift the crayon and place it down again close to where they want it. Scribbles begin to be joined into lopsided geometric figures. Control over the fingers is also slowly developing. The tight fist may be replaced by a looser grip, although some children may still have no particular hand preference.

As children persist in repeating motions and creating the resulting lines and figures, they develop skill and control, but something else is also happening. One day the child will look at the lines, the mess of scribbles, and say, "Look at my doggie," or "I made a bear." And although ten minutes later, the child may give a totally different name to the scribble, the lines, still unrecognizable to us, have developed meaning for that child. This development is tremendously exciting. We can "see" and "hear" the child thinking.

Now is when parents get enthusiastic. They study the drawings, trying to find what their child sees in the lines. They label the pictures and hang them up. Their child is an artist! Their child is communicating! But they are also bewildered, because it will be many months yet before they can find something recognizable in their child's work.

WHAT IS KNOWN ABOUT THE ARTISTIC DEVELOPMENT OF CHILDREN?

> One has to respect the time of maturation, of development, of the tools of doing and understanding, of the full, slow, extravagant, lucid and ever-changing emergence of children's capacities; it is a measure of cultural and biological wisdom.
>
> LORIS MALAGUZZI (IN EDWARDS ET AL., 1992, P. 74)

In the past hundred years, children's art has attracted the attention of many researchers. Some have collected samples of children's art and looked for patterns (Kellogg, 1969; 1970). Others have tried to use it as a way to measure intelligence (Goodenough, 1926; Harris and Goodenough, 1963). Many have used it as a means to understanding how children think (Gardner, 1991; Golomb, 1981; Winner, 1989). Over the years, general patterns have appeared and new insights have been offered. A review of the some of this research will shed some light on the relationship between children and their art.

The Work of Rhonda Kellogg

> If the observations I have made lead to increased study of children's art, I shall be delighted.
>
> RHONDA KELLOGG (1969, P. 12)

From the 1950s to the 1970s, Rhonda Kellogg (1969; 1970) collected over one million drawings done by children from the United States and other countries. These drawings provided the basis for her in-depth analysis of the patterns and forms found in children's art. Today these drawings can be found in the Rhonda Kellogg Child Art Collection in San Francisco. They represent a commitment to the collection of child art unparalleled in early art education research.

Kellogg was one of the first to recognize that the scribbles of young children were an important part of the child's development and that the marks made by young children the world over were more the same than they were different. Based on her collection, Kellogg identified several patterns that were similar in all the drawings she analyzed.

Basic scribbles. She isolated twenty kinds of markings *(Basic Scribbles)* made by children two and under. The Basic Scribbles consisted of all the lines the children make, with or without the use of their eyes, whether using a crayon on paper, finger paint, or scratching the lines in the dirt. She saw these strokes as representative of the neural and muscular system of the child and forerunners of all the strokes needed to make art and language symbols. Her descriptions of these Basic Scribbles were offered as a way to describe the art of the very young child.

Placement patterns. In addition, she looked at how children under two placed these scribbles on their paper. She felt that the placement patterns were the earliest evidence that the child was guiding the initial formation of shapes. She hypothesized that children react to the scribbles they make by seeing shapes in the drawing itself, rather then trying to represent the shapes seen in the world around them, and that visual and motor pleasure were a motivating factor in causing children to scribble.

Diagrams and combines. Between the ages of two and three, Kellogg found that children began to draw shapes which they then combined into groups. She termed these groups *Aggregates*. At this stage, children move from unplanned scribbling to being able to remember and repeat shapes they have drawn previously. These shapes become the basis of all the symbols later found in children's drawings.

Mandalas, suns, and people. Kellogg was most fascinated by the symbols that often emerged between the ages of three and four. She noted that the symbols seemed to follow a developmental sequence and felt that the mandalas and suns provided the stimuli for the child's first drawings of a person (figure 3–3).

Importance of Kellogg's work. At the time Kellogg did her research, most adults considered child art to be a poor attempt to represent objects and persons in the child's environment and therefore, worthless or in need of correction. Children were discouraged or even forbidden from scribbling, and encouraged to copy adult models. She felt that drawing was an expression of the growth of the child's physical and mental processes, that it was the process of drawing that was important. She argued that children need plenty of time for free drawing and scribbling in order to develop the symbols that will later become the basis of all drawing and writing.

Based on her observations, she felt strongly that "...the child who has frequent opportunity to draw without adult interference learns faster and increases his cognitive ability more than he would if he were denied the opportunity" (1969, p. 100). She added that it is wrong to label children's work for them, as when an adult looks at a *human symbol* and calls it "Mama" or "Daddy." She offered her terminology (e.g., human symbol) for the marks of the young child as an alternative to what she characterized as an adult tendency to seek real objects in the art of the child.

The Work of Lowenfeld and Brittain

> It is not the adult's answer, but the child's striving toward his own answer that is crucial.
>
> VIKTOR LOWENFELD AND W. LAMBERT BRITTAIN (1987, P. 11)

Lowenfeld and Brittain (1987) built on Kellogg's work with young children and expanded the developmental sequence through adolescence. They postulated distinct types of child art for each stage and warned against outside interference in the child's process of self-expression, such as the teaching of specific ways to draw. Instead children moved

FIGURE 3–3 Mandalas, suns, and people. Marker—Various children, ages 2-5

through these stages naturally as they matured and it was the teacher's role to provide the time and materials for children to explore on their own (table 3–1).

The Importance of Kellogg, Lowenfeld, and Brittain

The work of these thoughtful educators has had a profound influence on how educators approach the art of young children. The stages they developed are basically descriptive generalizations of the kinds of drawings children make at different ages. Scribbling, shape making, and the development of graphic symbols were found to be important parts of the normal development of children. Child art also came to be seen as an important facet for understanding how children think.

Art and Cognitive Development

Depiction of aspects of the world through drawings, constructions in blocks and clay, or other iconic vehicles is a symbolic avenue of great significance in early childhood.

HOWARD GARDNER (1991, P. 56)

TABLE 3–1 Developmental stages of child art, based on Kellogg (1967) and Lowenfeld and Brittain (1987)

AGE	STAGE	CHARACTERISTICS
2–4 years	SCRIBBLING	
A. 1–2½	Random Scribbling	Random lines are made using the whole arm Tool held with whole hand Lines may extend beyond paper
B. 2½–3	Controlled Scribbling	Begins to use wrist motions Stays on paper, makes smaller marks Controls where lines are placed
C. 3–4½	Named Scribbles	Holds tool with fingers Can make many different lines and shapes Names scribbles, but often changes name
4–7	PRESCHEMATIC	Develops a set of symbols to represent concepts May not resemble or be in proportion to real objects Learns pictures communicate to others Begins to value his product
7–9	SCHEMATIC	Drawing shows concept, not real images Baseline and skyline appear X-ray drawings appear
9–12	DAWNING REALISM	Objects are drawn smaller, with more detail Less concern for placement of objects Realizes symbols do not represent real images
12–14	PSEUDO-NATURALISTIC/REALISTIC DRAWING	Detailed figures, cartoon images Shading, proportion, and perspective appear, more or less successfully Spontaneous drawing ends, except for those who go on in art
14 +	ARTISTIC DECISION: ADOLESCENT ART	Some pursue naturalistic drawing Many copy or imitate various styles before developing their own

Child art as a multifaceted process. Instead of seeing artistic development as a sequence of levels leading to realistic art work, as Lowenfeld did, recent researchers have approached art creation as a multifaceted process, characterized by distinct drawing approaches that develop and then continue to exist and be utilized throughout the life of the individual.

Child art as an expression of cognitive growth. Howard Gardner has led the way in recent investigations into the cognitive aspects of early childhood art. In general, Gardner (1991) supports Piaget's idea (1959) that sensory learning dominates the first 18 months of life, and that this is followed by a symbolic period during the preschool years, in which children master the symbolic forms of language, number, and art. According to his theory of multiple intelligences, Gardner proposes that cognitive development takes place in waves rather than stages, with burgeoning knowledge developing within a specific intelligence and then overflowing into other intelligences.

FIGURE 3–4 "Route 79 going from my house to town." Marker—Matthew, age 5

The first wave. Sometime between the ages of 18 months and two years, Gardner believes children become capable of using symbols to communicate their knowledge that events consist of objects and actions. Although language-oriented, this symbolic realization "spills" into other intellectual domains. At this point, if asked to draw a truck, the child scribbles with the marker while making truck sounds.

The second wave. At about age three, a second wave called *topographical mapping* occurs. Now the child's graphic symbols can express the spatial relationships of real objects, such as showing two adjoining circles and identifying the top one as a head.

The third wave. Around the age of four, the child begins to utilize numerical relationships *(digital mapping)*. For example, children may draw four human figures to represent four people in their family or count the eyes on the drawing of a face.

The fourth wave. The most educationally important event occurs sometime during the fifth, sixth, or seventh year when children begin to invent their own notational systems. Children now draw pictures using graphic symbols of their own invention, for such purposes as to remember experiences or to "list" belongings. Gardner, although he points out the influence of seeing adults using notational systems, feels that there is an innate human propensity to create such systems.

Table 3–2 summarizes the relationship between cognitive growth and how it is expressed in children's art.

Artistic development as modality. Wolf and Perry (1989) describe five separate areas of development in children's drawings, each of which develops at a certain age, but then persists throughout life as a way of approaching art. Instead of disappearing with maturation, toddlers' playing with art media, and their expression of bodily movement through art, continue in the artwork of all adults, including professional

TABLE 3–2 Art and cognitive growth, based on Gardner (1991)

AGE	COGNITIVE UNDERSTANDING	ART PRODUCED
Causal Relationships		
1½–2	Discovers relationship between object and event	Draws a cat by scribbling and meowing at same time
Spatial Relationships		
2–3	Discovers spatial relationships	Draws cat by putting a circle (head) beside another circle (body)
Numerical Relationships		
3–5	Represents numerical concepts	Draws cat with four legs, two ears, and one tail
Notational Relationships		
5–7	Invents or learns meaningful symbols of the culture	Draws cat with tail, whiskers, and pointy ears and labels it "CT"

artists. The same is true of young preschoolers' labeling of presymbolic scribbles and their later use of relative sizes, shapes, and conventional symbols.

Incorporating these ideas, Kindler and Darras (1994) have proposed a model of artistic development which presents artistic production as a twofold process. One part of the process is comprised of biologically propelled physical and cognitive growth. The other is the social and cultural learning, including the formal teaching, to which the

TABLE 3–3 Multimedia modes of artistic production, based on Kindler and Darras (1994)

CHILD	Mode 1	Mode 2	Mode 3	Mode 4	Mode 5
Says:	Random sounds	Words	Matches sound & action	Naming	Story
Draws:	Random marks	Shapes	Action symbols	Object symbols	Pictures in cultural style (understandable without verbalization)
Moves:	Random movements	Conscious control	Self-imitation	Repetition	Imitation of cultural style
ADULT	Media exploration	Simple doodles	Complex doodles	Shorthand symbols (e.g., stick figures)	Detailed recognizable symbols in style of culture

FIGURE 3–5 Within an age group, children will be found who are working in all of the modes. (1) Exploration. Marker—Andrew, age 3; (2) Initial shapes. Crayon—Kelsey, age 3; (3) Action symbol. Marker—Ross, age 3; (4) Story symbols. Pencil—Michelle, age 3

child is exposed. Like Wolf and Perry, these researchers emphasize that in their model, unlike Lowenfeld's model of linear growth, individuals do not lose their earlier approaches to art production, but incorporate them or return to them as needed throughout their lives.

Based on the work of these researchers, the multimedia chart indicates the possible range of art behaviors a child might exhibit (table 3–3). Rather than specific ages or levels, artistic production is organized by modes of behavior. During one's lifetime an individual may function in one or more of these modes in varying contexts. For example, upon meeting an unfamiliar medium, most children and adults will operate in the exploratory mode, making random movements as they try to assess the nature of the material. Once they have learned to skillfully control a material, they will attempt detailed, graphic, and symbolic expression.

This model shows how a child's art is more than the picture on the paper. It is also what the child says and how the child moves. Art production is a *multimedia* blend of graphic, verbal, and kinesthetic expression that reveals the child's thought processes. Comparing the behavior of a particular child to the models presented here will help teachers plan suitable art experiences for that child.

WHAT SOCIAL AND CULTURAL FACTORS AFFECT ARTISTIC DEVELOPMENT?

> Young children are not alike, each has unique qualities and features that are evident early in life.
>
> SARAH HAMMOND LEEPER (IN LEEPER ET AL., 1974, P. 42)

An examination of social and cultural context in which young artists function reveals that there are many important ways in which guiding adults and other environmental factors influence young artists—some to good effect and some detrimentally.

Defining Art Materials

Adults determine what art materials are acceptable for children to use. We set the limits on what is creative art and what is not. Smearing finger paint on paper is encouraged; smearing cereal on the wall is not. Are egg cartons an art material? Should we

FIGURE 3–6 "A flower." These 12 pictures done by the same five-year-old show how skill and familiarity with media affect how the resulting artwork looks. The pencil and crayon drawings are far more controlled than the cut paper, yarn, and collage pictures. Laurel, age 5.

use food products in art? The cultural definition of what is an art material, and what is not, will be transmitted to the child. Because of cultural traditions, some art media have higher value than others. For example, an oil painting may be considered fine art, whereas weaving is considered craft, even though both involve the manipulation of art elements in highly skillful and creative ways.

Experience with Art Media

Adults also determine how much experience children have with a material. The more opportunity to use art media and tools children have, the more comfortable and adept they will become with those materials. All individuals, regardless of their age, need to spend time exploring a medium before they can use it expressively. Because in our culture young children usually have many opportunities to draw, they usually show their highest level of symbol development in their drawings. The same child may produce much less "competent"-looking artwork if asked to use an unfamiliar material. Children will quickly revert to scribbles in their first finger painting or watercolor (figure 3–6). Repetition and practice are the keys to improving skills at any level. Even adults with excellent fine-motor control find themselves scribbling the first time they try to draw freehand with a mouse on a computer.

Availability of Art Materials

Children are influenced by what is going on around them. They are more likely to be interested in doing art if other people around them are also doing art, and if art materials are visible and easily obtained. Young children may make drawings in mud and soap foam on their own, but they are not going to choose formal drawing, painting, or modeling activities unless guiding adults have offered such opportunities to them.

The Environment

Young children may not see the world in the same way adults do, but they are influenced by the pictures they see, the kinds of objects that surround them, and the artistic reactions of their guiding adults to these things. Children who grow up in places where most houses have flat roofs, draw house symbols that have flat roofs. Children who have seen that people come in many colors, whether in their community or in pictures, and are comfortable with that fact, are more likely to include skin color in their art. Exposure to a wide variety of interesting objects challenges the child to invent new symbols or refine existing ones. For example, after viewing a live bird, children may add more details to their symbols for bird.

Children who have seen examples of a variety of art forms and are taught to value them, are more likely to incorporate elements from these examples into their own art. Dennis (1966) found that children raised in environments with plentiful visual imagery, and surrounded by many drawings of people, had higher scores on the Goodenough Draw-A-Man Test. McFee and Degge (1977, p. 334) cite studies that indicate that children from cultures with stylistic drawings will learn to draw in that style.

Emotional State

How a child is feeling will greatly influence the artwork the child produces. A child who has just experienced a traumatic event may use art as a way to express deep feelings. Tornados, earthquakes, accidents, and death often elicit scribbling, stabbing at the paper, and splashing of paint from people of all ages. Art can serve as an emotional release for every individual. As guiding adults, we need to bring sensitivity to the artistic interaction. With understanding and encouragement, we can allow the child to work through these deep feelings.

Teachers also need to understand how their own actions and those of parents can influence how a child feels about art. Children who are pressured to make their art match an adult "ideal," or are frustrated by an art material that is beyond their physical ability to control it, may develop feelings of failure. Such feelings may lead to a reluctance to participate in future art activities. Similarly, children who feel their artwork is rejected or unacceptable also retreat from art activities. That is why it is equally important that teachers show their acceptance of the child's work and teach parents how to encourage their young artists.

Seeing the Whole Child and the Child's Art

All of these factors interact together with the physical and cognitive development of the child in order to produce the resulting art (figure 3–7). Each child is a unique combination of these factors. We can never assume that because a child is a certain age, or is offered the same materials as another, we can predict exactly what that child will do

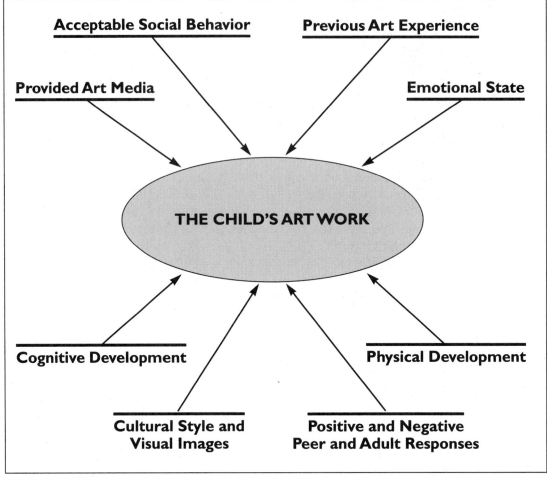

FIGURE 3–7 Influences on children's art

with them. This is what makes teaching art to children so exciting. Every day is full of fresh, new graphic images for the teachers to enjoy.

WHAT DO CHILD ART DEVELOPMENT MODELS TELL EDUCATORS?

The growth of young children from exploring scribblers to symbol creating artists is an amazing journey. Guiding adults need to provide art experiences that will enhance the child's journey. These models of children's artistic development have been provided to help teachers to better understand the art behavior of young children, so that they can offer the most appropriate art experiences.

Four Ground Rules

From these models, four ground rules emerge for teaching art to young children.

Set realistic expectations. These models enhance understanding of why children's art looks the way it does. Among young children, expect to see scribbling, named scribbles, and simple and complex graphic symbols. Within an age cohort the type of art produced by children may vary widely, depending on the mode of drawing being demonstrated, the children's cultural and visual perception experiences, and their familiarity with the media. For example, it is not at all unusual, in a group of four-year-olds, to have some children scribbling, some using a limited number of symbolic forms, and some drawing complex graphic symbols. We must accept the scribbler's approach to drawing as being just as valid and important as the more adult-pleasing graphic symbols.

Value child art as a developmental process, not a product. Teachers must find ways of recording and presenting not just the final static product, but the whole multimedia art event. Anyone who has watched and participated in a child's art activity knows that the final product is almost a letdown. Artwork needs to be accompanied by what the children said, the stages the works passed through, and how the children moved as they worked. This is a challenge for a busy, overworked teacher, but it is not impossible. (See chapter 12 for suggested ways to do this.)

Understand better what the child is thinking.

- A child banging and stabbing the paper with a crayon is exploring the medium.
- A child making engine sounds as the marker races around the paper is demonstrating, in a multimedia way, the understanding that objects can create events.
- A child drawing a horse, using two contiguous circles and three lines for legs, is showing an understanding of the basic spatial relationships of horses.
- A child carefully counting the fingers on a person symbol is demonstrating an understanding of numerical relationships.
- A child drawing a map of the room and using different-colored circles to represent each of the toys is inventing an original notational system.

Select activities that are suitable for particular children. The art activities teachers select must be open-ended. There must always be room for exploration as well as symbol production.

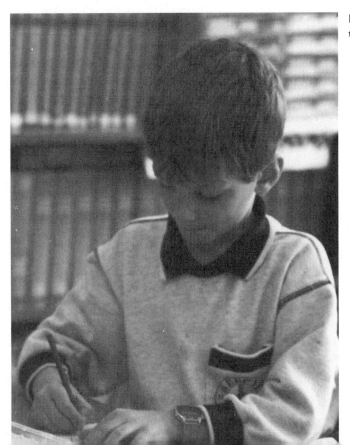

FIGURE 3–8 Children need to know their drawings are valued.

Types of Art Activities

Based on these models, there are three kinds of art activities that are most suitable for children under six.

Exploration activities. The base of all production, the first phase of development is the exploration of the medium. *Exploration,* therefore, must be the mainstay of early childhood art programs. Children need multitudinous opportunities to play with art media—to "scribble." Children who are scribbling, no matter what their age, need open-ended activities that allow them to learn about the medium. No one can be expected to produce wonderful artwork with an unfamiliar material.

The first phase of artistic development never disappears. Even accomplished artists spend time exploring a new material before using it in a piece of artwork. Children need to know it is okay to explore and that these explorations will not be judged.

Practice activities. Exploration must be followed by *practice.* Children need to be given many opportunities to use the same material over and over, in order to develop control. The common practice of putting out a new art material or "project" each week does not help children develop their ability to use art materials to express their thoughts. It is only after children are comfortable with an art medium, whether it is pencil, blocks, or paint, that they have the control needed to use it to express their thoughts.

Responsive activities. Once children are competent with an art medium, they need to be provided with thought-provoking experiences, visual stimulation, and multisensory happenings, followed by opportunities to use art in all its multi-media dimensions. *Responsive* activities stretch children's thought processes as they try to represent what they know using graphic symbols of their own invention.

Providing a Continuum of Art Activities

In the Art Focus sections that follow each chapter, ways to guide children's experiences with the common media of early childhood art education are presented. Each Art Focus begins with an exploratory activity intended for children who have had little or no experience with that medium. Following this are suggestions for practice activities using the same or similar materials. When children are skillful and confident in their use of a material, they will begin on their own to use the medium to respond graphically to their experiences.

Responsive art activities can be encouraged by making sure that familiar art materials are readily available, following such events as visitors to the class, stories that are read or told, science experiments, exciting field trips, and all the other daily experiences of a young child. Providing time to discuss the children's responsive art and recording their verbal descriptions will also encourage children to move from basic explorations to expressive graphic responses.

It is important to remember, however, that this is not an orderly progression from simplest art production to most complex. Exploration is as important as graphic representation. Each child will vary in his need to explore, practice, and respond. Some children will require longer periods of exploration. Others will move quickly from one mode of working to another. The same child may explore one day, create a detailed, responsive artwork the next, and return to media exploration on the following day.

Regardless of the children's ages, always present a new medium as an exploration and allow time for practice before presenting it as a responsive activity. For example, children should have many opportunities to freely explore drawing with chalk before offering them chalk to use to record their reaction to a walk in the woods.

Remember that although the children's artwork is starting to contain somewhat recognizable images, teachers must not demand that children produce a particular image. Activities that require the children to produce turkeys or rabbits or Christmas trees set both teachers and children up for failure. The fact that most young children cannot successfully produce such items is what leads well-meaning teachers to provide patterns, coloring-book pictures, or precut shapes to "help" the children. But they do not help. Instead they tell children that their symbols and explorations are unacceptable and not valued.

Development does not proceed at a regular pace. Teachers need to be sure that every art medium and activity they offer provides opportunities for each child to work in the way that is most appropriate for that child at that particular time.

SUMMARY: THE CHILD ARTIST

Once put down a line provokes thought.

SYLVIA FEIN (1993, P. 16)

Child art development models provide educators with a more encompassing view of the child as an artist. Contemporary research and thought (Gardner, 1991; Wolf and Perry, 1989; Kindler and Darras, 1994) emphasize that artistic development is not a separate process, but part of the total growth of the child. This development is a combination of the biological maturation patterns of the body and brain, mediated by social and cultural behavioral expectations and education.

Kinesthetic movement, language, and graphic images occur in unison as children create their own graphic symbol systems. Gardner visualizes this as a spilling over of symbol making from one intelligence to another. Kindler and Darras use the term

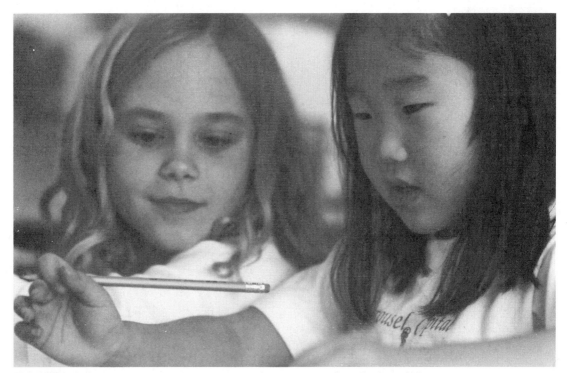

FIGURE 3–9 Drawing is not simply the creation of a static image, but a "multimedia" event.

multimedia to describe this simultaneous process, and this is the way early childhood educators must think about children's art. It is not the product that matters, but the process the child went through to make it.

Art creation for the child is more than the simple manipulation of materials at an art table. It is a culminating moment of kinesthetically, vocally, and symbolically defined action that expresses the child's thoughts. Child art is not the static image on paper so carefully described by the early researchers and so often displayed on the refrigerator door. Nor is it the same as adult art, in which artists skillfully manipulate the symbolic images and accepted media of their culture. Rather it is a multimedia, multifaceted growth process in which teachers, with all their cultural and educational beliefs, participate along with the individual responses of the child. It is our challenge to create the environment, to select the activities and delivery system that nurtures this multimedia event.

FURTHER READING

> Children's creative work is one of the most valuable and deeply interesting sources of insight into children's minds.
>
> BRENDA S. ENGEL (1995, P. V)

These books will provide further insight into the artistic development of young children.

Cherry, C., Godwin, D., and Staples, J. (1989). *Is the left brain always right? A guide to whole child development.* Belmont, CA: David S. Lake.
This book details the physical and mental development of young children and suggests a wide variety of appropriate activities.

Fein, S. (1984). *Heidi's horse.* Pleasant Hill, CA: Exelrod Press.
This beautiful book presents the drawings of a young girl, from infancy through early adulthood, with descriptions that place the drawings in the context in which they were created.

Gardner, H. (1980). *Artful scribbles: The significance of children's drawings.* New York: Basic Books.
In this book Gardner presents examples of child art and analyzes the nature of their creation.

Kellogg, R. (1969). *Analyzing children's art.* Palo Alto, CA: National Press.
This book presents Kellogg's descriptions of child art, illustrated with hundreds of children's drawings.

Lowenfeld, V. and Brittain, L. W. (1987). *Creative and mental growth.* New York: Macmillan.
In this textbook for art teachers, Lowenfeld and Brittain present their philosophy and the developmental stages of child art production.

Art Focus

FIGURE 3–10 "Elephants." Marker—Joey, age 4

EXPLORING DRAWING

Children vary greatly in maturity level and ability to concentrate on an activity. Appropriateness of an activity should be based on each child's day-to-day behavior, rather than chronological age. Drawing can be done by children of all ages, but in order for the experience to be meaningful, teachers need to set up the drawing activities to match the children's developmental levels.

The introductory "Drawing for Toddlers" presented here would be appropriate for children from 18 months to three years old, who have had little experience with drawing materials, still put objects in their mouths with regularity, or who have short concentration spans no matter what their age or experience.

The "Drawing Practice Activities" that follow are designed for children who have had several introductory drawing explorations. They are familiar with the medium, can be trusted not to put drawing tools in their mouths most of the

time, and can work on their own for a period of several minutes without immediate supervision.

How Children Grow through Drawing

In this and following Art Focus sections, the descriptions of the growth areas addressed by the activity are followed by a parenthetical reference to Gardner's "intelligences," when such a connection is appropriate.

Children will develop:
1. Physically, by using the large and small muscles of the arm and hand to draw (Bodily-Kinesthetic)
2. Socially, by working alongside other children and sharing art materials (Interpersonal)
3. Emotionally, by learning to enjoy the act of drawing and the ability to control a part of their environment (Intrapersonal)
4. Visual perception skills, by exploring new ways to make marks and responding to the visual effects they have created (Spatial)
5. Cognitively:
   • By learning a drawing vocabulary and using sound and language in combination with graphic production (Linguistic)
   • By seeing that their motions can cause the effect of making visual lines (Logical-Mathematical)
6. Art awareness, by becoming familiar with the ways drawing and lines are used in books and the artwork of others

Drawing with Toddlers

Toddlers need many opportunities to make their important marks. The following activity describes how to introduce drawing for the very first time.

Group composition. Work with one to three toddlers at a time. If there are more than that number, provide other activities that will allow the remaining children to play safely on their own or have another adult help.

Setup. Provide a low table for the child or children to sit or stand at while working. They may also work on the floor. Surfaces should be easy to clean. There should be a place for the teacher to sit comfortably, as close to their level as possible.

Materials. CRAYONS: For introductory explorations choose washable crayons in the thickest sizes. Crayons are durable and stand up well to the exuberant pushing, pulling, and pummeling of a toddler's first explorations.

PAPER: Paper should be fairly large, at least 12 inches by 15 inches or larger. The backs of large computer printout sheets work well because they are sturdy enough for the child's experiments. Large newsprint also works well, although it tears more easily. Whatever is chosen, have a large supply on hand, so the children can use as much as they like.

Transition in. For children this young, just putting out the drawing supplies may be enough to get their attention. If needed, personally invite a child to come explore: "Judy, would you like to draw with this red crayon?" If children seem interested, place the crayons in their hands, and show them the paper. It is not necessary to make every child draw. If they are not interested, do not force them. They will draw when they are ready. Just keep providing the opportunity.

What to do. At this stage do not be surprised if one child draws for only a few seconds and then wanders away, whereas another child makes 20 drawings. Some will draw without even looking at the paper. Others will put their faces right up to the paper or look at the back to see if the lines went right through. Children will react in their own unique ways to the drawing stimulus.

Sit with the children while they are working; smile and point to the lines and marks they have created.

NOTE: For their own safety be ready to gently move their hands away from their mouths, if they attempt to taste the crayon. If children refuse to do more than put the crayon in their mouths, then distract them and move them away from the drawing activity to one that will allow them to use the sense of taste to explore. While crayons are a relatively safe art material, children must learn from the beginning that art materials never go in the mouth.

What to say. It is not necessary to talk constantly while the children are working, but occasional statements or questions can increase the toddler's enjoyment and learning.

1. When speaking, be enthusiastic and descriptive:

   "Look at that red line!"
   "What a long line!"
   "What kind of line will you draw next?"
   "That's an up and down line!"

2. If the children put the crayon to their mouths, redirect their attention to the paper and say, "Crayons are only for drawing."
3. Use drawing as an opportunity to develop the child's vocabulary. Words to use include: draw, drawing, write, writing, line, lines, long, short, thick, thin, dark, light, colorful, the color names, crayons, dots, marks, paper.
4. Toddlers love songs and rhymes. Make up little poems, using the descriptive words, to go along with their art explorations and sing them to traditional tunes. (Consult Music Boxes for a possible idea.)

MY LINES

(sing to the tune "Are You Sleeping?")

I like drawing.
I like drawing.
Yes I do! Yes I do!
Long lines and short lines.
Red lines and green lines.
(substitute any colors)
Lines and lines. Lines and lines.

Transition out. At this young age the children will spend only a relatively short time, by adult standards, drawing. When the child loses interest, let him wander off to the next activity. If the drawing activity must end, do so by providing an attractive alternative:

"It's so nice out, let's go outside to play."
"It's time for lunch."
"Let's read a story now."

Drawing Practice Activities for Toddlers

Continue to provide similar drawing explorations for toddlers daily or as often as possible. Vary these initial explorations of drawing by offering different colors of crayons, and different types of paper. As the children mature and gain experience, allow them more independence. Move away from the artists for short periods of time. Offer more choices of colors of crayons and times and places to work. Eventually, drawing should become as much a part of a child's daily activities as playing with toys and eating lunch. How much an individual child will draw will always depend upon the unique interests of that child, but the drawing materials must be available for children to see and use, if they are to demonstrate an interest in drawing.

Once the children have reached the point where they have some control over their drawing tool and what it can do, they are ready for activities that allow them to practice these skills in new and exciting ways. There are endless variations on the basic drawing activity. By changing the drawing tool or the drawing surface, new activities are created based on the initial one. Just a few of the many possibilities are described here.

Drawing materials for toddlers. CRAYONS: Crayons have been the mainstay of early childhood drawing for many years. Their durability, relative safety, and ease of use will continue to keep them popular. The thick kindergarten size will prove most sturdy for grasping fists. However, other shapes and sizes can be slowly introduced over time. Breakage is to be expected and removing the paper wrappers expands their creative possiblities.

MARKERS: Markers are much loved by toddlers. Choose water-based, broad-tipped markers. They create broad sweeps of vibrant color with little pressure. Taking off and putting on the caps provide small muscle practice, although some youngsters may need help doing this for a while.

JUMBO COLORED PENCILS: Look for pencils with very soft leads. Using pencils makes young children feel grown up and lets them draw finer lines than they can with the other materials.

SIDEWALK CHALK: If the children are able to keep their hands out of their mouths while working, thick sidewalk chalk used outside on the pavement will provide an interesting color and texture change from using crayons and markers. Avoid the use of chalk on paper or any other surface when working with toddlers. The dust created is hazardous to their health (see chapter 6).

Special combinations. Offer a combination of markers, crayons, and pencils that are in the same color range, such as all reds or all blues. Talk about dark and light, and dull and bright.

Drawing surfaces for toddlers. PAPER: There are many ways to vary the paper offered to children. The size and shape of the paper will affect how the child uses it. Generally the younger the child, the bigger the paper should be, because smaller paper requires more muscle control to stay within its borders. Paper can be cut into squares, rectangles, triangles, and circles. Use paper of different colors and textures as well.

MURAL PAPER: Long rolled paper can be hung on a wall, inside or outside, to create a "graffiti" mural. A large sheet can also be laid on the floor and several children can draw together. At this age, toddlers are not fully aware of each other when they are drawing, but it is good to encourage the beginning of cooperative behavior by providing opportunities to work side by side at the same activity. (See chapter 10 for more mural and cooperative ideas.)

BOXES: Four children can work together drawing on the sides of a large box. To withstand the pushing of the artists, the box should be securely fastened to the table or floor, either with tape or by putting a heavy weight inside. A smaller box can be drawn on by one child. The decorated boxes can then be used for all kinds of play: as beds for dolls and stuffed animals, as a pull toy by attaching a string, and as furniture in a play corner.

SAND: If a sandbox or sand table is available, provide the children with tools such as sturdy smooth twigs, or thick stubby wooden dowels for drawing in the sand. The experience can be varied by wetting the sand. A thin layer of sand (or a similar material such as rice*) can also be placed in a shallow plastic dishpan or tray. Children can make marks in the material with their fingers or a tool such as a craftstick.

ROCKS: With the children, look for large flat rocks or smooth round stones on which they can draw with crayon or marker. Do not use chalk on rocks. Although it produces a beautiful effect, the chalk-covered rocks will be a health hazard for young children who cannot help overhandling them.

Connections. LITERATURE: Toddlers enjoy simple humorous stories about drawing such as *The Line Sophie Drew* (Barrett and Barrett, 1972), *The Chalk Box Story* (Freeman, 1976), and *A Very Special House* (Krauss, 1953). (See Appendix B: Children's Literature for more suggestions.)

To build vocabulary, look for examples of lines in the environment, such as cracks in the pavement or veins on a leaf. Use the same terms to describe their drawings.

ART AWARENESS: Point out examples of lines in the artwork of others. The work of Paul Klee is particulary appealing to toddlers.

Drawing for Children Three Years Old and Up

Once children begin to use graphic symbols, the nature of their artwork changes. No longer is drawing solely for the purpose of exploring the media and refining physical control, although these aspects will always continue to play an important role. Now drawings become a form of communication as well. Children at this stage are able to use drawing tools to express their feelings and ideas. They can also use their drawings to tell stories and to show their reaction to experiences. These new skills, plus the child's increasing independence and conformance to rules, will allow the introduction of more complex drawing activities.

Group composition. Children can now work side by side in larger groups. Four to six preschoolers or even larger groups of primary children can draw together if the table or paper is large enough.

Setup. Provide flat drawing surfaces, such as child-height tabletops or easels. A small, individual-sized chalkboard makes a portable drawing surface. Children can also work on a smooth floor.

Because they are less likely to misuse the art materials, children can also spread out more and do not need an adult hovering over them. Some children prefer to draw in more private spaces. (See chapter 4 for ideas on space usage.)

Materials. The following list provides suggestions for possible choices. All should be presented for exploration and practice before they are used in the kind of activities that follow this listing.

CRAYONS: Kindergarten-sized crayons continue to be excellent drawing tools. As the children gain better finger control, provide regular-sized crayons as well. Children can also be offered a much wider variety of colors. Fluorescent crayons, metallic crayons, and multicolored crayons will provide great enjoyment for children at this level. Two or three notches can be cut in the side of a large unwrapped crayon. Rubbed sideways on the paper, it will produce an interesting effect.

MARKERS: Unscented water-based markers should be the backbone of the drawing program. The smooth, fluid nature of markers allows a level of detail not possible with other drawing materials. Children now have the control needed to remove and replace the caps and should be taught how to put the cap on the end while working.

CHALK: In addition to sidewalk chalk, regular white and colored blackboard chalk can be offered, but only if the children draw outside or on wet paper. Liquid starch, milk,* water, or thinned white glue can be used to dampen the paper. Alternatively, the chalk can be dipped in the liquid and then used for drawing. Do not use dry chalk or artists' pastels. (See chapter 6 for a discussion of health hazards related to chalk use.)

PENCILS: Soft-leaded, regular and colored pencils in the thick kindergarten size should be made available on a regular basis.

PAPER: Provide paper in a range of sizes. Some children in this age group who have not yet developed control over their small muscles will continue to need paper 12 by 18 inches or larger. Newsprint and 50-lb. manila and 50-lb. white drawing paper should be provided for basic drawing activities. Used computer-printout paper can also be used for economy.

On occasion offer paper in different colors and textures. Colored construction paper makes a good background for wet chalk drawing. It also works well with crayon and marker. Try putting out dark-colored paper with light-colored or metallic crayons for contrast. Children are fascinated with the way marker changes color or even disappears when used on colored backgrounds. Paper placemats and paper plates provide a textured drawing surface for crayons.

BOOKLETS: Booklets can be made either from 9-by-12-inch paper or in "Big Book" size from 12-by-18-inch sheets. Staple the paper together on either the long or short side. Start with two pages; as the children develop their story-making skill, increase the number of pages. Tell the children that pages can be added if they need more to complete their story. Show the children how to fold back the pages so the booklet lies flat while they are drawing.

SHAPED PAPER: Paper can be cut into a variety of geometric shapes, but keep them large and simple. Squares, long thin rectangles, and large triangles are easy to prepare. A paper cutter is invaluable when working with a large number of children. Circles are much more time-consuming to cut and can be offered once in a while, perhaps to relate to a special theme.

TEACHER TIP

Avoiding Misleading Shapes

Avoid offering paper cut into the shapes of animals, plants, or other "real" objects. Besides taking up preparation time, such shapes, which have a right and wrong way to be held, are often confusing to young children. An adult-created silhouette or symbol for something such as a car may have very little in common with the child's concept of a car. A child who does not "see" what the shape represents may draw tires or other details in the wrong place.

Even if teachers are open to a wide range of "decoration" by the children, remember that often parents judge their children's intellectual ability by how well they have decorated such shapes. Parental comments such as "Why did you put the eyes on the duck's feet?" or "Don't you know the rabbit's tail belongs here?" are not beneficial to the growth of self-confident young artists.

OTHER SURFACES: Like toddlers, preschoolers and primary school children will enjoy drawing on rocks, on cardboard boxes, in sand and rice, and making graffiti murals. With their increasing fine-motor skills, they can also work on materials with more confining shapes and sizes, such as strips of adding machine tape and sandpaper. Scrap pieces of wood that have been sanded on the edges make an interesting drawing surface. Small decorated pieces may then be used in wood sculpture constructions.

Transition in. Introduce drawing activities by reading a book such as *Purple, Green and Yellow* (Munsch, 1992), or do a kinesthetic activity such as drawing with an imaginary crayon (see chapter 8).

What to do. Drawing materials with which the children are familiar should be made available at all times. Children should know where these are stored, how to obtain what they need, and how to put them back when finished.

What to say. When children share their work, provide supportive, descriptive comments.

> "You made many circular shapes!"
> "The bright colors in your picture really show how you felt."

Transition out. When children indicate they are finished, offer a descriptive comment, remind them to replace the materials, and direct them where to put the picture if this has not been done already.

Connections. LITERATURE: Read books that feature lines in playful ways, such as *Drawer in a Drawer* (Christiana, 1990), *Simon's Book* (Druscher, 1983), and *Monsters* (Hoban, 1989). *My Map Book* (Fanelli, 1995) will inspire children to draw maps of their special places, and *How a Crayon is Made* (Charles, 1988) will fascinate children as it illustrates how crayons are manufactured.

ART AWARENESS: There are many fine prints that illustrate drawings in all styles. Durer's *Rabbit* (Metropolitan), Van Gogh's *Harvest* (Take Five: Drawing) and the cave art of the Paleolithic (Modern Learning; Take Five: Horses) are all appealing to young artists.

Art Words

Kinds of Paper

Bogus drawing paper

A heavyweight gray paper (80 lb.) with a rough textured surface that provides a contrast to the smoothness of most other papers.

Construction paper

A medium-weight paper that comes in a wide variety of colors. It is available in the same standard sizes as white paper.

Kraft paper

Medium-weight brown paper like that of grocery bags. It is often sold in rolls. It is a sturdy paper for drawing and other art activities. Rolls of colored kraft paper are also available.

Manila paper

A medium-weight paper in a pale golden beige with a slight texture. Comes in the same sizes as white drawing paper and is less expensive. A durable paper for children's drawings.

Newsprint

A lightweight, inexpensive paper, slightly gray in color. It can often be purchased from small local newpapers at low rates.

Tag board

A stiff, smooth bendable board also called poster board or oaktag. Available in many colors, it makes a good surface for drawing, but is relatively expensive.

White drawing paper

A sturdy paper with a smooth surface. Standard sizes are 9 by 12, 12 by 18, and 18 by 24 inches. Although more expensive than newsprint it offers a durable surface for active drawing. Purchase 50-lb. weight.

Studio Page

LOOKING AT CHILDREN'S ARTWORK

Based on the models of artistic development described in this chapter, how would you describe the following examples of child art?

DRAWING 1

DRAWING 2

DRAWING 3

DRAWING 4

DRAWING 5

DRAWING 6

DRAWING 7

DRAWING 8

Studio Page *14*

For each drawing record how each of the following would describe the work: Kellogg, Lowenfeld, Gardner, Kindler and Darras.

DRAWING 1	DRAWING 2
Kellogg:	Kellogg:
Lowenfeld:	Lowenfeld:
Gardner:	Gardner:
Kindler/Darras:	Kindler/Darras:
DRAWING 3	**DRAWING 4**
Kellogg:	Kellogg:
Lowenfeld:	Lowenfeld:
Gardner:	Gardner:
Kindler/Darras:	Kindler/Darras:
DRAWING 5	**DRAWING 6**
Kellogg:	Kellogg:
Lowenfeld:	Lowenfeld:
Gardner:	Gardner:
Kindler/Darras:	Kindler/Darras:
DRAWING 7	**DRAWING 8**
Kellogg:	Kellogg:
Lowenfeld:	Lowenfeld:
Gardner:	Gardner:
Kindler/Darras:	Kindler/Darras:

Studio Page 15

IDENTIFYING ARTISTIC DEVELOPMENTAL LEVEL

Read each vignette and then write a description of each child based on what you have learned about artistic development.

1. Jeanine is sitting at a table busily "writing" a book. She has filled several pages with circles containing circular "eyes" and "mouths." One page has a large scribble that is darker in the center where she has gone over the lines many times. She reads her story to you. "This is my cat. She had three kittens." She points to the center of the scribble. "The kittens all died."

    _____

    _____

2. Antonio grasps a marker in his fist and pulls it across the paper. Nothing happens. He holds the marker to his eye. Then he tries the other end. Still nothing happens. He pulls on the end of the marker and with great effect the cap pops off. All smiles, he makes broad up-and-down strokes across the paper.

    _____

    _____

3. Sharla slowly draws a lopsided circle on her paper. Then she carefully draws another circle inside of it. Quickly she scribbles all over her circles.

    _____

    _____

4. Two children are drawing with marker on the side of a large box. "This is going to be a great car," Jonas says as he scribbles bright purple lines. "I'm making the tires," replies Bruce as he carefully draws several large circles.

    _____

    _____

5. Andrew is busy drawing with a black marker. "Whoosh! Bang! RRRRRRRR!" he shouts. Across his page he has drawn X-shaped figures. Now he pokes and stabs the paper, making wild marks and bending the tip of the marker in the process.

    _____

    _____

6. Martina has filled her paper with tiny people and a huge house and is now busy filling the space around them with scribbles.

    _____

    _____

Studio Page 16

DEFENDING A DEVELOPMENTALLY-BASED ART PROGRAM

Three-year-old Michelle's mother approaches you at the end of a class session. "Why does my daughter do nothing but scribble when she is here? Do you call this an art program? Michelle and I do exercises from the book *How to Teach Your Toddler To Draw Like Rembrandt.* Everyone agrees that her drawings of animals are outstanding. You are ruining my little artist!"

How would you respond to Michelle's mother? Use what you have learned about the developmental nature of artistic growth to defend your art program.

Studio Page

OBSERVATION: TODDLER DRAWING

1. Plan a drawing exploration or practice activity suitable for a toddler between the ages of 12 months to three years.

2. Obtain permission to work with one toddler either at home or in a child care setting.

3. Setup your activity and observe the toddler at work. If possible, take photos or videotape the activity (get permission first). With the child's permission, save one or more of the drawings for your own collection.

Age of Child:

Setup of materials:

Length of time of observation:

1. What did the child do first?

2. What did the child say?

3. How did the child manipulate the drawing tool(s)? (E.g., describe position of arm and hands, grip, any other body parts involved.)

4. How long did the child work? (Measure periods of concentration. If child stopped, why? How did the child let you know he or she was finished?)

5. Describe the art produced. (What did the child draw first? How many drawings were made? What was repeated?)

6. Compare your observations to the developmental models of Gardner and Kindler and Darras. What behaviors did you see that support their ideas?

Studio Page *18*

OBSERVATION: CHILD DRAWING

1. Plan a drawing exploration or practice activity suitable for a child between the ages of three and eight years.

2. Obtain permission to work with one child either at home or in a school setting. If possible, take photos or videotape the activity (Get permission first). With the child's permission, save one or more of the drawings for your own collection.

Age of child:

Setup of materials:

Length of time of observation:

1. What did the child do first?

2. What did the child say?

3. How did the child manipulate the drawing tool(s)? (E.g., describe position of arm and hands, grip, any other body parts involved.)

4. How long did the child work? (Measure periods of concentration. If child stopped, why? How did the child let you know he or she was finished?)

5. Describe the art produced. (What did the child draw first? How many drawings were made? What was repeated?)

6. Compare the art activity of this child to that of the toddler you observed. What similarities and differences did you notice?

7. How did this child's behavior fit Gardner's and Kindler and Darras' models.

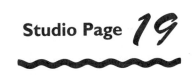

Studio Page *19*

COLLECTING CHILDREN'S ART

Everyone who works with young children should keep a collection of children's artwork. Use these guidelines in making your own collection.

Collect work that:

1. Comes from a wide range of children at different ages
2. Represents different art media
3. Contains examples of what children are capable of doing in a variety of learning situations
4. Comes from the same child over a period of time
5. Includes explorations, practice, responsive, and instructive activities done both individually and in group situations
6. Shows both typical and unusual approaches

Respecting the Artist

If you would like a particular piece from a specific child you must obtain the child's permission. You may not be able to get every piece that you would like, but remember that children are prolific artists; over time you will be able to build up a wonderful collection. The easiest art work to obtain is that of your own children or that of other family members. After it is displayed you can add it to your collection, or create a separate folio that may become a treasured keepsake in later years. Some artwork, particularly drawings, can be photocopied.

Organizing the Collection

In order to be useful, the collection needs to be organized in an orderly way. Three useful storage systems include a portfolio, an oversize book, and an oversize file box.

Book

File

Portfolio

Studio Page 20

MAKING A PORTFOLIO*

Materials:

2 pieces of corrugated cardboard cut to the size of the finished portfolio (A), 24 by 36 inches, will hold all but the very largest pieces

2 sheets of paper at least 2 inches larger in both directions than the cardboard (B) and two sheets the same size (C)

2 pieces of fabric, 4 inches wide and the length of the folding edge of the portfolio (D)

6 lengths of ribbon, about 12 inches each (E)

White glue

Scissors

1. Before beginning, select matching paper, fabric, and ribbon colors.
2. Glue together the sheets of paper (B).
3. Place both sheets of cardboard (A) side by side on top of the paper, as illustrated. Leave an even amount of paper projecting on all sides. Leave a 2-inch space between the boards in the center.
4. Place a small line of glue on the outside edges of the boards. Flip and glue down.
5. Cut off the corners as shown.
6. Fold over and glue down the flaps.
7. Attach ribbons as shown.
8. Glue the sheets of same size paper (C) over the glued-down flaps and ribbon ends.
9. Glue a strip of fabric (D) on the inside and outside of the folded edge. Make sure glue is only on edges of fabric, to maintain flexibility when folded.
10. Use your creativity to decorate the outside of the portfolio. Attach a pocket made from a large envelope to the inside to store a table of contents.

Note: This method can be used to make portfolios for storing individual children's artwork as well.

STEP 2

STEP 3

STEP 5

STEP 6

STEP 7   **STEP 8**   **STEP 9**

STEP 10

4

A Place for Art

Creating an Environment for Art

> **66** *Classrooms need to reflect how we ourselves value art and how it has meaning for us.* **99**
>
> •
>
> <small>MARJORIE SCHILLER (1995, P. 38)</small>

Questions addressed in this chapter:

What kind of environment is needed for art?

How should the art environment be arranged?

How should art supplies be organized?

How is an aesthetic environment created?

SUMMARY: Creating a Sense of Place

FURTHER READING

ART FOCUS: Art in Three Dimensions—Blocks, Boxes, and Papier-Mâché

Young Artists at Work

Michael takes his paper and crayons and crawls under the table. Lying on his stomach, he draws and draws and draws.

Katina slowly looks through the plastic bins on the shelf. Carefully she selects a piece of ribbon, a gold button, and a piece of shiny silver paper. Then she carries her treasures to the table, eager to make her collage.

Suddenly it grows dark and rain starts hitting the windows. The children stop what they are doing and run to the window. One boy puts his finger on the window and traces the path of the rain drops.

WHAT KIND OF ENVIRONMENT IS NEEDED FOR ART?

A site for art needs to encompass bold energetic expression and studied, time-consuming precision, solitary work and social kibitzing.

JIM GREENMAN (1988, P. 162)

Environment is anything that surrounds us and that exerts an influence over us. It consists of space and furnishings, time and organizing elements. Environment affects our social and emotional sense of well-being. We change to fit different environments. We relax in our living rooms and feel anxious in the doctor's waiting room. Children run and leap in open spaces and huddle under beds. In designing an environment in which young artists will work, it is important to consider how the surroundings, organization, and supply storage systems will affect these children.

Defining the Instructional Space

The instructional environment is the total space that is available for the children's use and how it is arranged. It includes the contiguous outdoor areas as well as any entrance ways or hallways that the children will pass through or use. The actual space is less important than its design. It does not matter if the art program is provided at home, in a mixed-age preschool program in a large room such as a church basement, or in classrooms designed especially for young children. Almost any space can be effectively arranged to provide an excellent experience for young artists.

Jim Greenman (1988) identifies the following characteristics as important elements of environments that surround young children: comfort, softness, safety and health, private and social space, order, time, mobility, and the adult dimension. Each of these can be viewed as essential to the presentation of art activities.

Comfort. Children feel comfortable when they can use their whole bodies and all their senses as they explore and learn. Kinesthetic activities and sensory experiences require open and preferably carpeted spaces for the children to move their bodies in many ways. Tables for art activities should be low enough for small children to kneel, sit, or stand at comfortably. Small, foot-high play tables that straddle the children's legs, picnic benches, and coffee tables all provide toddler-sized work surfaces.

Softness. There need to be places where the child can curl up and cuddle, handle plants and animals, and use soft, pliable art materials. Art media provide the important elements of wetness, mushiness, malleability, and stickiness, which toddlers and preschoolers need to have in their daily environment.

Safety and health. The children must be provided with a space that is safe and healthy, but with small risks allowed so that children have the opportunity to learn to manage themselves safely. By handling carefully selected art materials, children learn to deal with such small challenges as water cups that spill, paint that drips, and scissors that are sharp.

Privacy and social space. There need to be places where children can work in large groups, as well as a small private spaces where one or two children can work on a special project. Art activities should not be limited to the "art table." There should be times and places for children to take their crayons and paper and work off by themselves. The floor is always available as an artwork surface. Private spaces can be found under tables or beside a piece of furniture. The provision of "drawing boards" (small chalkboards work well) can provide a drawing surface in a carpeted area. Obviously some art media need to be confined to areas that are easy to wipe up or near a sink. But even these spaces can be arranged to provide more privacy for the young artist. Tables for a group of four can be mixed with tables for one or two. Low dividers or storage units can provide a sense of privacy around the easels or modeling areas, and at the same time contain these messier materials in a limited space.

Order. More than anything else, order—the structuring of space, time, and materials—reflects the educational goals of the teacher. If children are expected to work independently, then the materials and space need to be arranged so the child can self-select. If there are materials that children are not to use without adult supervision, such as firing clay (see chapter 6), these need to be placed in non-child-accessible places.

Order is especially important in art pursuits. Children need to understand where materials and tools are kept, how they are to take them, where to use them, and how they are to be returned. This order can not be introduced all at once to children; it must be built up over time, slowly adding new materials and tools as they gain competence in handling each new addition. For example, one drawing material should be introduced and used for a period of time, and then the next added, and so on until the children have access to a variety of drawing materials. They can then use the materials in combinations of their choosing. They should be able to obtain supplies, take them to the allowed work areas, and return them when they are done. This leads to much richer art possibilities than having crayons put out on a table for one week, markers the next, chalk the next, and so on.

Time. Time is also a part of the environment, and art explorations, in particular, require a different sense of time than other activities. Some art activities take just a few minutes; others take days. Some children will spend long periods at an art activity while others doing the same activity are done in a flash. Creating art requires a flexible time schedule. It needs to be part of a group of activities so that there are other choices for children who are ready to move on and there need to be provisions for the storage of unfinished work to be completed another day.

Mobility. Children need space to move in active ways within the environment. Outdoor areas are often underutilized for art activities. Children need to feel they can move their arms boldly and bounce around while painting, modeling, or constructing. Everyone feels bolder out-of-doors and there is less concern about damage. Out-of-doors is a good place for large projects such as murals and refrigerator-box constructions, and wet, messy projects such as papier-mâché and wet clay.

Mobility also refers to the furnishings. It is important that many elements of the environment be as flexible as possible, to allow teachers to adjust the arrangement to suit the needs of particular children at specific times.

The adult dimension. Children are not the only ones occupying the environment. Attention needs to be given to the adults who work there as well. There should be places teachers can sit comfortably when they are talking to children about their art, and where they join children when they too are creating art. There should be room for teachers to move as boldly as the children, and viewpoints from which they can see everything that is going on at once. Teachers need to feel comfortable in this space that they have created.

HOW SHOULD THE ART ENVIRONMENT BE ARRANGED?

> The consideration of the children's own needs and rhythms shapes the arrangement of space and physical environment.
>
> LELLA GANDINI (EDWARDS ET AL., 1992, P. 147)

Layout

Art activities should not be arranged independently of the other uses of the room. In some cases the art activities will overlap areas used for other activities. Some activities such as easels and computers require special exclusive locations, out of the flow of traffic. Other art activities, such as painting a mural or refrigerator box, will require large temporary locations (out-of-doors in good weather).

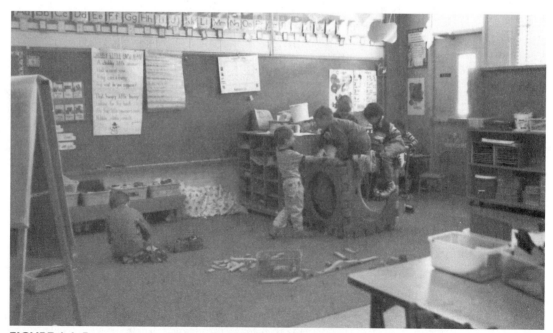

FIGURE 4–1 Environments for children should provide a variety of activity areas.

Instead of thinking in terms of the traditional activity areas such as blocks, dramatic play, art center, and so on, teachers need to view the total environment, considering its inherent qualities, and designing flexibility into the layout. There should be a quiet, relaxed area with soft furnishings where children can enjoy beautifully illustrated books and study art prints and interesting artifacts, an open space for kinesthetic movement and group activities, and an uncarpeted area for creative and constructive activities such as block building and collage making. Wet and messy activities, whether they are art or science or cooking, need to center around the sink or water source. In a home setting, bear in mind that such work areas might be located in a living room, a playroom, a workshop, and a kitchen.

Adequate Space

Plan enough space for children to move from one area of the environment to another and to spread out and work comfortably. Younger children need more space than older ones. Allow at least four square feet or more of artwork surface for each toddler, and at least three square feet for each older child.

Traffic Pattern

Consider how the children will move in the room. Will the activity areas attract them? Will there be sufficient room for children to gather around an interesting exploration? How many children can work in an area at a time? The more flexible the room arrangement, the less difficulty there will be if several children all want to work together. There should be ways to add more chairs, push two tables together, or even move all the furniture out of the way to accommodate children who wish to explore an art activity on the floor.

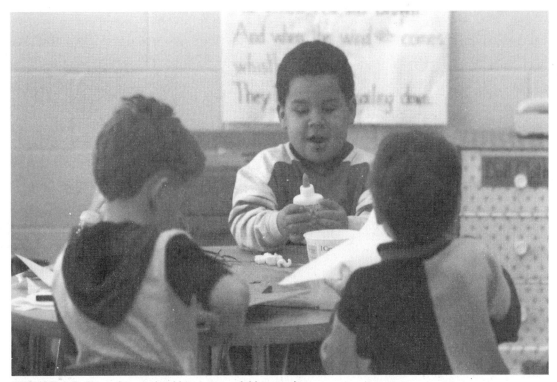

FIGURE 4–2 Places for art should encourage children to share.

Water Requirements

Art activities that require the use of water need to be located near a water source. The dirtier the children's hands will get, the closer they need to be to a sink or washing area. Finger painting and printmaking, in particular, require easy and clear passage to the sink. Dishpans and buckets of water can provide a preliminary rinse-off area when working outside or at a distance from a sink.

Separate from Food Areas

In all situations, art activities and cooking activities must be kept separate. As detailed in chapter 6, children need to learn from the beginning that art materials are never eaten, and separating these two activities is one way to do this. In a home situation, when the weather does not allow outside artwork, the kitchen may provide the only location for art activities requiring water. One way to separate art from food activities is to have a special low table, tray, or mat that is used only for art activities. If tables must be used for both food and art, put down a special covering for one of the activities, such as a plastic tablecloth for eating or an old shower curtain for art.

TEACHING TIP

ACTIVITY REQUIREMENTS

Activity	Needs
Drawing	Standing-height work surface or a child-size table and chair. Alternatively, the floor, a drawing board, or an easel may be used.
Painting	An easel or other raised slanted surface works well. Otherwise, a wall can be used, or a low table. The area must be near water. Protect surfaces.
Printing	Low table without chairs, close to water. Protect surfaces. Have a place to store wet prints near the work area.
Modeling	Low table with chairs, close to water. Special mats or trays can be provided to confine the material to a limited area.
Collage and Construction	Low table with or without chairs or, for larger projects, the floor. Close to supply storage and water and located near a place easy to store drying projects.
Mural	Wall or floor or blackboard area. Can be done outdoors if it is not windy. Protect surfaces when using paint or glue.
Computer	Child-height table and chair, far from water areas, paint, modeling, sand. There should be no glare from window or lights on screen.

HOW SHOULD ART SUPPLIES BE ORGANIZED?

How art supplies are arranged in the environment is more than just a convenience. Carefully considered storage not only provides a more appealing appearance, but also teaches. The art materials and tools should be displayed and stored so that children learn how to get what they need and put it back by themselves. Categorizing the materials by their unifying qualities teaches children visual perceptual skills as they learn to group similar items together. Toddlers do best with broad categories of storage units with easily distinguished appearances, while older children can handle more complex storage systems. The order in which materials are arranged also teaches, as when materials used in a particular sequence are ordered from left to right.

Location

Not all work spaces for art need to be at tables. Nor do all art activities need to be done in the same work space. Easels, for example, create a special place just for painting. Try to set them up in such a way that brushes and bottles of paint are beautifully displayed nearby.

Drawing has a far wider range of suitable places than some other, messier activities. Carpeted areas and durable pillows can entice children to sit and lie quietly while drawing. Places to crawl under and draw allow children private moments with their art. Encourage children to expand drawing activities by making small portable containers of markers and crayons, and by placing drawing materials in many areas of the room, such as by an aquarium or near a plant. Drawing should not be an occasional choice at the art table. Rather it should be ever present throughout the room—available to record the child's ideas and thoughts throughout the day.

Supplies should be stored as near to the area of use as possible. Materials that are stored near each other will tend to be used together. Paper, scissors, and drawing materials stored near the block area will increase the likelihood that children will make signs, maps, and other additions to their block creations.

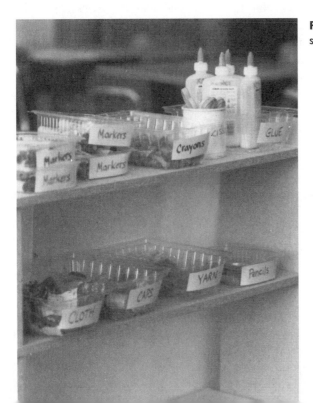

FIGURE 4–3 Clear containers help children find supplies quickly and easily.

Display

Supplies that are freely available to the children should be placed at child height and attractively displayed in sturdy, clearly labeled containers. When supplies are carefully arranged, children are encouraged to treat them more respectfully. Children will, for example, carefully consider which piece to take when cut-paper shapes are ordered in containers by shape and color, but they will root and grab from a box of mixed-up scraps.

Although supplies should be ample, avoid putting out huge amounts of any material. When children see large amounts of a material, whether it is paper or buttons, they are more likely to use the supply wastefully. It is better to attractively display fewer supplies and refill the containers more often.

Labels can be a way to introduce children to the printed word and should include both the word and a picture or sample of the object. Even though labeled, containers should be low enough and wide enough so that children can easily see what is inside from their low perspective. Clear plastic containers work well for many supplies, as do low baskets, cut-down cardboard boxes, and dishpans.

Storage

Closed storage, such as closets, cupboards, or boxes, is essential. Whatever children see and ask for they should be able to use as this encourages creative growth. When there are insufficient supplies of a popular material or when an item is not safe for children of that age, then those materials should not be offered to that particular group of children, and should be stored completely out of their sight.

Storing Finished Work

Before selecting any activity, consider carefully how the finished products will be handled. There is nothing more frustrating than trying to find space for items such as 25 dripping wet, papier-mâché-covered boxes or a 3-by-10-foot freshly painted mural.

Try to plan multiple-use areas. Tables can be used for working on during the session and for storing projects at the end of the day. The area under tables or on top of shelves can also be used. It is often better to leave wet projects to dry where they are, rather than risk damaging them. If projects must be moved, have the children work on trays or pieces of sturdy cardboard.

Cubbies or individual boxes for each child make a good place to store small projects, drawings, dry paintings, and collages. Placed near the door, they help remind parents to pick up their child's work. If cubbies cannot be used, a table by the door can hold work ready to go home.

HOW IS AN AESTHETIC ENVIRONMENT CREATED?

A teacher as an artist thinks and designs the classroom differently from a teacher as a researcher or a teacher as an administrator.

RENATE NUMMELA CAINE AND GEOFFREY CAINE (1994, P. 123)

There is more to designing a space for living or working than arranging the furniture in a functional way. This is particularly true of work spaces for children. In selecting the individual elements that make up the children's learning environment, we must consider the ways in which these elements will enrich the children's perceptions and thereby influence the children's aesthetic experience. Although people have different aesthetic senses, and room designs will reflect the uniqueness of personal experiences, the following guidelines, based on principles of color, design, and children's behavior, are intended as an initial direction from which teachers can create a beautiful work space for children.

Guidelines for Establishing an Aesthetic Environment

It does not matter if the work space is a large formal classroom or a corner of a family room or kitchen, these basic guidelines can be used to provide an aesthetic place for the child to do art.

Floor and walls. The floor is an important working area of the room. Carpeted areas provide softness and absorb sound. Tiles and linoleum areas are easy to clean up when wet or sandy and make a good surface for block building. Area rugs provide the most flexibility and can be used to divide areas visually and texturally.

The walls are also a major teaching area. They provide a place for wall-mounted activities such as easels and mirrors, as well as a display space for the children's work. But very often the walls are overused. When they are plastered with signs and artwork and garish commercial bulletin board displays, they overload the senses and make the room a tiring place.

Wall displays need to be carefully selected and hung at the child's eye level. It is an eye-opening experience to lower ourselves to the children's height occasionally, and see the environment we have prepared from their viewpoint.

Color and texture. View the walls and floor as background for the objects that will be displayed in the room. Bright or strongly colored walls or floor are limiting, especially if we consider that most children's toys and clothes are brightly colored. Bright colors make a room seem smaller and are tiresome after a while. Light neutral colors such as white, off-white, or soft gray will allow the color scheme of the room to be varied simply by changing the colors in the displays, and allow the colorful toys to stand out from the background. To add a brightly colored area, put up a temporary covering of colored paper.

Consider the textures and patterns of the various materials on the floor and walls of the room as well. It is good to have a variety, but to keep the effect from being overwhelming, keep the colors of these items closely related. Here again, neutral earth colors including beiges, grays, and browns will provide a unobtrusive background for brightly colored toys and art material.

Work surfaces. Light, neutral-colored backgrounds not only increase the aesthetic quality of the room but also make the space seem larger and provide an unobtrusive foil to the children's own choice of colors in their artwork. Avoid the overuse of bright and saturated colors and patterns in areas where children are creating art. Although initially attractive, they quickly tire the senses and make it hard for children to concentrate on their own color use in their art.

Tables that the children work on should be neutral colors such as beiges, browns, or grays. When covering tables with protective coverings, select plain ones when possible. Even newspaper, although certainly necessary for many activities, can prove wearing on the senses after a while. Try to avoid having surfaces constantly covered with it, and substitute plain white newsprint or brown kraft paper on occasion.

Storage items. Wood has a warm, neutral color and will blend into most color schemes. Baskets are art forms that provide a very beautiful way to store many items. Take the time to paint or cover any cardboard boxes that are used for storage. Choose a color that goes with the color of other items in the room. When using purchased plastic bins or containers, try to get them in similar colors, such as all blues or white. Clear containers are the most versatile and allow the children to quickly see the contents. Use labels to creating a color-coded sorting system. Clear package-sealing tape works especially well for attaching labels to a variety of containers (see Appendix A).

Displays. Rather than overloading the child's senses, place only a few carefully selected items on display at a time and change the displays often. Young children quickly lose focus if surrounded by too many things. They will jump from one thing to another with barely a glance. Select a special place for displaying each type of item. Less effort is needed in setting them up and keeping them orderly and neat when small displays are set up in limited areas. Use areas outside the children's learning zone, such as hallways and entrances, for large and/or permanent displays of children's art (see chapter 12, Art Focus).

Art prints. Choose a very visible location and put up only one large fine-art print at a time. Make sure it is at the children's eye level. (See chapter 9 for ways to encourage children to become familiar with the print.) "Cute" wall cutouts, stereotyped seasonal and holiday decorations, and purchased bulletin board items will not contribute to developing aesthetic awareness in young children and should be avoided. Small fine-art prints can be displayed in a housekeeping corner or the reading area.

Art artifacts. Put out one three-dimensional artifact at a time. Provide a special display base such as a small low table or large painted box on which it can rest. (See chapter 9 for suggested artifacts and how to present them.)

Beautifully illustrated books. Display a small selection of books by standing them upright on a low shelf or facing forward on a book rack so that the children can easily see them and handle them. Provide a cozy reading area that has a rug or small rugs for the children to sit on. Pillows and large cushions can add to the sensory quality of this area, and appeal to children who like to curl up in cozy areas. The "clean hands only" reading area could be separated with a beautiful screen, hanging streamers, or low bookcases containing attactively arranged puzzles and games in addition to books.

Nature objects. Adding live plants, aquariums, terrariums, and other displays of natural objects can also enrich the aesthetics of the environment. Set up slowly changing displays of natural objects, such as shells, leaves, or rocks. Arrange the objects by size, texture, or color and provide magnifying glasses or a Fresnel lens so the children can study them more closely. Quantities of small natural objects, such as acorns, seeds, and pebbles can be displayed on a shelf or windowsill. Use clear plastic jars and containers that allow the light to pass through and are safe for the children to turn, shake, and study how the objects move and re-form.

Children's artwork. Classroom displays of children's artwork are often overwhelming. To avoid having to put up everyone's work all the time, select one child to be artist of the week and put up a few pieces of child-selected artwork. It will make that one child's piece of work much more special, and eliminate the urge to compare the work of one child with the others. Make sure the works are displayed at child height and in a location where they will not be damaged by splashing water or wandering hands. A good location is in the "clean hands" area.

Theme-related displays of children's artwork can be incorporated into the children's activities. For example, children's drawings of fish can be displayed by the aquarium, along with fish books and photographs of fish, or made into a book about fish. Children should participate in creating these displays and deciding how they will look and where they will be placed.

Details. As much attention should be paid to the small details as to the larger objects in the room. In the play corner, are the dress-up clothes and the dolls' clothes and bedding made from cloth that looks and feels beautiful? Is there a variety of textures? Do the dishes and tableware match? Are the blocks carefully arranged by size and shape? Are the puzzles, games, and toys displayed so that each one is separate and clearly visible, instead of piled indiscriminately in a basket or box? It is better to put out only a limited selection of toys and games at a time and rotate them when the children begin to lose interest. Remember to remove and replace worn and broken items frequently.

Expressing Personal Taste

Our environments mirror who we are. The colors, shapes, and patterns appealing to one person may be different from what is appealing to another. What teachers consider the ideal environment for children may change as they learn new teaching approaches or visit other classrooms. In creating environments in which children will create art, there are unlimited possibilities. All of the above suggestions are starting points, not unbreakable rules. No two early-childhood environments need to be alike. Nor should they remain static. The environment should change as the children's interests and activities change, or as teachers explore new ways to create the ideal environment for children. The key element is flexibility. When flexibility is built into the room, then teachers can create the best environment for their particular children at that particular moment in time.

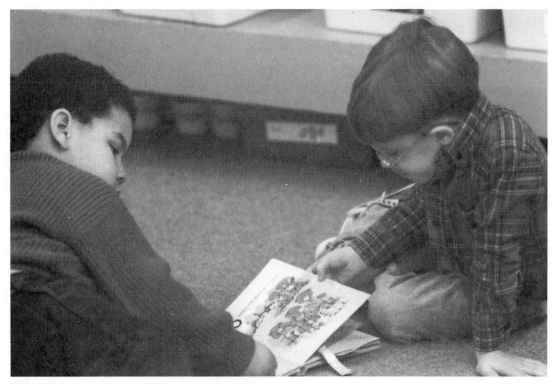

FIGURE 4–4 Children need beautiful spaces in which to learn.

SUMMARY: CREATING A SENSE OF PLACE

We shape our buildings; thereafter they shape us.

WINSTON CHURCHILL (TIME, SEPTEMBER 12, 1960)

For many years the emphasis on places for children has been on ease of cleaning and efficient functioning. This has been the model for most public schools in the United States. One large space is intended to serve all purposes. It is not surprising that in such an environment, art activities are limited to a multipurpose table that has to be cleared off at snack time, some boxes of junk, and perhaps a lonely easel. Cooking and art often go on at the same sink. In order to create an environment that is conducive to art creation, there need to be some major changes in how we build and equip the basic room.

The key to an enticing and functional place for children to do art is an environment where children can focus on the activities and supplies available, work independently, and clean up when done. Guiding adults want an environment that is safe and functional and in which children can learn. But most of all the space should show that adults value the role of art, not as a playtime activity, but as an important way that children show us what they are thinking.

Although every space is unique, with careful planning it can meet these requirements. It is well worth the effort.

- Children behave better in environments that consider their needs.
- Space that is arranged so that teachers can move about easily, and find needed supplies quickly, helps them become more relaxed and attentive to the children as they create art.
- Beautiful work places inspire both adults and children to do their best work.

FIGURE 4–5 "My house is flying." Marker—Brittany, age 5

On the whole, our society suffers from a lack of aesthetic vision. Many homes are decorated with an accumulation of well-liked things that do not relate to each other. Our educational settings mirror this. Adults often feel that children need all these things to use and learn from. But do they?

Sand boxes are filled with so many shovels and containers that there is no room for a child to just play with the sand. Styrofoam trays, wrapping paper, strips of carpet remnants, and some old yarn bits are shoved in a cardboard box and then children are expected to make something beautiful from them. Children are overwhelmed; they do not learn to focus in such an environment. Adults need to teach them that there is beauty in each part, and that each part relates to the others to make the whole.

FURTHER READING

The space has to be a sort of aquarium that mirrors ideas, values, attitudes, and cultures of the people who live within.

LORIS MALAGUZZI (EDWARDS ET AL., 1992, P. 149)

Church, E. B., and Miller, K. (1990). *Learning through play: Blocks.* New York: Scholastic. This book is a comprehensive guide to using blocks with young children.

Greenman, J. (1988). *Caring spaces, learning places.* Redmond, WA: Exchange Press. This sensitive book provides a picture of how to plan the total environment for young children, and should be read by anyone planning a place in which to teach.

Seefeldt, C. (1995). Art—serious work. *Young Children, 50* (3): 39–45. This article describes the way art is valued and presented in the Reggio Emilia Preprimary Schools of Italy.

Art Focus

ART IN THREE DIMENSIONS— BLOCKS, BOXES, AND PAPIER-MÂCHÉ

> The smooth shape of the blocks gave me a sense that never left me—of form becoming feeling.
>
> FRANK LLOYD WRIGHT
> (AS CITED IN WILLARD, 1972, P. 7)

Children, too, are builders. They create environments. They are the architects of the spaces they inhabit, often creating complex arrangements of toys and furnishings indoors, and shelters of sticks and grass out-of-doors. Frank Lloyd Wright (Willard, 1972, p. 7) attributed his interest in architecture to the gift of a box of Froebel blocks from his mother. But there is more in a box of blocks or in any three-dimensional art form than a possible future as an architect.

Much has been written on the importance of block play for young children (Church et al., 1990; Gelfer, 1990; Hirsch, 1984). In this section, the focus will be on the art learning that is developed in block play and through other three-dimensional construction activities.

How Children Grow through Three-Dimensional Art Activities

Children will develop:

1. Physically, by using large muscles in moving large blocks and boxes, by using the small muscles of the hand and arm in controlling the placement of smaller three-dimensional objects, and by using eye-hand coordination to effect careful placements (Bodily-Kinesthetic)
2. Socially, by sharing space and materials with others and by working cooperatively on large constructions (Interpersonal)
3. Emotionally, by gaining confidence through building substantial structures (Intrapersonal)
4. Visual perception skills:
   - By learning to see three-dimensional structures from a variety of viewpoints—

FIGURE 4–6 Blocks allow children to create their own environment.

inside and outside, top and bottom, and front, sides, and back
   - By using their eyes to measure spaces to be filled with other three-dimensional parts (Spatial)
5. Cognitively:
   - By learning a vocabulary for concepts of size, form, shape, location, and relationship, and by describing the nature of the structures through conversation (Linguistic)
   - By sorting objects by categories, by organizing them into patterns, by counting them, and by observing cause and effect as they try different solutions to problems (Logical-Mathematical)
6. Art awareness, by gaining an understanding of sculpture and architecture

Group composition. The number of children who can be in a block area will be determined by their ages and the size of the area. Two toddlers can work side by side if there are enough blocks and space. If there are only a few blocks in a small, enclosed area, bumping and grabbing may result. Preschoolers and primary children, who may become involved in cooperative building projects, often can work in larger groups. But attention must always be paid to each having enough room to move around and get more blocks without knocking over someone else's structure. Other factors that affect the group size are the size of the blocks and the floor surface.

Setup. A flat, low-pile carpet makes a good surface as it muffles the blocks when they fall. It is also more comfortable for the children to sit on while working. A smooth wood or tile floor, however, provides a slightly more stable base on which to work and allows smooth motion of wheeled vehicles. A well-designed block area should include both types of surfaces.

Storage. Like other supplies, blocks need to be arranged aesthetically and conveniently. Low shelves are essential. Blocks stored higher than the child's waist can fall and cause injuries. On the shelves the blocks should not be stacked more than several high and each different type of block should have its own location. Create a label for each location by tracing the shape of the block on paper and then attaching it to the correct shelf. Put the heaviest blocks on the bottom. Use the top of the shelves for accessories stored in clear plastic bins. Use masking tape to mark off a distance from the shelves in which building is not allowed, so that children can get blocks off the shelves without knocking someone's structure down.

Materials. Offer several different sizes of blocks. Many different kinds are available.

LARGE BLOCKS: Made of plastic, wood, cardboard, or foam, large blocks allow children to build structures they can sit on or inside. They are excellent for dramatic play and for balancing towers. They provide a fun way to discover spatial relationships by building walls to peek over, through, and around.

Child-decorated cardboard boxes stuffed with newspaper can be used as temporary building units as well. Empty cardboard boxes provide spaces to build within. Boxes with holes or the bottom cut out can be used for tunnels or structures to build through.

PATTERN BLOCKS: These small, flat, colored blocks of wood or plastic demonstrate many mathematical relationships. They are excellent for developing ideas of symmetry and pattern as well as for inventing creative designs and patterns.

UNIT BLOCKS: These blocks are usually wooden and come in a variety of geometric and architectural forms. They represent mathematical concepts, such as two triangles align to form a rectangle the same size as the rectangular unit block. This offers the children an excellent opportunity to investigate symmetry and geometric relationships.

Transition in. Most children need little introduction to block play. A beautifully displayed set of blocks is the best enticement. The book *Changes Changes* (Hutchins, 1972) can be shared before introducing the block area.

What to do. Block play is very simple to instigate.

1. Introduce the children to the layout of the block area and where the blocks can be used.
2. Show them how the blocks are to be put away when they are finished.

What to say. Choosing the right questions and words is one way teachers extend learning and help the child learn new vocabulary and concepts. Block play elicits conversations about form, space, shadow, balance, symmetry, top view, and side view.

1. Offer description.

   > "You are making your tower symmetrical. See, you have the same blocks on each side."
   > "You have made lots of spaces in your structure. Look, here's a square one."
   > "Your house is balanced. You put a tall brick at each end."
   > "Your building looks rectangular from the side, but round from the top."

2. Provide direction.

   > "What size block will you use next?"
   > "How can you make the base stronger?"
   > "Which block goes next in the pattern?"

3. Encourage children to include art in their building.

   > "From which view will you draw a picture?"
   > "Can you make a roof with this cardboard?"
   > "Do you want to make some signs for your road?"

TEACHER TIP

Adding Art to the Block Corner

Art materials can be added to the block area to increase the dramatic and architectural possiblities.

- **Paper, markers, and crayons** for making maps, and drawing pictures of the buildings
- **Blue paper and white pencils or crayons** to make "blueprints"
- **Cardboard pieces, tubes, and scissors** for the construction of roofs, signs, ramps, and more
- **Fabric pieces** to use for rugs and furnishings in houses
- **Nonhardening clay** to make people and animals
- **Bottle caps and thread spools** to add decorative patterns
- **Aluminum foil** to cover blocks for a sparkling effect

NOTE: These materials should be slowly added to the block area, so that the children have time to investigate the possibilities of each before being overwhelmed by too many choices.

Extending the learning: Architecture. Blocks and boxes introduce children to the world of architecture. It is natural for young children to build structures that mirror the buildings they inhabit and see around them. Encourage this connection by pointing out the relationships between the basic forms and their architectural counterparts.

1. Take walks through the neighborhood and find cylindrical columns, triangular roofs, rectangular bricks, arches, and more. Note how doorways are created by placing a crosspiece over two vertical supports (post and lintel) and point out similar constructions in their block buildings.
2. Invite an architect or architecture student to come and share their sketches, plans, and models of buildings they have designed.

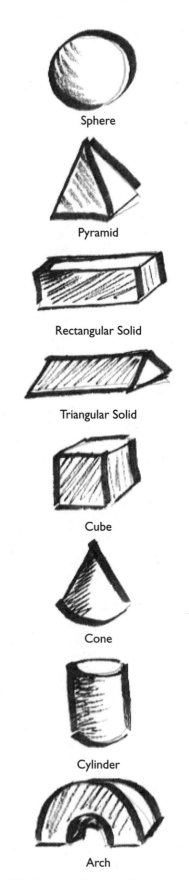

FIGURE 4–7 Basic three-dimensional forms

Such a visit will inspire the children to draw "blueprints" of their own. (See chapter 9 for visitor guidelines.)

3. Plan a day for older children to each be given a small section of the room in which to build their own private place using blocks, moveable furnishings, and other delineating materials to form the walls. Share the story *Roxaboxen* (McLerran, 1991) as the perfect complement to this activity.

Connections. LITERATURE: Other books to read that provide a link to architecture include *This Is My House* (Dorros, 1992), *Houses and Homes* (Morris, 1992), and *Building a House* (Robbins, 1984). *Architecture Colors* (Crosbie and Rosenthal, 1993) is particularly suitable for toddlers and can be read and then followed by a walk in the neighborhood to find the same forms.

The following books can be used to teach basic forms: *Brown Rabbit's Shape Book* (Baker, 1994), *Round Round Round* (Hoban, 1974), and *Of Colors and Things* (Hoban, 1989). (See Appendix B for other suggestions.)

The book *What It Feels Like to Be a Building* (Wilson, 1988) provides many ideas for kinesthetic activities that relate to architectural forms. Children can hold hands and form arches, windows, and doors for others to pass through. They can mime building imaginary buildings with "invisible" blocks.

ART AWARENESS: Hang a print of one of Frank Lloyd Wright's buildings. Tell the children about how he loved to build with blocks. If possible visit a piece of public sculpture or have a sculptor visit the children.

Boxes, Boxes, and More Boxes

Boxes of all kinds inspire the imagination of children. Small boxes can be homes for beloved stuffed toys. Appliance boxes can be turned into spaceships or submarines. Boxes can be glued together into animals, cities, and more.

Group composition. Depending on the sizes of the boxes and the purpose, box activities can range from individual projects to large cooperative ones. Two children can work together painting a small box. Four can work on a larger one.

Setup. Although small boxes can be used at a table, most box activities will require open floor space. If painting and gluing are to be done, the floor should be uncarpeted and covered with a protective covering such as an old plastic shower curtain. Newspaper can be used, although it sometimes slides or moves under the boxes when children handle them energetically.

Art Words

Architectural Structures

Arch
A curved structure supporting the weight of part of a building.

Beam
A long, straight piece of solid material, such as wood or metal, that supports the weight of some of the building.

Column
An upright support.

Post and Lintel
Two upright supports (posts) that hold up a horizontal piece of solid material (lintel), such as wood, stone, or metal, to create an opening such as a door or window.

Materials: Boxes of all types can be used separately or together.

TINY BOXES, such as ones jewelry or pudding mix comes in, can be used to make miniature houses to be arranged in a model of the neighborhood or town. They can also be made into homes for tiny toys or special treasures, or glued together into unique three-dimensional structures.

MEDIUM BOXES, such as shoe boxes and cereal, pasta, and oatmeal containers, can also be made into houses, homes for treasures, and creatures of all kinds. Attach a string to turn a box into a vehicle. Art can be created inside the box as well as outside. Holes can be cut so viewers can peek inside. Boxes can also be the base of puppets and masks (see chapter 11).

LARGE BOXES of corrugated cardboard can be used singly or glued together to create large elaborate structures. This kind of box activity is most suitable for pairs or small groups of children, to encourage them to work together.

GIANT BOXES are instantly appealing to young children, providing an immediate sense of privacy and drawing forth imaginative play. Painting larger boxes provides large motor movement for young children. Adding other boxes, cardboard pieces, paper, cloth, and other art elements can enhance the children's imaginative play.

What to do. Always have a supply of small- and medium-sized boxes available for children to use as they desire. Provide supplies for gluing them together, painting them, or using them with papier-mâché. (See Papier-Mâché below.)

On occasion provide large- and giant-sized boxes and create an open area for the children to explore and use them. Let the children play with the boxes—stacking them, pushing and pulling them, and crawling in and out—before offering art materials for the children to use with them. This gives them time to experiment with these larger forms without seeing them as just surfaces to "decorate."

What to say. As children play with the boxes, draw their attention to art elements and spatial relationships.

1. Describe the different forms.

"This box is rectangular."

"This box is a cylinder. That one is like a cube."

2. Describe location, size, and position.

"This box is on top. That one is on the bottom."
"You crawled into that box."
"This one is smaller than that one."

Extending the learning.

1. Add to the box construction by providing precut pieces of flat cardboard that can be glued on in various ways.
2. Take a field trip to the local grocery and have each child select a carton to bring back. Find out what the store does with the empty cartons.

Connections. LITERATURE: The following books feature boxes used in different ways: *Boxes, Boxes* (Fisher, 1984), *The Trip* (Keats, 1978), and *The Gift* (Prater, 1985).

ART AWARENESS: Share the box assemblages of Duchamp and Nevelson such as Nevelson's *Case with Five Balusters* (Take 5: Collage & Assemblage).

Papier-Mâché

Papier-mâché is a wonderfully sticky material that dries hard and paintable. It is the best way to convert flimsy cereal boxes into sturdy constructions.

Papier-mâché should be seen as a medium to be used when children have a specific problem or project in mind. For example, if children are frustrated because paint will not stick to the box they are painting, suggest papier-mâché. If some children want to build a box robot and the boxes will not stick together, suggest papier-mâché. Avoid doing papier-mâché as a whole-group activity. It takes a preconceived goal to motivate children to work through the difficulties of the medium and to see the end result over the intermediate newspaper-covered mess.

Group composition. Children are ready to do papier-mâché when they can stay in one place while working. Younger preschoolers can work in pairs on individual projects. Older children can work on large, oversized structures if they take turns working in groups of three or four.

Setup. Have children work at a low table covered with several thicknesses of newspaper and without chairs if doing individual projects. Large projects should be set up on a sheet of plastic or an old shower curtain on top of which are several layers of newspaper.

Cleanup. It is essential that the work area be located very close to water. If necessary, use a bucket for an initial rinse. Nothing is as slippery and dangerous as wet papier-mâché paste on the floor. Out-of-doors is always a good choice if the weather cooperates.

Materials. PASTE CONTAINER: Each child needs his or her own individual container for the paste. It should be wide-mouthed, such as a three-pound margarine container.

PAPIER-MACHE PASTE: This is also called art paste. See Appendix A: Sources. It is also effective to use thinned white washable glue.

BASE: A structure to cover, such as a cereal box, cardboard box, or styrofoam tray. Avoid curved objects such as balloons and tubes. Children need to build skill in applying the papier-mâché on stable objects before they can handle an object that must be held while the paste is applied.

NEWSPAPER: Pre-torn into two-inch strips.

Transition in. Papier-mâché activities can be related to a variety of occurrences. A walk to view buildings could lead into a project for some children who want to make buildings. A pair of children who want to make puppets can cover a cereal or spaghetti box, left open at one end so that it will turn into a puppet form to fit over their hands. A small group of children can make a stack of graduated boxes into a snowperson. A tray can be used to make a masklike shape. But regardless of the intended end, while the children are using the paste and paper they cannot help being involved in pure sensory exploration.

What to do.

1. Demonstrate how to dip a strip of paper in the paste and then place it on the box or tray.
2. Children should keep their hands over their paste buckets which should be set directly in front of them in order to catch drips.
3. Encourage the children to cover the box or tray completely, leaving nothing to show. One layer is usually sufficient for the first papier-mâché experience. In future experiences, children can be encouraged to put on more layers to make the base sturdier.
4. Place finished projects on a sheet of plastic to dry. They will stick to newspaper. Place them in a safe, dry place near a heater or in the sun, to speed drying time.
5. When the papier-mâché is dry, the form can be painted and/or collaged.

What to say. Use this experience to direct the children's attention to the different sides of the form. Children commonly miss sides and are surprised to find how many there really are on a cereal or cardboard box. Encourage them to look from different vantage points.

> "Did you put papier-mâché on the top?"
> "Did you look at the other side?"
> "How can you put that strip on to cover that place?"

Connections. LITERATURE: Read books that feature characters enjoying wet, messy things, such as *Muddigush* (Knutson, 1992).

ART AWARENESS: Share prints of or actual papier-mâché artifacts, such as masks from Mexico. (See Appendix A: Sources, for papier-mâché artifacts and mask prints.)

FIGURE 4–8 Papier-mâché challenges children to control a wet, sticky material and create three-dimensional projects.

Studio Page *21*

GOALS AND ENVIRONMENT

For each of the artistic goals below, describe the most conducive environment for young children:

• Emotional Growth:

_____

• Social Growth:

_____

• Physical Growth—Small muscles:

_____

• Physical Growth—Large muscles:

_____

• Physical Growth—Sensory:

_____

• Cognitive Growth—Spatial:

_____

• Cognitive Growth—Logical-Mathematical:

_____

• Cognitive Growth—Linguistic:

_____

• Creative Expression:

_____

• Art Integration:

_____

• Teacher As Artist:

_____

• Responding to the Art of Others:

_____

Studio Page

BECOMING SENSITIVE TO OUR ENVIRONMENT

The following activities are designed to provoke thought about the environments in which we exist and the effect they have on our feelings and behavior.

1. Make a list of places where you feel most relaxed. Categorize them as soft or hard, open or closed, private or social.

    _____

    _____

    _____

    _____

    _____

    _____

    _____

2. Make a list of all the different environments you spend time in each day, such as bedroom, kitchen, classroom, bus, and so on. Describe your behavior in each environment in terms of how you move, talk, dress, and whether you feel comfortable or not.

    _____

    _____

    _____

    _____

    _____

    _____

    _____

3. Based on what you wrote above, describe the perfect environment for you.

    _____

    _____

    _____

    _____

    _____

    _____

    _____

Studio Page 23

OBSERVATION: CHILDREN AND THEIR WORK SPACES

In this observation, study how children use the available space and materials that have been provided for them. Observe in any setting in which three or more young children have a choice of activities including using art supplies. The observation should last 40 minutes to an hour.

Date of Observation: **Length of Observation:**

Age of Children: **Size of Group:**

1. Draw a quick sketch of the room and indicate the location of the various activities and supplies.

2. How are the supplies stored?

    _____

    _____

3. Can children get their own art supplies and replace them with minimal help?

    _____

    _____

4. How do the children use the art supplies?

    _____

    _____

5. Did children move the art supplies to other areas?

    _____

    _____

Studio Page 24

THE IMPORTANCE OF SPACE

1. Using the data from your observation, decide if you think the room arrangement encouraged or discouraged the children from using the art supplies in a variety of ways.

_____
_____
_____
_____
_____
_____
_____
_____
_____
_____
_____
_____
_____
_____
_____

2. How would you change the space allotment, the furniture arrangement, and/or supply storage to increase artistic growth? Draw a sketch of your idea.

_____
_____
_____
_____
_____
_____
_____
_____
_____
_____
_____
_____
_____
_____

OBSERVATION: AESTHETICS OF AN ENVIRONMENT

Choose a room in a home or school where children do artwork. Examine this room's aesthetic effect. Use the information in this chapter as a guide.

1. What are the background colors in this room?

   Walls: _____

   Ceiling:_____

   Floor: _____

   Floor Coverings: _____

2. What is displayed on each wall? Be specific. Make a sketch if necessary.

   Wall 1: _____

   Wall 2: _____

   Wall 3: _____

   Wall 4: _____

3. Are there any sensory displays? If yes, describe them.

   _____

   _____

   _____

   _____

4. How are toys, games, and books displayed?

   _____

   _____

   _____

   _____

5. What is the total aesthetic effect of this room? Is there anything you would change to make it more aesthetically pleasing for children?

   _____

   _____

   _____

   _____

Studio Page **26**

MIND MAP OF AN ENVIRONMENT FOR YOUNG ARTISTS

Fill in this graphic organizer with your ideas for creating an aesthetically pleasing environment for children. On a large board, illustrate these ideas with sketches of displays and furnishings. Use clippings of color samples for walls, floor, and accessories.

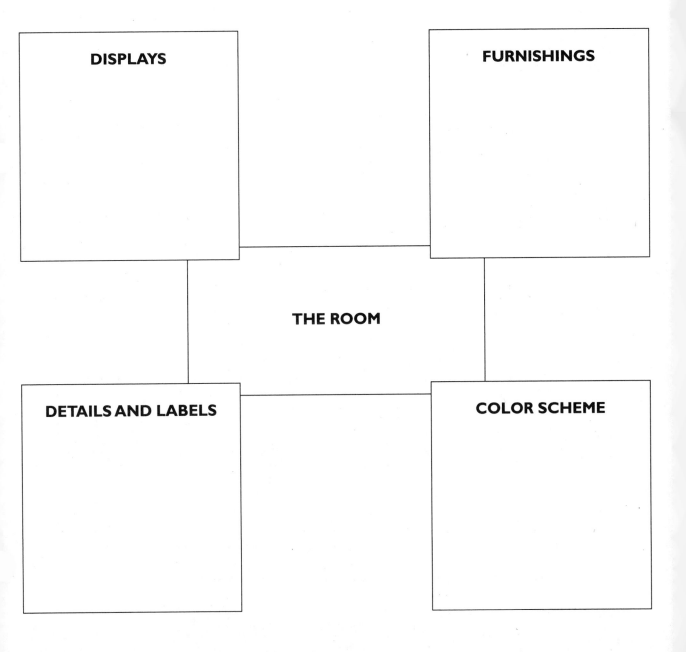

DISPLAYS

FURNISHINGS

THE ROOM

DETAILS AND LABELS

COLOR SCHEME

Studio Page 27

DESIGNING THE ENVIRONMENT

Keeping in mind what the children will be learning about art, design an ideal environment.

1. On this graph paper is outlined a room 14 feet by 20 feet. (Scale is one square equals one foot.)

2. Trace the scaled pattern pieces on Studio Page 28 or design your own.

3. Cut them out and try several possible arrangements to create an environment that would be ideal for young artists.

4. Plan areas for wet and messy activities, quiet, comfortable ones, creative and dramatic play, and kinesthetic movement.

5. Consider all the different art activities that could take place in each area and then indicate where supplies would be located.

SCALED FURNITURE PIECES

5

> ❝ *All children everywhere will become more skilled in those pursuits that engage their interests and efforts and that are valued by adults and peers in their environment.* ❞

•

HOWARD GARDNER (1991, P. 106)

Making Connections

Art and the Integrated Curriculum

Questions addressed in this chapter:

How can art activities be integrated into the total curriculum?

What is the thematic teaching approach?

What is the project approach?

SUMMARY: Making the Connection

FURTHER READING

ART FOCUS: The Painting Experience

Young Artists at Work

Dennis has found a dead butterfly in the grass by the swing. He bends over and picks it up gently. "Look!" he says, "I've found a butterfly." Several other children gather around.

"I've seen one like that."

"My sister caught a butterfly."

"Can I have it?"

The teacher notices the group of children and approaches. "Look at my butterfly," Dennis says proudly.

"It's so many colors!" responds the teacher. "I see gold and blue. What do you see? "

"Here's some red and yellow," answers Dennis.

"It has lots of feet," Tomas adds.

"Wow, there is so much to see! Why don't we take it inside and look at it with the magnifying glass?" suggests the teacher.

Inside, Dennis places the butterfly on a soft cushion of paper towels and the children take turns looking at it through the magnifying glass. Some children begin to pretend they are butterflies fluttering around the room. The teacher says invitingly, "Would you like to paint with butterfly colors?"

"Yes," say the children.

Gold, blue, red, yellow, and black paints are put out at a table. A group of children begin to paint enthusiastically. One paints a huge head and body with many legs and swirls of color around it. Another dabs his brush up and down lightly across his paper. "My brush is a butterfly flying from flower to flower," he says.

Another girl studies the butterfly, then runs over to the table. She makes a tiny dab of paint on her paper. Then she goes back and observes again. Back and forth she goes, choosing each color and stroke with deliberation. "My butterfly is the same size," she states with assurance.

Dennis is painting too. His paper is covered with bold strokes of lines and colors. "This is a butterfly day," he declares.

HOW CAN ART ACTIVITIES BE INTEGRATED INTO THE TOTAL CURRICULUM?

Through the multiple threads of many activities, learning can be woven into a whole cloth.

PEARL GREENBERG (1972, P. 85)

In order to produce meaningful art, young artists need to participate in an experience that will provide a basis for the work they will produce. The experience needs to be rich in sensory and visual stimuli. It should be memorable and full of opportunities for asking questions and making observations. Most important, the experience should flow directly into the art expression that relates to it.

The teacher adds to the value of the experience by taking an active role in increasing the children's interest, by modeling enthusiasm and wonder, and by asking tantalizing questions. Instead of dismissing Dennis' butterfly with a "That's nice," the teacher draws the children in by pointing out the colors and asking questions. Sensing the interest of children, the teacher brings the experience back to the classroom, discards the plans for the day, and instead provides some simple art materials and an opportunity for the children to express their observations. How much richer, how much more memorable, how much more exciting is this art experience than is putting out some butterfly patterns on a table and saying to the children "You can make some butterflies, if you want."

There are many possible ways to provide such experiences. This chapter presents ways of organizing art activities and the entire curriculum around stimulating learning experiences.

FIGURE 5–1 "Angry butterfly." Tempera paint—Nick, age 5

The Transition

The *transition* is a group experience in which all or some of the children participate, such as listening to a story or moving kinesthetically. This experience is then used to introduce a new art material for exploration or to set the stage for a responsive activity. For example, blowing bubbles can be a transition into exploring foamy soap paint, or it can inspire a mural that expresses the bubble-making experience.

Sometimes a transition may be unplanned. A surprise visitor or a sudden rain shower may create the opportunity for a teachable moment. If teachers have made flexible plans, they can often find a related activity, using the basic art materials available, which will take advantage of this situation, as the teacher did in responding to Dennis and his butterfly.

Designing successful transitions. Good transitions are designed to increase the child's perceptual awareness and cognitive understanding. Reading a story about how different colors mix to form new ones, such as *Colors* (Felix, 1993), will entrance children with the idea that certain colors mixed together make other familiar colors. Then when they paint, they relate what happens on their paper to what they heard in the story.

Transitions should not determine what the resulting artwork will be. A thoughtful transition allows for a wide range of artistic response. Reading a story about bears and then telling the children to paint a bear is not a transition. Instead, after reading a bear story, help the children mix up a batch of light, medium, and dark brown colors. Then invite the children to use the different "bear" browns in their paintings. Once the children are working, each will go in a different direction as they respond to the nature of the medium and their own internal need for self-expression.

Transitions are vital. Although putting art materials out on a table or having an easel set up in a corner will allow children to produce art, a transition provides a focus and enriches the experience. Use a transition whenever a new art medium is being presented, to rekindle interest in already available art materials, and to initiate responsive artworks. The younger the child, the less time should separate the transition and the art activity, and the more directly it must relate to the present interest of the child. Brief transitions, such as sharing a short poem or chant, painting with an "imaginary" paintbrush, or pointing out a pattern on a piece of clothing, take only a few minutes and are suitable for the short attention span of toddlers. They can also be used with older children, especially when time is limited.

With older children and more time, transitions can be much more complex. For example, a drawing activity could be introduced by reading a story about lines, such as *Billy and the Magic String* (Karnovsky, 1995), then moving kinesthetically in lines, and finally taking a walk and finding lines.

Successful transitions must be created to fit the particular needs and interests of our children. Sometimes the best transitions are those that occur at the spur of the moment. For example, a group of children is excitedly watching what happens when some paint mixes with water in the sink. Ask them what would happen if they put water on a piece of paper and then painted on it. At other times, a carefully planned transition can serve to spark or renew a less outwardly visible interest, such as sharing the story *Galimoto* (Williams, 1990), and then wondering aloud what kinds of toys could be invented from things in the classroom. There are many examples of transitions in the Art Focus sections of each chapter. Use these as guides in the process of creating inviting transitions into art activities of all kinds. Appendix B provides an annotated listing of children's books, many of which include suggested ways to use them as transitions into art activities.

Curriculum Connections

Connections are activities in other curriculum areas which can lead into or occur simultaneously with related art activities. For example, if children are experimenting with measuring water at the water table, they can also see what happens when they add different amounts of water to the paints. Cross-curriculum connections are a way of using the experiences gained in one area as a transition into another.

Art activities can also transition into other areas. The butterfly-painting activity described at the beginning of the chapter could be connected to reading books about butterflies, dramatizing their life cycle, hatching a cocoon, or creating a graph of the different butterfly colors observed. Examples of connections can be found in the Art Focus sections of each chapter.

Planning activities that connect across the curriculum helps us appreciate the interconnection of all knowledge and learning. Connections are a simple way to start to form an integrated curriculum. They can be created by focusing on the common elements in two or more areas. For example, both art and science require fine observation skills. Identifying patterns plays an important role in art, math, music, science, and literature. In the following section, these simple connections are built upon to create an entirely integrated curriculum through the thematic approach.

WHAT IS THE THEMATIC TEACHING APPROACH?

> Life should be a single whole, especially in the earliest years, when the child is forming himself in accordance with the laws of his growth.
>
> MARIA MONTESSORI (1967, P. 164)

Many educators would agree that learning is best accomplished when children are surrounded by activities, objects, and active experiences which relate to each other in a meaningful way. Caine and Caine (1974, p. 171) find that when a thematic approach is used, conditions are created that match optimum requirements for "brain-based" learning. As thematic-based curricula have become widely accepted in early childhood education, more teachers have found that unifying the activities presented to young children is both challenging and very rewarding. The use of themes stimulates both children and teachers to look at the environment around them in new ways.

Selecting a Theme

A theme-based curriculum is one in which many different subject areas are integrated by relating them to a carefully selected broad-based theme. For example, if the chosen theme is water, then books about water will be read. Children will experiment with water. They will paint with water, wash the dolls and toys in the play area, and splash in water at the water table. They may take a field trip to a stream or lake and talk about the animals that live in the water.

Setting up a thematic unit such as this can be quite time-consuming on the part of the teacher. It takes time to locate the books, set up the activities, and plan the field trips. This has led to a profusion of books that present ready-made thematic units, complete with patterns for bulletin boards and ideas for projects, which are often then carried out in lockstep fashion, week by week or month by month.

(1)

FIGURE 5–2 The children in this kindergarten class made a special visit to their playground. Together with their teacher they looked carefully at the different shapes and forms and noticed the spaces as well. Then they came back to the classroom and drew pictures in response.

(1) "I'm going down the twisty slide." Marker—Jamie, age 5
(2) "My friends and I like to ride the swings." Marker—Brittany, age 5
(3) "I like to run and jump all over the playground." Marker—Joe, age 5

(2)

(3)

Rather than following the thematic plan of a book, however, a successful and meaningful theme must grow out of the teacher's knowledge of the interests and experiences of the children and must represent a significant element in their lives. Just because there is a wonderful unit on penguins does not mean that this topic will interest a particular group of children, none of whom have ever seen a real penguin.

Guidelines for theme selection. The following guidelines will aid the selection of appropriate themes.

1. Begin by learning about the children and their interests. Watch them as they play and interact with each other. What do they talk about? What are their favorite things? Has someone gone on a trip or, like Dennis, brought in something to share that elicits enthusiasm from the others?

2. Decide if the theme is one that is rich in possibilities for expansion to the different curricula or growth areas. Are there many books on that theme? Are there related songs and poems? Will there be things to explore through science, art, drama, and play? Will children be able to use skills from the different growth areas to explore this theme? Some themes offer more range than others. The following list presents themes that reflect the interests of many young children.

   Building things (architecture, machines, construction)
   Colors
   Everyday life (e.g., shopping, going to the doctor, clothing)
   Families
   Feelings
   Growing things (plants, trees)
   Light
   Living things (animals, bugs)
   Moving things (things with wheels, flying things)
   Nonliving things (sand, mud, rocks, metals)
   Patterns
   People
   Shapes
   Sky (clouds, sun, moon, stars)
   Textures
   Water
   Weather

3. Survey the resources. Are the needed supplies available for certain activities? Are there places to visit or people who could talk to the children about this theme? Where can books be found on the theme?

4. Analyze the time available. The theme should be open-ended enough that if the children's interest wanes it will be easy to move on to something else. However, there should be sufficient time so that if the children become highly interested they do not have to be cut off to "move on." It is not the specific theme that teaches. The goal in early childhood education is not to make the children experts on the theme subject. The theme should be a vehicle that allows the child to explore and learn about his environment within a meaningful context.

Selecting thematically-related art activities. Themes provide an excellent way to unify the child's art experiences with the rest of the curriculum. However, it is very important to make sure that the art activities are open-ended. It is a real temptation for teachers to want to give the children thematically-related pictures to color and patterns to follow, but it must be remembered that such directive activities do not foster artistic growth no matter how attractive the results may be.

Open-ended art activities can be used to relate to themes in many ways. Regardless of the thematic unit, basic art supplies should be available at all times. Children should be free to choose to draw, paint, make a collage, or build throughout the thematic unit, whether as a personal exploration or as a reaction to a thematically-related experience. More focused open-ended art activities, such as making a quilt, painting a mural, or using firing clay, can also accompany a thematic unit.

Planning a Thematic Unit

Once the thematic unit is chosen and the materials collected, design a flexible plan that will respond to the interests of the children. There is no way to predict how a certain group will react to the experiences and activities related to the theme, so it is difficult to create a specific day-by-day plan in advance. Instead lay out a flexible, long-term plan with general ideas for possible activities. According to Becker, Reed, Steinhaus, and Week (1994, p.15), a well-organized thematic teaching unit includes:

1. Excellent literature
2. Multidisciplinary activities
3. Opportunities to work with others
4. Visible and tangible displays that make the room look different

Flexible planning. A flexible plan is essential for organizing and carrying out an integrated thematic unit. Although there is much work involved in writing plans, it is well worth the effort. The practice of writing plans orders our thoughts and allows us to play with ideas. It enables teachers to use their knowledge and experience more effectively. When they are with the children, having a plan will enable them to be *proactive* rather than *reactive*. This does not mean that teachers should be inflexible in adhering to the plan, but rather that they should have a basis from which to make decisions. Having a plan is like traveling with a road map. It keeps us from getting lost, and lets us make side trips with confidence that we will find our way back to the main road.

Art skills and processes build upon each other, and teachers need to relate them to the other experiences that will be happening in their programs. Visualizing the possible directions a thematic unit may take enables teachers to see beyond the isolated art "project." It forces them to focus on the specific goals they have for young artists across the curricular areas and leads to a program that naturally engages the children.

Graphic organizers. A graphic organizer such as a calendar, chart, or web is an excellent way to organize activities in terms of what children will be experiencing. Although this kind of planning is often organized by curriculum areas such as literature, math, science, and art, this only serves to create divisions between learning that are not really there. For example, many art and science activities are very similar. Activities described as art explorations in this book, such as texture walks, touch boxes, color mixing, eye-dropper art, and natural dyeing are also recommended by Williams, Rockwell, and Sherwood (1987) as part of an early childhood science curriculum. The organizing categories need to be broad enough to include activities with multiple learning dimensions.

To create a thematic unit that flows across the disciplines, organize activities by what the children will be learning. Categories based on the social, physical, emotional, creative, and cognitive goals of the program, and phrased in terms of the

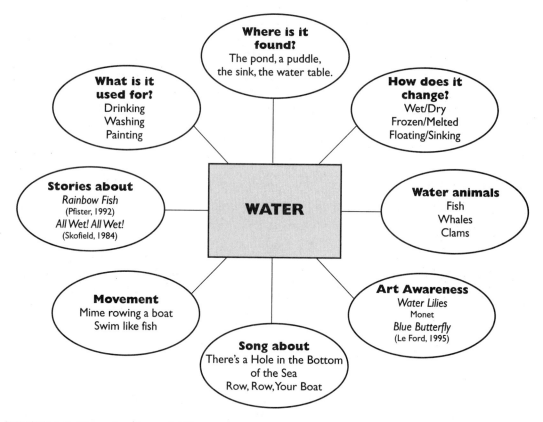

FIGURE 5–3 Thematic unit sample: Water web

vocabulary, observations, questions, discussion, experiments, explorations, and assessments to be used, will provide a focus on what is really important for the children to be doing.

Another approach to organizing thematic activities is to identify subtopics that relate to the theme and related activities for these topics. But no matter which organizing principle is used, there will always be activities that overlap others. This is not a sign of a problem, but rather reflects an activity rich in meaning (figures 5–3 and 5–4)

Teaching a Thematic Unit

Thematic units consist of the following components:

Setting the stage. Before beginning the unit, allow the children to become familiar with how the work space or room is organized, what behaviors are expected of them, and how the time is divided during the day. Once the thematic unit begins, the children will already know where the basic supplies are and what areas are used for certain activities. Taking time to allow for basic exploration of the environment and getting to know each other beforehand will make it easier for everyone to concentrate more on the theme. This also provides time for an idea for a thematic unit to grow naturally from the children.

The initial event. Once an interest has been identified and a theme selected, plan an initial event that will be stimulating and provocative. It should focus everyone's attention on the theme and be full of images, ideas, and feelings. The event may be one that takes the children beyond the walls of the room, such as a walk or field trip, or it may involve

EXPLORATION:
- Take a walk to the pond. Look at the water. Ask: "What color is it? Where did it come from? What lives in it?"
- Look for signs of life. Collect specimens.
- On return, put out specimens and art materials. Ask: "Would you like to make some pictures about our trip?"

WATER TABLE:
- Put out cups and bowls. Ask: "Which holds the most? The least?"
- Put out bottle and funnels. Ask: "What happens to the water in the funnel? How long does it take to fill the bottle?"
- Put ice cubes in the water. Ask: "What happens?"
- Put measured water in bowls and leave them out in the sun. Ask: "What happens?"
- Put out objects that sink and float.
- Have art supplies out. Ask: "Would you like to make some pictures that show how _____?"

EASEL:
- Put out water in a cup and paints. Ask: "What happens when you wet the brush first? What does the water do to the paint?
- Put out small amounts of paint and water. Let children add different amounts of paint. Ask: "What happens?"
- Put out wet sponge and demonstrate how to use it to wet paper. Invite children to try painting on wet paper. Ask: "What happens to the paint? How does it change?"

ART PRINT:
- Display *Water Lilies* by Claude Monet. Ask: "How does it look when you stand close? Far away? What colors did the artist use?" Read *A Blue Butterfly: A Story about Claude Monet*.

MUSIC:
- Sing "Row, Row, Row Your Boat." Make up new verses and actions to go with the song.
- Learn words to "There's a Hole..." Make up new words.

ANIMAL STUDY:
- Set up an aquarium. Assign the children different jobs to help take care of the fish.
- Observe how fish swim. Identify different parts.
- Read: *The Rainbow Fish*. Talk about fish scales and colors.
- Put out an Indonesian fish sculpture. Compare it to real fish.

AT THE SINK:
- Ask: "How does the water get here?" Trace the pipes coming into the sink. Study the faucets.
- Visit the water plant. Put out booklets for children who want to "write" about the trip.
- Comment on how water feels when children wash their hands. If a child makes a comment about how skin color does not wash off, use it as a teachable moment to discuss skin color.
- Wash toys and playthings.

RAINY DAY:
- Read *All wet! All wet!* Go for a walk in the rain. Look for puddles. Find reflections. Ask: "What looks different when it's wet?"
- Make paint-drip mural. (see chapter 10). Add water to make the paint drip faster or slower.

FIGURE 5–4 Thematic unit sample: Activity list

bringing something special to the children such as a visitor or animal or object. Rearrange the room and put out new materials and play items that carry through on the theme. The idea is to raise the interest of as many children as possible.

Activity integration. Thematic unit activities should be integrated into each of the learning areas offered, but should not replace them. Children need the continuity of knowing that sand, blocks, home-life/dramatic play, and easel painting will be waiting for them every day. Integrate the thematic unit into these areas in small ways such as changing the paint color or texture or the paint tools offered at the easel, providing different containers or toys in the sand, putting out theme-related toys, or providing different dress-up clothes, art to hang, or play food.

Although it may not be possible to integrate the theme into every area every time, try to find creative ways to touch as many areas as possible. The following examples give an idea of how this can be done.

Example 1:

Theme: The color red
Sand Play: Put out red containers and shovels and/or hide red blocks or red plastic objects in the sand.
Block Play: Put out pieces of cardboard that have been covered on both sides with red paper or contact paper and/or add red plastic toys to the block area.
Dramatic Play: Offer red dress-up clothes. Put out red play food, dishes, or art prints.
Easel: Put out red paint plus white and black.

Example 2:

Theme: Faces
Sand Play: Photocopy photographs of the children's faces. Mount the photocopies on cardboard and hide them in the sand for the children to find and play with.
Block Play: Put out people blocks or plastic people.
Dramatic Play: Put out masks and mirrors, and hang portraits on the wall.
Easel: Put out a variety of skin-colored paints

Ending a thematic unit. After all the time and effort spent on a thematic teaching unit, it should not be allowed to fizzle away at the end.

Celebrate! It takes extra effort, but a celebration of learning or a culminating activity at the end of a thematic unit helps solidify all the learning that has taken place. The culminating activity may consist of special activities that relate to the theme and/or it may include displays of work and photographs that reflect the activities that have taken place. The entire environment of the room may be changed for the day, and/or visitors may be invited. It should be a party that celebrates the joy of learning.

Evaluate. The end of a thematic unit is also a time for evaluating what has happened. What were the children's favorite activities? What do they remember best? What new things did they learn? What do they want to tell others about their experiences? What have the children learned and accomplished?

It is important to provide time for the children to share what they have learned with each other. Children can show art or projects they have done and tell how they made them. Consider trying a variety of formats. Although having the child stand up in front of the group is a common method, other possibilities include audiotaping or videotaping the child's presentation for sharing with the others. These tapes can then be shared with parents as well.

The children can also make displays that show what they have learned, and the children can circulate among them asking questions and making comments. To keep the group focused on the presentations, provide a simple checklist to mark or coupons to collect to show which displays they visited.

Young Artists at Work

Jamil and Corin are hunched over a large sheet of paper, engrossed in their drawing of dinosaurs and actively engaged in a conversation about the color of dinosaurs. As the other children play in the block area, put on dress-up clothes, paint at the easel or dig in the sand, the boys continue drawing, oblivious to the activity around them. Every once in a while the teacher passes by and, on occasion, makes a comment such as, "Wow, you are working hard. You have drawn so many dinosaurs!" or offers, "Here is a new dinosaur book I just found."

"I'll look for more dinosaurs and see what colors this book shows. You keep drawing," Jamil tells Corin.

"They have been working on that drawing for three days!" the teacher tells a visitor. "We read a book about dinosaurs and now those two are just so entranced by them."

WHAT IS THE PROJECT APPROACH?

The project approach has many similarities to the use of themes, yet it differs in significant ways. Katz and Chard (1989, p. 2) define a *project* as "an in-depth study of a particular topic that one or more children undertake." This approach, often used in the upper elementary grades and in art education classes, is attracting interest from

FIGURE 5–5 Purple dinosaur project. Working together with others to build a large project helps children develop independence and self-confidence.

early childhood educators because of the Reggio Emilia program. Gardner applauds the project approach, as demonstrated at Reggio Emilia, for the way it guides children in using all their "intellectual, emotional, social and moral potentials" (Edwards et al., 1992, p. xii).

It involves encouraging children to work in small groups of two to five on a project that reflects their personal interests, some of which may be far removed from their everyday experience, and from what the teacher might select. These groups establish a relationship with the teacher in which the teacher not only facilitates, but collaborates in the process directly by supplying the needed skills and direction. Examples of possible projects for children under eight include "writing" a book about a topic, building a sculpture out of boxes, creating puppets and performing a drama, or painting a mural.

The Value of the Project Approach

Katz and Chard (1991) have identified the following goals for the education of young children, which are best met through the project approach:

1. The project approach engages children's intellects by widening their knowledge and skills at their individual levels of understanding. The traditional format of learning through play, while beneficial, lacks intellectual challenge and underestimates children's ability to acquire wider meaning from their experiences. An academic approach, on the other hand, forces children to proceed in a lockstep sequence of learning skills and concepts, whether or not these skills are relevant or appropriate for the individual child.
2. Project work helps children learn in an integrated manner and breaks down the divisions between subjects or play areas.
3. The use of projects challenges teachers to be creative and to devise constructive solutions to educational problems.
4. Project work relies on the children's intrinsic motivation as it allows for a much wider range of choices and independent efforts on a topic of their choice.
5. Children can select work that matches or challenges their skill level.
6. Children can become expert in their own learning. They are in charge of finding information and using it in new ways.
7. When children reflect on and evaluate their contribution to a project, they become accountable for their own learning.

Initiating Projects

A project may start out very much like a thematic unit. The entire group of children participates in an exciting, multifaceted experience, after which they discuss and perhaps draw about their experience. Following this discussion, the teacher plans activities that reflect the interests expressed by the children or the children suggest possible activities that they would like to do. Based on the experiences of the Human Development Laboratory School at the University of Massachusetts, LeeKeenan and Nimmo (1992, p. 255) suggest the following basic components. These components can be used in any order and repeated as needed throughout the project.

Exploration. As with the initial event of the thematic unit, the exploration is a stimulating event or activity, related to the project, that involves the entire group. These can be used throughout the unit to restimulate interest or to answer questions that have been raised. For example, taking a field trip to the same place, after the children have explored and thought about what they experienced the first time, can lead to a deeper understanding as they notice new things or clarify memories.

Organization. Learning activities are planned that relate to the individual children's ideas and questions. These activities should allow open-ended exploration of project-related ideas, encouraging the children to observe, sense, explore, and experiment, both individually and with others. For example, after several children participating in a project on plants comment that all leaves are green, a variety of plants are put on display alongside containers of different green materials for collages. These activities are then available as a choice for all the children to investigate.

Discussion/representation. Time is set aside to talk about and share the children's ideas daily. These can be recorded by the teacher in various ways—in charts, graphs, dictation and through audiotaping. The children's changing ideas can also be documented through their drawings and constructions, and photographs and videotapes made of their activities. This is a very important part of the process; it is the way the different groups' learning is made visible to all the children.

Working on Projects

Children work on the projects as one of the choices they can make during free-play time. If projects continue over a period of time, children who have formed a group to work on a particular project may need to be reminded of their project and should be encouraged, but not forced, to finish it.

Culminating Projects

As with a thematic unit, projects need to be recognized in a special way. Concluding activities need to be carefully designed. One of the main dangers with the project approach is the temptation to focus on the finished product and to ignore the thought and process that went into it. Plan ways to share the children's work through displays of not only the project but also all the documentation of the process that went into it. (See chapter 12 for display ideas.) There also needs to be a time for the same kind of assessment as is done for thematic units.

Projects and Themes in Combination

Although these two approaches have been discussed separately, they are not mutually exclusive. Within the presentation of a thematic unit, small groups of children can initiate independent projects. These projects may relate to the theme or may go in a different direction. On the other hand, a project initiated by a small group of students can grow into a thematic unit if it attracts the interest of the other children.

Whether used separately or in combination, both these approaches integrate art into the total learning of the child. Art provides the graphic medium through which children can express what they have observed and thought about. Drawings record how a dinosaur was built. Paintings record color experiments. Prints show the child's understanding of pattern. But these artworks do not stand alone. They are richer and more intense because they are part of a total experience.

SUMMARY: MAKING THE CONNECTION

> Let the main ideas which are introduced into a child's education be few and important, and let them be thrown into every combination possible.
>
> ALFRED NORTH WHITEHEAD (1929, P. 2)

This chapter has focused on the "how" of teaching, by furnishing guidelines for developing theme-based units and projects that integrate art into the curriculum. Art, as a way of learning and communicating about the world, can enrich every aspect of an early childhood program. Presented with activities that are unified by a common theme, children learn to see and react to the world as an interconnected place. When children's interests dictate the starting point for designing art activities, the children see them as meaningful. Self-initiated projects help children develop independent thinking and working skills.

Setting up these kinds of opportunities takes a great deal of work and effort on the teacher's part. There is no published thematic unit or project list that will work with every group of children every time. Each class is unique in its interests and skills and the units teachers create must be customized accordingly. It is well worth the effort. When children's interests are aroused, when they are full of enthusiasm, and when they know they have a choice, they respond by thinking more deeply. They care more about what they are doing and they understand the world better. Integrating art into the curriculum also means that all learning becomes more meaningful.

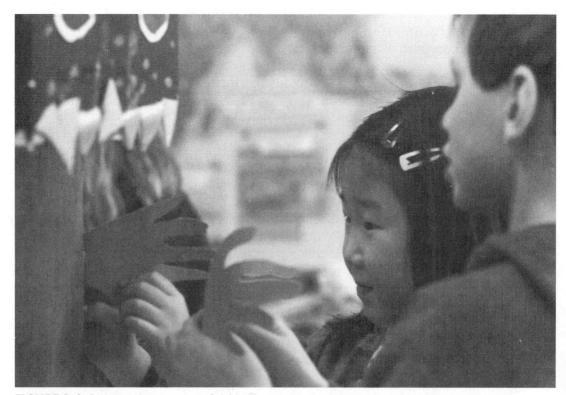

FIGURE 5–6 Activities that grow out of children's interests and experiences help children create more meaningful art.

FURTHER READING

> To produce art, children need many interesting experiences in classroom and community, and encouragement to think, talk, and create art in response to their experiences.
> CAROL SEEFELDT (1995, P. 40)

Cecil, N. L., and Lauritzen, P. (1995). *Literacy and the arts for the integrated classroom: Alternate ways of knowing*. White Plains, NY: Longman.
There are many ways to integrate art into children's learning. Cecil and Lauritzen present a wide variety of ideas to inspire teachers.

Edwards, C., Gandini, L., and Forman, G. (1992). *The hundred languages of children: The Reggio Emilia approach to early childhood education*. Norwood, NJ: Ablex Publishing.
This book describes the philosophy of the project approach as practiced in the Reggio Emilia Preprimary Schools, with examples from both Italy and the United States.

Katz, L., and Chard, S. (1991). *Engaging children's minds: The project approach*. Norwood, NJ: Ablex.
This book defends the use of themes in early education and presents ways to institute this approach in the classroom.

Art Focus

THE PAINTING EXPERIENCE

> Paint is different from other media. It is fluid; it has qualities of flow and freedom; it is spontaneous; it has feeling.
>
> KATE HART (1994, p. 2)

There is nothing else quite like it. Long tapered brushes dip into liquid color that flows and falls with abandon across a white rectangle of paper. For a moment the young artist is alone, focused on the interplay of mind and muscle, action and reaction. Painting provides the sensory link between the childish finger that plays in the spilled milk and the masterly hand that painted the Mona Lisa.

Before beginning a painting exploration with children, take a moment to make a tempera painting. Swirl and spread the paint, concentrate on the way the brush responds to muscular commands and the visual result created. Feel the way the brush glides over the surface and watch how the wet paint catches the light and glistens. Creating a painting is the perfect way to appreciate the importance of process over product to the young child for whom painting is first and foremost a sensory experience.

FIGURE 5–7 What happens when child, paint, and brush mix?

TEACHER TO PARENT

Sample Letter to Parents About Painting

Dear Family,

Painting is an important part of our art program and the children will be painting almost every day. In order for your child to have a wonderful time painting, please dress him or her in clothing that is easy to wash. It is important that sleeves can be pushed up above the elbows to prevent them from dragging in the paint.

Children will be wearing smocks when painting. However, accidents do happen. The water-based tempera paint we use will come out of most fabrics if it is washed in the following way:

1. Apply detergent to spot and rub.
2. Wash normally.
3. If spot still shows, repeat rubbing and washing.
4. Line dry. Do not put in dryer until spot is gone as the heat will set the color.
5. It may take several washings to remove the stain completely.

Painting activities help your child grow in many ways as they learn to control the paintbrushes and other painting tools. Please help your son or daughter enjoy painting without the worry of getting paint on clothing.

Your child's teacher,

How Children Grow through Painting

Children will develop:

1. Physically, by using the large and small muscles of the arm to control the paintbrush. (Bodily-Kinesthetic)

2. Socially, by learning to take care of the paint so that others will also be able to use it (Interpersonal)
3. Emotionally, by being trusted to control an easy-to-spill, messy liquid (Intrapersonal)
4. Cognitively, by learning a painting vocabulary and observing how paint physically changes when it mixes and dries (Linguistic; Logical-Mathematical)
5. Visual perception skills, by observing the visual effects of their motions and identifying the resulting colors, shapes, and lines (Spatial)
6. Art awareness, by responding to paintings done by many different artists

Painting Explorations for Toddlers

Children between the ages of one and three will approach painting completely on a sensory level. Combined with their limited control over hand and arm movements, they often create what to adult eyes is a "mess." With careful planning, however, this can be an exciting experience for both adults and children. Older children with special vision or muscle-control limitations require a similar guided introduction to painting.

Group composition. For an initial painting experience, work with one child at a time. After they have had some experience with the painting setup, two can paint at the same time.

Setup.

Smocks. It is important to protect the child's clothing as much as possible as even the most washable tempera or poster paint can stain some fabrics. Provide a smock for each painter (see Teacher Tip). Provide a low table for the child to stand at or an easel that is at the height of the child. Cover the work surface with newspaper. If using an easel, put heavy plastic underneath to catch the drips. Use spring-type clothespins to clip the paper to the easel.

Cleanup. Have a bucket, paper towels, and sponges nearby for quick wipe-ups.

FIGURE 5–8 Toddlers use their whole arms when painting.

TEACHER TIP

Painting Smocks

A good smock that will cover most of the child can be made from a large adult's shirt that buttons up the front.

1. Cut the sleeves very short.
2. Put it on the child backwards and fasten it together in the back with a spring clothespin.
3. Make sure the child's sleeves are pushed up above the elbows.

Materials. For a child's first painting experience provide the following.

BRUSHES: Thick-handled, stubby paintbrushes work well for toddlers.

PAINT: Provide two colors of thick, liquid tempera paint in plastic containers, such as yogurt comes in. (These have tight-fitting lids so unused paint can be saved for the next day.) Fill them half full. Place one brush in each color. If the containers seem to tip easily once the brush is inside, put them in a small box or plastic basket. Alternatively, cut a hole the size of the container in an upside-down styrofoam tray.

NOTE: If the paint is too thin, add a small amount of flour* to thicken it. It should not drip very much when the brush is taken out of the paint. A small amount of liquid detergent may be added to make hand cleanup easier.

SPECIAL NEEDS

Painting Modifications

Visual: Children with limited vision should work on a tilted surface or easel so they may have their eyes closer to the work surface. Choose the colors of paint that they can see best and add sawdust or sand so they can feel their finished painting. Different scents can be added to the paint to help in color identification.

Physical: Some children with orthopedic handicaps work best if they can lie on the floor when painting. Tape paper to the floor or other work surface so that it does not move while they are working. Wrap foam around the handles of the brushes to make them easier to grip. Use wide, low-sided containers for the paint such as cut-down margarine or frosting containers. If necessary use tape to hold paint containers in place.

Keep the paint thick and make sure all children have ample working space so if there are involuntary movements or lack of control, paint does not splatter on the paper or clothing of other children. (See chapter 11 for more information.)

Transition in. Paint is naturally appealing to young children. Introduce the idea of painting by giving the children small buckets of water and brushes and going outside to paint on walls or pavement. Mime painting while singing a song about painting or color mixing. Share a "Big

Book" about painting such as *Mouse Paint* (Walsh, 1989). When they eventually paint with the liquid tempera, their interest level will be high.

What to do. When children first begin to paint, they may hold the paintbrush awkwardly and have difficulty staying within the confines of the paper. This is normal and reflects the child's lack of control over the arm and hand muscles. Toddlers will use the whole arm stiffly to move the brush in up-and-down and circular strokes reminiscent of the first scribbles. As children gain muscular control, they will be able to stay on the paper and control the movement of the brush more effectively.

Stay near the child for the first few painting experiences. Give a few simple directions in the beginning. Otherwise do not interrupt the painting process until the child is done.

Do not worry if children mix up the paint colors. With practice they will learn to keep the brushes separate. It is sometimes helpful to label the brushes with the same color tape.

What to say. Keep initial direction very brief and let the children discover the joy of painting on their own. Only interfere if children put the paint brush up to their mouths or try to leave the table still holding it.

Vocabulary to use during painting explorations includes paint, brush, handle, color names, mix, mixing, drip, dripping, wipe, smooth, and wet.

The comments teachers make should focus on the effects of color mixing and the kinds of lines the child has made.

"Look what happened when the blue touched the yellow!"
"You made a thick green line with the brush."
"That yellow line goes from the top to the bottom of the paper."

Transition out. Children are usually very delighted with the effect they can create using colorful paints. Let them paint until they feel they are finished, then guide them to the place to wash their hands. Put the painting out of the way to dry. It is best if it can dry flat, to minimize drips. If space is a problem, however, paintings can also be hung on a low, wash-line-style drying rack, available from art suppliers. Instructions to make a homemade drying box are presented in figure 5–9.

Practice Painting Activities for Toddlers

Once the children have experienced painting, try to offer the opportunity to paint on a regular basis. Have the paint table or easel set up and ready before the children arrive. Since most toddlers only spend two to five minutes painting there is usually plenty of time for all of them to make a painting if they wish. There are many ways to vary the basic painting exploration and still allow the children to practice the basic skills.

Use different brushes. Provide different types of brushes such as wide, house-painting brushes, foam rubber brushes, and long-handled vegetable brushes.

Use different colors of paint. Once the child understands painting procedures, offer three colors at the regular paint setup. There is no rigid formula for selecting the color paints offered the children. Choose from the ones that are available. The primary colors of red, yellow, and blue are good choices to start with because these three colors provide exciting color mixes.

As the children gain experience, increase the number of colors offered to include a fourth color—either brown, green, purple, orange, black, or white. Sometimes the colors may relate to the theme of the program. If a specific color is the theme, offer the featured color and related colors at the paint setup. On purple day, for example, put out purple, lavender, and white paint. If the sea is the theme, try deep blue, green, turquoise, and white.

It is less expensive to buy the larger sizes of liquid tempera. To make the most efficient use of paint, buy the basic colors and then mix the other colors as needed. Start with red, yellow, and blue. The next choices should then be white and black. If funds are available, supplement these with green, brown, orange, and purple, in that order. Chapter 11 discusses the importance of having many varieties of skin-colored paint available. These can be purchased or mixed.

1. Select a box that is slightly larger than the paper children usually use.

2. Draw lines two to three inches apart on opposite sides of the box.
3. Cut halfway in on each line.

4. Cut "shelves" (from cardboard) that are four inches longer than the box. Measure in two inches from the edges and draw lines.

5. Cut halfway in on each line on the shelves.

6. Slide each shelf into the corresponding slots.

FIGURE 5–9 Making a paint-drying box

TEACHER TIP

Guide to Mixing Colors

THE PRIMARY COLORS

The primary colors are red, yellow, and blue. Primary colors, when mixed, make the secondary colors:

Red + Yellow = Orange
Red + Blue = Purple
Blue + Yellow = Green

ADDING WHITE

White plus any color makes it lighter or more pastel. Even a small amount of a color will change white. Add the color little by little until the tone is just right. More white will probably be used than any other color, so purchase double the amount of white.

Red + White = Pink
Blue + White = Pastel Blue
Green + White = Mint Green
Orange + White = Peach
Purple + White = Lavender
Brown + White = Tan

ADDING BLACK

Black plus any color makes it darker and duller. It takes only a small amount of black to change a color. Mix it in sparingly.

Black + White = Gray
Black + Red = Brown
Black + Yellow = Olive Green

OTHER COMBINATIONS

Orange + Yellow = Gold
Red + Green = Brown
Blue + Green = Turquoise
Red + Purple = Magenta
Blue + Purple = Deep Blue (Indigo)
Yellow + Green = Chartreuse

SKIN TONES

Skin tones can be made by mixing different combinations of black, brown, yellow, red and white. Always start with the lighter colors and add the darker ones.

Add textures to the paint. A variety of materials can be mixed into the liquid paint to give it a different feel. Once the children have some experience painting, the simple addition of a little more water makes a thinner paint and changes the sensory response of the brush as it moves on the paper. Some materials can be sprinkled over the wet painting. Paint will hold them on like glue, even when dry.

- Detergent, liquid starch, and corn syrup* added to the paint will make it spread differently.
- To make the paint thicker, add sand, sawdust, cornmeal,* flour,* oatmeal,* dry cereal,* or soap flakes.
- Salt* added to the paint will produce a bubbly effect.
- Salt* and Epsom salts sprinkled on the paint produce a glittery effect.

NOTE: Commercial glitter is not recommended for young children as it sticks to their hands and can be accidently ingested or rubbed in the eyes. However paint with glitter already mixed in can be purchased commercially and provides an exciting painting experience for young children.

Offer a variety of papers. In addition to the large newsprint, vary the painting surface by providing colored paper, cardboard, and smooth shelf paper. Cut the paper into a variety of large rectangles and squares, or occasionally a triangle or circle.

Painting Explorations for Children Three-Years-Old and Up

As the child develops more control over the fluid medium of paint, offer a wider variety of activities. In addition to the basic painting activities that are suitable for toddlers, offer more colors and kinds of paint.

Group composition. Once children can keep the paint within the confines of the paper, return the brush to the right color fairly consistently, and know how to clean up after themselves when done, they can paint in groups of three and up.

Setup. Provide a ratio of one easel for every five children (i.e., if there are 20 children, have four easels set up), or a table on which four children can paint at one time. Side-by-side easels provide the most opportunity for the children to interact.

FIGURE 5–10 Boxes provide multiple surfaces to paint.

Cover the table and easel surface with newspaper and put a piece of heavy plastic under the easel.

Cleanup. Have available a quantity of predampened paper towels, sponges, and a bucket for cleanups. The children should be shown how to wipe up any drips from the floor and how to move to the hand-washing area without touching anything. Children must wear smocks (as described for toddlers). Teach them how to help each other put the smocks on.

Materials. PAINTS: In addition to liquid tempera, other types of paint can be offered on occasion. Most of these will work better if used on a table rather than at the easel.

* Tempera blocks. This paint comes in dry cakes that fit in special trays. The children must wet the brush to dampen the cube for use. Choose the larger sizes in basic colors and fluorescents (see Appendix A for sources). Some adults like the fact that these do not spill. However, the colors and texture of the block paints are not as exciting as liquid tempera paints so these should never be the only type of paint the children use, but rather an interesting addition to the program.
* Paint "Markers." These small plastic containers have felt tips. Fill the container with tempera paint and use like a marker. The stubby shape of the bottles fits well in little hands and the paint flows out easily. Keep them tightly capped in a resealable plastic bag when not in use (see Appendix A for sources).
* Watercolors. The small size of the individual watercolors in a set, even in the larger half-pan

size, makes them suitable only for children with well-developed fine-motor control. Watercolors are also more likely to stain clothing than tempera paint. Before giving watercolors to the children to use, wet the color pans and let them sit a short time to soften the paints. Watercolors produce interesting effects when used on wet paper or on top of crayon drawings. Paper can be dampened with a sponge or paintbrush before painting.

PAPER: The paper for painting can provide an important sensory component to the child's exploration. Painting uses a great deal of paper, especially in the larger sizes. Although newsprint offers the most economical choice, try to offer different kinds and colors as well. Older children can begin to use smaller sheets of paper once in a while, but avoid always giving them small paper. They still need to use the whole arm as part of the painting process, just as adult painters do. Most of the paintings adults are familiar with from small reproductions are in reality quite large. Many of Monet's *Water Lilies*, for example, are over five feet long.

* Brown kraft paper (or a cut flattened paper bag) provides an absorbent surface with a color that contrasts well with the lighter colors that are often lost on white paper. Try it with pink, yellow, and white paint. Try wrinkling the paper and then smoothing it again, to create a bumpy texture that is fun to paint on, too.
* Colored construction paper in dark colors also offers a good contrast for light-colored paints.
* Burlap or fabric glued to a cardboard base serves as a challenging texture for painting. The book *The Mud Family* (James, 1994) features illustrations done using this technique. This would be a good choice for a thematic unit on textures.
* Children can make their own textured painting surface by gluing collage materials such as sand, textured papers, fabric, and ribbon pieces to a sheet of construction paper on one day and then painting over them the next.
* A sheet of plexiglass or heavy plastic, or a smooth, bare tabletop can be painted on directly. A piece of paper can then be pressed over the painting to save it as a monoprint—a one-of-a-kind copy of the painting.

- Cardboards of various kinds make interesting painting surfaces. Often these materials curl up when the paint dries and may need to be pressed. Cardboard boxes of any size can be painted for a variety of uses.

PAINTING TOOLS: In addition to the basic brushes suggested for toddlers, introduce long-handled easel brushes. These encourage the child to use more arm and shoulder movements.

Teachers can use their own creativity to come up with a variety of ways children can apply the paint.

Paint can be applied with all of the following items.

- Branches and twigs
- Feathers and feather dusters
- House-painting brushes
- Paint rollers
- Sponges
- Sponge brushes
- Squeeze bottles (such as empty mustard or shampoo containers)
- Craft sticks with cloth taped to the end

Transition in. Most children love to paint, but teachers still need to make them aware of the availability of the paints and the many possiblities they offer. An easel setup is ideal because it is clearly visible to the children as something different from anything else in the room. A paint table can be marked or labeled in some special way to attract attention.

Introduce the area by inviting the children to mime painting during circle time, by telling a story about a famous painter, or by reading a book about painting such as *A Painter* (Florian, 1993) which explains what a painter does via a simple, sensitive text.

Once their interest is aroused, it may be necessary to set up a situation for children to take turns. Because painting is an intensely sensory and personal experience, offer it as often as possible; every day is best. Children should awaken every day knowing that they will have blocks and toys, and books and paints to explore.

What to do. Preschoolers and primary school students still spend a great deal of time exploring the sensory qualities of paint. They may paint simple lines and shapes or cover the whole paper with one color. They may start out making sym-

bols for faces or houses and then, fascinated by how the colors accidently mixed, paint over their initial symbols. In painting the process is always more important than the product.

This does not mean, however, that the child is not interested in what happens to the finished painting. Because of its large size and bright colors, a painting becomes a very visible product of the child, even more so than a drawing. Children can be very possessive and proud of their paintings and they will demand that care be taken in handling their pictures.

1. Keep painting open-ended. It is very important to have a hands-off policy in regard to children's painting. Other than a few simple rules based on safety and cleanliness (such as "keep paint away from the face" and "keep the brushes in the paint containers"), children should be allowed to explore any way they wish.
2. Allow color mixing. Let them mix colors as they desire even if the brush gets "dirty." Let them hold the brush however they want.
3. Accept exploration. Adults must be careful not to show disappointment if the child paints over something they thought was a great picture. This freedom to explore allows the child to grow in self-confidence and creativity. In this way, children become familiar with the possibilities and the control needed to paint richer and more detailed pictures.
4. Foster concentration and reflection. Encourage children to spend time on their paintings. If children always seem to rush through painting, ask questions that will inspire them to add to their work, such as, "What do you think might happen if you used the smaller brush now?" A painting can also be put away overnight. The next day, ask if they wish to add to it with paint or with other art materials such as markers or chalk.

What to say. Use the painting experience to help the children focus on the art elements and the way that the paint functions. Remember not to interrupt children when they are absorbed in the painting process. Wait for them to look up, or save conversation for later, when helping to take the paper off the easel or returning the dry painting to take home or put in a portfolio. Sample questions include:

"How did you make this color?"

"Which brush did you use to make this line?"

"Why do you think the paint dripped like this?"

Transition out. Children know best when they are finished. They often announce this fact, with a great deal of satisfaction, to no one in particular. Show the children how to take off the smock, where to hang it, and how to move to the sink to wash up. After a few times the children should be able to do most of this on their own. In situations in which the paintings will be placed on the floor to dry, most children can be shown how to take their own paintings to that place. To prevent accidents when moving their artwork, remind them to keep the smock on until this chore is done.

Connections. LITERATURE: Share books that are illustrated with paintings such as *In a Small, Small Pond* (Fleming, 1993), *Chickens, Chickens* (Porte, 1995), or *Snow on Snow on Snow* (Chapman, 1994). Books about children painting include *No Good in Art* (Cohen, 1980) and *Peter's Painting* (Moss, 1995).

ART AWARENESS: Display and discuss paintings by artists from different times and cultures. Children respond well to the Nonobjective Print Set (Take 5) which features work by Hofmann, Jenkins, Klee, Merida, and Mondrian. See if children can figure out how the artists made the different colors.

Finger Painting

No early childhood art experience would be complete without finger painting. If painting with brushes is an intense sensory experience, then painting with the fingers is the ultimate. For some children, however, finger painting is at first a very confusing activity. These children have often been taught to keep their hands clean or may have taken to heart the directions to always wash paint off their hands. The idea of putting paint on their hands on purpose is bewildering. Never force a child to finger paint. Plenty of others are quite willing to dive in; often a reluctant child, after seeing the others' fun, will tentatively join them. Teachers can help such children by offering light colors of finger paint and showing them that adding detergent to it helps it wash off better.

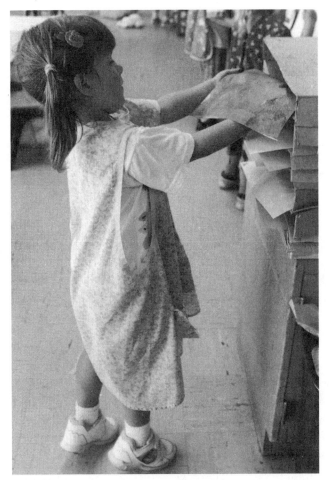

FIGURE 5–11 A drying box provides a convenient way to store paintings and other wet projects.

A great deal of the "messing" that children seem to do when they finger paint is not because finger painting in itself is such a messy medium, but because it is offered so rarely to children. Most children never get beyond the initial exploration. Imagine what the quality of finger paintings would be like if children finger painted as often as they drew with crayons!

Group composition. Keep the number of children working at one time very small: one or two toddlers at a time or three to four older children. Remember they will need to be supervised at the sink or wash-up area. Never have more children working than can fit at the sink.

Setup. Finger painting works best when children work standing at child-height tables. Finger painting may also be done on the floor. This gives the child the opportunity to make large hand and arm movements; however, there is also the chance that child will kneel in the paint. Floor painting works best if the children are wearing shorts so they do not get paint on the knees of their clothing. In warm weather try finger painting out-of-doors and then let children hose off. Always place newspaper under painting surfaces.

Cleanup. It may help to have a bucket of soapy water for children to soak their hands in before rinsing in the sink. Make sure there are plenty of damp paper towels available to wipe paint smears.

Materials. FINGER PAINT: Commercial finger paint provides vibrant color in a smooth, easy-to-clean formula and should be the main finger paint used. For other finger paint explorations, try shaving cream, or whipped soap flakes and liquid starch colored with a small amount of food coloring or tempera paint.

PAINTING SURFACES: Commercial finger paint paper is heavy, with a smooth shiny surface. Although relatively expensive, children should occasionally have the opportunity to finger paint on this paper. Freezer paper and shiny shelf paper can also be used. Paper may be dampened with a wet sponge to make the paint spread more easily.

Finger painting can also be done directly on smooth-surfaced tabletops or on a piece of plexiglass. Pictures can be saved by placing a paper over the artwork and rubbing, to create a monoprint.

Transition in. Read books that describe wet and unusual textures such as *I Touch* (Isadora, 1985).

What to do.

1. Before starting, make sure the child's sleeves are pushed up over the elbows and the smock sleeves are short enough not to drag in the paint.
2. Place about a quarter of a cup of paint on the paper. Add another quarter cup of water.
3. Encourage the child to mix and spread the paint.
4. Show how to use different parts of the hand to make marks.

What to say. Use words that describe the feel of the paint, such as cold, wet, or sticky. Encourage children to think of other things that feel the same.

Describe the different movements of their hands.

> "You moved your hand up and down."
> "You wiggled your fingers."

Transition out. As the finger paint dries, it will become harder for the child to make marks and the activity will naturally stop. Guide the child to the sink or wash-up area. Remove paintings from the newspaper to dry or they will stick in place.

Extending the learning.

- Give the children several colors and encourage them to mix them together to make new ones.
- Instead of putting the paint directly on their paper, put the finger paint on the newspaper next to the paper, or in a disposable tray. Let the children dip their fingers in and apply paint where they want it. This encourages more thoughtful placement of colors.
- Wet paper with a sponge before starting.

FIGURE 5–12 Finger paint provides a wonderful sensory experience for young children.

Studio Page 29

CREATING A THEMATIC UNIT

The Topic Web

Studio Pages 29 to 34 will guide you in developing an original thematic unit, suitable for young children, using a topic web and flexible plan format.

Steps in creating a topic web:

1. Choose a theme.
2. Brainstorm a list of words, questions, and related activities. Ideas can be written on small pieces of paper and physically moved into groups.
3. Order items and group into subcategories.
4. Transfer ideas to the sample web on Studio Page 30: Write the theme topic in the large shape in the center of the web. Write the subcategory headings on the lines inside the circles.
5. List items in each group underneath the topic headings.
6. Highlight all the areas that relate to art or can be expressed through art activities, such as drawings about a field trip.

Studio Page **30**

TOPIC WEB FORMAT

Studio Page **31**

SAMPLE THEMATIC UNIT PLAN FORMAT

List each activity on the web beside the related growth areas.

Time Frame: **Special Needs:**

Age(s) of Children: **Group Size:**

GOALS	ACTIVITIES
Physical:	
Social:	
Emotional:	
Perceptual:	
Cognitive:	

SUPPLEMENTARY MATERIALS

Make a list of materials that are related to the thematic unit.

Books:

_____

_____

_____

Songs and poems:

_____

_____

_____

Artworks:

_____

_____

_____

Places to visit:

_____

_____

_____

_____

Guests to invite:

_____

_____

_____

Food to serve:

_____

_____

_____

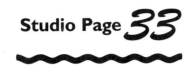

INTEGRATING ART EVERYWHERE

Describe how your selected theme will be reflected in each of these learning areas.

Block Play:

_____

_____

Sand Play:

_____

_____

Water Play:

_____

_____

Dramatic Play:

_____

_____

Easel Area:

_____

_____

Literature Area:

_____

_____

Out-of-Doors:

_____

_____

Movement Area:

_____

_____

Music Area:

_____

_____

DESIGNING TRANSITIONS

Design a transition into each of the following art activities:

1. Mixing white with other colors of paint at the easel

_____
_____
_____

2. Drawing with chalk on wet paper

_____
_____
_____

3. Painting with twigs

_____
_____
_____

4. Using chalk over a dried painting

_____
_____
_____

5. Painting on burlap

_____
_____
_____

6. Drawing on small smooth stones

_____
_____
_____

Studio Page *35*

OBSERVATION: LOOKING FOR CONNECTIONS

Observe a group of children in a child care or school setting for at least two hours. Note how the guiding adult transitions into the different activities planned for the day.

Date of Observation: **Length of Observation:**

Age of Children: **Size of Group:**

What to Observe:

1. How do the children transition from the large group to small group or individual activities?

   _____

   _____

   _____

   _____

2. How do individual children transition from activity to activity?

   _____

   _____

   _____

   _____

3. What transition techniques are used? (Reading a story, movement, questioning, and so on.) Which ones seem to be part of the daily routine?

   _____

   _____

   _____

   _____

4. Are themes or projects being used in this program? If not, how are learning activities connected for the children?

   _____

   _____

   _____

   _____

Studio Page 36

ANALYSIS: MAKING THE CONNECTION

Based on your observations, write a response to these questions:

1. How many different types of transitions were used?

_____

_____

_____

_____

2. Which transitions were the most effective?

_____

_____

_____

_____

3. What role do you think routine played in making transitions go smoothly?

_____

_____

_____

_____

4. Did any child not respond to a transition? What was the adult's response?

_____

_____

_____

_____

5. Was learning effectively integrated in this program? Why or why not?

_____

_____

_____

_____

6

Please Don't Eat the Art!

Making Art Safe for Young Children

❝ *It is easy to deal with a situation before symptoms develop. It is easy to maintain a situation while it is secure.* ❞

•

Lᴀᴏ Tᴢᴜ LXIV:152

Questions addressed in this chapter:

Young Artists at Work

Eric takes a piece of play dough and puts it in his mouth. "It tastes salty," he says in surprise.

Sallie picks up a cup of water in which a paint brush has been rinsed and takes a sip. "It looked like chocolate milk," she whispers sheepishly.

Darlena takes a scissors and snips a piece off Maria's bangs. "I'm a beauty parlor lady and I'm making her beautiful," she says smugly.

WHO IS RESPONSIBLE FOR CHILDREN'S SAFETY?

Plain old common sense is basic to safety.

SUSAN RODRIGUEZ (1984, P. 269)

What are the limits to a young child's exploration of art materials? Does allowing children to be creative entitle them to do anything that comes into their minds with everything that they find? Our common sense tells us definitely not. Young children need our protection. We do not let them put a hand in the fire to discover how hot it is. We do not leave poisons in places where young children will find them. Children are unaware of the dangers in their environment. Guiding adults must take responsibility for the safety of the children in their care.

Ultimately it is the adult who is working directly with children who must create a safe environment which they can explore without danger. Selecting safe art materials, organizing a secure work space, and establishing limits on how tools and materials are used will allow children to create freely without endangering themselves. Caregivers and teachers cannot rely solely on outside authorities to make the daily safety decisions that are required when interacting with active and creative young children. We are the ones offering the materials directly to the children, supervising the work space, and enforcing safe behavior among the children. The information in this chapter is designed to provide the information needed to create the safest environment possible for young artists.

WHY ARE ART HAZARDS A CONCERN?

Art stores and art catalogs offer a multitude of media for artists. Some have been used for thousands of years, such as chalk. Others are brand-new, such as pinking shears for kids. Not all of these wonderful materials, however, are safe to use with young children. Other dangers to children may come from nontraditional materials that are used for artwork, from bacteria-contaminated supplies, and from inexperienced or uncontrolled behavior.

Risk Factors for Children Under Six Years of Age

Because of their physical makeup and because of the way they explore their environment, young children's health is more at risk than adults' or older children's.

FIGURE 6–1 Enthusiastic exploration often puts children at risk.

Metabolism. Young children are in a period of rapid growth. They have a higher rate of metabolism than adults and therefore absorb toxic materials more rapidly into their bodies. Many toxic materials particularly affect the growing brain and nervous system of the young child.

Body size. Young children have a smaller body size so that the same amount of toxic material will be more concentrated in a child's body than in an adult's. Their smaller lungs are more likely to be affected after breathing in only a small amount of a toxic or irritating substance. Children have proportionately shorter torsos and larger heads than adults, so that when sitting they are closer to the work surface. Their mouths and noses are nearer to the art materials and any toxins, bacteria, or irritants that might be there.

Muscular control. Young children may not have sufficient muscular control to handle certain materials safely. Children who are frustrated by a glue top that does not open may decide to open it with their teeth. If children can not get a scissors to cut, they may push so hard they not only cut the paper but a finger as well. Children with special needs often have difficulty handling art materials in safe ways because of limited physical control.

Behavior. The wonderful creativity of young children also puts them at risk. In exploring all the possibilities of using art materials and tools, they often come upon ways that are dangerous to themselves or others. They are fascinated by interesting shaped bottles and containers containing unusual liquids or powders, by brightly colored materials or things that have interesting textures or smells.

Eating. Toddlers are particularly at risk because their sensory exploration of their surroundings includes putting everything in their mouths. Although children can be taught not to put materials in their mouths, they still have a tendency to suck or lick their hands and fingers or chew their fingernails regardless of what they have last touched. Young children are still relatively inefficient at washing their hands well after touching and using art materials. There is also a tendency for little children to swallow instead of spitting out especially when told to do so, as any parent who is trying to teach her child to spit out toothpaste instead of eating it well knows.

Sniffing. Children of all ages often put their noses into things they should not. Mists and powders floating in the air are quickly sniffed. Powders are shaken for the purpose of creating a cloud. Dust-covered hands are clapped so they can see the dust rising. Unknown odors are fully investigated. Young children have often not yet learned to identify certain smells with toxic substances, such as the smell of turpentine or ammonia, and finding such smells pleasant, take long, deep breaths.

Following directions. Even with the most careful instruction, young children cannot be trusted to always follow the best precautions consistently. They can easily become so immersed in an investigation they forget the directions or they may not be able to generalize a safety instruction from one very similar material to another. It is easy for them to become confused, especially if the materials seem similar but are handled differently, such as when they are given edible play dough one day and inedible play dough the next. It takes a great amount of experience with an art material, even for adults, before safe handling becomes automatic.

Environmental factors. Beyond the immediate exposure to unsafe art materials, several environmental factors affect the level of danger.

Health Factors. All children bring with them a unique set of factors that determine how susceptible they will be to toxin exposure. These include such factors as the child's previous health history; for example, a child who suffers from asthma will be very sensitive to any level of dust exposure, and solvents can induce epileptic fits in some sensitive children.

Exposure. Another factor is the child's frequency and duration of exposure to a material. Working with firing clay on a daily basis is more health-threatening than using it only once a year. The conditions of exposure are also important. Using dusty clay outside is less dangerous than using it in an enclosed unventilated room.

Body Burden. Previous exposure to toxins that are stored in the body may be a hidden factor. A child who already has a high lead level may be more severely affected by a visit to a stained glass workshop than a child who has a low lead level. Children whose parents smoke cigarettes may be more affected by irritating inhalants.

Routes of Entry into the Child's Body

There are three routes of entry for toxins: skin, lungs, and mouth.

Skin. Although the skin has a protective layer made up of a waxy coating, keratin, and dead skin cells, there are now many common chemicals in our environment and in art materials that can destroy this layer, causing reactions such as burns or rashes on the skin. Some substances may produce allergic reactions only after several exposures. Some of the more common skin irritants include ammonia, chlorine bleach, methyl alcohol, peroxide, turpentine, and most other solvents. Some of these chemicals, such as turpentine, toluene, benzene, and methyl alcohol, can even penetrate through the skin and enter the bloodstream.

In addition to chemical hazards, skin can also be injured in other ways. Sharp, jagged, and pointed objects are always a danger to young children.

Lungs. Inhaling toxins can cause respiratory diseases, asthma, and allergies. If the toxin or irritant affects the upper respiratory system, bronchitis can result. If it reaches the lungs, pneumonia. Allergies and chronic lung diseases are also possible results. Dusts, vapors, gases, smoke, and fumes can result from many art activities.

Aerosol sprays, airbrushes, and spray guns increase the likelihood of a toxin being inhaled, either by the person using it or by other people in the vicinity.

Substances used in art activities that can affect the respiratory system include: ammonia, cotton and fabric dusts, firing clays, fabric dyes, glazes for clay, lead, zinc, model glues, plaster dust, overheated waxes, formaldehyde, melted plastics and styrofoam, sawdust, and solvents of all kinds—alcohols, benzene, toluene, resin solvent, lacquer thinner, paint and varnish remover, plastic solvents, rubber cement thinner, mineral spirits, turpentine, and kerosene.

Mouth. Chemicals and bacteria can enter the body through the mouth directly or by contact with contaminated hands, food, work surfaces, and art tools. Dusts that are inhaled may also be swallowed. Young children who still put things in their mouths may be endangered by the chance of choking on small objects. Art materials that can be mistaken for food may also be eaten accidentally.

HOW ARE SAFE ART MATERIALS SELECTED?

> Many art materials recommended in children's art books are highly toxic and should not be used by children.
>
> MICHAEL MCCANN (1985, P. 62)

In order to allow young children the freedom to explore that is so necessary for their creative growth, the first step must be to make sure that any supplies offered are the safest possible. Every material must be chosen with great caution. Unfortunately there is no sole authority or one comprehensive list of safe or unsafe art supplies for young children. There are no legally mandated standards or labeling required for art materials and some chemicals that are regulated in the workplace are not regulated in art materials. Medical research is constantly finding new hazards in the environment. New art materials are designed and sold. Materials long considered safe are found to be dangerous. The following guidelines are offered against which every material should be evaluated before being offered to children.

Read the label. Research the ingredients in art supplies by reading the label or doing some research.

Nontoxic means that the material will not cause immediate death or severe injury, but it may be quite toxic over time, or may cause nonfatal disabilities, especially to a young child.

The Art and Craft Materials Institute has a voluntary labeling program. The *AP Seal* stands for a product certified to contain insufficient quantities of any material that is toxic or injurious to humans or that will cause acute or chronic health problems. The *CP Seal* means the product meets manufacturing standards. However, not all these products will be suitable in an early childhood art program. The labeling is designed for

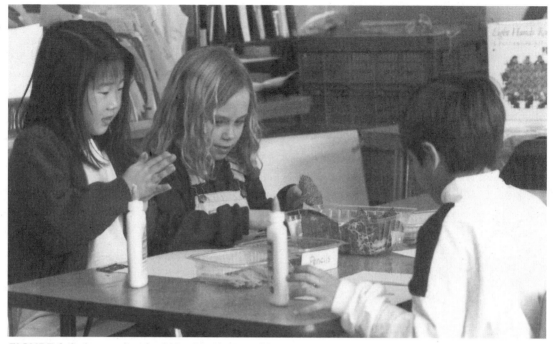

FIGURE 6–2 Art supplies should be the safest possible.

children of all ages and does not take into account the behavioral characteristics of children under the age of eight.

Any product that is labeled "Keep out of reach of children," "Flammable," "Avoid breathing vapors," "Do not take internally," or "Use in a well-ventilated area" should not be used by children. EVER!

Research unlabeled products. If an art product is not labeled, write to the manufacturer for a Materials Data Safety Sheet that will list the ingredients and health effects. Schools are required to have copies of these kept on file.

If the ingredients of any material are unknown, do not use it!

Choose children's art supplies. Use only art products specifically designed for young children. Art materials intended for use by adults often contain permanent pigments that are not safe for young children.

Use tools sized for a small child's hands.

Adult supplies may require more skill than a small child has to handle them safely, such as opening the containers, controlling dusts, or cleaning them up.

Products that are labeled for specific ages should be used only by children at that age. Items that do not meet the standard choke test are required to be labeled for restricted use (children aged three and up). A simple device to check the size of objects can be purchased from most school supply catalogs and stores. A general rule is that objects shorter than two inches in length and less than one inch in diameter should not be used by children under three years of age.

When working with mixed age groups, all art materials available to the children should be suitable for use by the youngest child in the group. This also applies if a child with special needs or with allergies would be endangered by any particular art material.

Avoid old art supplies. Standards for children's art supplies have changed dramatically in the last 10 years. It is not unusual to find or be given stockpiles of old art materials that have been stored away for a long time.

Discard any supplies that are old or that do not have current labeling even if they still look usable. It is not worth any amount of money saved to put the health of young children at risk.

Analyze material usage. After determining that the ingredients are safe, then determine if the material will be safe in use. Many materials can be used in a variety of ways, some of which will be more injurious to the children than others.

For example, chalk designed for children is safe if it is used on dampened paper or dipped in water first. But if it is used dry, the chalk dust easily becomes airborne and can irritate children's respiratory passages.

Painting with poster paint using a paintbrush is safe; blowing bubbles in the paint with a straw is not. There is too great a chance that young children will suck instead of blow, or put the painted end in their mouths, risking ingestion of the paint.

When looking for art activity ideas in books on art for children, remember that many ideas that are suitable for older children are not safe for young children who are just beginning to have physical control over art tools such as scissors and materials such as clays. Always try out the art activity before introducing it to the children.

TEACHER TIP

Material Safety Checklist

Examine the material and circle yes or no for each question:

1.	Is there a low chance that it will be ingested?	yes	no
2.	Is there little dust produced?	yes	no
3.	Does it wash easily off skin and surfaces with water?	yes	no
4.	Will no spray, vapor, smoke, or fumes be produced?	yes	no
5.	Are the ingredients known?	yes	no
6.	Is it designed for children?	yes	no
7.	Will children be able to handle it safely?	yes	no

Avoid any product that has one or more "no" answers.

WHAT ARE SOME SAFE ALTERNATIVES?

> We all know that risk can not be entirely eliminated in any environment, but it can be significantly reduced.
>
> RENE GRATZ AND PAMELA BOULTON (1993, P. 31)

This section provides possible substitutions for unsafe materials or methods for young children.

Solvents

Solvents are found in oil-based paints and paint thinners, varnishes and varnish removers, printing inks and lacquers, rubber cement and its thinners, epoxy, instant and model airplane glues, and in permanent felt-tip markers.

One tablespoon of turpentine can kill a child if swallowed, and two tablespoons of methyl alcohol (found in shellac) can blind a child.

ALTERNATIVE: Use only washable paints, printing inks, and markers. Make sure they are labeled *water-based* or *watercolor*. Use only school paste, white or gel glues, and homemade pastes.

Aerosol Sprays

Do not use spray glues, spray paints, or chalk fixatives which can be inhaled.

ALTERNATIVE: Use liquid white and gel glues, and water-based paint. To decrease chalk dust, cover chalk drawings with a piece of paper and rub off extra chalk dust. Then place the drawing in a folded piece of newspaper to keep the dust from rubbing off on the child on the way home. Chalk drawings also look beautiful if laminated or covered with clear contact paper.

Toxic Pigments

Toxic metals are found in colored pigments made from cadmium, lead, manganese, cobalt, and chromium. These pigments are found in artist-quality oil, watercolor, and acrylic paints, artists' pastels, and in glazes for firing clays. They are also used in copper enameling.

ALTERNATIVE: Use only water-based poster, tempera, and watercolor paints, and colored chalk intended for children. Although a teacher could glaze a firing-clay piece for a child, it is more creative to allow children to paint their clay with watercolor or tempera paints.

Copper enameling is not safe for children to do. Chapter 11 presents ideas for safe jewelry making for young artists.

Dusts

There is a wide range of art materials that create hazardous dusts.

Firing clay. Clay use produces a fine dust that is easily airborne and inhaled. It settles on surfaces and remains in the environment. Some clays containing talc may be contaminated with asbestos.

ALTERNATIVE: Air-dried clay should never be handled by young children. Have children use only wet, talc-free clay. They must be taught to keep their hands damp and away from their faces. Wipe all surfaces when done or use out-of-doors. Do not eat in the same room as used for clay work.

Glazes. Many glazes contain toxic pigments such as lead, copper, and cobalt. The dry glaze dust is very fine and easily airborne. The dust settles on all surfaces in the environment.

ALTERNATIVE: Have the children paint their fired clay with tempera or watercolors. If a more natural effect is desired, use different colored clays to make designs. If glazing is necessary it should be done by an adult. Choose only liquid, lead-free glazes. Never allow children to handle unfired glazed clay pieces.

Plaster. Plaster creates a very irritating dust; in addition, there have been cases of skin being burned when children have been casting body parts in setting plaster.

ALTERNATIVE: Plaster should only be mixed by the teacher, wearing a dust mask, outdoors or in a well-ventilated room away from the children. Choose activities that do not involve the children in handling dry plaster, carving or scraping molded plaster, or in casting hands or other body parts. Safe plaster activities include:

- Making casts by pouring plaster into depressions made in sand.
- Pouring plaster into a plastic bag and allowing it to harden (these odd forms can then be painted).
- Pouring plaster into dishes of various sizes and shapes, to a depth of three-quarters to one inch (when set, it can be painted with tempera or watercolor paint).

Powdered tempera paint. Dry, powdered tempera paint should never be used by the children. Avoid all activities that suggest that the children work directly with the powder. Some colors, especially in older paints, may contain toxic pigments.

ALTERNATIVE: Mix powder paint away from the children and always wear a dust mask. Liquid tempera and poster paint are safer alternatives.

Fabric dyes. Fabric dyes of all kinds can cause bladder cancer and severe allergic reactions. Artists who use dyes wear organic vapor filter masks. Never use over-the-counter, multipurpose dyes whose labels say they dye both cotton and wool.

ALTERNATIVE: Dye cotton fabric and wool yarn using dyes made from natural plant materials or food-quality dyes. See chapter 9 for safe dye activities.

Fumes and Toxic Gases

Harmful gases may be released when ordinary materials are heated.

Waxes. Natural waxes such as beeswax and paraffin are not hazardous by themselves. But when heated, they can vaporize into strong lung irritants such as acrolein and formaldehyde. Avoid activities that have young children working with melted wax (such as batik) or crayons (an old favorite—ironing crayon shavings between two sheets of wax paper).

ALTERNATIVE: If wax must be melted, do so in a well-ventilated area not used by children. Never let it get so hot that it smokes. Always melt the wax over hot water (in a double boiler), never directly on a heat source.

Instead of batik, children can decorate cloth with natural dyes or glue on felt and fabric shapes.

Instead of melting crayons between sheets of wax paper, use marker or crayon on tracing paper to produce a similar translucent effect.

Plastics. Plastics are safe when used as found. However, heating and sawing them releases toxic gases. Plastic glues contain solvents that actually melt the plastic together, creating fumes.

ALTERNATIVE: Attach plastics together by punching holes in them and tying them together with yarn, pipe cleaners, or wire. Attach styrofoam pieces together with toothpicks.

Bacterial Contamination

There are several kinds of bacterial contamination that can be a problem in art materials.

First is the danger of contamination from reusing styrofoam and plastic food containers that have held meat, fish, dairy products, or eggs.

ALTERNATIVE: Rinse containers and their lids in hot soapy water. Soak for one minute in a disinfectant solution of three-quarters of a cup chlorine bleach per gallon of water. A final rinse in warm water is necessary to remove the bleach solution. Cover clothing and protect hands from the bleach by wearing rubber gloves. Do not allow children to use this disinfectant solution.

A second form of bacterial or viral contamination can occur when young children touch their mouths, eyes, or noses and then touch modeling materials that are shared. ALTERNATIVE: If necessary, older children can be asked to wash their hands or use a tissue. For toddlers and young preschoolers, a good solution is to give the children their own pieces of modeling dough and their own storage containers or resealable bags.

Sharp Objects

A surprising number of materials can cut the skin or injure the eyes of children. While it is impossible to eliminate all the small injuries of childhood, and children need to learn to handle small risks, do check that the art supplies offered are as safe as possible.

The following items can cause injuries: cut or jagged edges on pieces of plastic, broken shells, sharp sticks, adult-sized scissors, unsanded wood, pins, needles, staples, and the ends of pipe cleaners. The younger the children, the more carefully the supplies must be selected.

TEACHER TO PARENT

Child Safety Information

Dear Parent,

All of the art materials used in our program have been carefully selected to be safe for young children. Some children, however, have special sensitivities. To help us select the safest art materials for your child, please answer the following questions:

1. Is your child allergic to anything?   yes   no
   If yes, please list:
2. Does your child have any respiratory problems?   yes   no
   If yes, please explain:
3. Is your child's skin sensitive to anything?   yes   no
   If yes, please list:
4. Are there any art materials that your child should not use?
   Please list and explain.

Thank you for taking the time to complete this form. Together we can make sure that your child will have a safe and fun time creating art.

Your child's teacher,

HOW CAN SAFE BEHAVIOR BE MODELED?

> Children have never been very good at listening to their elders, but they have never failed to imitate them.
>
> JAMES BALDWIN (NOBODY KNOWS MY NAME, 1961)

Being adult does not make teachers impervious to art hazards. It is as important to protect ourselves from the dangers that have been discussed as it is to keep the children safe. First and foremost, teachers need to preserve their own health. A sickly, ill teacher does not have the enthusiasm to inspire young artists. One of the important ways that children learn proper behavior is by imitating adults. If teachers practice unsafe behaviors, they are showing the children that safety standards are not really very important.

Guidelines for Safe Teacher Behavior

1. Any room or space used by children must be totally free of hazardous materials.
2. When there is a choice, buy the least hazardous art material that will meet personal needs. For example, choose:

   Water-based markers instead of permanent markers.
   Liquid paint instead of spray paint.
   White glue instead of rubber cement.
   Tacky craft glue instead of epoxy.

3. Keep all hazardous materials in a locked metal cabinet.
4. Do not use any art supply that is listed as hazardous in front of children. For example, do not use rubber cement while the children use safe white glue.
5. When working with dusty materials, wear a dust mask.
6. When working with skin irritants, wear rubber gloves.
7. When working with solvents or hazardous fumes, wear an approved face mask with the proper filters. This is essential when using fabric dyes or doing stained glass.
8. Adequate ventilation means out-of-doors. Unless there is a sealed glove box that is ventilated to the outside, never use hazardous materials at home or in the classroom, even if children are not present. An open window is not sufficient. Fumes and dusts can remain in the air or collect on surfaces and contaminate the children or teachers days later.
9. Handle sharp, dangerous tools with care. Pass scissors to children in a safe way. Store the paper cutter where children cannot see or touch it.

HOW IS SAFE BEHAVIOR PROMOTED IN CHILDREN?

Creativity doesn't mean doing whatever you want, it means finding new ways to work within a structure.

FRED ROGERS (1982, P .4)

Even the safest art material can be dangerous if it is used in the wrong way. A key element to providing a safe environment for young artists is to teach the children to use the materials in a safe way. *BE SAFE* should be the first and only rule for the young artist's explorations of art materials. All children need to learn that they are ultimately responsible for their own personal safety and for the safety of others.

It is important to remember that most unsafe behavior is not intentional but reflects the child's developmental level and unfamiliarity or inventiveness with the art material or tools. Toddlers taste play dough because they naturally want to use all their senses, not because they want to do something dangerous. The best way to foster safe behavior is to understand how children at different developmental stages act and to set up activities so that safe behavior is promoted.

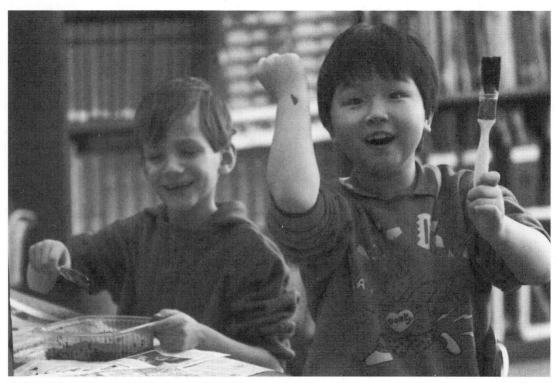

FIGURE 6–3 Children need to know what behavior is safe and acceptable.

Ways to Promote Safe Behavior

There are three ways to foster safe, creative behavior: prevention, redirection, and removal.

Prevention.

1. Offer only those materials and tools appropriate for the child's developmental level.
2. Keep materials and tools not on the child's developmental level out of reach and out of sight.
3. Provide each child with adequate space in which to work. Dangerous behavior often happens when children accidently bump or push each other.
4. Provide sufficient supplies, to prevent the children from grabbing for that one special item.
5. Closely supervise the children while they work, especially during initial explorations of new materials and tools.
6. Keep group sizes small until the children know how to work safely with that material or tool.
7. Keep supplies and tools orderly so children do not have to dig or grab for what they want.
8. Model safe handling of tools and supplies at all times.

Redirection.

1. If a child begins to use a tool or supply unsafely, gently state the safe way to use it and model correct use if necessary. For example if the child puts play dough up to her mouth, say, "Play dough is not food, we use it to make art."
2. If two children want the same supply or tool, provide other similar ones.

Removal.

1. When a child's behavior is developmentally appropriate and not unsafe, but annoying to the other children, such as when a toddler draws on other children's papers, gently move the child to a place near to the others but too far to reach their materials. Put the move in a positive light by saying, "You will have more space to draw over here."

2. If a child persists in unsafe behavior, redirect the child to another activity that is more appropriate for that behavior. For example, if a child is snapping the scissors open and closed, explain that the scissors are too sharp to be used that way, but she can open and close the toy pliers. Remove scissors and replace with the pliers.

3. When it is obvious that the tools or materials are inappropriate for the developmental level of the children, redirect them to another interesting activity and then remove those supplies. Just because a particular activity may be recommended for children of a certain age or has been successful for others does not mean it will be perfect for these particular children. It is better to say this is not working and clear it away then set up a potentially dangerous situation or one that will cause children to misbehave.

IS IT FOOD OR ART?

> Because many other materials are available, it is unwise to waste food by using it for art.
>
> LILA LASKEY AND ROSE MUKERJI (1980, P. 31)

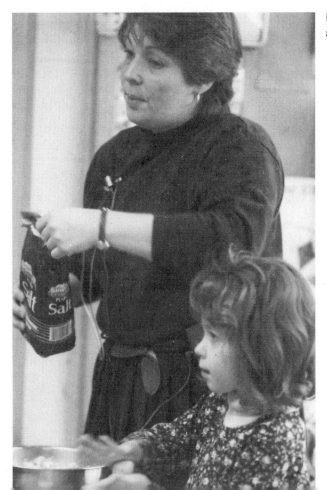

FIGURE 6–4 Is homemade play dough an acceptable art material?

A controversial issue in art for young children is the use of food and food products in art activities. Many people have very strong feelings on either side of this issue. Teachers need to decide where they stand so that they can defend their choices of art materials to parents and to other educators. One of the reasons that there is so much controversy is that it is not a clear-cut issue. While reading both sides of the argument, try to understand that while both viewpoints are based on concern for what the children are learning, each is based on a different set of values concerning the role of food.

Pro: Why Food Can Be Used for Art

- Many traditional art materials, such as egg tempera and casein paint, are made from food products.
- Some modern art materials, such as play dough and white glues, are made from food products.
- It is easier to find out the ingredients in food products than in real art supplies.
- Cereal, macaroni, rice, beans, and so on are readily available at the supermarket. Sometimes it is hard to find safe art supplies.
- There is no need to worry if children put their hands in their mouths after using food-based art materials, such as pudding finger painting or peanut-butter play dough.
- Art activities that use food products provide a multisensory experience in which children can use all their senses in a safe way.
- The children learn to appreciate the aesthetic qualities of the foods such as the shape of the macaroni, the color of the beans, the texture of cornmeal, and the pattern inside an apple.
- Food used as art can be used to relate the activity to the theme of the class, such as making apple prints when reading about Johnny Appleseed.
- Children are very motivated by food and have a lot of fun doing these activities.

Con: Food Should Never Be Used in Art Activities

- Most traditional art materials are not food-based, such as crayons, chalk, and paper.
- Food products used in commercial art supplies are usually inedible residues such as sour milk or whey.
- With a little research, teachers can find out the ingredients of all art supplies.
- Safe, commercial art supplies for children are widely marketed in department stores, drugstores, and through catalogs. There are also many free found items that can be used.
- Children become confused when they are told they can eat one art material but not another one that seems similar.
- The aesthetic qualities of food should be investigated in cooking activities, not art.
- Food is expensive and should not be wasted.
- Many food/art projects involve sugary foods and reinforce poor eating habits.
- People are hungry in our country and all over the world. Many children do not have enough to eat. It is cruel to have them make projects with food that could have fed them.
- Some ethnic groups are offended if food that is valued by them is used for play and not shown respect.

Making a Choice

A decision to use a food should not be made lightly. Those who feel strongly that it is morally wrong to use any food will have no trouble making their decision. Others are more comfortable if they base their decision on the appropriateness of the activity for the children, taking into account all the serious implications of food use. They are not willing to forego making homemade play doughs just because they are made from flour. They feel that modeling a soft, pliable material is important for the child's growth and that play dough can be safely handled by the children as an inedible art material.

Some food-based art materials are less objectionable than others. Throughout this book, food-based art materials have been marked with an asterisk(*). Consider the suggested approaches to dealing with the safety and waste issues before choosing to use it in an art activity.

Is It Safe to Eat It?

One of the main ways that children put themselves at risk from hazardous art materials is by ingesting them. This can occur either directly, by eating or tasting an art material, or indirectly, by putting their contaminated hands and fingers in their mouths. As those who are opposed to using food in art point out, using edible and inedible materials in similar ways is not a good way to teach children safe behavior. It is confusing for a toddler to be told she can eat her "candy dough" one day, but not her "play dough" the next. One way to develop the basic safety skill of keeping art materials away from the mouth is by helping children learn how to discriminate between edible and non-edible substances. In order to strengthen this health-preserving skill, present art activities in such a way that children can clearly identify what is food and what is art.

Ways to help children distinguish food from art supplies.

1. Avoid art materials that closely resemble foods or smell like foods.
2. Completely separate the areas that are used for food and art.
3. If the children will be making something from a food and eating it, it should be called "cooking" and done in the cooking area.
4. Never eat on tables that have been used for art projects. If tables must be used for both purposes, give the children trays on which to do their art, or cover the tables with plastic tablecloths when eating on them.
5. Enforce the rule that no art material is ever tasted, eaten, or drunk.
6. Supervise children and do not let them put their fingers in their mouths when working with art materials, or before they have washed them.
7. Mix and store art materials in containers that are visually different from those used for food. If a food container is being reused, cover the outside with a label or paint it.
8.   Insist that children wash their hands after they finish using art materials, and before they work with foods.

Avoiding food waste. Before selecting an activity, consider what kind of attitude toward food is being modeled, and whether or not what the children will learn can only be learned in that way. In a world where there are people who are hungry, we must consider what message we send children when they see edible food used in art activities and then often thrown away. The children themselves may be hungry and not understand why they cannot eat the foods intended for an art activity. Children who have been taught not to waste food may be dismayed and confused when asked to paint with a banana or to sprinkle their favorite cereal on their collage. As one little boy said as he looked in a wastebasket full of fruits that had been used in a printing lesson, "Why did we mess up so much good food?" Before using any food product in an art activity, consider whether or not a nonfood item will accomplish the same learning goals. See table 6–1 for suggested substitutes.

WHAT RECIPES WORK?

A concoction is something you cook up on the spur of the moment with a bunch of ingredients and only an idea of what it will turn out to be.

SUSAN PINKERTON (1985, P. 25)

Most homemade art materials are pale imitations of the real thing. Before cooking up a batch of finger paint or paste or any other art material, determine the cost, effort, and learning advantage of the homemade supply. Ready-made products are often cheaper and more attractive to the children.

There are a few recipes that have become traditions in early childhood art. These tried-and-true recipes have stood the test of time for several reasons. In some cases the recipe is cheaper than the commercial product. They use easily obtained ingredients that are safe for young children, and they are quick and easy to make. Most of these recipes are made from food products, but the resulting art material does not resemble food, nor are they designed to be eaten. These recipes are often mentioned throughout the Art Focus sections of this book, and Appendix A lists some basic recipes for homemade art materials.

There are hundreds of recipes in books and articles on art for young children. Teachers can make their own pastes, paints, and modeling doughs of all kinds. It is fun to mix up small batches of these just to see how they work. Remember that recipes, particularly those involving flour, may not consistently turn out the same. The particular set of ingredients, the cooking temperature, or the weather may all affect the results. Before making up a large amount for the children to use, experiment with the material in the way the children will.

For example, young children like to squeeze modeling materials very tightly in their fists. Surprisingly, some doughs that model well when gently patted and rolled turn into a sticky mess when squeezed or pressed hard. Also consider the work surface.

TABLE 6–1   Substitutions for foods in favorite art activities

ACTIVITY	SUBSTITUTE
Vegetable or fruit printing	Sponge or block printing
Collages made with macaroni, rice, cereal, etc.	Pebbles, sand, buttons, etc.
Seed/bean mosaics	Pebbles, shells
Edible doughs made from sugar, flour, cornmeal, etc.	Nonhardening modeling clay, purchased play dough
Cereal for stringing a necklace	Cardboard tube pieces, cut straws
Pudding finger paint	Purchased finger paint, detergent or soap finger paint

FIGURE 6–5 Making a homemade art supply can be an unpredictable experience.

Some homemade glues cause paper to wrinkle up; some play doughs will stick to a newspaper covering, but work fine on a smooth, bare tabletop. Cleanup is something to consider as well. Many concoctions, especially ones that involve flour, leave a residue that must be scrubbed off the work surface.

Start a collection of recipes that have been tried and document how much the materials cost, any difficulties in making it, and how successfully the children used it. Once the basic elements of the recipes are familiar, experiment with original ideas. Who knows? Maybe a new art material will be discovered that will become another child art tradition.

SUMMARY: BALANCING FREEDOM AND SAFETY

> Teaching about the hazards of art materials and how to work safely should occur when students first learn art techniques.
>
> MICHAEL McCANN (1985, P. 6)

In this chapter, ways to create a safe environment in which children will be free to be artists is presented. It is, indeed, a challenging task. Young children have more energy and more inventiveness than can be imagined. Adults are ultimately responsible for the health and safety of children in their care and it is easy to become overcome with guilt. A child cuts herself seriously with a scissors and requires stitches. A child has an allergic reaction to the scent of an art material, goes into shock, and becomes unconscious. An article is published that says an ingredient in an art supply teachers have used with the children for the last 10 years has been found to cause cancer.

The longer we work with children, the more likely something unfortunate will occur. But if the children are closely supervised, if teachers have enforced safe behavior and provided the safest art materials based on the best information they can obtain, they should not bury themselves in guilt. When an accident occurs, take time to analyze why it happened and correct the situation so it will not be repeated. If an art supply is suddenly deemed unsafe, stop using it. Read, listen, and learn from others. All teachers can benefit from sharing experiences with other people who work with children.

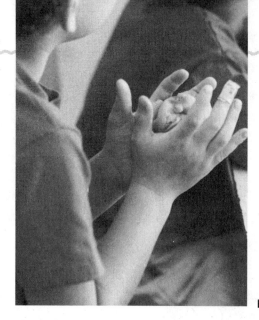

FIGURE 6–6 Children's safety is in our hands.

Art experiences encourage the child to explore freely. Children are ultimately responsible for creating their own learning. Although direct experience is a wonderful teacher, there are some experiences that are too dangerous for children to learn directly. The teacher has to be their *guiding* adult—caring, watchful, thoughtful, knowledgeable, and always prepared to gently redirect children who are endangering themselves or others.

FURTHER READING

Nothing's as good as holding on to safety.

EURIPIDES (PHOENICIAN WOMEN)

The following books will provide more detailed information on health hazards in art.

McCann, M. (1985). *Health hazards manual for artists.* New York, NY: Nick Lyons Books.
This book provides a simple outline of health hazards in art.

Qualley, C. A. (1986). *Safety in the artroom.* New York, NY: Davis.
This book is specifically directed to teachers of art and contains detailed information on making the art environment hazard-free.

Recipes for art materials can be found in many books. Choose recipes with care. Some recipes that can be used with young children may be found in these books and articles.

Kohl, M. F. (1985). *Scribble cookies.* Bellingham, WA: Bright Ring.

Kohl, M. F. (1989). *Mudworks: Creative clay, dough, and modeling experiences.* Bellingham, WA: Bright Ring.
These two books contain hundreds of recipes for all kinds of art supplies. Some are familiar, and some are surprising. Not all of them are safe or appropriate for children under eight. Select them with care.

Pinkerton, S. (1989). Concoctions: Creative mixtures to make and enjoy. *Day Care and Early Childhood, 17,* (2). 25-29.
This article describes the fun of inventing new recipes and provides several sample ones to try.

Miller, S. (1994). *Learning through play: Sand, water, clay & wood.* New York: Scholastic.
This book provides basic information on using modeling materials with young children.

Art Focus

EXPLORING MODELING MATERIALS

> Young fingers and growing sensitivities explore the very essence of shape. Form. How to mold a world.
>
> CLARE CHERRY (1990, P. 254)

Modeling, or working with three-dimensional pliable materials, is one of the great joys of early childhood. Soft, smooth clays and play doughs are just waiting to be squeezed and poked, to the great delight of the young artist. By giving children the opportunity to explore a material that has many sides, that can be turned over and around, and looked at from different points of view, teachers strengthen children's understanding of the spatial realm in which they exist. Three-dimensional art forms call upon different perceptual modes and different areas of skill development than do drawing, painting, and other two-dimensional activities.

When children draw or paint, there is a strong visual response to the marks they make on the paper. In working with modeling materials, although the visual element is still there, the children respond first to the tactile qualities of the forms as they create them. Young children working with play dough or clay will often manipulate the material vigorously while focusing their eyes on something else or staring off into space.

There is also a great deal of talking and noise-making that goes on as children explore clay. Children working on drawings or paintings will perhaps make a comment or two while they work or add a special sound effect, but many children at the clay table will pound and slap and talk incessantly. Modeling materials provide an opportunity for children to practice their social skills as they respond to each other's actions and exchange pieces of clay or tools.

Working with Modeling Materials

As in drawing, children go through modeling modes that mirror their physical and cognitive growth. The sort of forms that children can produce are determined by the amount of control they have over their arms, wrists, hands, and fingers, by their mental ability to imagine a form and then produce it, and by their previous experiences with the material.

Initial Exploration

When first confronted with a modeling material, children often approach it with caution that quickly turns to abandon. They push their fingers into it, pat it, pick it up and put it down, drop it, and squeeze it until it oozes out between their fingers. They may lick it and taste it, rub it on their faces, and stick it up to or into their noses

FIGURE 6–7 Poke it. Pat it. Squoosh it. Modeling provides a tactile experience.

for a good whiff. They will bang it with fists, peel it off their arms when it sticks, and throw it, if not stopped. There is no attempt to make the clay or dough into something, but only a pure multisensory exploration of this exciting material.

This purely exploratory behavior is seen in the youngest children, those between one and three years of age, and corresponds in some ways to scribbling in drawing. However, it is often seen in older children as well, especially as they first start to handle a new or unfamiliar modeling material.

For toddlers, the behavior reflects their lack of small motor control, the reliance on large motor movements of the arm and hands, as well as their sensory approach to learning about their environment. For older children, this initial exploratory behavior reflects an attempt to understand the material's possibilities and limits. Even adult artists spend time working freely with a medium in order to assess its parameters before beginning to create a sculpture in earnest.

Controlled Exploration

After the initial explorations of the modeling medium, children will begin to explore the clay or dough in a more systematic way. At this stage the children may flatten the clay into pancake-like forms using the palm of the hand. With their fingers, they may poke a series of indentations into the surface, or pull off small pieces and flatten them. They may stick the pieces back together or create a stack of them. One of the first forms that they can make due to the increasing control over their hands is a long thin cylinder created by rolling a piece of clay between the palms of their two hands.

One of the later forms that develops, sometimes in the fourth or fifth year, is the sphere or ball created by rolling the clay between the palms or between the table and one palm. This is a much more complex skill as it requires the child to move the hand in a circular motion and is often preceded by much experimentation. Once the ball is perfected, it often becomes the object of much manipulative play; it may be rolled across the table or several may be lined up in a row.

For children who have had many opportunities to use clays, *controlled exploration* reflects their increasing control over hands and fingers. Older children and adults may also repeat these

same manipulations as part of their preliminary explorations of modeling media.

Named Forms

The difference between a *named form* and controlled exploration is not one of form or physical control. It relates instead to the *cognitive* development of the child. The long thin cylinder becomes a "snake," the poked pancake becomes a "face," the clay balls become "snowballs." This naming of the modeled forms correlates to the naming of scribbled drawings and reflects the child's developing language skills and the growth of mental imagery.

The very manipulative nature of modeling materials allows children at this stage of development to pursue symbolic play in a way that they cannot with two-dimensional art media. Young children "cook" play-dough bits in the pots on a toy stove. They offer a "taco" to taste. They make mommy snakes and baby snakes that hiss and wiggle around the room and then turn into bracelets wrapped around active wrists. They "bowl" with their clay balls.

Although the child's creations may take on a life of their own, they still are to a large extent the result of unplanned manipulation. Once made, they are then "seen" to resemble or represent something. As in drawing, children will repeat these behaviors over and over as they perfect the skills needed to create the basic forms of sphere and cylinder at will.

Developing Three-Dimensional Symbols

In the final mode of modeling development, children are able to mentally plan the forms they will

FIGURE 6–8 "Man." Non-hardening clay—Nick, age 5

need to create an object. Instead of using the clay solely as a vehicle for sensory sensation and the release of feelings, the modeling material now becomes a means of self-expression for internal images. These images can be formed in several ways. Some are created by bending, flattening, or distorting one of the basic forms, for example making a "nest" by poking a hole in a clay ball. Others may be produced by joining simple or distorted basic forms together, as when a child creates a person from a clay ball and four flattened cylinders. As with the graphic symbols of drawing, the children are not trying to create actual representations of these objects, but rather the idea of the object. Once created, they assume a major role in the symbolic play of the child. Airplanes fly and drop bombs; animals eat clay bits from the clay bowl; birds sit on eggs in the nest and then fly off to find clay worms.

The kind of images that are produced will depend upon the amount of control the child has developed over the particular modeling material. All modeling materials are not the same; they differ in pliancy, stickiness, and rigidity. A child who has had a lot of experience with only one kind of clay or dough is often frustrated by trying to produce in a new one, and may engage in purely sensory exploration instead of creating symbols. Regardless of their age, children who have had very few experiences working with three-dimensional modeling materials may also need to spend time repeating the processes of each of the earlier modes before they can work on a symbolic level.

Using Modeling Materials for Emotional Release

The creation of modeled forms is often accompanied by their enthusiastic destruction. Pliant modeling materials give children the power to control a small part of their environment. Clay and play doughs are regularly used by children to release strong feelings in an acceptable way. Clay, unlike other children, bossy adults, or precious belongings, can be hit and smashed, slapped, pinched and poked, torn apart and put together again. Children who are having difficulty controlling their social behavior benefit from redirecting this behavior to the forgiving clay.

TABLE 6–2 The development of modeled forms

The Development of Modeled Forms

Mode	Child's Behavior
1. Initial Exploration	Manipulates material using all the senses; uses large motions of arm and hand
2. Controlled Exploration	Begins to make basic forms—pancake, worm, and ball; uses palms and fingers
3. Named Forms	Gives names and labels to modeled forms; begins to use them in symbolic play; uses fingers for shaping.
4. Symbolic Forms	Plans the forms that will be used; can attach forms together; can pull a form out of a larger piece of modeling material; can use fingers to create small details

How Children Grow through Modeling Activities

Children will develop:

1. Physically, by using the large muscles of the arm and the small muscles of the hand to manipulate the modeling material (Bodily-Kinesthetic)
2. Socially, by working alongside others and sharing materials and space (Interpersonal)
3. Emotionally, by learning that they can control this material and use it to release energy, tension, and emotion (Intrapersonal)
4. Visual perception skills, by exploring three-dimensional forms from differing viewpoints and learning that pliant forms change shape (Spatial)
5. Cognitively
   - By learning a vocabulary for concepts of size, shape, form, comparision, and relationship (Linguistic)
   - By observing cause and effect as their manipulation changes the nature of the form (Logical-Mathematical)
6. Art awareness, by examining three-dimensional modeled forms, such as pottery, that have been created by people from many times and places

Modeling Explorations for Toddlers

Most toddlers need many opportunities to freely explore soft, pliant modeling materials. The modeling material offered to toddlers must be one that contains no injurious ingredients because of the risk of ingestion. These young children still need to be closely supervised while they are working.

Group composition. The first exploration of a modeling material should be limited to one or two toddlers. Like paste, modeling materials are quite often tasted or eaten. Provide constant close supervision until they have learned not to eat the material.

Setup. A low, smooth-topped table that is easily washed makes the best working surface. There should be plenty of space for each child. If the tabletop is not appropriate for modeling or when working at home in a kitchen area, provide each child with a large tray to be used whenever they model or do other artwork. The low sides of the tray will help keep some of the pieces from falling to the floor.

There will be less mess on the floor if the children remain seated while working, so provide child-sized chairs. However, children can use more of their upper arm motion when standing, so occasionally allow them to stand while working as well.

FIGURE 6–9 Cookie and stick." Play dough—Ross, age 3

SPECIAL NEEDS

Children who are blind or who have very limited vision love the tactile nature of modeling materials. Provide a large tray with slightly raised sides for the child to work on. It will make it easier for the child to find small pieces of the modeling material.

Materials. The safest and most pliable modeling material for toddlers is play dough. Use a commercial brand or make a homemade version. There are many recipes available in books on art for children, or consult Appendix A: Recipes.

For the child's initial exploration, the dough should be a nonfood color and have a nonfood scent. A homemade dough has the advantage of being able to be made without scent for the first few explorations. Use only one color of dough for the first experience so the child can concentrate on the tactile qualities of the materials.

Provide each child with a baseball-sized piece of the modeling dough. If the dough will be reused, provide separate tightly lidded containers or resealable plastic bags, clearly labeled with each child's name.

Transition in. Offer the children a lump of play dough and show them where to use it. Explain that it is not food, but something with which to play. Let the children see it, smell it, and touch it.

What to do. Children will react differently to the stimulus of the play dough. Some will dive right in; others will approach cautiously. Some will pat and poke gently; some will squeeze it tightly in their hands. Often the first response is to try to taste or smell it.

1. Sit at the table with the children.
2. Squeeze and poke a piece of the play dough, too, but do not show them how to use the play dough.
3. Avoid making forms such as balls and snakes, which are beyond their developmental level.
4. Only interfere with their exploration for safety reasons. Be ready to stop them from putting the dough in their mouths. Remember that it

is important from the start to emphasize that art materials are never put in the mouth.

What to say. Use this activity to talk about the tactile qualities of the play dough. In an excited voice use words like soft, squooshy, pat, poke, push, pull, sticky, press, squash, and flatten. Modeling is a wonderful time to chant or sing with toddlers. Make up some modeling chants to accompany this wonderful activity (see Music Box).

MUSIC BOX

Modeling Chants

1. Push and mush.
    Pull and tug.
    Roll around,
    And mash it up.

2. Poke it. Pat it.
    Make it flat.
    Pick it up
    and put it back.

3. Today I play,
    With sticky clay.
    First I squeeze,
    Then I pat.
    Now I've made it nice and flat.

4. First I played
    Now I've stopped
    In goes my play dough.
    On* goes the top.

    (*If using a resealable plastic bag, substitute: "zip" goes the top.)

Transition out. Let the children spend as much time as they wish exploring the nature of the dough. When they lose interest, show them how to gather up the play dough and put it into its storage container. Show them where the containers will be stored and tell them it will be there for them to use it again.

Modeling Practice Activities for Toddlers

Once children are familiar with safe ways to use play doughs, the activity can be varied in many ways.

Color and scent. Toddlers love using play dough over and over again. Vary this experience first by offering a different color each time. Later provide colors that they can mix together. Once they have learned not to taste the dough, add nonfood scents. (See chapter 8 for a listing of possible scents.)

Textures. Find a recipe for homemade play dough that has a different texture or add a material to commercial play dough to provide a different tactile experience. Make sure that whatever is added is safe if it is ingested.

Provide tools. The majority of a child's modeling experiences should be done with the fingers only. Manipulating the play dough directly is the best way to develop hand and finger strength. On occasion, provide some very simple tools. Little children love to cut up play dough. A plastic knife provides a safe way for the child to feel grown up and trusted. A small wooden or plastic rolling pin is another tool that children enjoy and one that helps children develop hand-eye coordination.

Avoid giving the children cookie cutters to go with the rolling pin, however. Although these are commonly used in early childhood programs, in many ways they are similar to giving the children precut paper patterns on which to draw. They tell the children that adults do not think the forms they create on their own are as good as the commercial cookie-cutter designs. Cookie cutters also reduce the wonderful three-dimensionality of the play dough to two dimensions and so do not help develop the child's spatial abilities.

Their use is another case of trying to make children's artwork more pleasing to the aesthetic sense of adults. Unfortunately once cookie cutters are introduced, many children abandon their own creative exploration of the clay to develop skill in making the perfect cutout.

Connections. LITERATURE: Read *The New Baby Calf* (Chase, 1984). The illustrations in this book are created from nonhardening modeling clay. Have the children try and figure out how the different textures were made.

ART AWARENESS: Display a handmade clay bowl and supervise the children handling it, or use the bowl to hold a snack.

FIGURE 6–10 "Person." Play dough—Melody, age 4

Modeling Activities for Three-Year-Olds and Up

Children who have had some experience using modeling doughs are ready for a larger variety of activities. Children over three years are less likely to eat or taste the play dough or clays, so more types of modeling materials can be introduced. The following modeling compounds can all be used with older children, but please note the special cautions on safety that accompany them.

Modeling doughs and related practice activities. Like toddlers, preschoolers and primary age children like the soft, pliant doughs which are easy to form into a wide variety of creations. Both commercially made and homemade play doughs can be used.

Play dough. Children can be given several colors of play dough at a time, which they will mix together with great enthusiasm. Try to pick colors that when mixed, will form attractive new ones. For example, red and yellow make orange, and blue and yellow make green. Let the children color their own dough by squeezing a drop or two of food coloring or liquid tempera paint on uncolored homemade dough and then mixing the color in with their hands. (Homemade play dough recipes are in Appendix A: Recipes.)

Salt-flour dough. Children can also mix their own play dough. A salt-flour dough is the easiest for children to do on their own. NOTE: Salt may cause a burning sensation or irritate any small cuts or scrapes that children have on their hands. Check the children's hands first. If children complain about burning, let them wash their hands right away.

1. Work with a small group of three or four children that can be closely supervised.
2. Give each child a bowl and help them measure and pour one cup of flour and one quarter cup of salt. Add one quarter cup of warm water and let them knead it together.
3. If the dough is too dry, add some drops of water. If it is too wet, add more flour.
4. Show excitement and interest as the children respond to the changing tactile quality of the mixture. Children can add liquid tempera or food coloring to the dough as well.

Baked play dough: Several of the homemade doughs are suitable for air drying or baking. In general, children are much more involved in the process of using the modeling material than in creating a finished work. Usually it is best to save children's sculptures only when they request it. Many, however, are extremely fragile. Some may not even be able to be removed from the table without destroying them. In these cases the best way to save them is to take a photograph of the child with the sculpture. If the piece is sturdy enough, put it in a safe dry place to air dry, or bake it according to the directions of the recipe.

Try to avoid instances in which all the children are required to make something permanent, such as making gifts of baked play-dough paperweights. Many young children lack the skill to make something that will dry or bake well. Their pieces may be too thin, not well-attached, or more often so thick that they dry poorly, if at all. If teachers tell them they have to change what they have made to be bakeable, they may feel this is a criticism. Remember, if teachers have to personally "fix" children's artwork so that it can be baked, then this is not a creative developmental art activity for young children.

A better alternative is to prebake simple round pieces of dough which the children can then use as a base on which to paint or glue pieces of collage items in their own creative ways.

"Stick" sculptures. Another way that play dough can be used is for children to use a lump of air-drying dough as a base in which to insert materials such as sticks, toothpicks, pipe cleaners, cardboard strips, craft sticks, beads, buttons, drinking straws, and nature materials, such as pinecones, acorns, shells, dried grasses, and twigs. When the dough has dried, the objects will be securely fastened to the base.

Impressions. Give the children objects with interesting textures to press into the dough. Try berry baskets, plastic food trays, plastic forks, potato mashers, and any other washable items.

TEACHER TIP

Using Food Coloring

- Some food coloring will stain the hands the way lollipops stain the mouth, but the stain does not last long. Parents and children, however, may be upset by the stain particularly if they do not know what caused it.

- When adding food coloring to dough, always add a few drops at a time. Fold dough over the color rather than putting hands directly in it.

- There may be some children who are sensitive to food dyes; check with parents before using them.

Nonhardening clays. These oil-based clays, also called plasticine or modeling clay, do not dry out when exposed to the air. They are more rigid than play dough and are suitable for older children who have more developed finger strength. Modeling clay needs to be softened by warming it in the hand. This naturally fits the pattern of young children's behavior as it encourages free exploration before the expression of ideas. Very brightly colored modeling clays are available which are attractive to the children. Another major advantage is that the oil-based modeling compounds will hold sharper detail, remain more upright, and stay very flexible when rolled into extremely long, thin "snakes"-much to the

delight of young children. Soft play doughs often sag and crack when rolled thin, and their details slowly soften and fill in.

However, children who have used the much softer play dough often do not want to work harder to create something out of modeling clay. In order to encourage children to develop the finger strength needed, modeling clay should be offered exclusively for a period of time. Show them how to warm the modeling clay in their hands and slowly begin to knead it. If the room is chilly, it is sometimes helpful to break the clay into smaller pieces and then warm them.

It is well worth the effort to present modeling clay to young children who are able to create symbolic forms. They can be much more expressive with this flexible but strong modeling material, and can develop more sophisticated forms to work with, such as cubes (made by tapping a sphere on table to create the sides) and slabs (flat rectangular "pancakes"), which can be used in building structures. In addition, textured objects can be pressed into the plasticine and will leave clear impressions.

SAFETY NOTE:
- Make sure that the modeling clay colors that are chosen do not come off on the hands and are specifically designed for children.
- Look for safety labeling.
- Modeling clay should not be ingested. It is not suitable for children who still try to taste or eat modeling materials.

FIGURE 6–11 "Flower and nest." Non-hardening clay—Heather, age 5

- Make sure that children do not put their hands in their mouths while working and wash their hands well when they are done.
- Check that they do not have clay under their fingernails. Modeling clay will wash off in soapy water but may require a bit of soaking or scrubbing.

Firing clay. Firing clay is the real clay that comes from the earth and from which pottery is made. It has been used for thousands of years by people around the world. The china dishes we use every day are made from this substance. Although strongly advocated in many books on art for young children because of its mudlike tactile qualities, firing clay has lost popularity in many early childhood programs.

There are a number of reasons for this. One of the main reasons is the health hazard related to the use of firing clay. Another is the need for constant supervision as the children work and the difficulty cleaning up the resulting "mess."

In general, commercial and homemade play doughs and modeling clays can provide plenty of wonderful modeling experiences for young children and meet all the same growth objectives. They should form the backbone of any three-dimensional art activity program. Firing clay, although not essential to a well-rounded program, can offer a special occasional experience for older children. This is particularly true if it is related to a child-initiated interest in pottery, developed either through a visit to a pottery studio, from a guest potter, or from observation of handmade pottery dishes and bowls from different cultures. However, if a safe environment is not available for firing clay activities, then do not offer them.

Group composition. The fewer children who work with the clay at a time, the more closely they can be supervised. Try to work with no more than four children at a time. The ideal situation is to have one adult work directly with one or two children. It may be possible to arrange for a local potter or parent to provide this close attention. The adult can work with clay beside the child and offer assistance and encouragement as needed and help the child focus on the tactile qualities of the clay.

Materials. Purchase only talc-free, moist clay (see Appendix A for sources). Avoid all powdered or dry clay mixes. Figure one pound of moist clay per child. A 25-pound bag will serve 25 students. Each child will need a baseball-sized piece. Store unused clay in doubled plastic bags that are tightly closed and placed inside a covered plastic can. When used clay is returned to the bag, add a half-cup of water per piece to replace evaporated moisture. Clay will keep a very long time this way.

Setup. Children create the least mess when they work standing at a table covered with several layers of newspaper.

- Use wet firing clay out-of-doors, if possible.
- Provide the children with buckets of water in which to rinse their hands as soon as they get dusty.
- Never use firing clay in any multipurpose room or where food is eaten. Clay use produces a fine dust that settles on all surfaces.
- If a pottery studio is used, it should be damp-mopped and all surfaces wiped down daily.

Cleanup. The clay-covered newspaper will need to be folded up slowly so as not to spread the dust.

- Wash all tools and wipe down all surfaces to eliminate dust.
- Use buckets for the initial hand and tool rinsing so the clay-filled water can be dumped outside on the ground where it will not clog the sink drain.

Transition in. An excellent book to share with the children, either before or after experience with the clay, is *Little Indian Pottery Maker* (Clark, 1955) If you wish, make an original big book about firing clay. Discuss how clay changes when it is baked at a hot temperature and show examples of unglazed, baked clay and glazed, fired clay. Compare how the firing clay differs from the other modeling materials they have used.

What to do. Children who have had a lot of experience using play dough and nonhardening clay have great difficulty adjusting to firing clay. Unlike these soft, elastic materials, firing clay is stiff and cold and damp. It makes the hands feel very dry. It dries out and cracks when handled and turns to mud when too much water is added. Before beginning show children how to add small amounts of water by dipping fingertips in a small shallow water cup.

1. Have children wear smocks to prevent dust from collecting on clothing. Wash smocks after use.
2. Present the firing clay to the children as an exploration.
3. Encourage them to try different ways of using it and let them explore on their own. Do not expect them to produce any finished product.
4. Show them how to return the clay to its storage container when they are done.
5. Remind them to keep their hands away from their faces and to dampen them when they are dusty and dry. Children must never put their hands in their mouths or touch their faces when using the clay. They must clean under their fingernails as well as their hands when done. Do not allow children to clap their hands together raising dust.
6. Two pieces of clay will not join and stay together when dry without special preparation:

   • To join: apply water ("magic glue" is a good name for it) to each piece.
   • Press together.
   • Smooth joint so it cannot be seen.

7. The more the clay is handled the more it dries out. Overly dry clay cracks and will not stay together. Small amounts of water should be added as needed. It takes a lot of experience to know just how much water to add. Children will quickly learn that too much water reduces the clay to a mud pile. Use this experience to help children see cause and effect. Help them learn to add just a little at a time.

Extending the learning: Clay tiles. Most creations by young children are too fragile to survive firing in the kiln. Again they are best saved through photography. If, however, a kiln is available, a wonderful, cooperative culminating activity for the firing clay exploration is to make clay tiles.

1. Make one or several large flat squares of clay, about one-half-inch thick, and four to six per side. Children can help roll out the clay using rolling pins.
2. Have the children take turns drawing an original design or picture on the tiles using pencils or craft sticks. Caution children not to press too hard.
3. Alternatively, wet the clay surface and have children attach small pieces of clay, such as flattened balls and skinny snakes, combined to make a picture. Keep the height under an inch.
4. Poke holes in the top of the tiles so they can be hung up after firing.
5. Air dry completely—at least a week.
6. Low-fire the tiles in the kiln (1100-1500° F).
7. After firing, the tiles can be painted with watercolors or tempera paint or left natural.

TEACHER TIP

Kiln Safety

Kilns must be located in areas far away from where children are working.

They must be fully ventilated to the outside. Never use any kiln that does not meet these requirements.

Connections. LITERATURE: Share books that describe what clay is, such as *Clay* (Dixon, 1990) or *A Ball of Clay* (Hawkinson, 1974). After using the clay have children make their own big book about the experience.

SCIENCE/MATH: Make two equal lumps of clay. Wrap one in plastic. Fire the other one. Have the children compare the two pieces and describe how they are different. Use a balance scale and see which one is heavier. Discuss why.

KINESTHETICS: Have children imagine they are lumps of clay. Call out different forms and objects and encourage the children to mold themselves into those shapes.

ART AWARENESS: Share handmade pottery pieces. Have a potter visit or take a field trip to a potter's studio. Use handmade pottery to hold snack foods. Art prints to share include the Ceramic Print Collection and the Folk Art Collection (Crystal: Portfolio Prints). (See Appendix A: Print Sources.)

Studio Page *37*

SAFETY SEARCH

Art Health Hazards in Your Environment

- How safe are your home and workplace?
- Conduct an inspection using this worksheet.
- Check off any potential art hazards that you find.

	Home	Work
SOLVENTS		
benzene	❏	❏
carbon tetrachloride	❏	❏
lacquer thinner	❏	❏
mineral spirits	❏	❏
paint remover	❏	❏
paint thinner	❏	❏
resins/resin solvents	❏	❏
shellac solvent (methyl alcohol)	❏	❏
silk-screen solvents	❏	❏
turpentine	❏	❏
AEROSOL SPRAYS		
fixative	❏	❏
spray glue	❏	❏
spray paint	❏	❏
PAINTS		
enamels	❏	❏
latex paint	❏	❏
oil paint	❏	❏
varnishes	❏	❏

	Home	Work
GLUES		
epoxy	❏	❏
model cement	❏	❏
plastic cement	❏	❏
rubber cement	❏	❏
super glues	❏	❏
DUSTS		
artists' pastels	❏	❏
dyes	❏	❏
firing clays	❏	❏
glass powders (enameling)	❏	❏
glazes (clay)	❏	❏
plaster	❏	❏
OTHER		
lead solder	❏	❏
permanent markers	❏	❏
silk-screen inks	❏	❏

Studio Page 38

IS THIS A SAFE ENVIRONMENT FOR CHILDREN?

Using your checklist from Studio Page 37, answer the following questions:

1. Are all items that you checked in locked metal cabinets?   yes   no

2. Are these items used only in areas that are not used by children?   yes   no

3. Are there dust masks available?   yes   no

4. Is there a face mask with proper filters for safe solvent use?   yes   no

5. Are surfaces and floors in areas where these items are stored and
   used kept clean and orderly?   yes   no

6. Do you have a hobby that uses potentially hazardous materials?   yes   no
   (fabric dying or painting, silk screening, stained glass, copper enameling
   pottery, oil painting, furniture refinishing, etc.)

   If yes, what steps can you take to make your work area safe for yourself? _____

   _____

   _____

   _____

   _____

   _____

   _____

7. Which environment is safer for children: your home or work space? _____

   _____

   _____

   _____

   _____

   _____

   _____

   _____

   _____

   _____

   _____

   _____

Studio Page 39

RECIPE RECORD SHEET

Art Material:

Source of Recipe:

Ingredients:

Directions:

1. What was the cost of the ingredients in this recipe?

   _____

2. How much did it make?

   _____

3. How many children would it serve?

   _____

4. Is this homemade material more or less expensive than a similar commercial one?

   _____

5. Were the ingredients easy to find?

   _____

6. Was this recipe simple to make?

   _____

7. Is the material aesthetically pleasing and fun to use?

   _____

8. Is this material easily confused with food? Should it be a cooking activity or an art activity?

   _____

Studio Page 40

FOOD VERSUS ART

Where Do You Stand?

- Where do you stand on this issue?

_____

_____

_____

_____

_____

- What art materials do you think are appropriate for young children?

_____

_____

_____

_____

_____

- Using what you have learned in this chapter, justify your position on this issue. Explain why you would or would not have the children do the following:

    1. Use homemade play doughs:

    _____

    _____

    2. Finger paint with pudding:

    _____

    _____

    3. String cereal necklaces:

    _____

    _____

    4. Use vegetables for printmaking:

    _____

    _____

Studio Page

OBSERVATION: USING A MODELING MATERIAL

The purpose of this observation is to allow you to study how a child approaches three-dimensional modeling activities.

Setup

- Observe an individual child in a home or school setting.
- Provide a safe modeling material you think will be suitable for this particular child. Do not provide tools.

Observation

1. What does the child do first with the material?

_____

_____

_____

_____

2. How does the child move his/her hands?

_____

_____

_____

_____

3. What forms does the child make?

_____

_____

_____

_____

4. What does the child say?

_____

_____

_____

_____

Studio Page 42

POST-OBSERVATION ANALYSIS

1. Based on the forms the child made, at what modeling stage is the child?

    _____

    _____

    _____

    _____

    _____

2. Was this modeling material suitable for the child?

    _____

    _____

    _____

    _____

    _____

3. Did the child have any difficulties?

    _____

    _____

    _____

    _____

    _____

4. Did you have to remind the child of safe behavior?

    _____

    _____

    _____

    _____

    _____

5. What other modeling materials do you think this child could use? Why?

    _____

    _____

    _____

    _____

    _____

7

6 6 *Encouraging a person to discover their uniqueness and helping them develop its expression can be one of the greatest gifts we can ever give.* **9 9**

•

FRED ROGERS (1982, P. 10)

I'm Creative!

Nurturing Children's Creative Growth

Questions addressed in this chapter:

Young Artists at Work

Several four-year-olds are busy using paper and glue. The teacher has put out a tray of precut yellow squares. Stephen spreads glue all over his paper and then slaps on several yellow squares haphazardly. He pokes at one square, sliding it around in the glue. Maryanne carefully makes small dots of glue. Then she selects a yellow square and places it over the glue dots. With a crayon she draws eyes, a nose, and a mouth. Keith watches his friends at work, then picks up the glue bottle and makes a line of glue in the center of the paper. He chooses a square from the tray and sticks it in place. Then he adds more glue and another square. Soon his paper is covered with a line of gluey yellow squares.

WHAT IS CREATIVITY?

Creative thinking is not a station one arrives at, but a means of traveling.

MARY MAYESKY (1975, P. 6)

Even though each of these children is the same age and is working with the same materials, the artwork that is produced is undeniably unique to each child. It is not enough to understand how a child grows developmentally. Adults who work with young children must also understand, and value, the nature of the creative process and how it is expressed in the art of each child.

Defining Creativity

Creativity has been the subject of much research and analysis ; yet there is no generally accepted definition. Creativity has been viewed in many ways.

It can refer to the creation of an original product such as an artwork. For example, Bruner (1979, p. 12) calls creativity an act that produces "effective surprise" and Boden (1992, p. 40) depicts creativity as doing something that is beyond the accepted rules—"thinking the impossible" in a way that is understandable and acceptable to the wider audience. Malaguzzi (Edwards et al., 1992, p. 70) views creativity not as a separate mental entity, but as an integral part of the way people think about and process information. Gardner (Goleman, Kaufman, and Ray, 1992, p. 27) sees creativity not as a general characteristic, but as specific to each of the multiple intelligences. A person cannot just "be creative," but must be creative in something, such as being a creative painter or poet.

Creativity can also be seen as a set of skills that enables people to solve problems in new ways. Amabile (1983) sees creativity as something all people exhibit when they do something that goes beyond the ordinary. She identifies three basic characteristics of creative people.

FIGURE 7–1 "Hungry Man." Mixed media collage—Edgar, age 6

1. They have skill in a particular domain.
2. They have creative thinking skills:
    • the ability to imagine a range of possibilities
    • persistance
    • high personal standards
3. They are intrinsically motivated: doing something for personal pleasure

ARE YOUNG CHILDREN CREATIVE?

The kernel of creativity...is there in the infant: The desire and drive to explore, to find out about things, to try things out, to experiment with different ways of handling things and looking at things.

TERESA AMABILE (GOLEMAN ET AL., 1992, P. 57)

Most animals have inherited reflexes and responses that enable them to survive from birth. Human beings, on the other hand, must learn almost everything starting in infancy. The creative process can be seen as the mechanism by which people use past knowledge and learned skills to meet the needs of a new situation or to solve a problem. Young children are constantly dealing with fresh circumstances and "creating" a unique response to the situation. The infant finds a dab of spilled milk and creates a design by swirling her fingers through it. The toddler rolls his clay into a long thin cylinder, wraps it around his wrist and creates a body ornament. The preschooler finds a stone, adds some crayon marks and creates a "creature."

The nature of the creative artistic responses the child makes will depend upon many factors. The infant does not yet have the ability to create a landscape painting. The toddler cannot produce silver jewelry. The preschooler cannot carve a marble monument. Nevertheless, even though the children's responses are limited by their skill level and level of physical growth, their artworks are still highly creative. At any moment, each child is at a precise point in development, has a unique set of experiences, and a personal base of knowledge and skills. These combine to produce a particular set of responses to each specific stimulus that the child confronts. We should not find it surprising that a one-of-a-kind child produces one-of-a-kind art!

A Nurturing Environment

As the process of creativity is discussed in this section, it is important to remember that the behaviors being described come from within the child. These behaviors are not distinctly separate from each other, but are elements of the individual's whole approach to learning. They are not taught directly, but can be nurtured through the presentation of carefully designed, open-ended art activities.

Children need an environment that is conducive to the creative process. It is easy for habit-bound adults, intentionally or unintentionally, to react negatively to creative behaviors or for helpful adults to want to "solve" children's problems for them. One of the more difficult things for adults to learn is when to set limits, when to offer direction, and when to stand back and let children do it by themselves. Guiding adults must constantly set themselves the task of providing safe stimuli and a nurturing environment that allows creative learning in young children.

In the following discussion of the creative process we will see how teachers' behavior and attitude, and the decisions they make, affect the creative behavior of children. Activities focused on the art medium of collage provide examples of how teachers can foster creative expression through art.

WHAT IS THE CREATIVE PROCESS?

The creative process can be viewed as being composed of a combination of mental processes that lead to the final creative product or action. They consist of:

KNOWLEDGE: What individuals already knows about what they are exploring
MOTIVATION: The inner drive to accomplish something
SKILL ACQUISTION: The development of expertise
IMMERSION: Being intensely focused on creating something unique with this knowledge and skill
INCUBATION: A period of time in which individuals think and process what they know and what they wish to do
PRODUCTION: The tangible expression of the creative process

KNOWLEDGE: WHY IS IT IMPORTANT TO THE CREATIVE PROCESS?

> Giving the child opportunities to create constantly with the knowledge he currently has is the best preparation for future creative action.
>
> VIKTOR LOWENFELD AND W. LAMBERT BRITTAIN (1987, P. 5)

Whenever people face a new stimulus or problem, the first thing that comes into play is their previous knowledge. Young children have a much more limited knowledge base than adults, so their responses are often wildly different from those we might expect. The amount of knowledge children have about an art material or concept will influence what their creative response will be. For example, before expecting children to create collages using only flower pictures, they must first have many opportunities to identify and to sort mixed clippings of flowers and other subjects by type. Only after the children can do these activities successfully can they be expected to make a collage on such a specific theme.

How Do Children Gain Artistic Knowledge?

Children gain knowledge that will enable them to be creative in art through the exploration of art materials, physical objects, graphic images, and art concepts. Teachers help children gain knowledge in several ways.

Provide time to explore materials. In designing collage or other art activities, provide time for exploring the basic materials individually before they are used together in a piece of art.

Young Artists at Work

"Look!" said the teacher after sharing the book *Planting a Rainbow* (Ehlert, 1988). "Here are some pictures of beautiful spring flowers." He places on the table a basket of magazine clippings showing flowers. The children gather round and begin to cut and paste enthusiastically, while the teacher imagines a beautiful garden of finished collages to hang in the hall.

When the children are done they hurry to share their creations with their teacher.

"Oh," said the teacher seeing the finished collages. Where were the gardens? Instead of flowers, each child held a unique artwork. Some had irregular shapes covered with print or a lopsided face encircled with pieces of an advertisement.

"Each one of you used the clippings in your own creative way," said the teacher. "That is what makes art so exciting. You never know what will happen."

FIGURE 7–2 "Flower Garden." Mixed media collage—Shawnee, age 4

Talk about art concepts. Use a vocabulary rich in artistic language and point out examples of the art elements in children's artwork. Children who know they are making a line, and that there are many different kinds of lines, will be able to choose the particular line they want to use in their art.

Present the art of others. Knowing what other artists have done provides a basis from which children can take a new direction.

Accepting Individual Differences in Knowledge

In some cases a limited or different knowledge base will cause the child to use the offered art materials in a very unexpected way, as when children take the wadded-up paper towel they used to wipe their fingers and add it to the collage. Although adults may find the addition "unpleasant" from their personal aesthetic viewpoint, it is important to view children's work in terms of what they know.

In this case the children have demonstrated that they have learned that collages are made from a variety of textured papers glued onto a base paper. Incorporating the used paper towel demonstrates the child's ability to categorize it as a piece of textured paper and represents a highly creative action, equivalent to Picasso's using a piece of real newspaper to represent itself in his early Cubist painting—the result of which was equally unpleasant to art connoisseurs of the time.

Sometimes the child's creative solution will challenge the adult's tolerance for messiness and disorder, such as when children take a glue bottle and "frame" their pictures by squeezing glue on the table all around the outside of the collage. At other times the inventiveness of a young child will overwhelm us with awe. Remember when selecting and designing art activities for young children that they will each respond creatively, based on their personally unique previous knowledge, not the teachers' preconceived idea of what they will do.

MOTIVATION: HOW DOES IT DRIVE THE CREATIVE PROCESS?

> Spontaneous interest follows neither the curriculum nor the clock but rather, the timetable of the child's own growth schedule.
>
> DAVID ELKIND (1974, P. 109)

Motivation is the inner drive that causes an individual to want to do something. Young children are motivated by intense curiosity about the world around them. Everything is new and exciting to them. They want to touch everything, see everything, and try everything. How wonderful for the teacher!

Often the guiding adult only has to present the art materials and to give a few simple instructions, and the children's natural motivation to explore will do the rest. When motivation is at work, smiling, laughing children gather excitedly around us. They ask curious questions and cannot wait to get started. They spend a great deal of time on their explorations, and they want to do more and more.

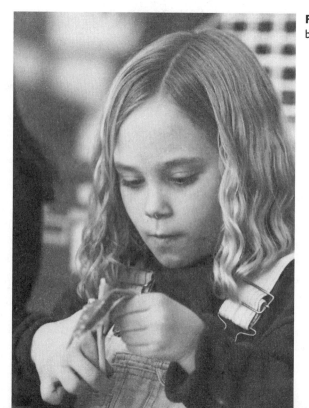

FIGURE 7–3 Motivation can not be taught. It must be inspired.

How is Motivation Stifled?

Unfortunately, motivation is a delicate force. It may be easily stifled by inappropriate organization or presentation of art activities. Overly restrictive art activities quickly dampen a child's natural curiosity.

Restricting choice. Materials that can be used in only one way, projects that must match a model, or actions that must conform to a fixed standard, all diminish self-motivation in children.

Boredom. Boredom arises when the child is constantly offered the same materials with little or no variation. For example, as wonderful as drawing with crayons can be, they cannot be a total art program for young children.

Competition. Rewards such as prizes or stars for "good" work or competition among students replace internal motivation with external motivation and do not belong in an art program for young children.

Conformity. Anxiety about making a mistake can prevent children from fully exploring an art material. The pressure to conform and to be like everyone else can make children afraid to be different and express themselves in a new way.

Fear. Fear of getting dirty or ruining something can cause children to be unmotivated to try the messier art materials. To discourage this, encourage parents to dress their children in easily cleaned clothing, provide smocks, and offer damp paper towels for wiping hands. Protect surfaces and only offer supplies that can be easily cleaned up.

Surveillance. If children feel that they are constantly being watched and evaluated, they may be less willing to take risks and try new ideas. If they think the teacher is going to interfere with their investigations, they will hesitate to pursue their own interests. If teachers solve the problem for them or do the work for them, they will expect that adults always will.

SKILL: WHAT IS ITS ROLE IN THE CREATIVE PROCESS?

> By selecting challenging, yet appropriate materials and by helping when necessary, the teacher can lead children into the development of skills that can serve rather than dictate their creative work.
>
> JUNE KING MCFEE (1961, P. 139)

The more skillfully children can handle an art material, the more they can concentrate on using the artistic elements of line, shape, color, and texture in a creative way in their artwork. A child using a new material or tool is often tentative and focused on controlling this new experience. The process of creating becomes secondary. As children gain skill their approach changes. They dive into the materials, no longer worried about how they will control them, but excited instead by the new way they can play with the artistic elements.

Designing Art Activities to Develop Artistic Skills

Art activities need to be carefully organized so that the skills required to accomplish them are appropriate for the skill level of the young child. If skills are new to the child,

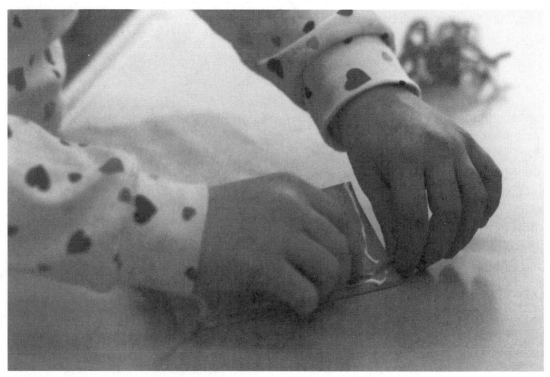

FIGURE 7–4 Skill develops with practice.

they must be within the physical and mental capabilities of the child to learn. Initial skills need to be presented in a structured format:

1. Materials should be aesthetically interesting, and limited to those that can be easily handled by particular children.
2. Children should be closely supervised when they are first introduced to new materials, tools, or techniques. Make sure the children are comfortable and understand what they will use, and how to do so safely.
3. Activities need to be carefully set up so that after new media and techniques are introduced, children can easily continue exploring and practicing with the materials and tools on their own.

Selecting practice activities. Successful initial explorations motivate the child to want to create again and again with those tools and materials. At this point, practice activities are extremely important in building up skill levels. At the same time, they allow the child to expand creatively.

In selecting practice activities, make sure that they do, in fact, utilize the same skills that were introduced in the explorations, so that children develop confidence in their own abilities. Children who are able to attach paper to the collage base may be able to glue down similar sizes and shapes of fabric as well, but may find the much different qualities of yarn make it more difficult to glue. In this case it is not enough to know how to apply the glue and place an item in it.

For example, picture a toddler who is trying to stick down a piece of string, but every time he lifts his gluey fingers the string is still stuck to them. He quickly becomes frustrated. He is no longer thinking about the creative fun of making a collage and how the different textures can be put together. He just wants the sticky string off his fingers. His frustration may grow to the point of furiously shaking his hand until the string goes flying across the room to stick to the wall or floor—a creative way, to be sure, of dealing with his problem, but one that is sure to bring repercussions from the nearest adult. For this toddler to be successful gluing string, he also needs to know how to wipe excess paste or glue from his fingers. Gentle guiding from an aware adult can help this child develop that skill as he creates.

Balancing Skill Development and Creativity

Skill development is often confused with creative processing, because they are so inter-related. Skills are needed to be artistically creative. At the same time, creative activities enable a child to develop skills. If activities are carefully thought out, children will develop the needed skills with a minimum of interference from adults, and they will be unhindered in their creative processing.

Activities that exist solely for the purpose of teaching or practicing skills, such as cutting along predrawn lines, coloring in teacher-drawn pictures or gluing together preformed pieces from a kit are not creative art activities. These same skills can be developed through open-ended art activities that allow for the expression of individual creativity. Children can draw their own lines and cut them out. They can color their own drawings, and they can cut out pieces and put them together in their own way.

It should be the goal of the teacher to offer only those activities that develop skills without dictating the end result.

IMMERSION: HOW DOES IT AFFECT THE CREATIVE PROCESS?

Children more naturally than adults enter that ultimate state of creativity called flow, in which total absorption can engender peak pleasure and creativity.

DAVID GOLEMAN, PAUL KAUFMAN, AND MICHAEL RAY (1992, P. 63)

Immersion is the state of being so completely focused on creating something that the passage of time is forgotten, as are personal needs and what is happening around us. In this state we feel relaxed and calm. Our ideas seem to flow effortlessly from our mind to

Young Artists at Work

A young child dabs some paste with her fingers and then begins to rub it across her paper in a swirling pattern. Although she is usually easily distracted, at this moment she pays no attention to the other children working beside her at the table. Instead of her perpetual chatter, she is silent. Her tongue projects slightly from her mouth as her eyes follow the movement of her hand. If we speak to her at this moment she may not even hear us, and if she does she may jump slightly or hesitate before responding to us. In the simple act of spreading the paste in a new way, this child has become immersed in the process of creation.

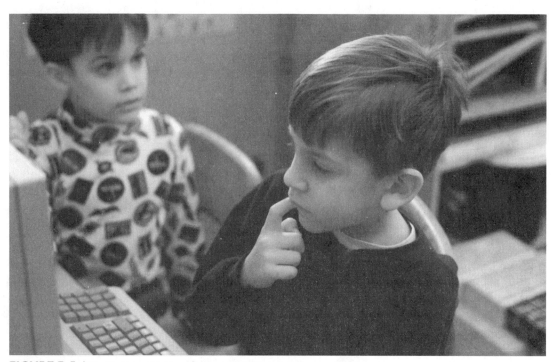

FIGURE 7–5 Intense concentration shows creativity at work.

our hands. We are not concerned with the end product, but only with the pleasure of the process itself. Creativity is at work! All the knowledge, skill, and motivation of the individual have come together to make this moment possible.

It is much easier for children to enter this state than adults. Adults rarely have uninterrupted, unlimited time in which to create. Some people, such as artists and writers, find that they have to go off by themselves to a "studio" or "garret" in order to work. Most people, however, spend their days surrounded by the pressure of social ties, of job commitments, and in tending basic human needs, with only rare moments to become immersed in the creative process. But adults must be careful that they do not impose such restraints upon children.

Providing Time. Anyone who has ever worked with young children knows that unlike adults, young children have little concern with time. Left on their own, children will immerse themselves for as much time as they need on a creative activity. In designing activities and interacting with the children, teachers must always be aware of the time factor in order to best meet the children's creative needs. Before children start an art activity, be sure that there will be sufficient time for them to become immersed in it. Especially when offering an activity for the first few times and it is unclear how long the children will need, present it at the beginning of the session. If children want to start an activity when they will not have sufficient time, it is better to redirect them to an activity that will involve less time.

Avoiding Interruptions. It is extremely frustrating for a child to be interrupted when immersed in the creative process. Unfortunately our society runs by the clock. It will happen, despite the best planning—children in the act of creating will need to be interrupted. If an individual child must be interrupted, do so gently. Try to make eye contact before giving a direction. Offer the assurance that the child can continue the activity at another time. It is essential to keep such interruptions to an absolute minimum. If this happens often enough, the child will eventually lose the motivation to create art.

INCUBATION AND PRODUCTION: WHERE DOES THE CREATIVE PROCESS LEAD?

> When a child is being creative he is fluent, flexible, original, confident, and adventuresome. He can redefine situations, is willing to work at things for a long time, will work hard, and can produce many possible answers to a single question.
>
> MARY MAYESKY (1975, P. 4)

The creative process is like a stew in which knowledge and skill are the raw ingredients that are brought together by motivation and immersion. Incubation is the slow simmering of this rich mix, which produces the creative ideas and products. During the incubation stage, young artists are actively engaged in trying out ideas, asking themselves questions and self-evaluating their actions. Outwardly they may study the materials, or handle them playfully. They may experiment with an idea and then cover it over or take it apart. They may test the limits of the material, or the rules, or the teacher's patience. At other times they may sit quietly and stare off into space or concentrate intently on what they are creating. Inside they may be thinking such thoughts as, "What will happen if I do this?", "How will these things go together?", "Wow, I didn't expect that to happen!", "I never saw anything like this before."

FIGURE 7–6 "Lady Cat." Collage—Laurel, age 5

All this leads to production, when the ingredients in the stew blend together to form something new, a flavor that has never existed before. At this point the children have become their creations. For each child's knowledge, skills, and motivation are uniquely different from every other child who has ever existed. Children's artwork is an extension of all that they are at that moment.

HOW DO TEACHERS FOSTER THE CREATIVE PROCESS?

Creation begins with vision.

HENRI MATISSE (MOGELON, 1969)

Adults will always be outside the child's very personal creative process. However, the role they must play is crucially important. Because it is so easy for a child's creativity to be stifled, it is the teacher's task to establish an environment in which the creative process is nurtured.

First, children's personal needs must be met so they will be ready to create. Sick, tired, or hungry children will not be able to concentrate. If children are worried or nervous, they will be unlikely to take the kinds of risks that creativity requires. Second, teachers need to personally value curiosity, exploration, and original behavior. Allow children to go at their own pace, to figure things out for themselves, and encourage them to try new things. Refrain from making models, from using children's materials in an expert, adult way, and from requiring children to produce artwork that fits an adult idea of what it should look like. Listen to the children and pay attention to what they are thinking. Observe the process that children go through in dealing with problems and pay less attention to the product of this process.

Lastly, provide the children with many opportunities in which they can safely explore and pursue creative activities without interruption.

How to Help Children Be Creative Artists

Teachers nurture children's creativity when they:

1. Help them accept change
2. Meet their physical needs
3. Help them learn that some problems have many solutions
4. Help them accept their own feelings and those of others
5. Help them appreciate themselves and others for being different
6. Help them develop perseverance and the courage to take risks
7. Help them feel safe and relaxed while working
8. Help them enjoy the creative process

How to Choose a Creative Activity

When selecting activities for young children, consider how they will allow the child to be creative. All activities need limits, but always make sure that the limits imposed on the children will foster creativity, not confine it. Preventing a child from eating paste will not stop him from making a creative collage. Offering a set of simple, precut shapes that children can arrange any way they want allows them to create an original collage.

There are infinite of ways they can arrange those shapes on the base paper. But offering precut shapes that can only be made into a clown face does not allow children any freedom to try something new.

When choosing art activities for young children, ask these questions:

1. Can children explore on their own?
2. Can children go at their own pace?
3. Can children figure out their own ways to do things?
4. Are there many possible ways to do this activity?
5. Are the rules based on safety and management, not on the product desired?
6. Is it challenging?
7. Can children set their own goals?
8. Will it be fun—will they laugh, imagine, and play?

Remember that young children usually try to please the adults around them. They do not want to be yelled at or embarrassed. They will do their best to follow directions. It is certainly possible, with enough preparation and structure, to get a group of children to make paper-bag elephant puppets, cotton-ball rabbits, and folded paper reindeers with antlers made of hand tracings, or whatever the teachers have in mind. Such activities are found in far too many books and magazines, and paper the walls of many early childhood classrooms. Young children will work hard on such projects and are happy that they can please their teachers and parents. But producing pseudo-art projects that please adult eyes is precious creative time wasted.

SUMMARY: CREATIVITY IN TEACHING

> What I like about [Marc Chagall]… is that after listening closely to my lesson he takes his paints and brushes and does something absolutely different from what I have told him.
>
> LEON BAKST (GREENFELD, 1990, P. 27)

Creativity is different from the other areas of growth that teachers try to develop in our children. It is not something we can teach directly, but we must foster it through our attitude, behavior, and activity choices. The entire learning environment must be designed around the elements that nurture creative processing. Teachers need to provide opportunities for children to gain knowledge and skill via the exploration of art media. Children need time to immerse themselves in art creation, motivated by their boundless curiosity and the search for solutions. Creativity is not found just at the art table, but also in the block corner, the housekeeping corner, and on the playground.

It takes a creative person to fashion such an environment. It takes knowledge, skill, and a great deal of motivation to fully enhance creative behavior in children. Like the child, the teacher will say:

"What will happen if I do this?"
"How will these things go together?"
"Wow, I didn't expect that to happen!"
"I never saw anything like this before."

No two individuals approach this task in the same way. This book and experience will provide the knowledge and the skills; educators must provide their own motivation.

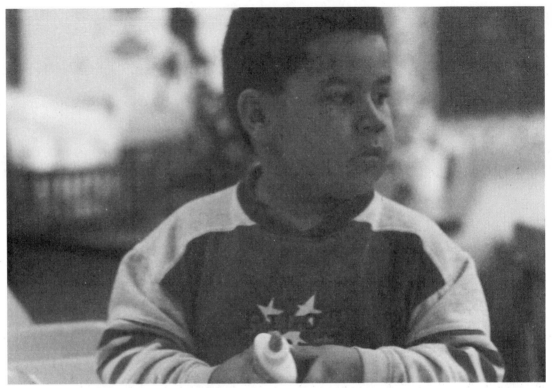

FIGURE 7–7 Children need time to immerse themselves in creative activities.

FURTHER READING

Teaching is a creative form itself.

LINDA CAROL EDWARDS (1990, p. 8)

Caine, R. N., and Cain, G. (1994). *Making connections: Teaching and the human brain*. New York: Addison-Wesley.
A brain-based approach to cognitive functioning, learning, creativity, and teaching methods that will help teachers design creative art programs.

Cameron, J. (1992). *The artist's way*. New York: Putnam's.
A step-by-step process of discovering and nurturing one's own creativity is presented in this book.

Edwards, B. (1986). *Drawing on the artist within*. New York: Simon & Schuster.
Personal creativity can be developed in many ways. Betsy Edwards uses art as a way to break out of habitual thinking patterns.

Goleman, D., Kaufman, P., and Ray, M. (1992). *The creative spirit*. New York: Dutton.
This inspiring book presents the thoughts of many people on the topic of creativity. It offers guidelines for developing personal creativity and includes examples of creative activities currently being used in business and education, including the Reggio Emilia preprimary program.

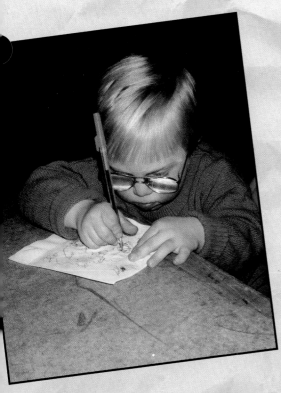

GROWING ARTISTS

What is the art of the young child?

"I'm making it go." MARKER—MATTHEW, AGE 2

IT IS A LINE MOVING ACROSS THE PAGE . . .

IT IS SHAPES FORMING INTO MEANING . . .

"I used all the colors."
TEMPERA PAINT—KIM, AGE 3

Kaitlin

"These are tall buildings. See how tall they are. They touch the top of the paper."
TEMPERA PAINT—KAITLIN, AGE 3½

IT IS TEXTURE, PATTERN AND COLOR

*"This is a great big bird.
He's going to sit on you!"*
TEMPERA PAINT—LAUREL, AGE 4

"It is spooky at night. You need big eyes. This is my cat." TEMPERA PAINT—JASON, AGE 4

IT IS CREATIVITY AT WORK . . .

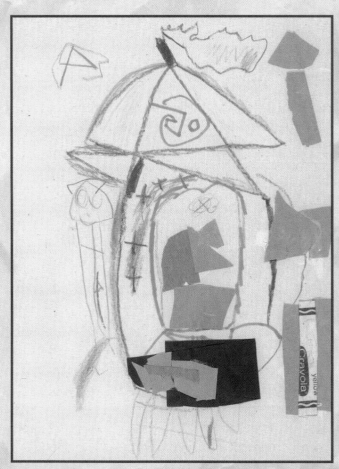

"This is a mixed-up house. I wouldn't like to live there. But the people are nice." COLLAGE AND CRAYON—LAUREL, AGE 4

IT IS DISCOVERING HOW TO COMMUNICATE FEELINGS AND EXPERIENCES . . .

"Here I am. I'm going to a party. That's why I'm smiling."
MARKER—LAURIE, AGE 4½

"This is an elephant. I saw one at the circus. They smell bad." TEMPERA PAINT AND CHALK—COURTNEY, AGE 5

"I mixed lots of colors and made different shapes all over, just like that artist did."
TEMPERA PAINT—MATTHEW, AGE 5

"Poppies."
TEMPERA PAINT—TOMMY, AGE .

IT IS BECOMING SKILLFUL AND SELF-CONFIDENT . . .

"It's a man in a hat. I had fun putting the chalk over the paint."
CHALK OVER PAINT—JAMIE, AGE 6

"I imagined him. It has dots and green horns." TEMPERA PAINT—NICOLE, AGE 6

IT IS LEARNING TO WORK WITH OTHERS, SHARING IDEAS AND JOY

"This is our purple monster. I drew long arms on Edgar so he could put the teeth on. We are all moving around working hard." CRAYON—DAVID, AGE 7

"The purple monster."
BOX SCULPTURE—EDGAR, AGE 6; DAVID, AGE 7;
ALISON, AGE 6; AND ERICA, AGE 7

Art Focus

COLLAGE EXPLORATIONS

> When the urge for creative aspirations starts to be felt, nobody knows what the result will be.
>
> SILVANO ARIETI (1976, P. 31)

Every art program for young children includes the art activity called collage. Children are offered various papers, magazine pictures, and small objects to glue onto their pictures. What is often not realized is that collage, from the French word for gluing, began as a radical reaction to the accepted fine arts of the time. In the early 1900s, artists such as Pablo Picasso and Georges Braque began adding cut-and-pasted scraps of various materials to their Cubist paintings. Their work in turn inspired the artists of the Dada movement of the 1920s. The Dadaists, such as Marcel Duchamp, created the first photomontages (art created from cutout magazine pictures and photographs), and art that featured glued-together objects from daily life.

The art philosophy of a good early childhood art program was shared by these originators of the collage: "The value of art was located more in the act of making it than in the work produced..." (Rubin, 1968, p. 15). In creating a new art form, these artists changed the nature of what was considered art, and provided a clear model of creativity at work.

Adults, when they are creating, are most like children. Picasso, Braque, and Duchamp *explored* the idea of adding real materials to their art. They were *motivated* to experiment with the different textures, colors, and shapes of the objects they found. They *immersed* themselves in their work as they investigated how their new idea worked in different themes and arrangements. They used their previously learned painting knowledge to "fool the eye" so that sometimes the real objects and the painted ones were difficult to distinguish. They became *skilled* in using their new techniques, and finally they *produced* many pieces of art in their new style. Like young children, these eminent artists played with art elements and materials.

Collage for Children

With this history, it is no wonder that collage has become one of the most popular art forms for young children. It is also one of the most creative. There is no limit to the ways young children can arrange their bits and pieces of collage materials. Adults do not expect children to produce "realistic-looking" collages and do not evaluate them in the same way as drawings. Teachers and parents are often more accepting of the exploration process and the resulting products in collage than they are in drawing or painting. Children are extraordinarily free of restraints as they become immersed in the creative process of making a collage.

Introducing Collage

The toddler has limited knowledge of paper and paste and its use to create art forms. Many

FIGURE 7–8 "I pasted shapes all over." Torn paper collage—Alex, age 3

preschoolers may also have had little opportunity to use paste and glue. As with drawing materials, introductory collage activities need to allow the child to explore the nature of the materials and to learn what can be done with them. In the beginning the child's focus will be on that wonderfully sticky, gooey paste.

The basics of collage consist of attaching paper or objects to a base using an adhesive of some kind. This action requires skill in hand-eye coordination. Children's first attempts at managing this complex coordination—putting the paste on their fingers, wiping it on the base, and picking up an item, and placing it in the glue—will often result in misplaced glue and papers, and require a great deal of patience on the teacher's part. It is important that children be allowed to develop their own independent skill in handling the paste, and teachers must be careful to provide enough supervision, carefully chosen supplies, and room for children to try out their own ideas.

How Children Grow through Collage Creation

Children will develop:

1. Physically, by using the large muscles of the arm to apply paste and tear paper, and by using the small muscles to use scissors and to pick up paper and objects and give them in a set place (Bodily-Kinesthetic)
2. Socially, by working alongside others, sharing materials, and learning to use scissors safely around others (Interpersonal)
3. Emotionally:
   - By learning to enjoy the act of collage making as a means of self-expression
   - By gaining self-confidence through being able to control a dangerous tool—scissors (Intrapersonal)
4. Cognitively:
   - By learning a vocabulary of size, shape, color, and placement and describing the artwork they make (Linguistic)
   - By observing that that paste and glue change over time, and that materials have different textures and can be sorted in different ways (Logical-Mathematical)
5. Visual perception skills (Spatial):
   - By manipulating a variety of textures and shapes and observing them from different points of view
   - By planning a shape and how to cut it out of a larger shape
   - By placing smaller shapes in different positions on larger shapes
6. Art awareness, by gaining familiarity with the way other artists have created collages.

Group composition. When first introducing pasting activities, limit the size of the group to one or two toddlers or four to six three- to eight-year-olds. Of all the art materials, paste and glue are the ones most commonly eaten by young children, probably because they closely resemble the texture of some foods. Until the children can be trusted not to put the paste in their mouths, provide constant supervision.

Setup.

Workspace. Provide a low table at which the children can comfortably stand or sit. The table-top should be bare and easy to wash up. If the table must be covered, use an old shower curtain or plastic tablecloth rather than newspaper, which can stick to the projects. A laminated sheet of construction paper also works well.

Because pasting with young children is a "messy" activity and one that can be confused with food, it is important to set up a place where pasting can be done away from food areas. This can be a special table that is near a water source. If working in a kitchen area, a large plastic tray or plastic tablecloth can be designated for pasting activities, and pasting can only be done when that surface is set up.

Cleanup. Have on hand an ample supply of damp paper towels so children can wipe sticky fingers before moving away from the work area.

Materials. For initial activities offer each child:
- A small amount of paste such as school paste or the homemade cornstarch paste described in Table 7–3.
- Use a small shallow container (such as a plastic lid from a margarine container) for each child. The small jars and applicator lids that paste is often sold in are too hard for toddlers and many preschoolers to use.
- Offer only about a tablespoon of paste at a time. It is easier to keep refilling the paste container than to clean up excess paste.

- Provide a base such as a sheet of manila or white drawing paper, about 12 inches by 18 inches in size, and a few simple, precut, construction-paper rectangles in two or three sizes and colors.

Transition in. With toddlers, sing a pasting chant to attract their interest. Older children may enjoy a story that features collage, such as *The Mixed Up Chameleon* (Carle, 1984), or *Imani in the Belly* (Chocolate, 1994).

🎵 MUSIC BOX

"PASTING"

(To the tune, "Mary Had a Little Lamb")

I am busy pasting, pasting, pasting.
(or gluing)
I am busy pasting,
Pasting all day long.

Watch me paste a triangle, triangle, triangle.
(Substitute other words for triangle - rectangle, yellow square, etc.)
Watch me paste a triangle,
On my paper now!

Now I wipe my fingers, fingers, fingers.
Now I wipe my fingers,
On my paper towel!

Now I wash my fingers, fingers, fingers.
Now I wash my fingers,

My collage is done!

What to do. Young children are fascinated by paste the first time they encounter it. It is so similar in texture to food and soap and yet it is used in such a different way. Their knowledge base may already include the "rule" that food is not smeared on paper.

It is the teacher's task to differentiate paste and its use from that of food. In the initial exploration, concentrate on the paste rather than the papers that will be glued. Later in the practice activities, help the children explore the textures, colors, and shapes of the collage items.

1. For the first collage exploration, show the children the paste. Let them smell it and feel it. Explain that it is not a food, but is used to stick paper together.
2. Demonstrate: Use fingers to place a small amount of paste on the base paper and attach a shape. Hold up the paper to show how the paper has adhered. Invite the child to use the paste to make a collage.
3. Until the children can be trusted not to eat the paste, an adult needs to sit close to the children. Be ready to gently stop them from putting their hands in their mouths. Repeat that paste is for sticking things together and not for eating. While the children work, smile and point to the different shapes and describe them.
4. Expect a wide variety of responses to the paste. Some children will be very hesitant to use it; others will quickly end up with both hands covered. Remember that toddlers will use the whole arm to move their paste-covered hands and as a result will not have much control over where the paste ends up.

It will be many years before most children can accomplish the complex task of applying paste to the back of a piece of paper, flipping it over, and then placing it in position on their paper. In the beginning years most children will put the paste directly on the base and then lay the shapes on top. Some children will become totally absorbed in spreading the paste on the paper and forget about adding shapes. Others will place shapes on top of shapes.

What to say. Use this activity to talk about the texture of the paste and the shapes and colors of the papers.

> "Does the paste feel smooth and sticky?"
> "You used a red square!"
> "You put the green shape next to the blue one."

Use a vocabulary that describes the materials the child is using. Words to use include: collage, paste, stick, stuck, attached, wet, gooey, sticky, smooth, cool, cold, damp, squares, rectangles, triangles, circles, and the color names.

As with drawing, make up songs and rhymes about the activity, and sing them while toddlers are working. Preschoolers can sing when they are done working and are busy cleaning up (invent a cleanup song), or they can sing and mime the collage activity during circle time.

Transition out. When the children tire of using the paste, help them wipe their hands on a pre-dampened paper towel and then go to the sink to wash off. This pre-wiping removes any excessive paste and also makes it quicker to wash off the remainder. As the children get more independent, the habit of pre-wiping will prevent items from sticking to their fingers instead of the paper. It will also help keep paste and glue from getting on their clothing and the furniture as they move to the sink. Knowing that they can quickly and easily get the paste off makes many children more comfortable investigating such sticky stuff, and it may also help discourage children's "automatic" wiping of their hands on their clothing.

Place the finished collages in an out-of-the-way place to dry. Chapter 5 outlines plans for a drying box that is very convenient for collages as well as prints and paintings. Paste does not hold very securely so handle the dried collages with care.

Extending the learning. The more opportunities the children have to use the paste, the more control they will develop. Vary the activity by offering different shapes made from different textures

of paper. Young artists can also tear or cut their own shapes. (See the followig section on tearing and cutting that follows.) Offer paste with different consistencies and textures. (See table 7–3: Adhesives for Collages.)

SPECIAL NEEDS

Other Ways to Paste

Some of the youngest children who have undeveloped small muscle control, or children with special needs, may have difficulty handling paste.

Another way to make collages is to use a piece of cardboard as a spreader to coat a base paper with thinned white glue. The children can then arrange their shapes by placing them on the sticky paper.

A different method is to remove the backing from contact paper and staple it sticky side up, to a heavy piece of construction paper. Both paper and small objects can then be placed on the sticky surface.

Collage Practice Activities: Skill Building

Every collage experience can be new and different. It is easy to vary the materials that are offered so the children's motivation to explore and practice will remain high. Children will steadily develop more control over the paste and glue if they are given many opportunities to make collages. The challenge of applying paste to objects of different textures and forms will help develop their hand-eye coordination.

Add other glues. When children can control paste, start adding white or gel glue to the collage experience. These glues will enable children to use heavier and irregularly shaped objects in their collages.

- Distribute glue in a plastic lid or a small, low-sided plastic container.
- Children can use their fingers or craft sticks to spread the glue. There are also plastic spreaders on the market.

FIGURE 7–9 Learning to wipe fingers after pasting is an important skill for collage making.

- Children who have developed hand strength can use bottled glue. The four-ounce size works well. Glue can be bought by the gallon to refill the smaller bottles.
- Do not use paintbrushes for glues. The glue stiffens up the brush making it unusable for painting; more, important, it confuses the children. If they see a brush being used in the glue, they think all brushes can be used in glue, which can lead to the ruin of many good paintbrushes.

Introduce new materials. In the beginning offer only limited types of materials at a time. Slowly, as the children grow in skill, introduce materials that are more difficult to paste or glue. Once they can paste down stiff materials, such as construction paper, oaktag, posterboard, and cardboard, offer some pieces of lighter paper such as the following.

Magazine clippings	Newsprint
Newspaper	White tissue
Paper doilies	

Irregular objects, like leaves, yarn, and string, can be added once the child can position these items fairly accurately in the paste or glue. Remember that young children often put a large quantity of paste and materials on a single collage. If the glued items will end up being somewhat heavy, provide a stiff base such as cereal-box-type cardboard, chipboard, or corrugated cardboard. If a base proves too light, it is easy to slip a piece of cardboard under the child's finished collage and staple it to provide support.

Magazine clippings. Initial selections should focus on color, texture, or pattern, rather than objects. They should be cut into simple shapes. Be prepared for the children to paste them down with either side facing up. Because the paper is lighter, some children may have more difficulty picking the pieces up especially if they are lying flat on a table top. Place the pieces in a flat, low-sided basket to make them easier for the children to manipulate them.

Theme collages. Young children can be offered simple pictures on a theme. Before they begin collage making, however, take time to introduce the pictures. Play simple guessing games or identifying games with them, such as, "Can you find a yellow flower?" or "Put your finger on the blue car." It helps if the pictures relate to the children's interests. For example, if at the moment they are very involved in car play, pictures of cars would be a good choice for a theme. Once the children are successful at identification, invite them to use the theme-related pictures in a collage.

Regardless of how competent the children are at identifying the pictures, expect some to be placed on "upside down" or "backwards." It is an advanced skill for a child to turn a picture over and put paste on the "back." Limiting picture selection to a theme is also a very difficult concept, requiring sophisticated sorting skills that should not be expected in children under four.

Textured paper. Keep the children interested in making simple collages by offering shapes cut from a variety of papers. Look for papers that are brightly colored or with interesting patterns. Unusual papers are often found in packaging or in advertising brochures. For young children just learning how to paste, select stiffer papers. Corrugated paper, oaktag, and cardboard all work

---

TABLE 7–1 Suggested Collage Papers

Advertising brochures	Art boards
Binders' board	Blotter paper
Candy wrappers	Cardstock
Cereal-box cardboard	Charcoal paper
Chipboard	Coffee filters
Computer paper	Construction paper
Corrugated cardboard	Corrugated paper
Doilies	Drawing paper
Fluorescent paper	Foil paper
Fadeless construction paper	Gift wrap
Graph paper	Holographic foils
Kraft pages	Magazine pages
Manila	Marble paper
Mat board	Metallic paper
Napkins	Newspaper
Newsprint	Oaktag
Paper placemats	Paper plates
Paper towels	Photographs
Poster board	Rainbow construction paper
Rice paper	Sandpaper
Shelf paper	Tag board
Tracing paper	Typing paper
Velour paper	Wallpaper
Watercolor paper	Waxed paper
White tissue paper	

Safety Note: Crepe paper and colored tissue paper are not recommended. When wet, the color bleeds out of them and may stain skin and surfaces.

Table 7–2 Suggested Collage Objects

(White glue is recommended for most of these items.)

From Nature: acorns, feathers, flowers, leaves, pebbles, sand (under special conditions), seashells, seeds, stones, twigs, walnut shells

From Home: aluminum foil, bottle caps, cardboard, carpet pieces, cork pieces, cotton, cotton balls, dried beans,* jar lids, macaroni, nails and screws, tubes from paper toweling or toilet paper (cut into short one-half-inch to one-inch slices), rice,* string, styrofoam packing beads

From Crafts: beads, buttons, cotton and polyester batting, craft sticks, fabric, foam pieces, fun fur, gift wrap bows, jewelry pieces, leather scraps, paper confetti, pompons, ribbon, rickrack, sponge pieces, spools, stuffing (polyester), tiles, wood scraps, wood shavings, wooden ice cream spoons (also called craft spoons), wool fleece, yarn

Safety Notes:

Not all objects on this list are safe for children under three. Use the choke test to be sure.

Glitter and metallic confetti are not recommended for young children. These items stick to children's hands and can get rubbed into the eyes.

Lick-and-stick papers should also be avoided. They give the children the impression that it is all right to put art materials in the mouth.

TABLE 7-3 Collage Adhesives

Recommended Commercial Adhesives:

School Paste (also called White Paste)

Advantages: This is the traditional thick, white paste of early childhood. It is inexpensive, safe, and has a pleasant scent. It is available in pint, quart, and gallon sizes as well as small individual jars with a plastic applicator top. It does not stain clothing and is easily cleaned up with water. It provides "instant" adhesion for most papers and dries quickly.

Disadvantages: This type of paste does not provide strong adhesion and is not suitable for heavier objects. When applied heavily, as is commonly done by little children, this paste wrinkles the paper, and becomes crumbly when dry. The small jars and applicators are difficult for the younger children to handle. They do better when they can use their fingers.

White Glue (also called School Glue)

Advantages: This is a strong, durable adhesive that can be used to glue all kinds of objects. Choose only the type that indicates it washes out of clothing. White glue can be thinned with water and spread on a base to provide a pre-glued surface for collage. It will stay wet five to ten minutes. It easily cleans up with water and it is available in a wide variety of sizes and of bottle designs. It dries clear.

Disadvantages: The runny consistency makes this glue more difficult for young children to control. When applied heavily, it wrinkles the paper. Its major disadvantage is that it dries very slowly. Projects must be dried flat for at least 30 minutes before they can be handled. (Tacky or craft versions of this glue can be used in specific situations when instant adhesion is required, but it does not wash out of clothing.)

Gel Glue

Advantages: This glue is transparent and may be lightly colored. It dries clear, leaving a shiny mark on the paper. It is strong enough to hold a variety of lightweight and medium weight objects. It cleans up with water and does not stain clothing.

Disadvantages: This glue is runnier than white glue and is hard for the children to control. When gluing fabric, for example, the glue quickly comes right through and wets the fingers. It is available in bottles similar to that of the white glue as well as in roller and tube forms. It dries slowly and wrinkles the paper.

Other Adhesives

There are many other pastes and glues on the market. Many of them are not safe for young children (see chapter 6). Others are difficult for the children to handle such as the mucilage, cellulose, and wheat pastes which are very sticky or runny. Glue sticks, pens, and rollers are much more expensive (often three times the cost of white glue!) and work best with children who are skilled in handling drawing tools. See Appendix A for recipes for homemade pastes.

Tape

Avoid the use of masking tape and transparent tape. Even though tape is easy to use, it is neither a permanent nor an artistic way to hold art materials together. Unfortunately, once children become accustomed to using tape they do not want to use the messier and more challenging paste and glue.

---

well for beginning independent pasting. Textured paper can be offered mixed with construction paper or on its own. Make up an attractive basket of papers that relate to each other in some way, either by shape, color, or pattern. For example, offer squares of yellow construction paper, with a yellow-patterned wallpaper and a gold metallic gift wrap.

Occasionally offer a textured paper, such as a paper placemat, as a base for the collage. If the paper is flimsy, such as gift wrap, glue it to a piece of construction paper or thin cardboard first.

Cloth and yarns. Textiles make interesting additions to collages. Most young children cannot cut such materials so precut them into simple shapes. In addition to fabric, offer ribbon pieces, rickrack, lace, thick yarns, and strings. Cut all these linear items into short lengths, no longer than six inches, to make them easier for young children to handle.

Simple paste will not hold these items very securely. If the children are experienced with paste, this may be the time to introduce white glue with these new materials. White glue is much messier for children to handle than paste because it is runnier. Always choose the washable type. Put a very small amount of white glue on the plastic lid just as was done with the paste. Demonstrate how to dab the glue with fingers.

Assorted objects. Many three-dimensional items can be added to collages once white glue has been introduced and handled successfully. Items for children under the age of three must pass the choke test. Be on the lookout for collage materials both inside and out-of-doors. (Table 7–2 provides some ideas to get started.)

Connections. LITERATURE: Read books that are illustrated with collages such as: *My House* (Des-imini, 1994), *Where the Forest Meets the Sea* (Baker, 1987), *Windows* (Baker, 1991), and *Mole's Hill* (Ehlert, 1994). *Lucy's Picture* (Moon, 1994) describes how a little girl chooses to make a collage instead of a painting by collecting objects in her school yard. Have the children identify the different materials used by the artists in their collages. (See Appendix B for more books illustrated with collage.)

ART AWARENESS: Share the work of Picasso's Cubist period, in which he used collage, such as *Three Musicians*. Children like to hunt for the different materials, such as pieces of newspapers that he used in his pictures.

Developing Cutting and Tearing Skills

Once children are able to skillfully paste and glue precut papers, begin to introduce tearing and cutting skills to the collage-making process. Tearing paper is appropriate for toddlers who do not yet have the fine motor control needed to use scissors. Cutting with scissors is more appropriate for children who have developed control over their fingers. However, all children enjoy the physical sensation of tearing paper and opportunities for torn-paper activities should also be planned for them.

How Children Grow through Cutting and Tearing

Children will develop:

1. Physically, by learning to move the arms, hands, and fingers in opposition while tearing paper and/or using scissors (Bodily-Kinesthetic)

TEACHER TO PARENT

Collage supplies can be contributed by families. Send a letter home (like the one below) or post a sign in a place where parents congregate. Change the list of items to match what is needed. Have clearly labeled containers ready so children can practice sorting when they bring in supplies.

Dear Family,
One of the children's favorite art activities is making collages. Could you please check around your home and see if you have any of the following materials that we can use in making collages?

> Bottle caps
> Buttons
> Cloth scraps
> Ribbon
> Spools
> Styrofoam packing beads (any shape)
> Wood shavings
> Wrapping paper
> Yarn

All contributions are greatly appreciated!

Your child's teacher,

2. Socially, by participating with a group in tearing and cutting paper and learning to enjoy working with others (Interpersonal).
3. Emotionally, by obtaining satisfaction from successfully tearing and cutting the paper (Intrapersonal)
4. Cognitively:
   - By learning a vocabulary to describe the different actions and by practicing shape names (Linguistic)
   - By learning that dividing up a whole creates parts, and that the parts are smaller than the whole and by counting shapes (Logical-Mathematical)
5. Visual perception skills, by visualizing characteristics of a shape before and after tearing it out (Spatial)

FIGURE 7–10 Using scissors is a complex skill.

6. Art awareness, by learning that torn- and cut-paper collages have been used to illustrate books

Torn-Paper Collage

Introduce young children to torn paper collage by starting with a group tearing activity.

Group composition. This is a fun activity to do with a small group of two to four toddlers or a larger group of older children.

Setup. Gather the group of children around a box. Toddlers can sit on the floor. Older children can also work at a low table without chairs. Choose an area that is out of the traffic flow and will be easy to sweep up when done.

Materials. Provide a large sheet of newsprint or newspaper for each child. Have extra sheets available. Set up a collage table or collage area with paste and a base paper for each child. Brightly colored construction paper makes a good contrast to the plain newsprint or newspaper. Have damp paper towels conveniently placed. (Note: this exploration can also be used as a transition into papier-mâché—see chapter 4.)

Transition in. Invite the children to help solve a problem. "Let's use this old paper for our collages. How can we tear it into smaller pieces so we can use it?"

What to do.

1. Give each child a paper. Those who know how to tear will start right in. Some toddlers may need help getting a tear started.

2. Demonstrate: If necessary, gently hold their hands and show them how to pull one hand toward them and push the other away. If children have been scolded for tearing a book or paper before, they may be hesitant to work. Encourage these children by saying, "This is old paper we can use for collages. It is okay to tear it up. Always make sure, before you tear something, that no one else needs it."

3. Actively join in the tearing process with the children. Sit or stand with them around the box and model for them how to tear pieces and put them in the box.

4. If a piece of paper drops on the floor, model how to pick it up and put it in the box. Explain that paper scraps on the floor are dangerous because someone could slip on them. If some children tear up their papers more quickly than the rest give them extra papers to work on.

What to say. Once the children begin tearing, describe the size and shape of the pieces they have created. "That piece is long and skinny." "This one is a little triangle." Vocabulary includes: tear, torn, jagged, long, short, narrow, wide, and all the shape names.

Transition out. When most of the children have completed tearing their papers, start asking them about the shapes in the box.

> "Can you find two shapes about the same size?"
> "How many rectangles are there?"
> "Is there any unusual shape?"
> "What animal does this shape look like?"

After everyone is finished, take the box to the collage table and invite them to use these interesting shapes to make a collage.

Extending the learning. Provide paper for tearing and a "collection" box on a regular basis. Sometimes children will want to tear without making a collage immediately afterward. Torn paper in the collection box can be added to the regular collage materials. Some of the pieces can be used to decorate the collection box.

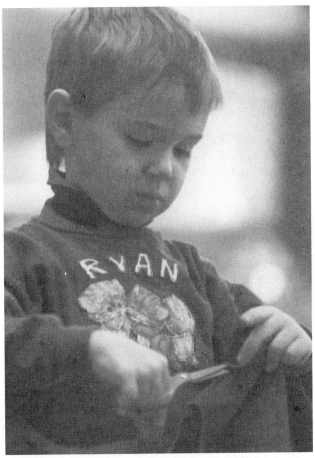

FIGURE 7–11 Cutting requires serious concentration.

Tearing Practice Activities

Once the children know how to tear, start offering different kinds of paper to tear. Newspaper, magazine pages, construction paper, wallpaper, and kraft paper all tear in different ways. Children enjoy making paper confetti and sprinkling it on a paste- or glue-covered base. To help them make small pieces, give them pre-cut strips of paper to tear.

Connections. Read books illustrated with torn-paper collages, such as *My First Animals* (Paterson, 1990) or *little blue and little yellow* (Lionni, 1959).

Activities Using Scissors

Young children are not ready to use scissors until they have control over their wrists and fingers. Children who are not physically able to use scissors find trying to cut extremely frustrating. Within a normal group of young children there may be children who may not yet be ready to cut,

some who may be just beginning to develop sufficient control, and some who are expert cutters. It is important to design open-ended activities in which cutting always remains an option. Collage activities provide a wonderful way to slowly introduce cutting skill practice.

Introducing Scissors

When a number of the children seem ready to manipulate scissors, introduce them as a tool that will be available for their use. Show the children where the scissors will be permanently stored. Scissors can be hung on a peg board with other tools, stored in a storage rack, or in an attractively decorated can or box. Explain that scissors can be used for cutting paper and collage materials. Set up clear safety rules for using the scissors, including: keeping them in a designated area, moving safely with them, and cutting only collage materials with them.

Demonstrate how to handle the scissors safely by always holding them with the hand clasped around the closed blade. Have the children practice handing plastic or model scissors around a circle with the blade closed and tipping the handle toward the next child. The child receiving the scissors should also grasp them by the closed blades. Make up a scissors rhyme such as "The Scissors Passing Song," and sing or chant it while they practice. Once the children are familiar with the location of scissors and the safety rules, begin an introductory cut paper collage exploration.

 ## MUSIC BOX

"The Scissors Passing Song"
(to the tune of "My Bonnie Lies Over the Ocean")

Scissors are made for cutting,
And handle them safely I must!
When passing the scissors to others,
I must always be holding them shut!

Group composition. Depending on the skill level of the particular children, they can work in groups of four to six. Choose a smaller group size if most of the children are just beginning to cut and a larger one if most of the children are competent with scissors.

Setup. The cutting area can be a low table with or without chairs. The surface should be bare. Have a wastebasket, paper recycling bin, and/or paper scrap box nearby; along with a dustpan and broom for quick cleanups.

Materials. Choose one of the kinds of scissors listed in Table 7–4. Provide construction paper cut into rectangular strips about 1-by-12-inches. Regular construction is the easiest for children to

---

TABLE 7–4 Cutting Tools

Scissors

Select scissors that are lightweight and move easily at the pivot. They should be sharp enough to cut paper with very light pressure. They should have a blunt tip. Scissors should be designed for use in either the left or right hand.

All-plastic scissors are best for toddlers and younger preschoolers. These scissors will not cut hair, skin, or fabric. Older children can use pairs with lightweight stainless steel blades with plastic handles. They can also use the new children's scissors that make decorative cuts.

Training Scissors

For toddlers or children with impaired finger dexterity, select training scissors that have blunt tips and spring-apart, plastic-coated handles.

Double-Ring Training Scissors

These scissors have a pair of outer rings so that as the child holds the scissors, you can guide the actual cutting. They are most useful for children who have the dexterity and strength, but do not turn the wrist enough to hold the scissors vertical to the paper. This problem is usually manifested when the child tries to cut, but instead the paper folds. Usually they only need to use them once or twice. If there continues to be a problem, have the child try the training scissors.

Rotary Hand Cutter

This cutting tool is very sharp and must be used with close supervision, however it may be the only way some children can cut. Make sure the blade is covered and the handle easy to grasp. Look for ones with an automatically closing cover. It must be used with a cutting mat underneath at all times.

Teacher's Scissors

Adults are always cutting many unusual items for collages. Invest in the best quality all-purpose snips to be found. These usually have stainless steel blades, spring-apart blades, and a lock mechanism, which makes them safer to have around young children. They should be able to cut through heavy cardboard, all fabrics, carpet, leather, branches, pipe cleaners, wire, and more!

---

learn to cut. Lighter papers, such as newsprint, are more difficult because they bend easily, and heavier papers, such as tag board, require more hand strength. Individual allotments of paste and base paper (such as manila or white, about 12-by-18-inches) should be set out on the table. Have damp paper towels readily available.

Transition in. The children should have had some experiences with paste and tearing paper before they are offered scissors. They should be familiar with the collage process and how the materials are set up for their use. When they are comfortable making collages on their own, introduce the scissors.

The book *Let's Make Rabbits* (Lionni, 1982) is a good introduction to the idea of cutting paper for artwork. Talk about how drawing is different from collage, but both are ways to create art. Leo Lionni uses collage for many of his illustrations. Display several of his books and challenge the children to find the different kinds of paper he used. Other books that feature torn- and cut-paper illustrations are *The Grouchy Ladybug* (Carle, 1977) and *The Snowy Day* (Keats, 1962).

What to do. Once scissors are introduced, the children will naturally be motivated to try out this new tool. There is a fascination with the cutting process as the children derive a real sense of power from being allowed to handle a (somewhat) dangerous tool.

1. When helping children learn how to hold scissors, it is useful to understand the position of the hand when cutting. Take a scissors and open and close it as if to cut something. Notice that just to use the scissors requires a turn of the wrist. The fingers move in opposition to the thumb. Try cutting a piece of paper. The hand muscles tighten to hold the scissors steady. Children may need assistance in positioning the scissors. If necessary, gently guide their hands into the proper position.

2. Initially most young children will cut with just the tip of the scissors, which is why narrow strips are offered at the start. When the children are more competent, offer other shapes for them to cut up. At this stage most children will be able to cut short straight cuts. Curves and being able to follow drawn lines are advanced skills that many children will just be

approaching by the end of their fourth year. They will also not yet be competent at coordinating both holding and turning the paper, which is necessary to cut out shapes. Do not plan activities that require children to cut out teacher-specified or predrawn shapes. If, on occasion, the children choose to cut out something they have drawn on their own, that will serve as a more creative way to learn these more advanced skills.

3. It is important to closely supervise the initial cutting activities of each child. Because the children will be at various stages, they will need different kinds of help.

   - HESITANT: If children have been forbidden to use scissors in the home, they may be hesitant to begin at first. Give them gentle encouragement to try the scissors.
   - DIFFICULTY HOLDING SCISSORS: Watch for children who are having difficulty holding the scissors vertically to the paper. Check that they are using the thumb and index finger to hold the scissors. If they are, gently guide their scissors into the correct position. It may help to hold the paper for them to practice the first few snips. There are also trainer scissors that can be used to give them a start. Sometimes the scissors are too heavy for the child's hand. In this case the scissors will tip or wobble unsteadily, and the child will not be able to cut paper. Light plastic scissors should be made available to the children.
   - HAND POSITION: Some children may need help positioning the hand that is holding the paper. Make sure that they learn to keep their fingers out of the path of the scissors.
   - PAPER BENDS: One of the most frustrating things for a young child is when the paper bends instead of being cut. This often indicates that they are not exerting enough pressure as they close the scissors. If they keep trying to cut in the same spot, they will never succeed. Suggest that they try cutting in another place or use a different piece. Check that the child is holding the scissors in the correct position as poor hand position often causes the paper to bend.

4. Demonstrate for the more advanced cutters how to make simple shapes by cutting off the corners of a piece of paper using a straight cut, and how to make a "fringe" effect by making a row of straight cuts along one side of a paper.
5. As they gain hand strength, encourage them to open the scissors wider with each cut so that they can cut a longer snip with each hand motion.
6. Make sure to give general reminders to everyone that they can tear paper as well, so that children who have not yet mastered cutting understand that tearing is also appropriate.
7. Most children will be so involved in cutting the first few times that they will put little time into the actual collage. Once they become confident in their cutting skills, they will go on to create their collages again.
8. Although this sounds like constant interaction with the children, actually this assistance only takes a brief moment or two. Move from child to child giving help as needed. There will be plenty of time to step back and observe the children working. Make sure the children are given time to explore and learn on their own. Step in to help only when the child asks for help or is obviously frustrated.

What to say. When children need help, quietly show them how to do it while saying, "It might be smoother if you did this," or "Let's drive your scissors this way."

Vocabulary to use with cutting activities includes: cut, snip, divide, side, edge, pieces, change, larger, smaller, jagged, sharp, straight, half, and all the shape names.

Transition out. When children are done cutting and pasting their pieces down on the base paper, they should clean up the leftover paper clippings. Remind the children to wipe their fingers on a wet paper towel before they handle the scraps.

Introduce sorting the paper into good scraps that can be used again and sticky ones that have to be thrown away, but do not expect perfect sorting at this age. The scrap box that is created in this exploration can become a regular offering for collage activities. When the scraps are picked up, the children can rinse their hands at the sink.

Extending the learning. Continue to make the scissors and paper to cut available on a daily basis.

Cutting is a skill that only improves with practice. In addition to cutting shapes for their collages, children can also practice cutting in a variety of other activities such as puppet making, mask making, printing activities, and constructed sculptures.

Connections. LITERATURE: Read these books, illustrated with cut-paper collages: *At the Beach* (Lee, 1994), *The Lion's Whiskers* (Day, 1995), and *Sea Shapes* (MacDonald, 1994).

ART AWARENESS: Use the book *The Block* (Hughes, 1995) to introduce the collage art of African-American artist Romare Bearden.

SPECIAL NEEDS

Other Ways to Cut

Children who have difficulty using their fingers, hands, or wrists will find cutting with a traditional scissors difficult. Scissors that are squeezed together between thumb and all the opposing fingers, and that open automatically with a spring work well for some children. These are often called "snips." Try to select the lightest-weight pair with the bluntest point.

Another option is the use of a rotary cutter, similar to that used by quilters. Look for ones designed for use by children that have a protective cover over the blade. A cutting mat to protect the surface is needed. This mat should also provide a gripping surface to hold the paper still while the child cuts. This setup will allow a child who can only grip with a fist to become quite proficient at cutting. But since the blade is very sharp, provide watchful supervision.

Practice Cutting Activities

Once the children have become competent using the scissors to cut construction paper, offer different weights of paper for them to try. Drawing paper, manila, wallpaper, and kraft paper are in the same range as construction paper. The lighter papers, such as newsprint, tracing paper, and metallics, are a little more difficult.

The majority of children under six cannot cut papers as light as tissue paper, and they also have great difficulty with cardboard, fabric, and yarn. To cut these items the children need to open the scissors as wide as they go and the scissors need to be sharp. If these materials are available in the collage area, the children will try cutting them. If they seem frustrated, assure them that special scissors are needed to cut some materials.

Always have precut pieces available in a variety of sizes and shapes. If any children are having trouble cutting, help them find other pieces they can use.

FIGURE 7–12 "I cut these shapes and then I glued them. Some glue came out over here. The glue was gooey. Now it is hard as a rock." Torn and cut paper—Brian, age 4½

Studio Page *43*

CREATING AN ART NOTEBOOK

In order to create a wonderful art program for young children, you need to have knowledge and skill. No one, however, can carry everything about teaching art to young children around in his or her head. By creating your own original notebook on how to teach art to young children, you will create a personal knowledge base that will guide you in a way no commercial book can. At the same time, creating such a notebook will allow you to personally experience the same creative process that your young artists do, as you develop your own art skills.

Your notebook should contain the following parts:

1. **An attractive, durable cover:** You will probably be using this notebook for many years. You may want to share it with other teachers or parents. Make sure you have plenty of room for expansion, for it will never be done!

2. **A table of contents:** Before you begin, prepare a list of what you want to include in your notebook. As you put the book together, you will be able to see which areas you know a lot about and which you need to study more.

3. **A way of organizing the information:** Design some kind of divider that clearly marks off each section. The knowledge in your notebook is useless if you cannot find it readily.

4. Information from books and magazines on art for young children: Make a collection of ideas, research, and new techniques that relate to teaching art.

5. **Observation notes:** Any observations that you make about children should be saved in your notebook. Also record anecdotal accounts of your interactions with children and parents. These will form a comparative base from which to design plans and determine your future behavior.

6. **Unit plans and activity plans:** It takes a lot of time to write plans. Save all your plans as they will guide you in writing the plans for the next group.

7. **Recipes:** In this section make a collection of recipes that you have tried and that worked well for you.

8. **Sample projects:** If you try out any activities or materials, save the samples in this section. You can also include children's work. Make sure you label these samples—how, when, what—or they will be useless as a reference.

9. **Illustrations:** Words are fine, but pictures can often say more than words. Sketch, photograph, or clip illustrations for all sections from magazines and catalogs. Art supply catalogs are a good source of material.

10. **Bibliography:** Record the bibliographic information for any books or articles you have found helpful. You never know when you will need them again.

11. **Personal diary of experiences:** You will be creating this notebook for yourself. It will be only as useful as you make it. If you do not write down the great rhyme about gluing you just made up, or note how many minutes it took to wash the hands of 20 three-year-olds, you may lose that knowledge.

Studio Page 44

OBSERVING THE CREATIVE PROCESS IN YOURSELF

After you have worked on your notebook for several weeks, answer these questions.

1. What knowledge do you need to create this notebook?

   _____

   _____

   _____

2. What is motivating you to make this notebook?

   _____

   _____

   _____

3. What skills do you have that will help you create this notebook? What skills do you need to learn?

   _____

   _____

   _____

4. When do you find is the best time to work on this book? How do you feel if you are interrupted?

   _____

   _____

   _____

5. How do you feel when you figure out how you will include something in your book? Did you have fun designing a cover and making the illustrations? Did you include anything funny—cartoons or anecdotal stories? Did you include anything about which you care deeply?

   _____

   _____

   _____

6. How do you feel about your notebook? Would you like it to be graded or compared to someone else's? Why or why not?

   _____

   _____

   _____

Studio Page **45**

DEFINING CREATIVE BEHAVIOR

Just how broadly creativity is defined is critical to any program planning, for far too often creative ideas are ignored, or worse yet, actively squelched when well-meaning educators are only watching for a creative product that matches their aesthetic standards.

NANCY LEE CECIL AND PHYLLIS LAURITZEN (1995, P. 28)

Analyze each of the following behaviors in terms of whether or not you would consider it creative and what action you would take, if any, to change or control the behavior.

- A child eats a piece of play dough because "it looked like a banana."

_____

_____

_____

- A child glues his paper to the table because he "didn't want it to slide off the table."

_____

_____

_____

- A child runs around the room biting everyone with his paper "snake."

_____

_____

_____

- A child pours glue into a box of collage papers.

_____

_____

_____

- A child uses a scissors to cut the hair of another child.

_____

_____

_____

Studio Page

CHOOSING CREATIVE MATERIALS

1. For each material below, brainstorm many different ways that it could be used in art activities:

    - A piece of paper

    _____

    _____

    - A jar of purple paint

    _____

    _____

    - A magazine

    _____

    _____

    - A piece of cardboard

    _____

    _____

    - A paper fastener

    _____

    _____

    - A duck-shaped stencil

    _____

    _____

    - A booklet of blank pages

    _____

    _____

    - A crayon

    _____

    _____

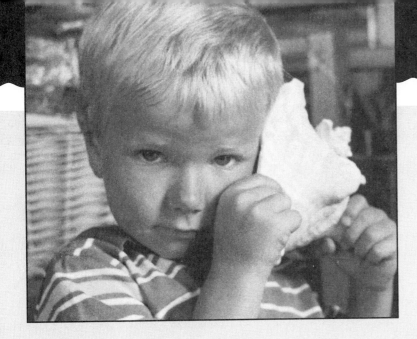

8

Anyone Can Walk on the Ceiling!

Aesthetic and Sensory Experiences for Young Children

> ❝ *It was the most imaginative, rich childhood you could ever want. That's why I have so much inside me that I want to paint.* ❞
>
> •
>
> ANDREW WYETH
> (MERRYMAN 1991, P. 21)

Questions addressed in this chapter:

What is beauty?

How does an aesthetic sense develop?

What are the elements of art?

How is sensory perception developed in young children?

What is the best way to present sensory experiences?

What is kinesthetics?

SUMMARY: The Sensitive Teacher

FURTHER READING

ART FOCUS: Printmaking

Young Artists at Work

"What a beautiful painting!" exclaims the preschool teacher, as she takes the dripping painting off the easel. Three-year-old Michelle smiles and runs off to the sand table, while the teacher carries Michelle's large sheet of newsprint covered with wiggly lines of lime green and black to the storage shelf. Soon Michelle's parents arrive to take her and her painting home. They too declare the painting beautiful and proudly hang it on the refrigerator door in the kitchen. When Michelle is eighteen and getting ready to study art in college, she finds her preschool painting. "Why did they save this old thing?" she chuckles.

WHAT IS BEAUTY?

Beauty is no quality in things themselves. It exists merely in the mind which contemplates them.

DAVID HUME ("OF THE STANDARD OF TASTE," 1757)

FIGURE 8–1 "My house." Tempera paint—Mercedes, age 4

Is this painting really beautiful? Why was it hung on the refrigerator instead of over the living room couch? Why does grown-up Michelle no longer think it is beautiful?

The Webster's College Dictionary defines beautiful as "delighting the senses or mind." When we judge something beautiful we are describing its effect on our sense of sight, touch, smell, taste and/or hearing—its aesthetic quality. But there are many factors that determine what impact a piece of art will have on our senses. No two people make identical judgments about art. People find beauty in different styles of painting or other art media because of their personal beliefs, knowledge, or experiences. The preschool teacher thinks Michelle's painting is beautiful because she knows that it represents an initial experiment with crossing wet lines of paint. Michelle's parents think it is beautiful because it was their beloved child who created this new visual image. However, they will not hang it over the sofa because the colors do not "go" with their beautiful living-room color scheme of rose and blue. Eighteen-year-old Michelle laughs because she thinks her current art is so much more mature and therefore, more beautiful than her childish beginnings.

HOW DOES AN AESTHETIC SENSE DEVELOP?

> Aesthetics refers to a person's ability to sense and gain beauty and wonder from his environment. It can be done with any or all of a person's five senses as well as his imagination.
>
> MARY MAYESKY (1975, P. 11)

Children are not born knowing what is beautiful. If that were true then every human being would have the same standards of beauty. However, children are born with a sense of wonder that makes them curious about their surroundings. As they explore with their senses they learn to identify pleasing experiences with beauty. At first children may discover what the important people around them think is beautiful. Parents, siblings, grandparents, and peers may express a personal view of beauty to the young child in statements such as, "Look at that beautiful sunset!", "Isn't that a gorgeous vase?", "There are wonderful designs on this sweater", and "Feel the beautiful quilt Grandma made you."

As children grow they are also influenced by the environment around them. The natural and human-made objects they encounter can provide pleasing or interesting sensory experiences that will shape their view of what is beautiful. Things that feel familiar, that are comforting or exciting become incorporated into an aesthetic belief about what is beautiful.

Many ideas about beauty are held in common with other people with whom the child shares a similar heritage. When a group of people hold the same ideas about the beauty of some object or experience, this represents a cultural aesthetic or style. Style can be based on shared lifestyle, history, or experience. Styles can be handed down from one generation to another, such as the Amish tradition of making quilts only from solid-colored fabrics. Style can also denote artwork that is based upon a common aesthetic belief, such as the style of Realism, in which artists try to represent real objects as they look on our retinas, or Surrealism, in which objects are shown as they look in our dreams and fantasies.

Although childhood experiences and cultural styles form the core of an individual's aesthetic philosophy, each person's definition of beauty is always changing. Some cultural styles change over time. Eighteenth-century European men felt beautifully dressed when wearing long, curled, and powdered wigs. Sometimes one group of people or an individual will copy or adapt a style from another group such as when non-Native Americans wear T-shirts decorated with traditional Native American symbols. Children are constantly bombarded with often conflicting ideas about beauty, from books and on TV, in movies and in commercials. These too are added to children's internal brew of aesthetic experiences and judgments. Taken together, all these diverse influences form a personal aesthetic philosophy which determines what they think is beautiful and what they like.

But liking a piece of art is not the same as understanding and valuing it. The word beautiful is not a simple adjective, but is also a word of judgment. Not all art is beautiful. Some art assails the senses with distorted or unpleasant images, or strong emotional statements, which makes it difficult to separate how we personally feel about a piece of art from its aesthetic value. Sometimes it is hard to separate our feelings about an artwork from its value as a creative statement by an artist. We may not like every piece of artwork done by every child with whom we work. But we can appreciate, and we can help children appreciate, the aesthetic elements in that piece of art by developing their sensitivity to the elements of art around them.

Guiding adults need to be aware of how they influence children's perception of beauty and the development of their aesthetic philosophy and judgment. This impact can be felt in two ways. One way that adults can affect young children's aesthetic perceptions is by creating a pleasing environment with carefully selected, beautiful objects. The other way is to expand children's definition of beauty by pointing out the aesthetic and sensory qualities in their art and environment, and by providing experiences that foster sensory awareness. The goal should be to help children grow into adults who love beautiful things, who value all kinds of art, and who can still find wonder in the beauty of the world.

WHAT ARE THE ELEMENTS OF ART?

> The moment we interact with our environment... our biologically growing brain also builds new connections based on what we experience.
>
> RENATE NUMMELA CAINE AND GEOFFREY CAINE (1994, P. 32)

When looking at a beautiful piece of artwork or a wonderful part of nature, we are overwhelmed by the total effect. But to recreate this experience for someone who has not seen it, we must describe it in terms of the artistic ingredients of which it is composed. These ingredients, or *elements* of art, are the building blocks of the artist. Line, shape, color, pattern, form, and space are found to varying degrees in almost every piece of art and throughout nature. When we react to something aesthetically, the senses are being affected by the way these elements have been brought together at that moment in time.

The creation of art is the process of playing creatively with these elements and arranging them in an aesthetically meaningful way. This is what young children are doing when they explore art media. However, they also need to learn how to identify and describe these elements so that they can talk about, understand, and make aesthetic judgments about artistic works.

The following descriptions of the art elements will increase the educator's ability to describe children's artwork and talk about natural forms. Each element is followed by suggestions for activities that help children focus on these elements in art and their environment.

FIGURE 8–2 "I made circles and diamonds." Object print—Shane, age 4

Line

A line is a mark made by a tool moving across a surface. It can be curved or straight, zigzag or wiggly. Lines can be thick or thin, long or short, and are used by artists to make shapes and symbols and by writers to form letters, words, and numbers. Lines can show direction—horizontal, vertical, or diagonal. Lines are present in artwork of all media, and in the environment. Lines are the mainstay of children's earliest drawings and will continue to remain an important element in all their art.

Playing with lines. Have fun with the children looking for different kinds of lines. Find straight lines between the tiles on the floor, curved lines hanging from the electric poles, and zigzag lines in the cracks of a frozen puddle.

Have the children line up one behind the other and make a line that moves, wiggles, and sways as they walk in an open space or around furnishings.

Connections. LITERATURE: Read some of the many children's books that feature lines, such as *You're a Genius BLACKBOARD BEAR* (Alexander, 1995), then put out blank booklets for the children to draw their own "line" stories.

MATH/SCIENCE: Compare the length of different lines in the children's artwork or line examples from nature: Lay pieces of yarn along a drawn or painted lines and cut to length. Use them to make a graph. Tape all the yarn pieces on a sheet of paper; label with the source.

Color

The world is full of color. The white light from the sun is made up of a spectrum of colors. As light bounces off different objects, some of the color rays are absorbed and others are reflected into the eyes. When there is no light, then there is no color. Young children love the bright colors red, yellow, and blue. When given a choice they will often choose the brighter color paint or paper, but they also like strong, saturated colors such as deep purple, vivid pink, rich turquoise, and black. Make sure they always have access to media in a wide range of colors.

Playing with color. Take time every day to notice the colors in the environment. Comment on the color clothing children are wearing, the color of the grass, leaves, and sky. Use descriptive or comparative words to identify a color, for example, "Your sweater is as green as the leaves on our tree," and "Today the sky reminds me of the color of a robin's egg."

Children love to mix colors together. Finger painting with two or three colors is a very tactile way to combine colors, as is mixing several colors of play dough together. Colors also get mixed intentionally or unintentionally when painting and printing. Mixing new colors gives the child a sense of power. It is wonderful to be able to make such a noticeable change in the characteristics of an object in this simple way. Never discipline or show frustration with a child who is exploring what happens when colors come together.

Not everyone sees colors in exactly the same way. Children who are color-blind need to be identified so that they do not feel uncomfortable during color activities and games. Art materials can be scented to help children who have visual difficulties. To

SPECIAL NEEDS

Color Blindness

Children who are color-blind often have difficulty with color-related activities. These children quickly learn to try and hide their color discrimination difficulties, especially if they are laughed at by other children when using a color the wrong way, such as drawing a purple tree. Often adults mistakenly think the child does not know the colors yet and try to force the child to learn them. It is important to identify these children as early as possible.

Once identified, help these children by using scented crayons and markers, and adding scents to paints. It also helps to always have the colors in the same order at the easel and to line up the markers and crayons in the same color order. When doing color games and activities, have these children work with the colors they can identify.

help children understand that colors can appear differently, tape yellow cellophane over a hole cut in an index card. Looking through this window will make all the colors look a little bit different.

Connections. LITERATURE: There is an incredible number of books about color for young children. One book that is a must is an old classic, *Hailstones and Halibut Bones* (O'Neill, 1961). This book of poems, each about a different color, provides perfect transitions into color activities. For the very young, read the book *White Rabbit's Color Book*, (Baker, 1994) which depicts a beautifully drawn rabbit playing in paint and discovering new colors. At the end of the book the rabbit covers himself with all the colors and turns into a beautiful brown rabbit. It is a charming way to teach color mixing and help children appreciate the color brown. Use the book to transition into color-mixing activities.

MATH/SCIENCE: Provide premeasured amounts of different colors of paint, let the children mix them together, and then compare the results. For example, measure out a quarter cup of white to mix with a teaspoon of red, and vice versa. Make a labeled chart of the resulting colors and then use them to paint with at the easel.

MUSIC: With the children, make up songs about the different colors using a familiar tune (see Music Box).

MUSIC BOX

"Colors"

(To the tune, "A Hunting We Will Go.")

Red is the color
Red is the color
Red is the color of Michael's shirt.*

*(*Substitute any name and item)*

Texture

Texture is the way something feels when it is touched. Surfaces can be hard or soft, rough or smooth, bumpy or jagged. Texture is found in all artwork and is an especially important element in collage and modeling activities.

Playing with texture. Invite the children to compare the textures of different items in the classroom or in the collage offerings. Ask, "Is it soft or rough?", and "Which is stickier: the paste or the glue?" Use words that describe textures as the children play. There are many more texture activities in the touch and kinesthetic sections that follow.

Connections. LITERATURE: Toddlers will enjoy any of the books available that contain actual textures to touch. In *The Petting Zoo* (Hanna, 1992), animals are covered with pieces of cloth that approximate how the animals actually feel. Children love identifying the different textures in the collages that illustrate *Smoky Night* (Bunting, 1994) and *Snowballs* (Ehlert, 1995).

MATH/SCIENCE: Invite younger children to sort pieces of material with different textures. Glue them on a chart or make them into a class book. Older children can find magazine pictures of things that have different textures, such as clippings of a dog (furry), a pillow (soft), and then make a similar chart or book.

MUSIC: See Music box for an example of a texture-play song.

MUSIC BOX

"Touch-It Song"

(Sung to the tune of "Go in and out the windows")

Let's go find something soft.*
Let's go find something soft.
Let's go find something soft.
Something soft to touch.

*(*Substitute any texture word)*

While the children sing, one child may find and touch something with that texture before the song ends.

Shape

Everything has a shape. A two-dimensional shape has height and width and may be geometric, organic, symbolic, or free-form.

- Geometric shapes follow mathematical principles, such as squares, rectangles, circles, and triangles.
- Organic shapes come from nature, as in the shape of a leaf or butterfly.
- Symbolic shapes have a special meaning, such as that of letters or numbers.
- Free-form shapes are invented shapes that follow no rules.

Each of the four categories of shapes may contain some shapes that are symmetrical. These are shapes that if a straight line is drawn through the center, will be exactly the same on both sides. Squares, butterflies, the letter "A," and hearts are all symmetrical shapes. All of these shapes will be found in children's artwork and the classroom environment.

Playing with shapes. Play games with the children that involve finding shapes. Talk about the qualities of these shapes. Are they big or small, short or tall, colored or textured? There are hundreds of art activities that use shapes. Many will be described throughout this book.

Connections. LITERATURE: Almost any children's book can be used for a shape hunt. Name a shape that is used in one of the illustrations and then ask the children to look for it as they listen to the story. *My Very First Book of Shapes* (Carle, 1974) provides an excellent way to introduce the names of the shapes to toddlers.

Children who are using graphic symbols love *A Wing on a Flea* (Emberly, 1961) and *The Secret Birthday Message Book* (Carle, 1972), in which a secret message is made up of shapes.

MATH/SCIENCE: Let children sort shapes by size or number of sides. Make charts or books about the characteristics of shapes. Ask children to count the number of shapes they used in their artwork.

MUSIC: Display pictures of different shapes. Use a different clap or vocal sound to go with each one. Point to the shapes in varying order and have the children make that sound. Give children a chance to make up the sounds and point to the shapes. The "Touch-It Song" can also be used with shape names.

Pattern

A pattern is a design made from repeated shapes, lines, and colors. Patterns occur naturally, as in the designs on a leopard's skin, or are invented by artists. Children should be encouraged to see the patterns they create in their art explorations.

Playing with pattern. Encourage the children to find examples of pattern in the environment. Comment on patterns found on the clothing they are wearing. Help the children see that a pattern is made up of smaller elements. Find the shapes, lines, and colors in the patterns. Patterns are not only important in art; being able to find and to understand patterns is also the basis of mathematical understanding.

Connections. LITERATURE: *Dots, Spots, Speckles and Stripes* (Hoban, 1987) is a fun book for toddlers. After sharing the book, go on a pattern hunt. For children with longer attention spans, try stories that are filled with different patterns. Challenge them to find all the patterns in books such as Polacco's *Renchenka's Eggs* (1988) and *Thundercake* (1990), and *Tar Beach* (Ringgold, 1991).

MATH: Invite children to use an object to make a repeated print. (See Art Focus: Printmaking.) Count the number of prints on each child's paper. Order the prints from smallest to largest in a class book.

SCIENCE: Look for patterns in nature, such as on butterfly wings, leaves, and flowers. Children who are ready for responsive art activities can record the organic patterns in their drawings.

MUSIC: Listen for patterns in the words, melody, and rhythm of favorite songs. Chart the patterns using colors or shapes. For a responsive art activity, suggest that children record the song's pattern using art media.

Form

Form is the three-dimensional quality of objects. Forms have height, width, and depth. There are spheres, pyramids, cubes, cylinders, and rectangular solids. Children need lots of exposure to a wide variety of forms. Most objects in our world are three-dimensional. Children's early physical handling and examination of many forms allows them as adults to recognize the nature of forms just by looking at them.

Playing with form. Forms are complex. They are not always the same in back or on the bottom as they appear from the front. Block play and modeling activities are excellent ways for children to explore form. Construction activities and papier-mâché involve three-dimensional forms. Kinesthetic activities also help children learn to judge spatial elements in their environment.

Connections. LITERATURE: Many of Tana Hoban's books are ideal for introducing the idea of form. The clear photographs help focus on the form rather than the use. Try *Round, Round, Round* (1974) and *Of Colors and Things* (1989). Use these to teach the different words that describe geometric forms (see figure 4–5). Children can find pictures of objects with different forms and create a class book.

MATH: Order forms such as balls from smallest to largest. Make a collection of boxes and stack them in size order. Use blocks to compare different forms. Look at the number and shape of the sides. Play a form-finding game. Name the shape of one side of a solid, then find the matching block, such as circle = cylinder, triangle = pyramid.

SCIENCE: Fill hollow forms of different sizes and shapes, such as boxes, oatmeal containers, and bottles, with sand or Styrofoam packing material. Have children predict which holds the most and least. Empty and measure to find out.

MUSIC: Look at the form of different musical instruments. Compare how they look to how they sound. Challenge the children to think about why instruments such as a bass and violin sound different when they have a similar form.

Space

Artists do not just see shapes and forms; they also see the space that surrounds them. This may be the empty space of the paper or the open spaces in a sculpture. Young children find this space when they look through a tube and see the view in a circle or look through a hole poked in play dough.

Playing with space. To help young children see space in their artwork, make comments such as, "You have left a rectangular space in the middle of your painting," or "You have made round spaces in your play dough. Can you see through them?" Cut differently shaped holes in pieces of poster board or cardboard covered with contact paper for durability. Encourage children to look through them at anything in the environment including their artwork and block buildings.

Connections. LITERATURE: Children love books with cutout windows through which to glimpse parts of the next picture. Two particularly clever ones are *Opposites* (Felix, 1992) and *Color Zoo* (Ehlert, 1989). (See Appendix B for more.)

MATH: Ask children to count the spaces in their block buildings.

SCIENCE: Take two equal pieces of play dough and poke holes in one. Have children compare the weights using a balance scale. Let them experiment with this idea by letting them weigh things that are full and empty, solid and poked with holes.

MUSIC: Point out that silent moments in a song (rests) are like holes or spaces. Listen for them in different pieces of music.

HOW IS SENSORY PERCEPTION DEVELOPED IN YOUNG CHILDREN?

Young Artists At Work

"The sand is singing," says Bruce as he pours the sand into a pail with a soft whir.

Mariah looks at the teacher through a tube. "I made you round," she remarks.

Allen lies down on the grass and says quietly, "I smell the grass growing."

The child is father to the man in a manner that may be irreversibly one directional, for to make up a bland impoverishment of experience early in life may be too great an obstacle for most organisms.

JEROME BRUNER (1979, P. 1)

It is through the senses that we learn about the world. Research (cited in Bruner, 1979, pp. 142-3) indicates that early sensory deprivation in animals prevents them

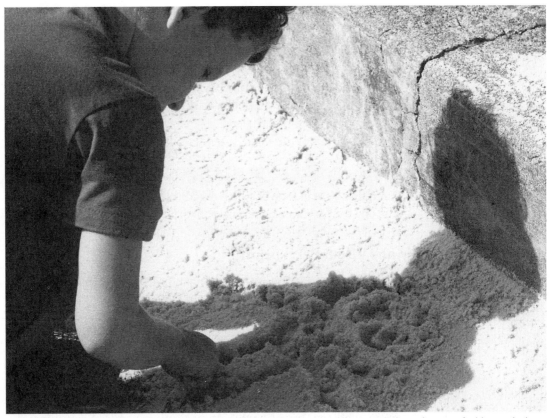

FIGURE 8–3 A drawing in sand holds a moment of awareness—the damp sand, the soft grainy feel beneath the hand, and the warm sun forming a shadow.

from developing an adequate model of the world in which they will eventually live. In the same way, children need to have the opportunity to experience many sensory activities in order to develop not only their aesthetic beliefs, but also their cognitive map of the world. A child who has never seen, touched, smelled, heard about, or tasted ice cream will not have a concept of what ice cream is, will not be able to understand stories, poems, or songs about ice cream and certainly will have no basis upon which to develop a symbol to represent ice cream in an artwork.

It is easy for adults to forget what it is like to focus entirely on a sensory stimulus. In our busy lives it is rare to take a moment to focus completely on the aesthetic qualities of objects—the many greens in a lawn of grass, the rough texture of a concrete block wall, the smell of rain on hot pavement, the sound of the refrigerator humming, and the taste of our toothpaste in the morning. But in order to guide young children's aesthetic growth, adults need to be able to become aware of these qualities again with childlike wonder.

Sensory awareness is not something that can be put out on a table like crayons and paper. Daily interactions with young children should be peppered with statements and questions that show wonder and valuing of the sensory qualities of the environment. Adults cannot verbalize these qualities to the children if they do not experience them themselves. Like an artist, who reminds us of the colors of a beautiful sunset or the texture of sand through a painting, adults must bring that same focus to what they say to the children.

There is a sensory element in every activity in which the children are involved. Instead of seeing blocks, see shapes and forms, instead of glue, notice stickiness. Listen and learn from the children.

Young children do not hesitate to invite us to "feel this" or "smell that," and we must do the same with them. Find a sensory element and express it:

"Look at how the light is shining on your wet paint!"
"Oh, the sand is so cool and damp today!"
"These flowers smell like a summer day!"

And of course, lavish the young artists with comments about the sensory quality of their work:

"That red and green look beautiful together!"
"Your clay ball feels so wonderfully round!"

Developing Sensory and Visual Perception

In addition to finding and celebrating the sensory qualities of children's ordinary activities, adults need to provide extraordinary and unexpected sensory experiences for children. These explorations often cross the boundaries of particular subject areas, providing not only artistic and aesthetic growth but also cognitive growth in the linguistic and logical-mathematical domains, as well as the bodily-kinesthetic and musical intelligences through the manipulation of a wide variety of objects and materials. For this reason, these kinds of activities should be part of all early childhood programs. The following list provides only a partial listing of a multitude of possible sensory activities. These can be used as springboards for designing original activities.

The ones presented here have been selected for their close relationship to art activities and are grouped by the sensory mode that is their main focus. Many are multisensory. It is almost impossible to eliminate the input from all senses but one, without placing great limits on the freedom of exploration of the child. In fact, many young children dislike being restricted from using any of their senses. They want to peek over blindfolds and taste things before being told to do so. They should never be punished for such natural curiosity. Instead, take care in setting up these experiences so that peeking and bold explorations are part of the fun.

Children often seem to spend only a short amount of time investigating these sensory activities before dashing off to something else. Remember that time for a young artist is not the same as time for an adult and that the value of an experience cannot be measured by the clock. Even a minute or two of investigating an unusual texture or visual perception, or challenging the senses in a new way, is of utmost benefit to a child's cognitive growth. The child's new information about that exploration will enrich that child in a way that constant exposure to familiar and everyday objects will not.

It is well worth the effort to spend time preparing these explorations. Offer them regularly and change them often. Do not be afraid to repeat an exploration after a passage of time. Young children grow quickly and will experience these activities differently at later stages of development. With careful planning and careful construction many of the sensory materials mentioned here can be reused many times over the years.

Vision

We begin with the sense of sight. Through our eyes we sense the art elements of line, shape, color, pattern, value, form, and space. All art activities can be experienced through visual input. Refer to the art elements when describing children's artwork:

"You used bright colors."

"You made a pattern when you pressed the potato masher into the clay."

The visual images that enter the brain become the basis for the mental images we create. Children need a wide variety of challenging and enriching visual experiences. Seeing familiar things in a new light or a new way prepares children to be more accepting of the unfamiliar images they will encounter in life. Learning to discriminate between different colors or different shapes helps them see the world with more definition and meaning.

Playing with visual elements. A window gives freedom to see through a wall and yet at the same time limits us to seeing only a part of the total view beyond the wall. The following activities do the same. They force the child to see only a small selected part of something. In doing so that part becomes important—it becomes a whole, like a picture framed in a camera's viewfinder. Children have this same type of "photographic" experience by looking through child-sized window frames or viewfinders.

TUBE VIEWFINDER: At its simplest the viewfinder can be a plain cardboard tube rescued from the trash. Set out an attractive basket or container full of long and short tubes and encourage the children to look through them and describe what they see. Give them an attractive name such as "viewscopes" or "looking tubes." For another experience, prepare some tubes ahead of time by taping colored cellophane to one end. Try taping black paper over an end and poke several small holes in it. The children can use art materials to decorate their viewscopes.

CARDBOARD WINDOWS: Make viewfinders with differenty shaped openings by cutting holes in stiff cardboard cards. The holes can be made small, for one-eye viewing, or large enough for the child to use both eyes. If possible, laminate these for durability or cover them with clear package sealing tape. Vary this activity by taping colored

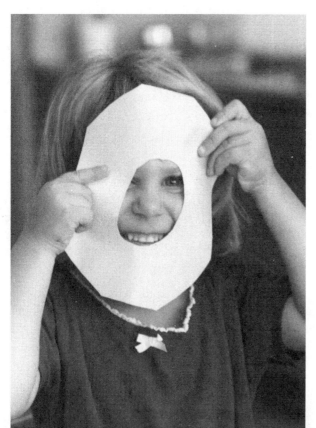

FIGURE 8–4 Visual elements invite playful peeking at new views of the world.

cellophane over the openings. Try overlapping several colors of cellophane in strips across the opening for another unusual effect.

PICTURE FRAMES: Prepare a set of construction paper or cardboard "frames" with varying sizes, shapes, and placement of holes cut out of them. These can also be laminated for durability. Children can use these to cover a piece of artwork, an illustration in a book, magazine pictures, or even games and puzzles for the thrill of seeing the detail of a small part. Young children love the peek-a-boo effect they can create and like turning the frame in different ways to see how the effect changes. On occasion add colored cellophane to these, as well, or create frames with multiple openings for a different experience.

ENVELOPE OF HOLES: Cut out magazine pictures and mount them on heavy construction paper or poster board. Wildlife and nature magazines provide excellent sources of interesting scenes, animals, and people. The mounted pictures should be slightly smaller than an 8½-by-11-inch brown mailing envelope. Study the picture and cut a hole in the envelope in a location where an interesting detail will show, such as an eye, a mouth, or a flower. Place the picture in the envelope. Children can study the detail and try to imagine the rest of the picture before pulling it out of the envelope.

BOOK OF HOLES: To make a book, create "frames" by cutting holes in pieces of construction paper. Place two mounted magazine pictures back to back, then a frame, then two more back-to-back pictures and another frame. Add a front and back cover, both with well-placed holes, and staple the book together. Place the holes in creative and interesting ways, or try using more than one frame between pictures. Several beautiful children's books such as *Look Again* (Hoban, 1971) and *Go Away Big Green Monster* (Emberly, 1992) use this same idea and can inspire teachers to make a masterpiece of their own.

LOOK-ABOUT TABLE: Set out, at the children's level, an object that encourages looking in new ways. Possible items include: smooth and crinkled aluminum foil mounted on cardboard, crystals, Fresnel lenses, magnifiers, kaleidoscopes, fly's-eye viewers, liquid crystals, mirrors, optical lenses, colored plexiglass, sunglasses, color paddles, holographic metallic papers, prisms, nonbreakable mirrors, transparent colored or textured plastics, plastic water globes, or even a small fish bowl, complete with fish.

COLOR LIGHTS: Set up a small table lamp in one corner of the room. Vary the color of the light bulb and encourage the children to look at their familiar toys, book illustrations, and artwork in a "new" light. *Color! Color! Color!* (Heller, 1995) uses color acetates between pages to create similar effects.

To change the total room environment for a special occasion, cover overhead lights or windows with loosely draped, colored tissue paper.

Touch

The tactile sense is very powerful. The entire surface of the human body is sensitive to pressure and temperature, as well as to the textural qualities of the matter that makes up the world. Young children rely heavily on tactile exploration to acquire knowledge about the characteristics of individual materials and objects and to develop an understanding of how things are spatially arranged. The environment and activities offered to young children should provide continuous opportunities to touch.

Playing with touch. Most art activities involve input from the tactile sense. Finger paint, modeling dough, textured collage materials, and sticky glue are explored with sensitive fingers. Art tools such as brushes and scissors, printmaking objects, and smooth-gliding drawing tools are felt both texturally and through the pressure that is sent back and forth from hand to object as they are used.

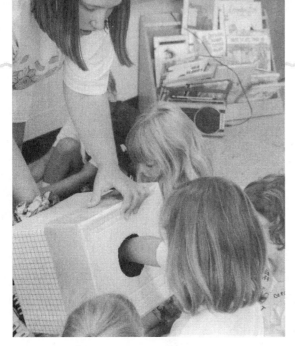

FIGURE 8–5 A touch box helps children focus on the tactile qualities of objects.

As children explore art media, teachers should increase children's awareness of these tactile qualities through what they say. Use texture words such as silky, soft, smooth, squishy, metallic, bumpy, and rough. Refer to the temperature of the materials: "Oh, this finger paint feels cold!", "The play dough is warm from your hand," as well as making them aware of the pressure they are using: "You pressed hard with your crayons," "You are using effort to push your scissors through the paper," or "You touched the paintbrush to your paper very lightly."

Other ways to provide tactile explorations include:

TOUCH BOX: Touch boxes can be made in several ways. One way is to glue different textures to each outer side of a box or cardboard cube. Cubes can be made from six square pieces of corrugated cardboard taped together at the edges. (Use clear, package-sealing tape.) Use textured items that are fairly flat, such as a variety of fabrics, carpet, and sandpaper. Make several, and children can use these for stacking and matching activities.

Another type of touch box encourages children to feel an object without using the sense of sight. Cut a hole large enough for a child's hand to fit inside of a box (shoe boxes work well). Cut the hole in the smaller side. Cover the hole by taping a piece of cloth over the top of the hole on the inside to form a flap. Glue an object with an interesting texture to the bottom of the box, put the top back on; and close with a rubber band. Encourage children to reach inside to feel the object first and then peek inside to see it.

Make the box more versatile by cutting pieces of cardboard the size of the box bottom and gluing a different object to each. Change the objects regularly by simply lifting out one cardboard and putting in another. A beautifully decorated touch box can become a regular stop for children as they explore the environment that has been prepared for them.

Objects for touch boxes should be at least palm-sized and durable enough to take a great deal of handling. Use both natural and human-made objects that have a variety of forms and textures. Check that objects do not have sharp or jagged edges. Some suggested objects include: aluminum foil ball, block, bone, box, candle, coral, cotton, crumpled paper ball, fabric (especially velvet and corduroy), lid, metal toy, netting, pinecone, plastic toy, polyester stuffing, rubber ball, rug piece, screwdriver, shell, spoon, stone, twig, and wax (canning). To use an item that spoils or is hard to glue, such as an apple, lemon, orange, or potato, place it in the box without glue. The children may need help holding the box while they find the object, as it will roll around easily. Use creativity to find objects that will make the touch box a wonderful experience for each child.

STUFF BINS: Partially fill a basket, dishpan, or large, clear plastic storage container with "stuff," through which the children can move their hands. Items for wet and dry stuff bins are listed in Table 8–1.

PLEASE-TOUCH TABLE: Set up a small low table on which to display one or a few items. Select these natural and human-made items with care. They should be individually beautiful items that are less familiar to the children and will attract their interest. To encourage a relaxed exploration make sure the items are not very valuable and will stand the children's nonexpert handling. Possible items might include: a large conch shell, a piece of brain coral, a large rock with fossil impressions, a large gear from an old machine, the inside of a clock, a carved Peruvian gourd, a feathered mask, an African wood carving, or an intricately woven basket. Invite the children and parents to contribute items to this table, too. Encourage the children to make tactile observations of these items by asking questions such as:

"What part feels smooth?"
"Is it cold to your touch?"
"Are there places you can put your fingers?"
"Does it feel differently on the bottom?"

TABLE 8-1 Ideas for Stuff Bins

Dry Stuff Bins:

cardboard squares	cornmeal*
cotton balls	craft sticks
crumpled white tissue paper	excelsior
fabric scraps	flowers
grass	gravel
leaves (green or dry)	lids (plastic, metal, juice)
macaroni*	marbles
metal washers	nylon netting
oatmeal*	pebbles
pennies	plastic caps
plastic "Easter" grass	polyester stuffing
popcorn*	raffia
ribbons and bows	rice*
sawdust	short pieces of yarn or string
shredded paper	Styrofoam packing material
tiles	wood shavings

NOTE: After being explored in the stuff bin, these materials can be added to the collage choices. (Remember to use only items that pass the choke test if working with children under three.)

Wet Stuff Bins:

bubble mixture (dish detergent and water)
cornstarch slurry (heat while stirring: one part cornstarch to five parts water until creamy, let cool)
goop (mix one part cornstarch to one part cold water)
shaving cream
unflavored gelatin mixture*
water (vary the temperature)
whipped soap (beat with hand mixer: two parts soap flakes to one part water).

Food coloring may be used to color these materials to excite the visual sense. After initial explorations, cups, containers, and other tools for the children to use in manipulating the material may be added.

NATURE SCAVENGER HUNT: Take the children for a walk outside to find objects with interesting textures. Ask toddlers to find objects with just one texture, such as something smooth, shiny, or wet. Alternatively we can say, "Find me all kinds of objects with different textures or that are interesting to touch." When they find items, we can describe the texture to them: *"Oh, you found a bumpy rock!","What a shiny cap you found."*

Three-year-olds can look for two contrasting textures such as something hard and something soft. Older children can find several objects and then sort and group them. Remind the children not to damage any living plants. Look over the area before taking the children out to make sure it is safe and to get an an idea about what kinds of objects they might find. It may be necessary to limit the area of the search to just grass or playground. Even in a small area many interesting textures can be found, such as a rough piece of bark, a bottle cap with bumpy edges, or a smooth shiny candy wrapper. Collect all the objects they find and bring them in to use in their collages.

TEXTURE CARDS: Glue pairs of sample textures to large cards made of heavy poster board or cardboard. If possible try to use textured items that are similar in color. A variety of fabrics works well. The children can try to match cards while closing their eyes and feeling the textures. Oversized dominos with textures glued on them instead of numbers can also be made.

SAND: Few children can resist the tactile qualities of sand. Dry sand runs through the fingers; wet sand sticks. Sand is a material that young children feel they can control. They can make their own textures in the sand by pushing and pulling, and patting and pressing. They can pour it and mold it. A sand table or covered outdoor sandbox is an essential piece of aesthetic equipment for young children.

To increase the children's tactile exploration of sand, vary the equipment and dampness of the sand. Remove the traditional sand toys occasionally and substitute more unusual items such as natural objects (seashells, stones, twigs), large kitchen tools (slotted spoon, potato masher, spatula, turner), tools (screwdriver, mallet, wrenches, large bolts), cardboard (boxes of different sizes, strips, and squares of corrugated cardboard), and caps and lids of all kinds.

To introduce sand play or to go along with it, read one of these delightful books about sand: *Story in the Sand* (Myrus, 1963) or *The Sand Lady* (Reed, 1968). Both these books take place on the beach. If there is a beach nearby, take the children there to experience play in a giant sandbox. Encourage them to create bold sand drawings and collages inspired by the books.

Children will enjoy *At the Beach* (Lee, 1994) in which cut-paper collages illustrate a story about children learning to write Chinese characters in the sand.

Smell

The sense of smell is also involved in the creation of art. The waxy odor of crayons, the minty smell of paste, and the slightly ammonia scent of white glue are an integral part of art exploration. Although the sense of smell is often less valued than the other senses, it is a very powerful one. A whiff of a familiar odor from the past can bring back a memory. The scent of school paste can make adults feel like they are in kindergarten again. Opening a box of new crayons can bring to mind a drawing made at the age of five. The smells that surround the children as they do artwork will be associated with art for the rest of their lives.

Make sure the classroom itself is always clean and fresh smelling. Check for allergies and then select an air freshener, potpourri, or disinfectant that leaves a pleasant odor. Open the windows in fair weather.

As the children explore the art activities, make comments about the smells of the materials they are using:

"The paste smells so fresh and clean!"
"This play dough smells minty."
"The yellow paint smells like a field of flowers."

Try to associate the smells with pleasant experiences, but avoid references to foods that might cause the children to try to taste the material.

Scents can be added to homemade materials or paints. Choose scents, such as different shampoos, dish detergents, potpourri, and scented oils. Food-related spices can also be used—cinnamon, allspice, nutmeg, cumin, coriander, thyme, marjoram, cloves, savory, and the mints. These strong-smelling scents are not as likely to be tasted.

Scented crayons and markers are available, but they should be used with great caution. The scents are too exciting for most children. They smell like candy, tempting young children to taste them, and cause a problem when children stick them in their noses or someone else's for a better whiff. For children with limited vision, however, the scents help them to identify the colors.

SCENT JARS: Scent jars can be used as a focused exploration on the sense of smell. Prepare cotton balls by sprinkling each one with a liquid scent. Another method is to glue powdered spices to a piece of paper. Place the scents in plastic containers, such as yogurt cups or icing containers, that have tight fitting lids. Cut a small hole in the lid and tape the lid on to the container. The scents will remain strong for several days. Ask the children if the smells remind them of anything.

As an extension, mark each container with a different symbol. Make a chart with the children of the smells they liked the best. Use the most popular smells to scent paints or homemade recipes. Another variation on this activity is to make pairs of scents and have the children try to match the pairs.

Sound

Some art activities are very quiet; others are quite noisy. A young child painting at the easel is a model of quiet. That same child actively exploring play dough bangs and slaps with glee. The sounds that surround art activities rise and fall as children enter the creative state of immersion or chatter happily with their friends. Several activities follow that will encourage children to interrelate art and sound.

RHYTHM INSTRUMENTS: Collect containers with tight fitting lids. Let the children fill them with different small objects such as sand, rice,* beans,* or pebbles. Then put on the lids, shake them, and listen to the sounds they make. Use tin cans and cardboard tubes for different sound effects. Cover the open ends with a piece of paper, and affix it with package-sealing tape. Children can decorate them with paint, crayon, marker, paper, and/or collage materials.

RESPONDING TO MUSIC: Set up a tape recorder while children are working in the easel area or at the drawing table. Music can also accompany some of the group mural activities described in chapter 10. Play tapes that feature a variety of sounds and rhythms from many cultures and traditions (see Table 8–2). Let the children respond to the music in their own ways. When they are done drawing or painting, ask them how the music made them feel. At other times, let the children choose the kind of music they want to hear while working.

TABLE 8-2 Suggested Music for Art Explorations

Artist:	Title:
Africa Fete 3	*Selections*
Benedictine Monks of Santo Domingo De Silos	*Chants*
Hamza El Din	*The Water Wheel*
Claude Debussy	*The Snow is Dancing, Play of the Waves*
Edward Grieg	*Peer Gynt*
Ferde Grofé	*Grand Canyon Suite*
Tokeya Inajin	*Dream Catcher*
Inti-Illumani	*Imagination*
Nikolai Andreyevich Rimsky-Korsakov	*Scheherazade*
Modest Petrovich Mussorgsky	*Pictures at an Exhibition*
Michael Oldfield	*Tubular Bells 1 and 2*
Rumillajita	*Wiracocha*
Camille Saint-Saens	*The Swan*
Igor Stravinsky	*Petrushka*
Bob Zander	*Almost Oriana*

These are just a few of a multitude of musical selections that can inspire young children as they create art.

Other ideas for relating music and art can be found in the section on Kinesthetics.

Taste

Taste is the only sense that children should not use when they are engaged in art experiences. Instead, emphasize the aesthetic qualities of food as it is served and eaten. Describe the visual and textural appearance of different foods, such as the rich pink and green of watermelon, the circle shape of a sliced orange, and the bumpy surface of a chocolate-chip cookie.

WHAT IS THE BEST WAY TO PRESENT SENSORY EXPERIENCES?

We know that children learn in active, not passive, ways. The sense of belonging to the environment is part of each one. It is only later that children learn that it is often a do-not-touch, do-not-see, do-not hear, do-not-taste world.

LARRY KANTNER (1989, P. 45)

In planning how to present these visual and sensory experiences, it is important to consider how to capture the children's attention. Some tubes sitting in a basket cannot compete with a bright and shiny toy unless the teacher adds that special touch, perhaps an intriguing comment, to attract the child. Place the sensory table in a highly visible place where there is frequent traffic, perhaps near the door so it is one of the first things the children find when they arrive. Make a comment about it as children arrive: "Look, we have a beautiful conch shell from Florida on the Look-About Table today!"

These items can also be introduced at circle time and then placed on the observation table or other selected location. For example, show an "envelope with holes" to the group and have the children take turns describing what they see. Then show them where there are more envelopes in a basket for them to explore. To introduce a conch shell, read *Bimweli and the Zimwi* (Aardema, 1985), a tale about a conch shell in an African setting.

Do not overwhelm the children with too many choices. Put out only one sensory exploration at a time. The key is to change the displays and items often, but repeat them regularly with slight changes or in new combinations. The more these kinds of experiences are offered, the more comfortable teachers become using the language and formulating the right questions. Teachers owe it to the children to offer these special experiences that allow them to touch, taste, smell, listen, and see in new ways.

WHAT IS KINESTHETICS?

Young Artists at Work

Martina, age 6, stands in front of the art print her teacher has hung on the door. Intently she studies the face of the child in the painting. She touches her own face. Slowly a new expression comes over her face. It matches the one in the painting.

We inhabit our whole body, and our whole body is a source and reservoir of experience.

GAIL NEARY HERMAN AND PATRICIA HOLLINGSWORTH (1992, p. 9)

Kinesthetic awareness refers to how people internally sense the feeling and location of their bodies in space. It is different from the other senses in that it combines the information received from the senses of touch, sight, and hearing with input from the internal body—organs, muscles, skin, and joints. The kinesthetic sense helps people remember the way they have moved, where they have been, and the sensory feelings they experienced along the way. Like smells, certain muscular responses that mimic ones felt in the past may trigger memories.

Young children learn with their whole bodies. The movement of their arms as they move a brush across the paper or stamp a print with a sponge are an integral part of the art experience. As in all the sensory areas, teachers need to draw attention to these motions and make children more aware of their own actions as sources of these sensations. For example, when a child is painting the teacher might say:

"You are making bold strokes, moving your arm up and down!"
"Now you are making lots of tiny strokes. Look how quickly you are moving your arm!"

FIGURE 8–6 Children mime moving like trees.

Kinesthetic awareness can also play an important role in reinforcing and expanding art activities that involve the other senses. By combining movement activities with aural, visual, or tactile elements, we come closest to the natural way that young children learn on their own. Kinesthetic explorations are powerful motivators and make wonderful transitions into other activities. They can also stand on their own as integral experiences for young children.

Designing Movement Activities

The following kinesthetic activities provide just a few examples of how movement and art can be combined. After trying some of these or ones found in other books, educators should design their own. Some of the best kinesthetic activities are based on spur-of-the-moment reactions to the needs of the children and the teacher's own kinesthetic sense and do not require any special preparation.

For example, imagine reading a book about a bird to a group of young preschoolers, but a few of them are having trouble sitting still. As they hear about the bird flapping its wings, ask the children to flap their arms like the bird. Continue to encourage the children to imitate the actions of the bird during the story and end by asking them to fly slowly to an activity of their choice. By bringing into play the kinesthetic sense we add more meaning to the words and to what the children are hearing, and at the same time channel the healthy bodily energy of wiggly children.

Combining Movement and Visual Elements

SHAPE TRAIL: Outside on a paved area, paint or draw with chalk a series of crisscrossing trails of foot-sized shapes. Use one repeated shape for each "trail." Challenge the children to follow a trail by stepping on only one kind of shape.

BODY SHAPES: Ask the children to lie down on the floor and make their bodies into a shape such as a circle or triangle. Be accepting of all their creative responses. Sing a song such as *"The Body Shape Song"* (see Music Box).

MUSIC BOX

"The Body Shape Song"

(Tune: "Mary had a Little Lamb")

Now I am a circle, circle, circle.*
Now I am a circle
Lying on the floor.

*(*Repeat with different shapes)*

BODY VIEWFINDERS: Ask children to create differently shaped "windows" to look through using parts of their bodies. They can try touching the fingers of one or both hands together in different ways, or putting a hand on another part of the body and looking through the opening.

PICTURE POSE: Invite children to look at a photograph, poster, or fine-art print of a person and try to imitate the position or expression of the pictured person. For a variation, use a picture of an animal.

PEOPLE MIRROR: Have each child work with a partner. One child is the model, the other the mirror. The model strikes a pose and the mirror tries to imitate it. Then have them reverse roles. An adult or older child can partner with a toddler.

PEOPLE CAMERA Have each child work with a partner. One child is the camera, the other the photographer. The camera closes its "shutters" (eyes), and the photographer slowly turns the camera around to face a view. When the photographer says, "Click," the camera opens the "shutters" for a moment, looks at the view, and closes them again. Then they may reverse roles.

Combining Movement and Texture

INDOOR TEXTURE HUNT: This simple game can be used to assess the children's identification of different textures. Start with the children in a circle. Ask them to find something in the room that is smooth. When they find it, they are to put their hand on it and stay there until everyone has found something. Encourage them to help each other and remind them to walk safely. When all the children are touching something, call out another texture for them to find and touch. Do not correct children who touch the wrong texture, but make a mental note to introduce more activities that involve that one. This game can also be played outdoors. To add to the fun, ask the children to "move smoothly to a smooth object," "walk bumpily to a bumpy one," or "take rough steps to a rough one." Be inventive and the children will too! (Note: This game can also be played with shapes, kinds of lines, or colors.)

MY TEXTURES: Ask the child or children to touch different textures on their bodies or clothes as they are named. For example, if "soft," is the word, they might touch their hair or skin. "Bumpy" could be the bottom of their shoes. After the teacher names a few, each child can take a turn calling out a texture. (Note: Colors, shapes, or kinds of lines can be substituted for textures in this activity as well.)

Combining Movement and Hearing

RHYTHMIC LINES: Have a small group of children sit around a large piece of paper. Let each one choose a crayon or marker. As them to make their lines "dance" to the rhythms or sounds that they hear. Tap a rhythm on a small drum or even a covered margarine container or coffee can. After a few seconds change the rhythm. A set of bells or a child's xylophone can be used to add pitch. The children can also take turns making the sounds for each other. Music can also be used but they need to be very short bits of a variety of musical pieces. Prepare a tape of short selections ahead of time.

This activity can be done with the children using finger paint or paint and brushes, and with play dough. When using play dough, encourage the children to pat and poke the dough according to the rhythm they hear.

> Fifty percent of a child's learning capacity shuts off when made to sit still.
>
> CLYDE GILLESPIE (TURNER, 1990, P. 243)

SUMMARY: THE SENSITIVE TEACHER

> He was like an orchestra conductor, telling them to savor each moment, take their time, look at the lights, make everything count.
>
> RICHARD MERRYMAN (1991, P. 25)

All of us have treasured memories of something exceedingly beautiful. Perhaps it was a sunrise we saw driving to work, or the image of our mother's face. Our children, too, deserve such memories. It is up to the adults who work with young children to help create these images. Some suggestions include:

- Sharing beautiful objects from nature and artists' hands

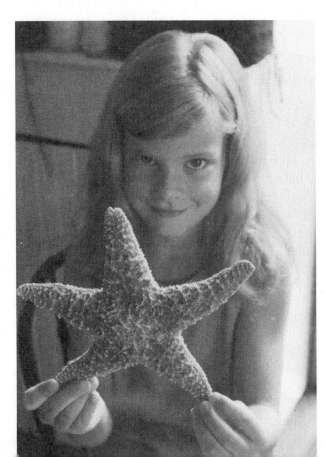

FIGURE 8–7 Sensory awareness cannot be put on a table like a box of crayons. It must be found in the world around us.

- Teaching children to see the elements of line, shape, color, form, space, texture, and pattern in the world around them
- Providing activities that develop children's sensory perception skills
- Providing opportunities for children to use their imaginations in new ways
- Pointing out the sensory, kinesthetic, and aesthetic elements in the children's own work and in the artwork of others

The sensory and kinesthetic activities presented in this chapter may seem different from more "traditional" art activities for young children. Some of them may cross into other curriculum areas; others do not use the expected art materials. Nevertheless, these explorations form the basis of what art will mean to young artists and upon which they will make aesthetic judgments about the world.

The guiding adults of early childhood are the most important ingredients in forming a child's initial opinion about art. It is only when children feel safe and confident that they are able to learn aesthetically. It is the teacher's job to create an environment that is open to exploration, that is full of wonderful experiences that allow the children to gain pleasure as they use their senses, and that rewards children for using their natural learning style.

Teachers must bring excitement and enthusiasm with them daily. Adults must be open to the aesthetic wonders that surround them—the pattern of the raindrops on the window pane, the rainbow in the spilled oil in a puddle, the warm fur of a kitten—and share these with children. Every experience can be an aesthetic one. Learn to see with the eyes of an artist and the heart of a poet. Anyone can walk on the ceiling, fly with a bird, or dance on the ocean floor, through the power of imagination. Teachers must visualize themselves as enthusiastic nurturers of young artists' sensory and kinesthetic development, and know that their style of interaction, and the environment they create, will make every day special for a young child.

FURTHER READING

> Things are pretty, graceful, rich, elegant, handsome, but until they speak to the imagination, not yet beautiful.
>
> RALPH WALDO EMERSON ("BEAUTY" *THE CONDUCT OF LIFE*, 1860)

The following books will help readers develop their own personal aesthetic sense.

Bender, S. (1989). *Plain and simple: A woman's journey to the Amish*. San Franciso: HarperCollins.
Bender describes how she learned to see beauty in simplicity from making quilts with the Amish.

Cameron, J. (1992). *The artist's way: A spiritual path to higher creativity*. New York: G. P. Putnam's Sons.
This book discusses the meaning of art and provides methods of enhancing aesthetic and creative self-awareness.

Stoddard, A. (1988). *Living a beautiful life*. New York: Avon Books.
This simple book will inspire readers to add beauty to the environment that surrounds them.

Art Focus

PRINTMAKING

Remember that art is process. The process is supposed to be fun... At the heart of this play is the mystery of joy.

JULIA CAMERON (1992, P. 154)

Printmaking is any art form that involves making a copy of something. Some printing techniques can produce multiple prints, others only one copy (monoprint). Printmaking can provide another way for young children to explore the sensory characteristics of objects. Before offering printing activities to young children, it is important to understand the nature of the technique and how young children approach this art form.

The Art Medium: Printmaking

The first prints were handprints found on the cave walls of 20,000 years ago. Handprints and fingerprints are also the first prints of our children, as

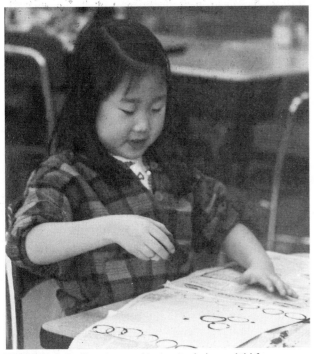

FIGURE 8–8 Creating an object print helps a child focus on the characteristics of the object.

anyone who has had to clean up after little ones with dirty hands can attest. To make a clear handprint, children have to first put paint on the hand either by dipping or spreading it on. Then they must press it down, hold it still, and lift it up again off the paper. It is this pressing down, holding still, and lifting up pattern of action that is the key to printmaking.

Books on art for young children are full of all kinds of wonderful printing techniques. However, many adults who try to do these with young children are quickly disappointed. Many young children do not press, hold, and lift; instead they treat the printing object as a paintbrush and smear the paint over the paper. In the process they also spread the paint over table and hands, and usually end up leaving excellent handprints on the sink, but few "prints" on their papers.

If we consider the physical development discussed in chapter 3, we find that this is easily explained. Toddlers who do not yet have wrist control will find the press, hold, and lift action difficult to accomplish. Children who draw scribbles will naturally move their arms in circular or up-and-down motions across the page. Toddlers and younger preschoolers will want to explore the nature of the paint, rather than focusing on the nature of the object that is used to apply the paint. They do not yet have enough art experience to differentiate a brush from some other paint applicator, or to differentiate between a printing tool and an object with which to paint.

Young children also have difficulty understanding the idea of making multiple copies of something. They are concerned with the process, not the product. They see little reason to make duplicates of something when they could be creating something new and different. Often they will make one stamp with a printing tool and consider themselves done.

To provide satisfying printmaking activities for young children, teachers need to consider the children's physical control and experience when selecting or designing printing activities. Once an activity has been presented, teachers need to allow the children to use the printing tools freely

FIGURE 8–9 "This is a circle picture. I kept making more and more circle prints. It was fun." Print—Shawnee, age 4

and creatively even if they are not making true "prints." It is the sensory experience of printmaking that is of most benefit to the children. The following explorations and practice activities emphasize this objective of printmaking.

A Printmaking Exploration

Printmaking is another way that young children can use their senses in a kinesthetic way to learn more about objects. The children use their sense of touch as they handle the object and apply pressure to make the print. They can compare the stiffness of the object with the slippery wetness of the paint. The print provides a visual image of the texture, pattern and shape of the object, and the stamping process often creates a rhythmic sound. Printmaking is also a very active art form that requires the children to move their arms with vigor and apply pressure sensitively.

How Children Grow through Printmaking

Children will develop:

1. Physically, by using the large and small muscles of the arm to apply paint to an object and then move the object on the paper (Bodily-Kinesthetic)
2. Socially, by sharing the printing tools and paint trays (Interpersonal)
3. Emotionally, by learning to enjoy making prints as a means of self-expression and by seeing themselves as competent people who

can control "messy" paint (Intrapersonal)
4. Visual perception skills, by exploring new ways to arrange print marks on a paper and by matching an object to the shape of its print (Spatial)
5. Cognitively:
   • By learning a vocabulary of printing words and by describing their prints (Linguistic)
   • By learning that different objects and materials make different print marks, depending on their texture and shape (Logical-Mathematical)
6. Art awareness by becoming familiar with prints as used in book illustrations and other artwork

Group composition. For initial printmaking explorations, limit the group to one or two toddlers or four older children. Once the children are familiar with the technique and can work more independently, the group size can be increased for the practice activities.

Setup. Provide a low table that the children can work at while standing. Children usually only spend a few minutes making prints and can do so standing up. This also enables them to reach the trays of paint and objects more easily. Cover the table with newspaper. Have all materials set out before inviting them to begin. Place the trays between the papers or down the middle of the table, depending on the size and shape of the table. Have smocks ready for the children to wear. (See chapter 4 for a discussion of smocks.)

Materials.

• Paint: Choose several colors of very thick tempera paint or finger paint. Make sure that the paint colors will not stain hands. White is always a safe choice, as are pastels that are mixed using white and a few drops of a color. If the paint is thin, it can be thickened by adding flour. Paint thickened in this way must be used up quickly or it will spoil. Place a small amount of paint in each tray.
• Trays: Put the paint in low-sided trays. Use Styrofoam or plastic food trays that have been sanitized (see chapter 6) and have sides no higher than half an inch.
• Printing Tools: For the first exploration, pro-

vide the children with large, easily-grasped objects that they can dip in the paint, such as a variety of potato mashers or long cardboard tubes. Place one tool in each tray.

- Paper: Use paper in the 9- by 12-inch size range. Larger paper makes it difficult for the children to reach the trays and objects without leaning in their prints. Have plenty of extra paper so that children can make more than one print if they wish.
- Drying rack: A cardboard-box drying rack (figure 5–8) or other wet project storage unit placed near the printmakers will provide a quick place to put the prints to dry while still supervising the children. With experience, the children can put their own prints away.

Transition in. Have the printmaking materials set out on the table. Ask the children what kind of mark they think the object will make if it is dipped in the paint. Invite some of the children to try to make a print.

What to do. Many children will begin their exploration very hesitantly. They may study the paint-covered end or the resulting print. Once they have an idea of the result of their actions they may try other ways of moving the object on the paper.

During the initial explorations do not interfere except for safety reasons. Allow the children to investigate this technique in any way they wish.

What to say. When children are done, comment on the shapes they have made: "Look you made circles," or on the way they moved the tool: "You moved the tube up and down." Or relate the mark to the object: "Which mark did the tube make? What made this mark?" When children say a paper is finished, ask if they wish to make another.

Use a vocabulary that describes the marks made by the objects and the actions the child has used. Words to use include: shape (and all the shape names), pattern, texture, repeated, lift, press, stamp, hold, move, and place. Say a printing chant with toddlers and mime it with the older ones.

Transition out. As the children finish, help them put their prints in a place to dry. Then guide them in removing the smocks and washing their hands. After the printmaking experience, set up a matching activity in which the child matches a print

MUSIC BOX

"Printing Chant"

Stamp, stamp, stamp.
Press, press, press.
Printing.
Printing.
It's the best!

with the object that made it. Older children can match the object with its print in their artwork. Talk about how the print is different from, but similar to, the original tool that made it.

Extending the learning. Make a Big Book about pattern, using prints made from the objects the children have used, and share it with the children.

FIGURE 8–10 Printmaking allows children to explore how shapes can be put together in new ways.

Have them match the print to the object that made it.

Practice Printmaking Activities

After the exploratory activity, offer printmaking on a regular basis. Vary the printing tools, combining new ones with familiar ones. Toddlers need larger printmaking tools than three- to eight-year-olds, but no matter what their age, children find small objects messier than larger ones.

Sponge prints. Sponges make great printing tools. Cut the sponge into simple geometric shapes. Avoid precut stereotyped shapes such as dinosaurs, rabbits, or letters. Although these may give "meaning" to the artwork for the adult viewer, such shapes have little meaning for the child who benefits more from sensory experiences with the basic shapes. Attach a clothespin to the top of the sponge shape, or using craft glue, attach a spool "handle" to the sponge.

"Rubber" stamps. Commercial rubber stamps are too small for little hands to grasp, but larger ones are easy to make. Cut out simple geometric shapes—square, circle, triangle, rectangle, oval, and so on—from heavy Styrofoam trays. Use craft glue to affix these shapes to sanded wood blocks.

Roller prints. Wrap and glue string, yarn, or rick-rack to cardboard tubes or juice cans. When dry, roll the decorated cylinder in paint and then roll it in the paper. This is a very messy, but exciting exploration.

"Gadget" prints. Almost any object can make a print. When selecting objects for young children, look for ones that will be easy for the child to grasp, and have smooth edges and an interesting texture. Toddlers require ones that can be grasped with the fist and are very sturdy.

Avoiding food items for printmaking. Many books recommend using fruits and vegetables for printmaking. Consider carefully the message children receive when told to put food in paint and then see the food thrown away. Although a carefully made print of a sliced orange or apple may make a beautiful print that allows the shape of the fruit to be

---

TABLE 8-3 Printmaking Objects

Berry baskets
Blocks (building or interlocking)
Bristle blocks
Cans (with smooth edges)
Corks
Corrugated cardboard (cut in rectangular pieces)
Erasers
Forks
Feet
Film cans
Garlic press
Hands
Juice cans
Lids and tops
Ornamental corn
Pinecones
Plastic cups and containers
Potato masher
Rocks
Shells
Shoes
Sponge ball
Sponges (in simple geometric shapes, not pictorial)
Spools
Toy trucks
Tubes
Wood blocks

---

seen in a new way, young children do not have the skill to create such a print. This is not an aesthetic experience for children. (See chapter 6 for further discussion on this topic.) Table 8–3: Printmaking Objects gives plenty of ideas for printing explorations that do not use foods.

Connections. LITERATURE: Have children try to figure out what was used to make the prints in books such as *Swimmy* (Lionni, 1963), and *I Was All Thumbs* (Waber, 1975). Invite children to cut their prints into shapes and paste them into a booklet. If they wish they can then add drawings and a story to go with them.

ART AWARENESS: Look for silk-screen prints by Native American artists of the Northwest coast, such as Tim Paul, Bill Reid, Tony Hunt, and others. Also seek handprinted fabric from India and Africa. Indian wood blocks, used for printing the cloth, be found in import stores.

Studio Page 47

WHAT IS YOUR PERSONAL SENSE OF BEAUTY?

Make a list of things that you think are beautiful. Next to each item record whether it is from nature or human-made. Also note how you decided it was beautiful. From whom did you learn to appreciate its beauty? What qualities about it make it beautiful?

Item of Beauty	Source	Why It Is Beautiful.

Review your list. Can you find any relationships among these items? What senses do you use in experiencing these beautiful things? What has been the greatest influence on your personal sense of beauty?

_____

_____

_____

_____

_____

_____

_____

_____

_____

Studio Page

REVIEWING THE ART ELEMENTS

Draw an illustration for each of these art elements.

Line	Shape
Color	Texture
Pattern	Form
Space	Symmetry

Studio Page

DESIGNING A BIG BOOK ABOUT ART

A big book is the perfect size to read to a group of small children. The large pictures can be easily seen by everyone. The Appendix at the end of this book suggests many commercial big books you can use. However, you will not find books on every topic you may need, nor will the books exactly fit your chosen activities. The ideal solution is to use your creativity and make your own!

Guidelines for Creating a Big Book on an Art Topic

1. Select a topic based on one of the art elements or senses.
2. Limit the book to five or six one-sided pages.
3. Use just a few words.
4. Illustrations should be made from the same materials that the children will have to use.
5. Illustrations should be large, bold, and simple. Avoid cute, stereotyped, or cartoon-type drawings.
6. Plan the book so that the children can interact with it. For example, include pockets that contain hidden shapes or holes to look through.
7. Make the pages from heavy oaktag, poster board, or corrugated cardboard. Join the pages with metal looseleaf rings.

Suggested Ideas for Your Big Book

Topic: Color. Feature a different color on each page. For each color, cut out a variety of shapes from different kinds of paper in that color. Write the color names in crayon and marker in that color. At the back of the book attach an envelope containing shapes in each color. Have children find the correct page for the "lost" shapes.

Topic: Pattern. Use gadget or sponge prints to illustrate the following concepts.

All patterns are made of repeated shapes.
Some patterns are made from one repeated shape.
Some patterns are made with two repeated shapes.
Some patterns are made with three or more repeated shapes.
Some patterns are made in only one color.
Some patterns have lots of colors.
Some patterns are made of differently sized shapes.

Use yarn to attach samples of the objects used to make the prints to the book. Invite children to match them to the patterns.

Topic: Line. Use marker, crayon, or paint to draw different kinds of lines on each page. Some to include are: straight, curved, zigzag, jagged, thick, thin. Try to have each line be a continuation of the one on the previous page. On the last page, put all the different lines together in a wild line "party."

Studio Page *50*

PLANNING YOUR BIG BOOK

Use this page to plan your big book.

Title:

Topic:

Studio Page 51

OBSERVATION: A SENSORY EXPERIENCE

Choose one of the senses and design a sensory experience for children. Present the activity to two or three children and record what the children do.

Date of Observation: Length of Observation:

Age of Children: Size of Group:

1. Describe the sensory experience:

    _____

    _____

    _____

    _____

2. What is the first thing the children do?

    _____

    _____

    _____

    _____

3. What do you say and do?

    _____

    _____

    _____

    _____

4. What do the children do and say?

    _____

    _____

    _____

    _____

5. How long do the children investigate the activity?

    _____

    _____

    _____

    _____

Studio Page *52*

POST-OBSERVATION ANALYSIS

Using the information in this chapter and what you learned from the observation, defend the inclusion of sensory art activities in an early childhood setting.

_____
_____
_____
_____
_____
_____
_____
_____
_____
_____
_____
_____
_____
_____
_____
_____
_____
_____
_____
_____
_____
_____
_____
_____
_____
_____
_____
_____
_____

9

Mommy, It's a Mola!

Introducing Children to the Art of Others

Questions addressed in this chapter:

What do children learn from the art of others?

How should artworks be selected?

Why should the program include art from other cultures?

How can teachers build their collections?

How are artworks, prints, and artifacts used with children?

How can community resources be used?

How can children's literature be used to teach art?

SUMMARY: Becoming an Artist

FURTHER READING

ART FOCUS: The Fiber Arts

Young Artists At Work

"What are those things?" Brian whispers.

"I think they're spaceships," his friend Allen replies.

"No, silly, can't you see they're whirlies?" says Shannon.

"What's a whirly?"

"That's when you take a brush and whirl it all around."

"Oh," says Michael thoughtfully, "I do that when I paint too."

"Well," says the teacher, coming up behind the children, "I see you have discovered our new print, Van Gogh's *Starry Night*. Come over to the rug and I'll read you a story about the artist. It's called *Camille and the Sunflowers* (Anholt, 1994).

WHAT DO CHILDREN LEARN FROM THE ART OF OTHERS?

Fine taste in the arts, or in any other aspect of life, cannot be specifically taught nor suddenly acquired. It develops slowly and subtly as a result of frequent exposure to examples which various cultures and generations have recognized as significant.

ALINE D. WOLF (1984, p. 21)

The aesthetic experiences that teachers present to children sensitize them to the qualities of objects in their environment. In selecting those objects we must look not only to nature, but also to the artwork and artifacts that express our cultural and historical roots. The graphic images and human-made objects that surround children when they are young will have an impact on how they will judge other artwork they encounter throughout life. People tend to like those things with which they feel comfortable and to reject the strange and unfamiliar. It is a basic principle of good advertising to bombard customer's senses until the product is so familiar, they choose it almost automatically. Educators must decide what they would like the objects in their children's environment to advertise.

Expanding the Child's Definition of Art

Children absorb many meanings from the objects in their environment. The illustrations in the books teachers select to read, the pictures they hang on the wall, and the knickknacks on the shelf all show what artistic images those teachers personally value. Do not think children are too busy playing to notice. Watch what happens if they are told not to touch something that has been sitting "unnoticed" in the room for several weeks or an "ignored" picture that has been hanging on the wall for two months is turned upside down.

Through the display of carefully selected artworks, children learn that art is more than just "messing around for fun." The children learn that art is not just what they do when they paint at the easel or draw with crayons. They learn that when they are exploring art forms they are participating in a long chain of human creativity. Young

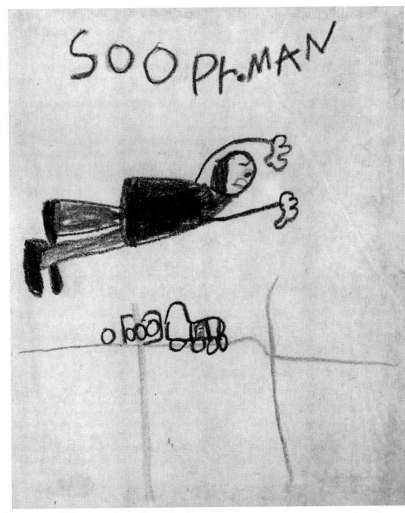

FIGURE 9–1 "Soopr.man." Crayon—Laurel, age 5

children naturally create art as part of their way of interacting with and learning about the world. Exposure to the art of others helps them understand why art is created, who is an artist, and how art is a part of their everyday environment.

Participating in the process of making art is only one facet of a total art experience. Surrounding children with exciting artworks to explore with all the senses provides them with the impetus to practice the cognitive skills of describing and responding to art.

How Do Young Children Perceive the Art of Others?

Initially, children respond to artwork in a sensory way, seeing colors, shapes, and textures. Children consistently prefer the brightest colors and are strongly attracted to colorful artwork (Parsons, 1987; Winner; 1982). Although children as young as two years old can identify pictures as representations of objects (Winner, 1989), they often prefer abstract artwork. They like to free-associate imaginary ideas or memories from the picture's image (Parsons, 1987). When viewing representational artwork, young children tend to prefer simpler and more direct pictures, whereas adult "art experts" would select more complex and intricate ones (Gardner, 1973). Young children tend to have "favorites," works that are personally pleasing. They judge artwork as good based on whether or not they like it (Parsons, 1987). Although they cannot readily identify different art styles, children recognize that art can show imaginary subjects (Gardner, Winter, and Kircher, 1975).

Children also have many misconceptions about art. Even though they, themselves, may have made art from similar media, many children may not be able to identify how an artwork they did not witness being made was created. They also may not be familiar with museums and what kind of artwork is exhibited there (Gardner et al., 1975).

Educators can utilize young children's initial attraction to colorful graphic images to attract them into looking at a wide variety of artworks. The artworks themselves will invite them into conversation about the qualities of the pieces. The ability to understand artworks extends far beyond seeing the subject of the piece. Teaching children to notice the way different artists have used the elements of art—line, shape, color, texture, pattern, form, and space—sets the stage for a more sophisticated understanding of art.

HOW SHOULD ARTWORKS BE SELECTED?

If young children delight in looking at picture books of bunnies, babies and bears, why not paintings such as Da Vinci's "Mona Lisa," Van Gogh's "Starry Night," Renoir's "Girl with a Watering Can" or Chagall's "Peasant Life."

JOYCE MESROBIAN (1992, p. 19)

In order to select the best art images to share with the children, teachers must rely on more than their own personal values about what kind of art is pleasing to them. The children already bring with them the aesthetic values of their family and culture. Teachers must expand their knowledge of art so that the children will be exposed not only to the style of art with which their heritage and upbringing have made them comfortable, and the art that reflects their background, but also those works that allow the children to experience a wide range of artistic inventiveness.

Criteria for Selection

It should be the goal of every guiding adult to help children value the very essence of artistic creation, regardless of the artist of its origins. By exposing children to a wide range of art forms, we prepare them to be accepting of others' creativity wherever they encounter it, throughout their lives. As Gardner (1991, p. 101) states,"...models initially encountered by children continue to affect their tastes and preferences indefinitely, and these preferences prove very difficult to change."

Selected artworks should illustrate the following concepts:

1. People of many different ages create art.
2. Art has been made by people from many places and times.
3. Art tells us about the lives of other people.
4. Art is made from a wide variety of materials that reflect the environment and choice of the artist.
5. There are many ways or styles of doing art.
6. Art is found in many places in our environment.

Sources of Information About Artworks

Teachers must take the time to learn all that they can about the history and stories that relate to each piece of art that they present to the children. The more they know about

Art Words

Major Styles of Western Art

Abstract Expressionism

Art having no recognizable subject, with a focus on color and media, often applied in a kinesthetic way. *Artists:* Willem De Kooning, Hans Hofmann, Jackson Pollock, Wassily Kandinsky

Abstraction

Art that is based on real images but uses them as design elements. *Artists:* Constantin Brancusi, Lyonel Feininger, Paul Klee, Henry Matisse, Henry Moore, Joan Miró

Cubism

Art that represents three-dimensional objects as if made of geometric shapes and forms. *Artists:* Paul Cézanne, Georges Braque, Pablo Picasso

Expressionism

Art that focuses on showing emotions. *Artists:* Paul Gauguin, Edvard Munch, Vincent Van Gogh, Georges Rouault

Folk Art

Art done by people who have not had formal training in art or who use nontraditional art media. *Artists:* David Butler the "Tin Man," Grandma Moses, Henri Rousseau

Impressionism

Art that focuses on capturing the effect of light. *Artists:* Mary Cassat, Edgar Degas, Claude Monet, Pierre Auguste Renoir

Kinetic Art

Art that moves or has moving parts. *Artist:* Alexander Calder

Nonobjective

Art based on geometric and organic shapes and forms. *Artists:* Piet Mondrian, Hans Hofmann, Franz Kline

Op Art

Art based on visual illusions and perceptions. *Artists:* Frank Stella, Victor Vaserly

Pointillism

Art that uses small dots of different colors that the eye blends together. *Artist:* Georges Seurat, Camille Pissarro.

Pop Art

Art that is based on images from everyday life and popular culture, such as soup cans, clothespins, and cartoons. *Artist:* Jasper Johns, Roy Lichtenstein, Claus Oldenburg, Andy Warhol

---

Art Words (continued)

Major Styles of Western Art (continued)

Realism

Art that focuses on showing reality. *Artists:* John Audubon, Leonarado DaVinci, Winslow Homer, Edward Hopper, Georgia O'Keefe, Maxfield Parrish, Rembrandt Van Rijn, Grant Wood, Andrew Wyeth

Romanticism

Art that attempts to make everything look more beautiful and wonderful than reality. *Artists:* Albert Bierstadt, William Blake, John Constable, John Copley, Eugène Delacroix, Jacques David, William Turner

Surrealism

Art that focuses on fantasies or dreams. *Artists:* Marc Chagall, Salvadore Dali

---

the art, the more confidently they will be able to present it to the children. There are many wonderful children's books on specific artists and types of art that can be consulted. They can provide interesting facts to share about the selected pieces. Refer to Appendix B for specific books about artists and their art. Become familiar with the major styles of Western and non-Western art, and the different subject matter and media that artists have used.

Starting a Collection

Every adult who works with children should have a personal collection of art prints and artifacts. This collection can be supplemented with some works provided by a school, another teacher, or even borrowed from an artist, but most of it should consist of individually selected pieces that have been chosen because they relate to what the teacher wants to share with particular children and which meet the criteria stated above. The collection does not have to be large, although over the years it will slowly grow as new pieces are found that speak to the teacher and the children.

Start with one or two pieces of art that are interesting, perhaps some prints or artifacts, and learn about them. Then pick a piece that is unfamiliar, perhaps disconcerting, and find out why it causes those feelings. To start, use the list of art in Table 9–1. Strive for a balanced collection of artworks representing different subject matter, art media, styles, and places of origin. As prints and artifacts are added to the collection, research each one. Slowly expertise will develop. Teachers do not have to become art historians overnight, just experts on one piece of artwork at a time.

Make sure that each piece is engaging for young children. It does not matter if it is a great masterpiece, represents an important culture, or is our favorite artwork; it will not interest children if the subject matter or meaning is too complex for them to understand.

No matter what style is used, children relate best to pictures that have subjects that they can identify with on a very basic level, such as faces, children, and people involved in activities, animals, nature scenes, and places. This does not mean that the pictures can only show familiar subjects, but they should have something on which children can base their understanding. Children who have never seen a red poppy can relate to the flower element of Georgia O'Keefe's *Red Poppy*. They do not have to have lived in the sixteenth century to identify with the child in Rembrandt's *Girl with Broom*. They will also enjoy abstract and nonobjective works that resemble their own artwork, and works such as René Magritte's *Raining Cats and Dogs*, that involve visual puns or tricks.

WHY SHOULD THE PROGRAM INCLUDE ART FROM OTHER CULTURES?

> How can we teach the essence of a people—Native American people, for instance? We can't, but we can do better than bows and arrows.
>
> PATTY GREENBERG (1992, P. 80)

Art communicates more than stereotypes or bald facts. Children learn more about a culture and its people from looking at its art, learning about how and why it was made, and coming to understand the use or importance of artwork in that culture, than they do from making stereotyped symbols of that culture. It is important, when selecting pieces for a personal art collection, to include examples of artwork from a diversity of cultures.

Art Words

Art Subjects

Abstract
A picture emphasizing shapes, colors, lines, and texture over subject matter.

Cityscape
A view of a city.

Interior
A picture showing the inside of a room.

Landscape
An outdoor scene.

Portrait
A picture of a person.

Seascape
A view of the sea.

Still Life
An arrangement of objects on a surface.

Art Words

Art Media

Acrylic

A painting made from acrylic polymer paints.

Collage

A picture containing glued-on objects or paper.

Crafts

Art that is based on traditional handcrafted techniques such as basket making, embroidery, glassmaking, quilting, pottery, tin work, weaving.

Drawing

A picture made from any linear art material: pencil, marker, charcoal, pen and ink.

Fresco

A painting made in wet plaster.

Mixed Media

A picture or sculpture made from a combination of materials, such as paint, paper, wire, and fabric.

Mobile

Three-dimensional art that moves.

Monoprint

A picture made using a technique that produces only one print.

Oil

A painting done with oil-based pigments.

Pastel

A chalk drawing.

Print

A picture made using any one of the printing techniques that produce multiple copies including woodcut, serigraph (silk screen), etching, and lithography.

Sculpture

A three-dimensional artwork. Sculpture can be made from a limitless variety of materials including wood, stone, clay, metal, found objects, papier-mâché, fabric, plaster, wax, and resins.

TABLE 9-1 Engaging Art Posters for Young Children

These exemplify the type of artwork that appeals to young children. Most are readily available from the sources listed. Addresses are listed in Appendix A.

TITLE	ARTIST/CULTURE	DESCRIPTION	SOURCE
The Acrobat	Marc Chagall	Floating man.	Modern Learning
Banjo Lesson	Henry O. Tanner	Boy learning banjo from grandfather.	Modern Learning/Dale Seymour Portfolios: African American Artists
Beasts of the Sea	Henri Matisse	Cut-paper collage of sea life.	Take 5: Collage
Blue Boat	Winslow Homer	Fishermen in blue canoe.	Boston
California	John Outterbridge	Sculptural assemblage of car.	Take 5: African American Art
Cat and Bird	Paul Klee	Abstract cat with a "hidden" bird to find.	Metropolitan
Children at Beach	Mary Cassat	Two toddlers dig in sand.	National
Hope Street: Church Mothers	Marie Johnson-Calloway	Black women dressed for church.	MAPS Set: Crystal
Decorated Eggs	Ukranian	Psyanky.	Dale Seymour
Diamond in Red, Yellow and Blue	Piet Mondrian	Geometric design.	National
False Face Mask	Iroquois	Carved wood mask..	Mask Set: Crystal
Girl with Watering Can	August Renoir	Impressionism— young girl in garden.	Metropolitan
Going to Church	William H. Johnson	Black family goes to church.	African-American set: Crizmac
Goldfish	Henri Matisse	Colorful abstract of fish in a glass jar.	Metropolitan
Hilltop Farm	Maxfield Parrish	Blue-toned evening winter landscape.	Boston
Hopi-Tewa Vessels	Nampeyo	Pottery bowls.	Take 5: Native American
Improvisation 31	Wasily Kandinsky	Pastel non-objective.	National
Reclining Mother and Child	Henry Moore	Stone sculpture.	Take 5: Sculpture
Red Horses	Franz Marc	Three red playful horses.	Boston
Red Poppy	Georgia O'Keefe	Giant close-up of red poppy.	Boston
Robinson Garcia Laguna	Kuna People of Panama	Mola of appliquéd cloth showing two boxers.	Folk Art Set: Crystal
Soap Bubbles	Jean-Baptist Chardin	Realistic view of boy blowing bubbles.	Take 5: Children
Standing Bison	Douglas Mazonowitz	Prehistoric cave art reproduction.	Modern Learning
Storyteller	Pueblo (Native American)	Folk Art: pottery sculpture of storyteller with children.	Print Set: Crystal
Tar Beach	Faith Ringgold	Black family group.	Take 5: Urban Environments

TABLE 9-1 Engaging Art Posters for Young Children (continued)

TITLE	ARTIST/CULTURE	DESCRIPTION	SOURCE
The Circus	Georges Seurat	Pointillistic circus scene in pastels.	Metropolitan
Sunflowers	Vincent Van Gogh	Thickly textured, yellow-toned still life.	Modern Learning
Tropical Forest with Monkeys	Henri Rousseau	Imaginary jungle scene.	National
War Wolf Helmet	Tlingit (Native American)	Carved wood headpiece.	Mask Set: Crystal
Water Lilies	Claude Monet	Impressionistic view of water.	Boston

Note: Some prints are available only in sets. Other prints in the sets may also be useful with young children.

When children see that the art of their culture and the art of other cultures contain many similarities, that culture becomes less strange and more appreciated. A simple woven basket from Botswana can link a small African village where baskets are used for carrying and storing grains, fruits, and peanuts, to a preschool where similar baskets are used to hold some of the art supplies. African masks can be compared to the masks worn by people on Halloween and by characters on TV and in plays and movies. All over the world artists have created art for the same purposes—to beautify their homes, to make everyday things distinctive, to make a personal statement, to tell their stories or record their history, and to express their spiritual beliefs. Art binds together all of humankind.

What Do Children Learn From Multicultural Art Examples?

> The art of a people can introduce the sense of pride in one's own heritage that is so badly needed by so many minority children. It can also introduce respect for other's achievements, which is equally needed by all children.
>
> ELAINE PEAR COHEN AND RUTH STRAUS GAINER (1995, p. 223)

When children see the art of their heritage displayed and honored, they feel valued as people. When children see the art of others treated with esteem, they learn to respect people who are different from them. Children model their behavior on adults' behavior. As teachers add pieces to their collection of artworks, they must consider the message their selection and focused discussion about them will give the children. Before we can teach children to relate to the art of the world, we, ourselves, must come to love and understand the art of others. We will always have our personal favorites, just as the children will, but as we live and work with each piece, it will become an old friend from which we will not wish to part.

In selecting artwork for the collection, make sure that it is representative of the art of everyone and that each piece is accorded respect and understanding.

1. Examples of multicultural art should be displayed in our rooms every day. Do not trivialize the art work of others by showing it only in the context of a particular holiday or art project.

2. Strive for balance. Do not collect most of the examples from one racial or ethnic group.
3. Respect the integrity of the artwork and the particular time, place, and person who created it. Do not disconnect the artwork from its creators by having the children copy the symbols or the design of the work. Making a paper copy of an African mask in a school setting is not the same as the ritualistic carving of a wooden mask by the African artist.
4. Avoid stereotypes. Collect artwork that shows different racial and ethnic groups involved in all kinds of common activities. Make sure that the examples are not just from the past but include art that was made by living artists.

HOW CAN TEACHERS BUILD THEIR COLLECTIONS?

> Children feel a certain magic about the real thing. You hear their breath draw in, see their eyes widen, hear their respect and wonder… Nothing really substitutes for this experience.
>
> Jo Miles Schuman (1981, p. 1)

There are several types and sources of art examples from which teachers can build a collection. Try to include pieces of each kind so that the children will experience a breadth of art media in a variety of formats.

Original Artwork

Children need to see and touch "real" pieces of art. They need to feel the texture of an oil painting, the flowing form of a stone carving, and the exhilaration of blowing on a mobile. They will have many of these experiences in the context of creating their own art. They also need, however, to see that it is not just little children, in this room, at this time, who make art. There are many art media and forms that are not safe for or within the skill level of children, but which they can experience on an aesthetic level, such as a welded metal sculpture or a piece of stained glass. Original art forms can be obtained in the following ways:

Other children. The teacher's personal collection of children's art can provide pieces for the current group of children to study. Permanently mounted in public spaces such as the hall and lobby, group-produced pieces such as clay tiles (see chapter 6) or mobiles provide a tie to the children who have come before.

Artists in the community. Every community has wonderful artists who work in all kinds of art media. Most of these people are willing to lend or donate a piece of art. A donated oil painting or wood carving has an advantage over borrowed pieces in that the children can handle as well as look at the piece. The piece does not have to be the artist's most cherished or even completed. An unfinished painting or sculpture can be more interesting for young children to explore than an elaborately framed artwork that they cannot touch. Children are concerned with process, and unfinished works mirror their own approach to art.

Teachers' artwork. If teachers have done original art of their own, they may have a piece to share with the children. It could be a picture drawn as a young child or a piece of pottery made in a workshop. Sharing a piece of their own artwork is very different from providing a model they have made and expect the children to copy.

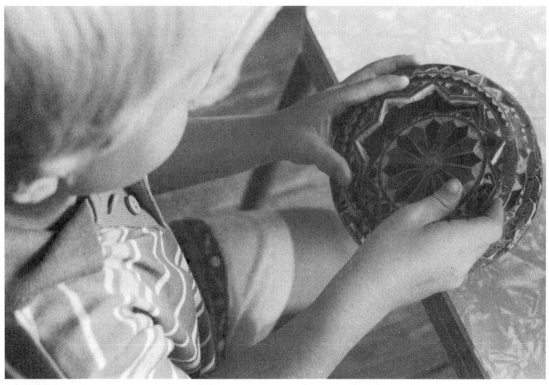

FIGURE 9–2 Children need many opportunities to experience the art of others. A Peruvian carved gourd, with a lid that fits in only one way, fascinates a toddler.

Display the art, and discuss it with the children. Do not then have the children do an art exploration with the same materials, as that would be too much like providing a model. Remember that as educators we stand in a unique relationship with the child. There are many things that we do teach by modeling. We expect children to copy the correct shapes of letters and numbers. We want them to copy our manners and the way we are sensitive to others. We do not want them to copy our art.

What teachers can do, when sharing their artwork, is model how artists share their creative efforts. The children learn that people they know and care about create art. Share how it felt to make it, why it is special, and where it is kept at home. By being proud of their own work, teachers model self-confidence. Use this experience to lead into a discussion about what the children might like to share about their own art.

Fine Art Posters

In recent years, inexpensive but high-quality prints of artworks from around the world have become widely available. Posters have the advantage of being large enough for a group of children to experience at one time and durable enough to take many years of handling. Sources for art prints and suggested titles that appeal to young children are listed in Table 9–1 and Appendix A. Fine-art prints can also sometimes be borrowed from libraries.

Medium-sized prints. Smaller art prints can be obtained inexpensively from some of the many beautiful calendars that feature artworks of all kinds, and from a variety of magazines and catalogs. These prints are too small for large group study or public display, but are perfect for use with small groups of three or four children.

Miniart prints. Museum postcards and pictures clipped from museum catalogs and mounted on tag board can be used for a variety of activities by one or two children. These prints are just the right size for small hands, and the freedom they have to handle them makes them very popular with children.

Art Books

There are many books written especially for children that contain numerous examples of art. Books are best used for sharing the art with one or two children at a time, or for a child to use independently. Children gain nothing from observing the small prints in a book when it is shared with a large group. Showing a group of children a picture of an African mask from a heavy adult art book, and then expecting them to show appreciation for this art form is ridiculous. For a child the miniature picture in the book has no relationship to the powerful, life-size piece of art it represents.

When reading a book about an art form to a group of children, try to have a related large print or artifact to share with them as well as the illustrations. Otherwise, share the book with just a few children at a time or put it in the reading area for children to enjoy on their own.

Art Artifacts

An artifact is a handmade, three-dimensional, cultural art form. Examples of artifacts include baskets, quilts, and wood carvings. They are often unsigned, made for daily use, and may be considered a form of collective folk art. They are not usually unique one-of-a-kind pieces, but are representative of a class of articles from the everyday life of a people. These are the cultural art forms that represent the ethnic heritage of a group of people. They are often handed down from one generation to another and carry the family's story with them.

In American culture, examples of contemporary artifacts include handmade quilts, weavings, and pottery. Although they may not be considered fine arts because of the element of repetition of traditional forms and designs, high-quality handmade artifacts retain the creative touch of the artist. They are not made from precut or purchased patterns; they represent a creative variation on a piece that follows a cultural tradition.

When selecting artifacts, choose those that reflect the artist who created it. Each handmade and designed artifact will have a different color, form, and perhaps decorative element from the others. Artifacts are made from materials that are found in the locality in which they were made. A quilt might be made from a family's old clothing or a weaving from the neighbor's sheep wool.

Sources of art artifacts. These items are intended for home, community, or ritual use, not for public display outside the culture. Teachers may have some artifacts that have belonged to their own families or that they have made themselves and can share with the children. If teachers are willing to share personally valued artifacts, such as Grandmother's patchwork quilt, others are more likely to do so. The families of the children may wish to bring in a special artifact to show the group. If friends have traveled widely or are collectors of a specific type of artifact, they may be willing to let the children see one or two pieces or might invite the children to visit the collection. (See the following section on using community resources for specific guidelines.) Sharing cultural artifacts is an excellent way to bond people of different heritages together.

TABLE 9-2 Multicultural Artifacts

Banners	Baskets
Beads	Beadwork
Calligraphy	Cloth, hand-painted, hand-dyed, or hand-printed
Cornhusk items	Crocheted items
Decorated eggs	Dolls, handmade
Embroidery	Ethnic clothing
Figurines, modeled clay, stone, wood	Furniture, handmade
Games, hand-carved or modeled	Glassware, hand-blown
Gourds, carved	Handmade papers, also cast paper
Jewelry, handmade	Inlays, wood or stone
Knitted items of original design	Lacquerware
Masks	Mats, woven fiber
Mosaics	Musical instruments
Papier-mâché	Pottery, hand- or wheel-built, not slip cast
Puppets	Quilts
Sand painting	Scrimshaw
Straw designs	Tapestries
Tinware	Weavings
Wrought iron	Yarn paintings

On occasion, a particular artifact may be purchased that will either expand the cultural experience of the children or relate to an activity. For example, share an Indonesian shadow puppet before making shadow puppets with the children. If cultural artifacts are being sold, it should be to benefit the family or community that made them. Beware of items made for the "souvenir" market. Especially on imported items, look for labels that indicate the country of origin. Avoid those that look like they were mass produced. Before buying an artifact, research its culture to find out if this item is one that is used in the daily life of the people. Artifacts of all kinds are available from many sources such as department stores, importers, charitable organizations, and craft fairs. Charitable organizations are a good source because they usually provide information about who made the item and how the money will be used to help the artisans. Craft fairs provide the opportunity to buy directly from the creator and to collect the story that goes with the piece.

Many artifacts are relatively low-cost and durably made. After all, they are intended to survive the wear and tear of a normal household. Children will especially benefit from being able to touch and perhaps even to use the artifact, such as using an African basket to serve crackers for snack, eating soup from a hand-thrown tureen or sitting under a handmade quilt for story time. Try to have a few such usable artifacts in the collection. Table 9–2 suggests some of the types of artifacts that teachers might seek. Appendix A provides a list of artifacts and their sources.

HOW ARE ARTWORKS, PRINTS, AND ARTIFACTS USED WITH CHILDREN?

There are activities in a developmentally appropriate curriculum that can take art to another level, one of discussion and understanding.

MARJORIE SCHILLER (1995, p. 38)

How a piece of art is presented is as important as the selection process that went into obtaining it. Hanging a Van Gogh print on the wall or displaying a piece of Burmese

FIGURE 9–3 There are many ways to share fine art with young children. Showing just a tantalizing part of an artwork adds an element of surprise. "Rembrandt Bear" helps introduce the print Goldfish by Matisse using a peekaboo window.

lacquerware is just a start. If teachers do not focus the children's attention on the artwork and relate it to their lives and artistic heritage, it will have no more meaning than the cartoon characters that decorate so many classrooms. Teachers must engage children in the process of looking, questioning, and thinking about each piece. The following activities will provide models that can be expanded to accompany any artwork selected for a collection.

Setting Up a Masterpiece Corner

Select a prominent place in the room in which to display a featured piece of artwork on a regular basis. The area should be free from distractions like toys, competing signs, and other wall decorations, and be in a "clean hands" area. Store related fine-art manipulatives, art books, and prints on shelves nearby. There should be room for several children to gather. Like the sensory table, a good location is near the entrance to the room where it will attract the children's attention as they enter with fresh eyes each new day.

It is important to place the print or artifact at the children's eye level. Leave one artwork on exhibit for a length of time. If the subject corresponds with a theme focus, leave it up during that theme period.

After several days of display or if several children become very interested in the piece, involve the children in one of the following suggested art appreciation activities.

Using a Puppet or Stuffed Animal

The key to engaging the children's interest in a piece of artwork is in the way we express our personal enthusiasm and interest in the work. Our voices need to be full of energy and excitement as we discuss the artwork with the children. Some people find it helpful to use a puppet or stuffed animal. Just like children, adults often feel less inhibited when having "Rembrandt Bear" or "Art, the Aardvark" talk to the children.

Convert a simple stuffed animal or purchased puppet into an "art expert" by adding a few small details such as a beret, a smock (with paint splotches, of course), and by sewing a crayon or paintbrush onto a "paw." An original puppet can be created using a sock, papier-mâché, or cloth. It helps if the "arms" can be moved so more expression can be added to the presentation. The "art expert" should be constructed durably as it will prove a popular friend to the children, who will often model the teacher's art discussions in their play. Make sure to give it a personal history that tells how it came to be so expert in art.

Questions to Ask

Although the specific questions will depend upon the particular piece that has been selected, the following list of questions suggests some ideas to get started.

What does it tell you about? These questions focus on the subject matter or the story of the artwork.

- What is the season? Weather? Time of day?
- What kind of place is this?
- What is happening in this picture?
- Who is this person? Who are these people? What are they doing?
- What is this animal? Tree? Plant? Building?
- What objects in the picture do you know? Use? Are there any you do not know? Use?

How was it made? These questions help children learn about the different art media.

- How do you think the artist made this? How can you tell?
- Does this look like it was made with any art materials that we use?
- What do you think the artist used to put the paint on her painting?
- How did the artist make this texture? Color? Line? Shape? Pattern?
- How did the artist carve this hard stone? Wood?

Can you find? These questions give the children practice in using art vocabulary.

- Can you find a line? Shape? Color? Texture? Pattern? (Be specific, e.g., red rectangle, rough texture.)
- Can you trace with your finger a line? Shape?
- Can you touch or point to a line? Shape? Color? Texture? Pattern?

How does it make you feel? Young children are not always able to express their feelings verbally. Be accepting of any responses that the children make to these questions. Trying to imagine how the people in artworks, particularly portraits, and how the artists feel, helps children become more sensitive to the feelings of others.

- If you were in this place, how would you feel?
- How does the person in this picture feel?
- How was the artist feeling when she made this?

- How do you feel when you look at this?
- Do you ever feel that way when you paint? Draw? Model?

What comes next? These questions challenge children to make predictions based on the visual clues they see and allow them to practice creative visualization. In designing these questions, make sure there are enough clues to give direction to the child, but that there is no one right answer. Be accepting of all responses.

- What do you think will happen next? Happened before?
- What do you think this person (animal) will do next? Did before?
- What will the weather be later?
- Who do you think lives in this building?
- What is inside this building? Box?
- What is behind this tree? Building? Fence? Curtain? Door?

How many? Questions can also relate to other curriculum areas such as math, language arts, social studies, and science.

- How many red circles (blue squares, etc.) can you find? (Math)
- Tell me a story about this picture. (Language Arts)
- Why are these houses made from reeds? (Social Studies)
- Do these clouds look like rain clouds? (Science)

Can you do? Asking children to respond kinesthetically to art helps them develop their mental imaging skills and allows them to become more involved in the artwork. There are no right answers to these questions; accept all of the children's responses.

- Can you make your face look like this one?
- Can you stand (sit) in the same position as this person? How would this person walk?
- Can you imagine you are climbing this tree? (Mime climbing up a tree.)
- Can you imagine opening and closing this door? Looking in this window? (Mime.)
- Can you imagine you are touching this animal? (Mime.)

What is the same or different? These questions encourage the children to develop skill in visual comparison. For very young children, keep the comparisons very general and obvious. Older children will enjoy trying to solve trickier ones.
In a single artwork:

- In this picture which person (house, animal) is bigger? Older? Younger? Smaller?
- Can you find the biggest (smallest) square (triangle)?
- Can you find the longest (shortest, thickest, thinnest) line?
- Can you find the brightest (dullest, lightest, darkest) color?

Comparing two artworks:

- In which picture is there a person? A house? An animal? A rectangle? the color pink?
- Which picture looks more real?
- Which artwork is round (three-dimensional)? Which is flat?
- Which artwork makes you feel happy? Sad?
- Which artwork have we seen before?

Personal taste. These questions allow the children to express their personal reaction to an artwork based on their aesthetic response of the moment. Asking children to pick their favorite is a good way to spark interest in an artwork. It is a useful assessment technique to ask the children for their personal opinions when first displaying an artwork, and then again after it has been on display awhile and discussed. Notice if negative initial reactions have changed or become tempered as the child becomes more familiar with the piece. Be accepting of all responses.

Do not tell children they must like something, but do make them justify their response by asking "Why?" Young children may not be able to express verbally why the piece elicits a certain personal response and may respond with, "Because..." or "I don't know, I just do." However, asking "why" sets up a pattern in which the child learns that a feeling about an artwork is always based on something. Some of the sophisticated justifications young children can make are quite surprising, especially after they have looked at and discussed several artworks.

- Do you like this? Why?
- Which of these is your favorite? Why?
- Would you like this artwork to hang in your home? Bedroom? Why?
- Would you like to meet this artist? Why?
- Would you like to make an artwork like this? Why?

Presenting Artwork From Another Culture

When presenting an artwork from another culture, have the children focus on its universal artistic qualities first so that it is clearly identified as a piece of art. Ask a selection of questions from any of the art categories before asking about the cultural element. Questions should focus on finding similarities with familiar art forms and investigating possible uses such as:

- How is this artwork similar to one we use? Make?
- How do you think it is used?

Remember that young children under eight have a minimal knowledge of the world. They do not know specific geographical information. They respond best when descriptions of how something is made and used in another place are embedded in a story. Children can identify with common human themes such as family, food, and homes; they love stories that contain animals. Consult Appendix B for some suggested story books or write an original story.

Designing a Big Book About Artworks

If a children's book about the specific artwork to be presented cannot be found, the teacher can make a big book for the children. In designing such a book, try to find photographs in magazine articles or calendar illustrations, or draw simple pictures or make collages that show the steps in making the artwork. If possible, glue on real samples of the materials used to make the artwork, such as wool and yarn for a book about weaving, or palm leaves for a book about basket making. Many craft stores carry art materials from around the world. When presenting an artwork from another culture, research details such as children's names, customs, and daily life so that the story will be accurate.

Children like repetitive and cumulative text books. Here is a sample of a repetitive text based on information about basket making in Botswana from *Native Artists of Africa* by Reavis Moore (1993):

> Nangura of the Mbukushu goes to the river,
> To get the palm leaves,
> For a basket to store her grain in.

Nangura of the Mbukushu collects the bark
To dye the palm leaves,
For a basket to store her grain in.

A cumulative text is an excellent format for describing the creation of artwork that is done in a series of steps, and the repetition of each step helps the children learn the sequence of how the article was made. Hand or body motions can be designed that mime the process to go along with the text. Using the same information as was used in the repetitive sample, here is a brief sample of a cumulative text.

Nangura of the Mbukushu goes to the river, (Mime walking.)
To collect the palm leaves, (Mime reaching up for leaves.)
For a basket to store her grain in. (Mime holding a basket.)

Nangura of the Mbukushu goes to the forest, (Mime walking.)
To collect the bark to dye the palm leaves, (Mime pulling bark.)
For a basket to store her grain in. (Mime holding basket.)

Nangura of the Mbukushu fills up the kettle, (Mime pouring water.)
To boil the dye, from the bark she collected, to dye the palm leaves, (Mime stirring a hot kettle.)
For a basket to store her grain in. (Mime holding basket.)

Nangura of the Mbukusku gathers up the dyed leaves (Mime gathering leaves.)
that were boiled in the dye, from the bark she collected, to dye the palm leaves, (Mime stirring the kettle.)
For a basket to store her grain in. (Mime holding basket.)

Engaging Children with Art Prints

The following activities are designed to help a small group of toddlers or a larger group of older children become engaged with an art print.

Using a peek-a-boo window. This activity can be done with a large print (12 by 18 inches or larger) that has been on display or one that the children have never seen. From a sheet of paper the same size as the print, cut out a "window" in any shape that corresponds to a particularly interesting part of the picture. For example in a painting such as Matisse's *Goldfish*, highlight one of the fish. In a portrait or mask accent an eye, a mouth, or a decorative element. In an nonobjective art work choose a shape or a color. Place the window paper over the print and fasten it securely at the top so it lifts easily. Then ask a series of thought-provoking questions about that part and what might be in the rest of the picture.

If they have seen the print before, ask questions that challenge their memories.

- Do you remember what this _____ was a part of?
- What other_____ are in this artwork? (colors, shapes, lines, details, textures, animals, people, plants, or any other visual element that relates to the artwork.)
- What is special about this one part of the artwork?

If it is new to them, ask questions that entice them to predict.

- What do you imagine this _____ is part of?
- What else do you think might be in the artwork?
- What other _____ do you imagine are in this artwork? (colors, shapes, lines,

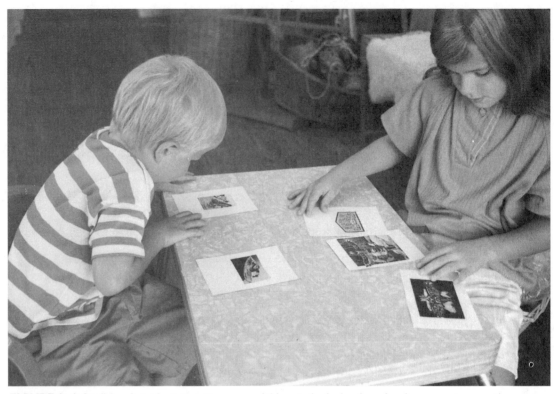

FIGURE 9–4 Small, hand-sized prints entice young children to look closely and make comparisons as they sort and group them.

details, textures, animals, people, plants or any other visual element that relates to the artwork.)

It is not necessary to ask a lot of questions. If the children are very excited about seeing the rest of the artwork after only one or two questions, end the questioning by saying: "Let's look at the artwork and see what the artist chose to do." The children will respond by comparing what they see to what they thought. This is an excellent way to develop mental imagery skills. Often they like to raise and lower the window several times. They also like to be able to touch the artwork. Leave the print covered for a while after the session so children can explore the window effect on their own.

"Envelope (or book) of holes." Medium-sized prints (about 8 by 10 inches) can be used in the same kind of cutout envelope or window book that was described in chapter 8. Medium-sized prints are easy to find. There are many calendars that contain reproductions of art, and people are happy to donate them when the year runs out. Magazine pages are just the right size and a wide range of art is found in magazines such as *The Smithsonian* and *Natural History*. The National Gallery also sells inexpensive prints in this size.

Art to hang. Laminate or cover four or five medium-sized prints with clear contact paper. Punch two holes in the top of each print and attach a string or piece of yarn. Hang a child-height hook in the homelife area or play corner and let the children select and change the displayed art at will. If possible try to get copies of the larger prints that have been discussed with the group, making sure the assortment represents a variety of art forms. Store the prints in an attractive basket or a box decorated with a collage of miniart prints. On occasion substitute or add a new print.

A blank wall or divider in one area of the room can be turned into a "museum" by providing a group of varied medium-sized prints and a row of child-height hooks. Large blocks can be used as bases for any three-dimensional artworks that are durable enough for the children to handle, such as baskets, weaving, and tinware.

Two books to share with the children as they explore the museum area are *Matthew's Dream* (Lionni, 1991), in which a young mouse decides to become an artist after visiting a museum, and *Visiting the Art Museum* (Brown and Brown, 1986).

This area can also become a gallery or crafts fair. Children can "buy" new art to hang in the homelife area, or they can select favorite pieces to take home to share and to enjoy for several days. The yarn hanger makes it easy for parents to display the print on a doorknob or other convenient hanging place. Attach a brief history of the artwork, the artist's name, and any special facts about it to the back of any artwork that is sent home.

Art bags. Sew simple cloth bags with a handle or decorate sturdy paper bags with miniprint collages. In each bag, place a medium-sized print or a durable, inexpensive artifact along with a book that relates to the artwork and a toy, game, clothing, or food item that relates to the theme. It is important to select artwork from a variety of heritages, so that parents as well as children become familiar with the art of others.

Children can take a bag home for a special treat such as a birthday or holiday. Set up a sign-out system. Make sure that the artwork is labeled and provide a notebook in which parents can write their comments before they return the bags.

Living portraits. After sharing several prints of portraits, place an empty, unbreakable picture frame in the area where the dress-up clothes are kept. Children can take turns

TABLE 9-3 Suggestions for Art Bags

ARTWORK: *Still Life with Apples on a Pink Tablecloth* by Henri Mattisse
BOOK: *Who am I? Looking through Shapes at Apples and Grapes* (Dillon and Dillon, 1994)
ITEM: Apple wrapped in a pink piece of cloth

ARTWORK: *Girl with a Watering Can* by Auguste Renoir
BOOK: *Planting a Rainbow* by Lois Ehlert (1988)
ITEM: A packet of flower seeds and a toy watering can

ARTWORK: *Key West, Hauling Anchor* by Winslow Homer
BOOK: *Sail Away* by Donald Crews (1995)
ITEM: A toy sailboat

ARTWORK: *Peaceable Kingdom* by Edward Hicks
BOOK: *The Land of Many Colors* (Klamath County YMCA Preschool, 1993)
ITEM: Animal finger puppets

ARTWORK: Native American basket
BOOK: "Mandan Gardeners" in *Children of Earth and Sky* by Stephen Krensky (1991)
ITEM: Cornmeal chips

ARTWORK: Wood carving of an elephant, from Kenya
BOOK: *I Am Eyes * Ni Macho* by Leila Ward (1978)
ITEM: Peanuts

ART WORK: *Diamond Painting in Red, Yellow and Blue* by Piet Mondrian
BOOK: *Color Zoo* by Lois Ehlert (1989)
ITEM: Set of colorful blocks

Note: All prints mentioned are available in size 11-by-14 inches from the National Gallery of Art.

"posing" behind the frame. Keep a camera handy, so as not to miss some of these creative portraits.

I see a... Play a game modeled on "I see a color...," in which one child names a detail in a print and others have three guesses to find it. The one who finds it goes next. If it is not found the same child goes again. Encourage the children to select art elements such as "I see a red square," or "I see a zigzag line." An exciting variation is to give each child a cardboard "looking" tube to use while playing this game.

Puzzles. Glue an inexpensive, medium-sized print to a piece of corrugated cardboard. Laminate or cover with clear contact paper. Cut it into a few simple shapes that follow the shapes in the picture. Make a frame for the pieces with two sheets of cardboard slightly larger than the print. In one piece cut a window the size of the print. Glue the window frame to the base and fit puzzle pieces inside (see figure 9–5).

Sorting activities using postcard-sized prints. Postcard-sized prints can be purchased; alternatively, glue small copies of prints from art magazines, calendars, and museum catalogs to postcard-sized tag board. If possible have them laminated for durability. Aline Wolf, in her book *Mommy, It's a Renoir!,* explains how to prepare special folders to store sets of miniart prints, and how to create sorting activities for children that increase in difficulty as the children become more familiar with the artworks. Sorting sets can consist of two to four pairs of miniprints that feature contrasting features.
   Some examples of sorting sets include:

- Pairs of duplicate pictures
- Pairs that are predominately the same color, such as two mostly blue artworks and two mostly yellow
- Pair a print that features mostly one color with a card bearing a shape in that color.

FIGURE 9–5 Puzzle construction.

- Pair a print of an artwork that has a basic shape—round, square, etc.—with a matching shape card.
- Pairs of different subjects, such as two portraits, two still-lifes and two landscapes.
- Pairs that show different art forms, such as two African masks, two Navajo weavings, and two Kuna Indian molas.
- Pairs that show the same art form created by different cultures, such as two baskets from Kenya, two Micmac baskets and two American willow baskets.
- Pairs that show the same subject, such as a sun or face, done in different media, styles, or cultures.

Sorting sets are most appropriate for children three and up. Three-year-olds will probably enjoy just looking at the miniprints and doing the simplest matching activities. Older children will enjoy working alone or in pairs trying to match the more challenging sets. Place the sets in attractive folders, clear plastic page protectors, small baskets, or decorated card boxes, and keep them in the "clean hands" area. To make the sorting activity self-checking, place matching symbols on the back of each pair of prints. When children think they have a match they can peek on the back to check themselves.

Sorting game board. A variation on this sorting activity is to create a game board by gluing six miniprints on a piece of cardboard and laminating it or covering it with clear contact paper. The board can be decorated to resemble a museum with different wings such as painting, sculpture, Asian art, and so on. For an easy level provide duplicate miniprints for the children to match with the ones on the board. For a more advanced level provide miniprints that are similar to the ones on the board. Glue a sturdy envelope on the back of the board to store the cards.

Miniprint group games. HOT AND COLD: Postcard-sized prints can be used to play the traditional game of "Hot and Cold." Instead of using a piece of colored paper, a child places a miniprint in plain view somewhere in the room while one or more children leave the room or cover their eyes. Then they try to find the print while the other children tell them if they are getting warmer (closer to the print) or colder (farther from the print).

PRINT MATCH: If several miniprints that match large or medium prints are available, play this matching game. Hang the large or medium prints on the wall and have the children sit in a circle in front of them. In the center of the circle, place the miniprints face down in a basket. Place all the children's names in a basket or use choosing sticks. (Choosing sticks are craft sticks with the child's name written at one end. Place the sticks name-end down into a small container. Pull a stick to choose a child.) The chosen child picks a miniprint and tries to match it to the larger print.

This game provides an excellent opportunity to explain to the children that prints are photographs of real artworks that are in museums. Demonstrate this by showing a real basket and a print of a basket or some similar artwork, or if there are prints that match some of the artifacts, play the Match Game and have them match the print to the real object. To demonstrate enlargement, show a snapshot-sized photograph of something familiar to the children (such as themselves) and an 8-by-10-inch photograph of the same subject. Matching commercial Big Books with the regular versions is another way to reinforce the concept of enlargement. Give the children plenty of time to explore these examples. These are new and difficult concepts for many young children, especially if they have not had much experience with photography.

Miniprint collections. Encourage the children and their parents to begin collections of art postcards. Start them off on a lifelong hobby by giving each child a miniprint in a folder that they can decorate. Postcards are widely available, and families can add to their collection when they travel or visit museums. Provide an information sheet for the family about why and how they should create the collection so that it is clear that the postcards should show artwork and not views or local-interest pictures. Provide time for the children to share their collections and interest them in playing sorting games with their own card sets.

Miniprint gifts. Another way to bring the art of the world into the children's lives is to give them gifts that feature great art. Birthday cards and bookmarks can be made by gluing reproductions of prints clipped from magazines and catalogs onto various sizes and types of paper. Very small prints can be glued to heavy tag board and made into magnets by sticking magnetic tape on the back. If there is access to a badge maker, make art pins for gifts as well. Whenever giving a print as a gift, be sure to label it with the artist or culture that made it.

HOW CAN COMMUNITY RESOURCES BE USED?

> Trips… give children an opportunity to see for themselves something they will learn more about later in pictures or in books or through conversation.
>
> RHONDA REDLEAF (1983, P. 3)

One way for children to learn about other art forms and the role of art in adult life is for them to meet working artists and to see art in the community. Because most young children have short attention spans, these kinds of activities need to be carefully planned.

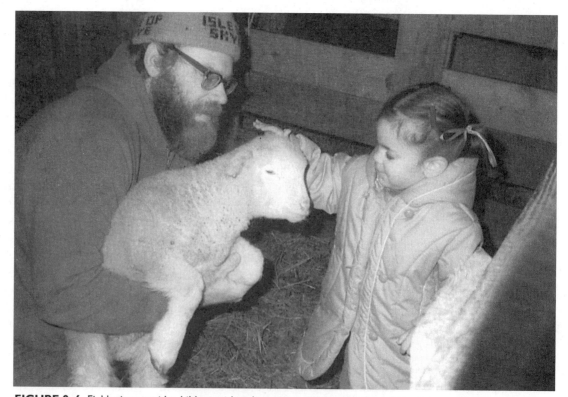

FIGURE 9–6 Field trips provide children with rich sensory experiences that add meaning to their art.

Although a bad experience can do more harm than no experience, it is not difficult to organize a successful artist visit, art-related field trip, or museum trip. The key is to design the experience so that it meets the attention level of the particular children.

Guest Artists

The guest artist can be a friend, a colleague, a family or community member who creates original art that is relatively portable and not injurious to the children's health. It would not be a good idea to have someone oil paint in the children's room or solder stained glass. The person should genuinely like young children and their infinite curiosity. When inviting artists to visit, make sure to prepare them for the particular group of children and explain clearly what they should share and say.

It is a good practice to have an information sheet prepared ahead of time to give to parents and artists who will visit the class. The information sheet should list the times of the various daily activities, the number of children, their ages, and any particular information about items such as special needs. There should also be a brief outline on how to design a program for children this age.

Presenting to toddlers. Toddlers respond best to artists who create fairly large pieces that change appearance quickly. Basket making, painting, drawing, pottery, weaving, and sewing quilt squares together are examples of this kind of art activity.

Setup. Rather than planning a group program, squirmy toddlers respond better if the teacher announces the visitor's arrival and directs the artist to a quiet corner. The artist then sets up and begins to work on a sample piece of art. This kind of presentation mirrors Gardner's "skilled master" model (1991, p. 204).

What the guest should say. Toddlers can gather around to watch and ask questions. The visitor should be prepared to answer the children's questions in a simple, understandable way without talking down to them.

Samples. The visitor should bring sample materials and child-safe tools that can be touched by the toddlers. Any dangerous tools should be put away out of sight after each use or if possible not used during the demonstration. For example, a quilter could substitute small blunt scissors for sharp shears when cutting threads.

Presenting to three-year-olds and up. Children three and up can benefit from a slightly longer and more complex visit. Before the guest arrives, tell the children about the visit and ask questions to find out what they already know about this art form. Relate the visit to any explorations or art activities that the children have done by asking intriguing questions such as, "Mrs. Kahn will be showing us how she paints landscapes today. I wonder if she will use an easel like you do when you paint?" or "Mr. Chang will be showing us Chinese calligraphy today. Calligraphy means beautiful writing. Do you think he uses a paintbrush or a pencil?"

Setup. When visitors arrive and have set up their work, gather the children around and introduce them. Let the guests explain what they do and give a brief demonstration if the art form is suitable for a large group to see clearly, such as working on a large painting or making a good-sized basket. The toddler format can be used for demonstrations that are best viewed by small groups of children at a time. If the process is very long, the guest might bring several samples in various stages of completion and then work on one that is just about complete.

Artists should limit the number of displayed finished pieces to only one or two. More than that is too overwhelming for the children. If the pieces are fragile or breakable they will need to be displayed in a location where the children cannot touch them.

The artist should bring a sample of materials that the children can touch as well. For example, a calligrapher could let the children touch the brush and the ink stone instead of the finished calligraphy.

What the guest should say. Rather than a lecture, the guest should be prepared with interesting questions to ask the children. For example, a quilt maker might ask, "How many pieces do you think are in one square?" or "How big do you think this quilt will be when I have sewn these six squares together?" A calligrapher might ask, "Do I hold the brush the same way you do?" A basket maker might say, "What do you use baskets for?" Teachers may want to offer possible questions to the guest ahead of time.

The guest or teacher may want to read a children's book that relates to the visit, or visitors may have interesting stories to share about when they were young or how they became artists.

Samples. Just like toddlers, it is important for older children to be able to use their sense of touch as much as possible. Encourage guests to bring a small sample the children can take home with them. A quilter could offer a scrap of cloth that matches the quilt, a basket maker a piece of reed, and a weaver some yarn. Painters can apply paint that matches the painting to a piece of paper; when dry they can cut it into simple shapes and sign them for the children.

Concluding the visit. Prepare a brief letter to send home to parents about the children's experience. This helps parents understand the child's new knowledge. The child's "souvenir" can be attached to the letter as well so that it will have a context of meaning once it is home.

After the guest has left have the children participate in making a thank-you card. A nice thank-you is a photograph of the visit. Also take photographs to keep in a scrapbook so that the children can "read" and remember the experience.

TEACHER TIP

It is well worth the effort to create an information sheet to send to guests before they visit. A sample follows:

Guidelines for Guest Artists

1. Bring an unfinished piece to work on and samples of your artwork at various stages.
2. Avoid dangerous tools if possible. If you must bring anything sharp or hot make sure you have a childproof container for it.
3. Children are more sensitive to toxic materials than adults. Do not bring any solvents, permanent markers, solvent-based glues, oil paints, varnishes, sprays, or dusty materials.
4. Bring only one or two finished pieces that you feel will appeal to little children. Consider how you will display them safely.
5. Bring samples that the children can touch.
6. If possible bring a "souvenir" of the process that the children can take home.
7. Keep your presentation very simple. Prepare questions about your art that you could ask young children. Young children have short attention spans. Plan for no longer than fifteen minutes.
8. You may also wish to write a letter telling parents about your demonstration for the children to take home.

FIGURE 9–7 Visits from guest artists teach children that many different people create art.

Visiting an Artist's Studio

Taking a group of young children to an artist's studio can be a major undertaking and is most suitable for older children or a small, mixed-age group with ample supervision. The advantages of such a visit are that artists are often more comfortable working in their own surroundings with all their supplies at hand. The children also get to see the working environment that the artist has created.

The disadvantages are numerous. The work space may not be large enough or safe enough for young children and there may be many items that they cannot touch. In cases where artists use materials that are hazardous for young children, a visit to the studio is not advised unless those materials can be cleaned up and put away. The workplace of a painter, illustrator, calligrapher, weaver, spinner, basket maker, quilter, woodcarver, and stone sculptor should all be relatively safe with minor adjustments. A printing studio, stained glass studio, pottery studio or metal workshop may need to be carefully cleaned up, certain processes not demonstrated, and the children closely supervised.

In considering such a field trip, always visit the artist's work space ahead of time. Check for the following features:

1. SPACE: Is there a space large enough for all the children to gather and observe the artist or must they take turns? What can the children who are waiting their turn look at or do?
2. SAFETY: Are there any dangers that cannot be removed? What areas does the artist need to clean up? What parts of the process are dangerous for the children?
3. PREPARATION: What do we need to tell the parents and children so they will be prepared? Do they need special clothing? What should they look for and point out to the children?

Make sure there is ample supervision for the children. Parents and other supporting adults should be invited to come and oversee one or two children each. Use the guidelines for guest artists to plan the actual presentation.

Visiting Museums

Most museums are not set up to deal with groups of young children. The look-but-don't-touch nature of the displays usually mean that the children cannot use their natural learning impulses and spend the visit constrained and unhappy, leaving them with a dislike for museum-going that may last all their lives. The exception is the children's museum of which numerous versions have sprung up around the country. These museums are set up to engage children of all ages in activities that involve the arts and sciences. If such a museum is in the vicinity, do take advantage of the wonderful features it offers. Again, make sure to visit the site ahead of time and arrange for adequate supervision.

Other Places to Visit

Young children may also enjoy a visit to a piece of public sculpture if there is an example within walking distance. Public sculptures are often found in parks or near government and university buildings. Outdoor sculpture gardens attached to museums may also make a good experience. When visiting these locations, go prepared with a list of questions to focus the children on the visual elements of the pieces and find out something about the artist who made it. Separated from the artist and very different from their own art, children often have difficulty recognizing these sculptural forms as art and treat them more like unusual playground equipment. Expect such visits to be brief, and perhaps tie them in with a trip to another location.

Reconstructions of older historical homes or farm sites may demonstrate traditional handcrafts from earlier times such as wool spinning or candle making. These places are usually set up to handle groups of people and may shorten and customize their presentation for young visitors. There is often a real story to make the place come alive for children.

HOW CAN CHILDREN'S LITERATURE BE USED TO TEACH ART?

Art is a universal language. It tells about history, human nature, natural wonders, fantasy, as well as the ordinary.

SUSAN W. BROOKS AND SUSAN M. SENTORI (1988, P. 4)

Even if teachers do not own any art prints, do not know any artists, or live far from suitable museums, they can still introduce children to great art. The picture books that teachers read to children are also pieces of art. For many children it is the pictures that first entice them to the world of books, and books for the very youngest children are often wordless. In selecting the books to share with young artists, always consider the importance of the pictures not just as illustrations of the story but also as aesthetic statements.

Picture books can be chosen on the same basis as artworks. Make sure that there is a variety of artistic media, styles, and cultures represented in the books that are offered. Specific descriptions of a multitude of children's books are found in Appendix B. Make sure to have some examples from the following categories to introduce to the children.

1. CALDECOTT WINNERS: The Caldecott award is given each year to an outstandingly illustrated children's book. Select those that are on the children's level (see Appendix B).
2. MEDIA: Look for books that illustrate some of the less common art techniques, such as *Red Leaf Yellow Leaf* (Ehlert, 1991), which uses natural materials in collages to create three-dimensional images. *Sing a Song of Sixpence* (Reid, 1987) has illustrations made from plasticine, *Draw Me a Star* (Carle, 1992) uses painted and printed papers in collage, and *Bitter Bananas* (Olabye, 1994) features chalk over cut-paper collages.
3. MULTICULTURAL: Include books that feature art forms from other cultures, such as *Totem Pole* (Hoyt-Goldsmith, 1990), which tells how a totem pole is made, and *Abuela's Weave* (Castaneda, 1993), which tells how weaving fits into the life of a girl and her grandmother in Guatemala.
4. BIG BOOKS: For group sharing, have several Big Books in which the children can easily see the illustrations. More and more books are now available in this format. Appendix B indicates books that are available as Big Books.

Sharing Books with Children

It is not necessary to read every word or the whole book. If the children are wiggly, simplify the text. Talk about the pictures. Point to objects and say their names. If there are unfamiliar objects in the pictures, introduce them slowly—only a few at a time. Compare them to familiar things that the children know.

Children enjoy books with repetitious and rhythmic text. After several readings they will read along. Use an expressive voice. Change the tone for different characters. It is not necessary to read a book as written. Use the illustrations to inspire storytelling and different uses for the book. Ask children to predict what will happen next, before the page is turned.

SUMMARY: BECOMING AN ARTIST

You paint what you are.

ANDREW WYETH (MERRYMAN, 1991, P. 64)

Art is much more than the physical act of manipulating art materials. Art is also looking at, talking about, and appreciating the art of others. If teachers are dedicated to educating the whole child, then they must provide children with opportunities not only to explore the process of art, but also to experience a broad range of artwork. In doing so they introduce children to the artistic heritage of humankind and the long continuum of creativity that it represents.

It will take effort on the teacher's part to do this. Putting markers out on a table is simpler and more immediate than learning about a piece of artwork and the culture that created it, and then designing a way to explain it to young children. But adults who work with children must never stop learning. We must dedicate ourselves to becoming as knowledgeable about art as we can be. Our lives will be richer, as will the lives of the children we touch. Together we will approach the crayons on the table, the play dough on the tray, and the paint at the easel with a new respect and sense of purpose.

FIGURE 9–8 Children need to experience a wide variety of art forms. Bringing the art of the world to our children enriches us all.

FURTHER READING

> When children are surrounded by artworks, photographs, collections of beautiful things—and all their own attempts are encouraged—they will begin to value art.
>
> GAELENE ROWE (1987, P. 5)

Brooks, S. W., and Sentori, S. M. (1988). *See the paintings!* Rosemount, NJ: Modern Learning Press.
This book is a guidebook to presenting reproductions of paintings to children. Although it is directed to elementary level students, many of the ideas can be adapted to younger children as well.

Mesrobian, J. (1992). Rediscovering the Ninja Turtles' namesakes. *Day Care and Early Education, 20*: 18-19.
A practicing teacher describes how she introduced fine-art prints to her preschoolers.

Parsons, M. J. (1987). *How we understand art.* New York: Cambridge University Press.
Based on his research, Parsons presents the way children at different ages respond to different types of paintings.

Wolf, A. D. (1984). *Mommy, it's a Renoir!* Altoona, PA: Parent Child Press.
This book presents a systematic approach to introducing children to fine art through the use of art cards.

Art Focus

THE FIBER ARTS

> To be a whole, he must create his own version of the world, using that part of his cultural heritage he has made his own through education.
>
> JEROME BRUNER (1979, P. 116)

Fiber art refers to any art form that involves the use of yarn, cloth, or the raw materials that are used to make them. Because fabric plays such an important role in everyday life in terms of clothing and furnishing, it is often seen as a functional object rather than an art form. Yet even the most simple piece of clothing bears the mark of unnamed artists who determined the shape of its pieces, the drape of the fabric, and its texture and pattern.

The Art Medium: Fiber

Introducing fiber art to children helps them appreciate this often "hidden" and ancient art, which has found unique expression and form throughout time and across cultures. It is an excellent example of an art medium that can serve as a unifying theme for young children. In this section the activities have been organized around a theme unit on clothing, to serve as a model. Some of these fiber activities can also be used as part of thematic study of texture, line, pattern, and growing things. Not all the suggested activities have to be done as part of this unit. Select those that best fit the needs, interests, and skill level of the particular children. The activities can also be used individually.

When Are Children Ready to Do Fiber Art Activities?

Most fiber art activities require specific fine motor and visual perception skills. In order to be successful at most of these activities the children need to have certain abilities. They should be able to:

1. Pick up or grasp small objects with thumb and index fingers
2. Rotate an object in one direction at a constant speed
3. Push and pull small objects with thumb and index fingers
4. Identify top and bottom, front and back, inside and outside
5. Repeat a patterned motion

How Children Grow through Fiber Art Activities

Children will develop:

1. Physically, by using hand-eye coordination and small muscles in repetitive patterns (Bodily-Kinesthetic)
2. Socially, by working with others to create fiber art, and by sharing materials (Interpersonal)
3. Emotionally, by using fiber art materials in an expressive way (Intrapersonal)
4. Visual perception skills, by working with patterned space in three-dimensional fiber materials (Spatial)
5. Cognitively:
   • By learning fiber art terms and by talking

FIGURE 9–9 "A little quilt. I used the scraps from my mom's big quilt." Fabric collage—Susan, age 5

about the fiber art of their own creation and that of others (Linguistic)

- By observing and analyzing changes in raw materials as they are processed, and by learning to identify and create patterns (Logical-Mathematical)

6. Art awareness, by gaining knowledge about the art of others, through touching and talking about different examples of fiber art

Group composition. The number of children who can participate at one time in many of these activities will vary depending on the age and skill of the children. Fiber art activities are particularly successful with mixed-age groups. Some of the activities here may be too complicated for toddlers or younger preschoolers to do on their own, but they may be able to do a part of the activity when paired with older children or adults. The activities in this section have been labeled as suitable for a whole group (15 to 25), a table group (4 to 6), and pairs.

Transition in. A series of fiber arts activities can form the core of a thematic unit. A unit on cloth and clothing can be introduced in many ways. The type and kind of clothing worn daily is an important facet of a young child's life. Getting into and out of complicated clothing, bundling up in cold weather or dressing lightly in the heat, and feeling comfortable or irritated by the fit or texture of a garment, all directly influence how a child feels.

Begin the thematic unit by building on this interest. There are many ways to do this. One way is to wear a hand-knitted sweater or other interesting piece of clothing that attracts the children's attention or to comment on a new garment one of the children is wearing. Compare this piece of clothing with that worn by other children. Notice the colors and textures in the different garments. Make charts and picture graphs of the clothing they are wearing. Ask them how they think it was made and how it was colored.

Follow this with an exciting introductory event. Have a fiber artist such as a spinner, weaver, knitter, embroiderer, quilter, or dressmaker come for a visit. Try to have this visitor make a complete garment from beginning to end so the children can see the entire process. A small piece of clothing for one of the children's

dolls or stuffed animals would be particularly involving for the children.

Once the children's interest is aroused, present a wide range of activities that focus on clothing. The sample activities presented here are ordered from initial processing of fibers to final use in garments, but they do not have to be done in a particular order. Pick and choose those that best meet the interest and skill level of the children. The "Connections" section that follows each activity provides tie-ins to other learning areas. The books in the literature section can be used as a transition into these activities. It may be necessary to simplify the text in some of these books to make the process more understandable for young children.

Washing Wool

Raw wool can be obtained from a sheep farmer or consult the sources in Appendix A.

Group Size. Pairs or table group.

Materials.

- ½ pound raw wool
- Three dishpans
- Detergent
- Fabric softener

Setup.

1. Fill each pan with warm water.
2. Add ¼ cup detergent to first two pans.
3. Add a capful of softener to last pan.
4. Place pans in row on table, low counter, floor, or outside.
5. Children will move from pan to pan down the row.

What to do. If possible, visit a sheep farm or observe sheep at a zoo. Watch a video of sheep and shearing. Compare shearing to cutting hair. Children are often concerned that shearing hurts the sheep. Fill the room with pictures, toys, and models of sheep, and examples of wool yarn and clothing.

1. Have child take a small handful of wool.
2. Place in first pan and pull it apart.
3. Squeeze gently and move it to second pan.
4. Pull it apart and move it gently in water until clean.

5. Rinse in last pan.
6. Place near heater or in sun to dry. Turn often.
7. When dry, fluff by pulling it apart. Use it in collage, in a stuff bin, or for dyeing and spinning.

What to say. Ask: "Why does the wool change color when it's washed?" and "How does it feel before and after it is washed?" Words to use: wool, fleece, fiber, grease.

Connections. LITERATURE: Read *Charlie Needs a Cloak* (dePaola, 1973). Even the youngest children love the delightfully mischievous sheep in this simple story of converting wool to a cloak.

SCIENCE/MATH: Measure the temperature and/or quantity of the water used for washing the wool.

ART AWARENESS: Display and discuss a handwoven woolen garment or piece of fabric.

Dyeing

This activity can directly follow the washing of the wool or be done after it is spun into yarn.

Group size. Table group.

Materials.

- Washed wool or yarn (Cotton fabric can also be used. Results will be paler and less permanent. Cut the fabric into small four-inch squares.)
- Dye materials: Unsweetened, dry packaged soft drink mix* such as Kool-Aid, or natural plant materials (see Table 9-4)
- Crock-Pot (set up on a counter where children can see the process but not touch the pot when it is hot)
- Water
- Wooden spoon or tongs
- Rubber gloves
- Dishpan

What to do. Transition into this activity by going for a walk and collecting some plant materials that produce dye. Serve drink mix for snack and encourage children to wonder about the color. Create a chart showing the children's predictions about which color the different materials will make on the wool or cloth.

1. Have children place a small amount of wool, yarn, or a cotton square in Crock-Pot.

2. Cover with water.
3. Sprinkle one or more flavors of drink mix over the materials, or add the plant materials. Allow children to select colors or plant matter.
4. Move the Crock-Pot to the counter, turn on high, and cover.
5. Stir plant dyes occasionally. Do not stir drink-mix dyes.
6. Heat until it simmers. Check color. If saturated enough, remove and place in dishpan, using rubber gloves and spoon or tongs. If it needs to cook longer, turn Crock-Pot to low and simmer until color is deeper.
7. Once removed, rinse in cool water. Let dry near heater or in the sun.
8. Make a chart showing a piece of the plant material and then a sample of the dyed wool, yarn, or cloth, and then the dyed materials in a collage, stuff bin, or another fiber activity.

What to say. Ask: "How long do you think it will take to change color?" and "What color will it be?" Words to use: dye, dyed, color names, hot, cool.

Extending the learning. Using cloth, create a tie-dyed effect by wrapping sections of the cloth with tightly wound rubber bands. Cloth pieces can later be sewed or glued together to create a quilt.

Connections. LITERATURE: Read the dyeing section in *Songs from the Loom: A Navajo Girl Learns*

TABLE 9-4 Safe, Natural Dye Sources for Young Children

Plant	Color Produced
Apple leaves	Green, Yellow
Blackberry shoots	Green, Yellow
Carrot tops	Green, Yellow
Dock (edible weed)	Yellow
Grape leaves	Yellow
Indian corn (the black kernels, also blue corn)	Blue, Gray
Onion skins	Orange
Tea	Brown, Orange
Walnut hulls	Brown

to Weave (Roessel, 1995, pp. 34–36). If necessary, simplify the story for younger children.

SCIENCE: Identify the different plant parts used for dyeing: leaves, stems, skin of root (onion), seed case (walnut).

MATH: Time how long it takes for the wool to change color.

ART AWARENESS: Display hand-dyed yarn and/or cloth.

Picking and Carding Wool

Before wool can be converted into yarn and cloth, it must be cleaned. Picking is the process of removing debris from the fleece. Carding is like combing hair to remove tangles.

Group size. Whole group or table group. Have children sitting in a circle or around a table.

Materials.
- Washed and/or dyed wool
- Handcards or dog combs

What to do. Following washing of the wool:

1. Demonstrate how to pull it apart to make it fluffy and pick out any large pieces of hay or other vegetable matter.
2. Give each child a small piece of wool to "pick."
3. Place picked wool in center of table or circle.
4. Demonstrate how to card the wool by pulling it across the teeth of the cards or combs to

FIGURE 9–10 "I liked playing with the wool except when it stuck to my fingers. We made it blue with that drink mix stuff." Fleece collage—Susan, age 5

straighten the fiber.

5. Pass cards or combs around the circle. Invite children to take pieces of picked wool from center and try carding. Colors may be mixed to create new blends. Other children can continue picking while waiting a turn to card.

What to say: Ask: "How is this like combing your hair?" and "How does if feel before and after carding?" Words to use: wool, carders, picking.

Extending the learning. Use picked and carded wool for collages, stuff bins, or spinning.

Connections. LITERATURE: Children aged four and up enjoy the story *A New Coat for Anna* (Ziefert, 1986). The story's theme of cooperation can be compared to how the children cooperated in carding the wool.

Spinning

Handspinning is an ancient process. In cultures where handspinning is still done, children learn at very young ages. Successful spinning requires the repetition of a simple movement pattern. Children are thrilled when they see fluffy fiber turn to yarn.

Group size. Pairs. This activity works extremely well with mixed ages, such as a five-year-old and a three-year-old. Have children sit opposite each other at a table.

Materials.
- Spindles: Screw a cup hook into the end of a 12-inch length of a quarter-inch diameter dowel.
- Spindle whorls: A whorl is the weight that goes at the end of the spindle. Stick a potato or an apple on the end. (This is a traditional practice in South America and Europe.) A wheel from a toy vehicle or a plasticine ball can also be used. If firing clay is available, spindle whorls can be made by flattening a ball of clay and poking a dowel-sized hole in the center. Making clay whorls to use for their spinning is a good project for children four years old or older. Have the children draw designs in the whorls and then fire them unglazed.
- Washed and carded wool, stretched out into thin pieces; each about 12 inches long (or use commercial roving).

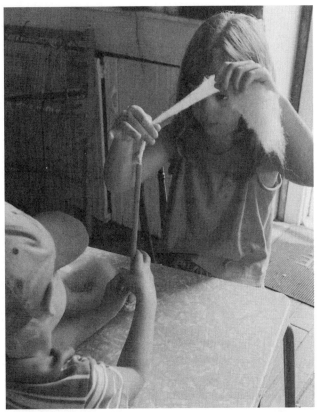

FIGURE 9–11 Spinning yarn is a wonderful partner project. Children are fascinated to see the fluffy wool turn to yarn.

What to do. Transition into this activity by inviting a spinner to demonstrate, or use a connection activity.

1. Demonstrate how the wool can be twisted into yarn with the fingers, then let the children try it.
2. Attach finger-twisted yarn to hook of spindle by wrapping it around several times.
3. Tell the children that one will be the "pincher" and the other will be the "spinner." Later they can switch roles so both get a turn at each job.
4. The pincher will pinch the wool about one inch above the hook. The other child holds the top of the spindle while resting the bottom on the table. The spinner then turns the spindle five or six turns.
5. The spinner stops the spindle and the pincher slides his fingers up about an inch. The pincher must never let go completely or the wool will untwist. Then the spinner spins again.
6. Repeat this pattern—pinch wool, turn spindle, stop spindle, slide fingers up—until a

length of yarn has been spun. It helps if the children chant "Pinch. Turn. Stop. Slide," as they work.

7. At this point if the children are very young, remove the yarn from the spindle. For older children demonstrate how to remove the yarn from the hook, wrap the wool around the spindle, and reattach the end to the hook. Then holding the end and a new piece of roving, give it several turns to attach the new piece.
8. The yarn will tend to untwist when removed from the spindle. Take the two ends together and let the yarn twist into a "two-ply" yarn.

What to say. Ask: "How does the wool change?" and "Which way is it stronger, before or after spinning?" Words to use include: pinch, spin, yarn, thick, thin, fast, slow, lumpy, smooth, twist.

Extending the learning. Use the yarn in a collage or for weaving.

Connections. LITERATURE: *The Goat in the Rug* (Blood and Link, 1980) is another appealing story about fiber processing for young children.

 TEACHER TIP

The following simplified steps can be repeated over and over until the pattern is learned. It usually takes children about five to ten minutes to learn to work independently.

Spinning Steps

1. WRAP (Wrap carded wool around hook).
2. PINCH (Pinch wool above hook).
3. SPIN (Turn spindle).
4. HOLD (Hold spindle still while partner slides finger up about one inch).
5. PINCH (Pinch wool again).
6. Repeat steps 2 to 5.
7. To make yarn longer: Unwrap from hook and wind around spindle.
8. Reattach end to hook.
9. Hold wool and yarn end together and spin several times.

SCIENCE/MATH: Measure or compare the finished lengths of yarn.

KINESTHETICS: Invite the children to imagine that they are spindles, spinning.

ART AWARENESS: Display and discuss skeins of handspun yarn and/or a garment or cloth made from handspun yarn.

Weaving

Many young children have difficulty with weaving activities that require them to go over and under in a regular pattern. The following activities allow children to see how the weaving process is done, but are open-ended enough that all the children can participate successfully.

Group size. Pairs.

Materials.
- Yarn, ribbon, shoe laces, or string
- Commercial vertical floor or table loom (see Appendix A) OR
- Large frame with fine chicken wire or yarn stretched across it and mounted vertically on floor or table. If using chicken wire, make sure rough edges are covered with tape.

What to do. Transition into weaving by inviting a weaver to bring a small loom for the children to see and try operating, or pull apart a piece of cloth (burlap works well) to see the yarn from which it is made.

FIGURE 9–12 Partner loom

1. Set up the loom. Chicken wire is easier for the children than the yarn. The activity may be introduced with the chicken wire first and then later set up with yarn.
2. Have two children face each other with the loom between them. One child pushes a piece of yarn or other material through the holes in the chicken wire or between the stretched yarns. Then the other child takes the end and pushes it back though to the partner. If necessary, wrap tape around the ends of the yarn. Use the song "Go in and out the Windows" to reinforce the pattern. Children may weave in any direction.
3. As the weaving grows and changes, take time to talk about the patterns that form.

What to say. Ask:

> "What is the texture of the weaving?"
> "How do the different yarns change how it feels and looks?"
> "What patterns do you see?"

Words to include: over, under, back, front, yarn, weave.

Extending the learning. Plastic berry baskets can be used for weaving by individual children.

Connections. LITERATURE: Read any of the books listed under Wool Washing, or share *The Rug Makers* (Allan, 1991), which describes in simple language a day in the life of a young boy from India.

MATH/SCIENCE: Compare different lengths and kinds of yarns.

KINESTHETICS: Play "In and out the Window." Have all children but one stand in circle holding hands. Children lift their arms as the child weaves in out between them as the song is sung. Continue until all children have had a turn to "weave."

ART AWARENESS: Display and discuss handwoven fabrics. Guatemalan, Mexican, and South American textiles are available from many sources (see Appendix A).

Stitching and Sewing

Children do not often notice how clothing is put together. Have an embroiderer, seamstress, or tailor visit and demonstrate sewing work. Or wear an embroidered garment or point out one a child is wearing. Take an old garment apart at the seams to see how it is put together. Have children find seams and stitches on their own clothing.

Sewing two pieces of cloth together is too difficult for many young children. The following activity helps them develop skills that can later be used with cloth.

Group size. Table group.

Materials.
• Sanitized Styrofoam trays
• Large-eyed three-inch plastic needles
• Yarn

What to do.

1. Thread a large number of needles with different colors of yarn, in 12-to-16-inch lengths. Double the yarn and make a large knot at the end.
2. Demonstrate: Show children how to punch holes in the Styrofoam or paper with the needle, and how to pull the yarn through from one side to the other.
3. Invite children to select a threaded needle and push it in and out of the tray. Do not expect children to make neat stitches. For most, this will be an exploration. It will take many stitching explorations before a child understands how to go from front to back in a patterned way. If children are to acquire this skill they need many opportunities to practice it.
4. When the yarn is used up, cut off needle and tape end to back of tray.

What to say. Ask: "How many stitches have you made?" and "Look how the yarn makes lines." Words to use include: in, out, front, back, needle, stitch, yarn.

Extending the learning. Pre-punch holes in a piece of cardboard for children to use.

Connections. LITERATURE: Read *Nine-in-One, Grr!* (Xiong,1989), a folktale of the Hmong people of Southeast Asia. This book is illustrated with stitched and appliquéd storycloths, traditional Hmong narrative needlework.

MATH/SCIENCE: Measure items in a room using equal-length pieces of yarn. Create a pictograph.

KINESTHETICS: Have children hold hands in a line. First child is the needle and threads through the line, ducking under the uplifted arms. Still clasping hands, others follow.

ART AWARENESS: Hmong embroidered and appliquéd pieces can be displayed and discussed. Embroidery is also used in the traditional dress of many cultures such as Ukrainian, Greek, Chinese, Indian, and more.

Appliqué

Applique is an art form in which cloth shapes are sewed on top of other cloth pieces.

Group size. Table group.

Materials:
• Precut felt pieces (in a variety of colors and shapes)
• Glue
• Heavy paper, cardboard, or felt base (about 9 by 9 inches or larger)

What to do. Invite an appliqué artist to visit. Or wear an appliquéd garment or point out one worn by a child. Talk about how one piece of cloth is put on top of another. Identify shapes found in an example of appliqué.

1. Place materials at a table.
2. Encourage exploration of how different pieces look when placed over and under others.
3. Glue down into a collage.

What to say. Ask:

"Which shapes are on top?"
"Which are underneath?"
"What textures do you feel?"

Words to use include: under, over, overlap, shape names, texture words.

Connections. LITERATURE: Read *Mole's Hill* (Ehlert,1994). This book features traditional Native American appliqué designs.

MATH/SCIENCE: Have children sort felt shapes by color, size, or shape before using them in their appliqué.

ART AWARENESS: Display and discuss examples of appliqué—in a handmade quilt, in

Hmong needlework, or in a mola from Panama (see Appendix A).

Yarn Pictures

Because of the linear nature of yarn, it can be used to create a "drawing."

Group size. Table group.

Materials.

- Yarn (different colors and thicknesses, 4 to 12 inches long)
- Contact paper (stapled sticky-side up to a paper or cardboard base) OR
- Paper (on which white glue has been spread)

What to do. Collect short pieces of yarn and put them in a stuff bin. Invite the children to explore the way they can bend and twist the yarn together. Do this activity immediately after spinning yarn.
1. Demonstrate: Show children how to press the yarn onto the contact paper or glued surface.
2. If using the glued surface, provide damp paper towels to wipe fingers so yarn does not stick to them.

What to say. Ask:

> "How did you get the yarn to stay there?"
> "Did you put the glue on the paper first?"
> "Do any pieces of yarn cross other ones?"

Words to use include: line descriptions; thick, thinly stretched, bend, folded.

Connections. LITERATURE: Read sections from "Mariano Valadez of the Huichol Tribe" in *Native Artists of North America* (Moore, 1993), or create your own Big Book based on this information.

MATH/SCIENCE: Measure each child's height using a piece of yarn. Invite the children to use the yarn to find other things that are about the same height.

KINESTHETICS: Have children imagine they are pieces of yarn. Imagine they are stretched, bent, folded, twisted, and so on. Have them join hands to form longer pieces of yarn and then wrap around furniture in the room, or trees and playground equipment outside.

ART AWARENESS: Display and discuss Huichol yarn paintings (see Appendix A). Find lines, shapes, symmetry, and patterns.

Quilting

Because quilt making involves creating a whole from parts, it is an ideal art form for cooperative activities. Quilts often represent family traditions and cultural heritage. There is a rich body of children's literature that features quilts.

Group size. Whole group.

Materials.

- Squares of cloth (Have each child bring in a 9-inch square.)
- Glue OR
- Invite someone to sew it together.

What to do. Have a quilter visit or share a handmade quilt with the children. Read a story about quilting. Point out the patterns in the quilts.

1. Have children stand in a circle with their quilt squares.
2. Invite them to take turns placing their squares on the floor, in the center of the circle, so that it touches the other ones.
3. Describe the patterns that are created.
4. Challenge the children to place their squares so that a rectangle is formed.
5. Have children retrieve their squares and then create a new arrangement. This can be repeated several times in a row or on different days. Use this opportunity to develop two concepts: (1) a whole is created from its parts and (2) pattern is created from the repetition of an element.
6. After several rearrangements, ask the children to make a final arrangement for the finished quilt. If the quilt will be glued together, put out a large sheet of paper. As children place their squares, apply glue to the paper in those spots. Emphasize that each piece must touch another.
7. If the quilt will be sewed, arrange the pieces on the floor and then gather them up by rows. Have a parent or volunteer sew the pieces together during class time, so the children can participate in the excitement of seeing the quilt grow together. The quilt top can

be left as it is and used for dramatic play, or it can be stuffed and finished, destined to become a favorite spot to cuddle. Or give it as a gift to a nursing home or other needy group with which the children have a relationship.

What to say. Ask:

"Can you count the squares?"
"How many are in a row?"
"What patterns do you see?"

Words to use include: quilt, pieces, pattern, row, repeated, stitch, bind.

Extending the learning.

- Have children use white or light-colored cloth squares and draw on them with crayons. Iron the crayoned cloth (not in the same room as the children, because of the fumes) to make it permanent.
- Use equilateral triangle-shaped cloth pieces.
- Use fabric squares that have been tie-dyed in tea.
- Use fabric squares that have been printed by the children.

Connections. LITERATURE: There are many books about quilt making. *The Boy and the Quilt* (Kurtz, 1991), features a little boy making his first quilt. Young children will enjoy his delightful independence. *Eight Hands Round: A Patchwork Alphabet* (Paul, 1991) presents different quilt patterns and their history.

MATH: Offer pattern blocks and color tiles with which to make sample quilt patterns.

SCIENCE: Look for patterns in nature—on a turtle's back, a tiger-striped cat, on insects, and more.

KINESTHETICS: Have children line up in an alternating pattern, based on their clothing, such as light and dark or long sleeves and short sleeves.

ART AWARENESS: Display and discuss quilts of all kinds, such as the work of Harriet Powers, Faith Ringgold, Michael Cummings (MAPS: African-American), Amish quilts, Early American quilts, and more. Create quilt matching cards from catalogs and calendars.

ARTWORK STUDY

Select an original piece of art, a print, or an artifact that interests you.
Record the following information:

TITLE _____

ARTIST/CULTURE _____

MEDIA _____

DESCRIPTION/STORY _____

_____

_____

Based on this artwork, write an example of each type of question you could ask children.

1. What does it tell you about?

    _____

2. How was it made?

    _____

3. Can you find? (art elements)

    _____

4. How does it make you feel?

    _____

5. What comes next?

    _____

6. How many? (related curriculum question)

    _____

7. Can you? (kinesthetic response question)

    _____

Studio Page 54

COMPARING ARTWORKS

Select two pieces of artwork that share some similarity, such as subject, media, colors, artist, or culture. Describe each piece:

ART WORK 1:   TITLE _____

ARTIST/CULTURE _____

MEDIA _____

DESCRIPTION/STORY _____

_____

_____

ART WORK 2:   TITLE _____

ARTIST/CULTURE _____

MEDIA _____

DESCRIPTION/STORY _____

_____

_____

Write three questions that would help children focus on the similarities in each artwork.

1. _____

2. _____

3. _____

Write three questions that would help children focus on the differences in each artwork.

1. _____

2. _____

3. _____

Studio Page 55

CREATE AN ART BOOK FOR CHILDREN

- Select an artwork or artifact from another culture.
- Research how the artwork was made and learn something about the culture that made it.
- Write a simple text about the artwork that will appeal to young children.
- Use the layout sheet on the next page to show how the book will look.

TITLE _____

ARTIST/CULTURE _____

MEDIA _____

DESCRIPTION/STORY _____

_____

_____

Studio Page *56*

ART BOOK LAYOUT

MY ARTISTIC HERITAGE

What is your cultural background?

_____

_____

What artwork did you have in your home when you were growing up?

_____

_____

As a child did you know anyone who was an artist?

_____

_____

As a child did you visit museums?

_____

_____

As a child did you have any favorite piece or type of art?

_____

_____

As a child was there any artwork you hated?

_____

_____

In your home, now, you have the following pieces of artwork:

_____

_____

Do these pieces reflect your artistic heritage, another family member's, and/or choices made based on what you have learned about art as an adult?

_____

_____

MY VIEW OF ART NOW

I think it is important to learn about art created by others because:

_____
_____
_____
_____
_____
_____
_____
_____
_____
_____

I would like to learn more about the art of:

_____
_____
_____
_____
_____
_____
_____
_____
_____
_____

If I could own any piece of artwork ever created, I would choose:

_____
_____
_____
_____
_____
_____
_____
_____

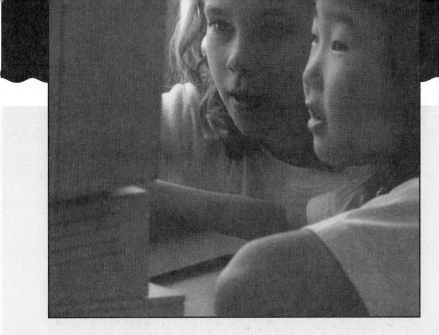

10

Growing Together

Cooperative Art Activities
for Children

> ❝ *Working in a*
> *group can help*
> *you produce something*
> *more, to think*
> *more widely,*
> *to enrich you.* ❞
>
> •
>
> TIZIANA FILLIPINA
> (GOLEMAN ET AL., 1992, P. 85)

Questions addressed in this chapter:

What is cooperative art?

How can children be encouraged to work together?

What is involved in making a mural?

How can young children use the computer to create art?

SUMMARY: Cooperative Art Binds People Together

FURTHER READING

ART FOCUS: Computers, Children, and Art

Young Artists at Work

"Your monkey has real long legs."

"So does yours."

"That's because he's trying to climb up this tree."

"My person is up in the air. He's jumping. You need long legs to do that."

"Yep. My monkey is going to jump when he gets to the top of the tree."

"Oops, the paint is dripping."

"Hurry. Catch it before it runs over Sari's picture."

"Sari will be mad if the paint drips on her dog."

"You are working hard on your paintings for our mural," says the teacher. "I see that you have used two different sizes of brushes."

"Yes, I used Mandie's little brush to paint the buttons and she used my big brush to paint the long, long legs."

"See," says the teacher, "When we share things we have more choices of things to use in our art."

WHAT IS COOPERATIVE ART?

Creative actions celebrate the individual, even when the actions are part of a group effort.

CLARE CHERRY, DOUGLAS GODWIN, AND JESSE STAPLES (1989, P. 133)

The traditional view of the artist is that of a socially inept loner, creating in isolation. In actuality, most art that has been produced over the span of human history, from the Egyptian wall paintings to the environmental art of Christo, has involved the cooperative efforts of groups of artists with different skills and interests. Cooperative art is art that is created by two or more people. The individuals explore the art media in their own personal way, but they also act and react to the exploration of their cooperative partners. The artists may work at the same time, in series or on different sections. Well-designed cooperative art activities allow children at different ages and skill levels to work together to create something uniquely different from what they would create on their own. When carefully planned, adults can even participate in many of these activities. There is great satisfaction in feeling a part of a successful group art activity.

Children need to learn that art is not always done by just one person. This is best learned by participating in many group art experiences. The most common cooperative art activity is the mural. This chapter will also describe many other ways for young artists to cooperate.

FIGURE 10–1 "All my friends are playing jump rope." Section of mural, marker—Joanne, age 4

HOW CAN CHILDREN BE ENCOURAGED TO WORK TOGETHER?

At two they will play in parallel, but by three they will play together.

DOROTHY EINON (1985, P. 79)

Toddlers

Children begin life totally self-centered. Infants know when they are hungry and demand to be fed. Toddlers see a toy they want and nothing short of physical restraint will prevent them from grabbing it. Children between birth and age two perceive themselves as the center of the universe. Toddlers work best in situations where they can pursue their own explorations under the watchful eyes of caregivers. Adults can promote social growth by providing activities in which toddlers can work alongside others. Setting up activities in which two toddlers or a toddler and an older child are painting at the same table, or are smashing play dough together, helps toddlers learn that they can do artwork in close proximity to other children.

As toddlers work beside each other, they begin to become aware of each other's actions. One child will begin to pound the clay and another child will imitate the same action. One child will see another using scissors and will demand a pair too. Imitation is one of the ways that children learn skills and behaviors. Adults and other children can serve as role models for the young child.

Three- and Four-Year-Olds

Many three- and four-year-olds can work together on all kinds of projects, from building a block city to painting a mural. They become enraptured by the excitement of the collective moment and yet, are interested in and "see" only the part they personally created. Cooperative activities for these children, therefore, do not have the same meaning as those designed for older children and adults in which ideas are arrived at jointly, and the project is viewed as a whole. Young preschoolers work best on projects that do not have definite end goals, but instead allow each child to play an individual part in the process.

Five-Year-Olds and Up

When children gain the ability to value and differentiate their own products from those of others, they can start to see that each contribution is a part of something larger—a whole—which is different from each small part but which is still partially theirs. Teachers can tell when children reach this stage, because they start to notice the artwork of the other children and will comment, "That is my friend's painting," or "That is Cheri's," when referring to a piece of art they see. They use the terms "we did..." instead of "I did..." when referring to group projects. They can identify who did the different parts of a project. When children reach this stage they are ready for more complex group activities.

These children are able to plan ahead of time which part of the project they will work on and enjoy working on projects that involve a common idea, such as building a castle out of blocks or building a box robot together. They may, however, still need adult guidance in learning how to incorporate the ideas of each member in a gracious way.

How Many Children Can Work Together?

Group size is a critical factor in determining if children will work together successfully or come to blows. At the Reggio Emilia preprimary schools they have found that different group sizes create different dynamics. Pairs of children can engage in intense social and cognitive interactions. The addition of a third child can produce solidarity but also conflict. Groups of four and five have other dynamics. (Edwards et al., 1992.)

In many overcrowded, understaffed early childhood programs it is difficult to set up opportunities for the children to work together in small groups. Teachers cannot expect small groups of children to work together on their own without careful adult observation and interaction. Teachers need to be there to teach resolution skills when two children both want to put the tower on the castle or both children want to make the robot's head. A caring adult is needed when a two-year-old wildly paints across a four-year-old's carefully done mural painting. A strategic question can make the difference in how the children decide to carry out an idea. In order for group work to be meaningful for young children, it needs to be carefully thought out, adequately supervised, and based on the interests and needs of the children.

Promoting Cooperative Behaviors

There are many benefits to learning how to work with others which will make people more successful in life. Young children can gain skill in small behaviors that will help them grow to be more effective group members. Working on group art projects will help children grow socially by:

1. Developing the ability to concentrate on a task in the presence of others
2. Developing the ability to wait for a turn
3. Developing the ability to share materials with others
4. Gaining the knowledge that working with others is a pleasant, joyful experience

Teachers can encourage the growth of these preliminary cooperative skills in a number of ways.

Toddlers.

1. Provide opportunities for two or three toddlers to work at the same table. Make sure they each have plenty of space for bodily movement without interfering with each other.
2. Place supplies in a common container from which children must select their pieces. Provide sufficient amounts of the supply so that children can have as much as they wish. Encourage children to take one item at a time.
3. Have children take turns working in pairs on a mural, a drawing, or painting a box. Make sure each child has plenty of space in which to work.

Three- to five-year-olds.

1. Have children work in groups of four to six at the same table or workspace.
2. Have pairs of children share some supplies such as glue or hole punches.
3. Offer supplies in common containers and encourage children to develop the independent behavior of taking only a few items at a time. This can be encouraged by giving children small trays on which to place their selections.
4. When a supply is limited, ask children to share fairly, such as having the children check that each has a red paper square or a similar supply of blocks.
5. Plan activities to which each child can contribute such as the mural suggestions that follow.

Five- to eight-year-olds.

1. Provide opportunities for children to work independently in teams of three to five to accomplish a set goal. Start with simple tasks such as painting a box or sorting colored paper scraps by color. After the children learn to work together successfully, advance to more complex activities such as making a poster, putting on a puppet show about a book they have read, or building a papier-mâché sculpture out of boxes.
2. When working on group projects, always have the children meet and plan ahead of time what part each child will do. Teach children that in a team each member can contribute in different ways. Have children assume roles within their team. In a group of four, one child could be in charge of getting supplies, the second could be assigned to returning the supplies, the third could record the group's accomplishments—either by writing or making illustrative drawings—and the fourth could report orally to the class. There is a large body of literature on teaching cooperative group skills to children five and up. (See Further Reading at the end of this chapter.)
3. Children at these ages are also ready to participate in large group cooperative behaviors. Have the whole class participate in deciding how the art materials should be cared for and organized. Then have individuals or pairs of children assume responsibility for taking care of a specific supply.

Mixed-age and ability groups. Groups that contain a range of ages actually offer one of the best settings in which to develop cooperative art behaviors. The older children and adults can model respect for each other's artwork and at the same time supervise the more impulsive little ones.

1. Select activities that each individual, no matter what his or her ability level, can participate in fairly equally. Most of the activities in this chapter are suitable for mixed groups and can be used in childcare situations, in family groups, or for child-parent art workshops.

2. Have members of the group take turns working in pairs or in groups of three. The older members should help the younger ones find a place to work and supplies to use.

3. Allow the youngest group members to go first as older members will be able to work around one another's artwork whereas the young children may not "see" the work already there and may work on top of it.

Enjoying Working Together

Always include an element of fun when working together. Songs, laughter, and excitement should all be part of the experience. It is the group experience that is important, not the finished product. Avoid the trap of planning an end use for the cooperative project before it is started. Do not be a boss telling people to do this or work on that so that a beautiful piece of artwork results. That is not a model for cooperative art. The teacher's role is to be the guide. Provide the location, the materials, the excitement, and the beginning of an idea, then let the participants take over. Teachers can even participate themselves! The result will be a true expression of each individual's creative moment as a part of that group, at that time, and in that place.

WHAT IS INVOLVED IN MAKING A MURAL?

> Creative energies are contagious.
>
> FRED ROGERS (1982, P. 10)

Well-designed mural activities can provide an excellent way to introduce children to working in a group. The word *mural,* although technically defined as a "wall painting," in literature on children's art usually refers to a very large, two-dimensional piece of artwork created by a group of children. That is the definition used here. Children can make murals using a variety of media, from drawing to collage, and can work not only on a wall, but on tables, floors, and windows as well.

It is important that the children are familiar with the medium to be used on the mural and have had many practice experiences with it. A mural is not the place to explore a material for the first time, but instead provides an opportunity to take pride in using a skill, and creating something that requires a level of control. It is important that murals be designed to be open-ended activities, so that every child can participate fully.

There are three basic types of murals that can be done successfully with young children: collection, shared space, and thematic murals.

The Collection Mural

This type of mural is an excellent initial group art activity. Because the children are attaching objects rather than creating original artwork directly on the surface, they can concentrate on how they will place the object in relationship to the others. This mural teaches two important concepts. First, a mural is an artwork made up of many parts; second, each artist must respect the work of the others and take care not to cover up any parts that other people have already put on the mural.

Nature collage. Take a walk in the woods or a park. Provide each child with a small paper bag in which to collect natural objects such as pebbles, leaves, and acorns. Discuss the

FIGURE 10–2 Mural making provides the perfect opportunity to practice sharing materials and space with others.

objects with children and then invite them to decide where to glue them on a large piece of paper or cardboard.

Connections. LITERATURE: Read *Outside Inside* (Crimi, 1995) or *In a Small, Small Pond* (Flemming, 1993). Have children make booklets about the things they saw on the walk.

SCIENCE: Classify the objects found by size, shape, texture, living/nonliving, purpose, etc. Put special objects in a minimuseum made from small, stacked boxes.

MATH: Count the objects found.

KINESTHETICS: Depending on what the children see: Move like a falling leaf, grow like grass, scamper like a squirrel, etc.

ART AWARENESS: Display Henri Rousseau's *Rendezvous in a Forest* (National Gallery).

Color collage. Declare one day a special color day. Ask everyone to wear something in that color. Fill the room with objects in that color. Read a book about that color (see below). Put out a collection of objects, art papers, and materials in that specific color. For a higher level activity, have children find objects in that color for the mural. Have children glue objects to a background paper in the same color.

Connections. LITERATURE: For red read: *Seeing Red,* blue: *Feeling Blue*, Yellow: *Hello Yellow* (Wolff, 1968a, 1968b, 1968c); for brown: *White Rabbit's Color Book* (Baker, 1994) and the individual color poems in *Hailstones and Halibut Bones* (O'Neil, 1961).

SENSORY ACTIVITIES: Fill a stuff bin with a material in that color. Serve a snack in that color: strawberries for red, bananas for yellow, blueberries for blue, gingerbread for brown, etc. Loosely cover lights and drape tissue in that color across the windows.

ART AWARENESS: These prints are appropriate with specific colors.

RED: *Red Poppy*, Georgia O'Keefe (Boston), *Red Horses*, Franz Marc (Boston)
BLUE: *Waterlilies*, Claude Monet (Boston), *Starry Night*, Vincent Van Gogh
YELLOW: *Sunflowers*, Vincent Van Gogh (Modern Learning)
GREEN: *Tropical Forest*, Henri Rousseau (National Gallery
BROWN: *The Guitar Lesson*, Henry Tanner (Modern Learning), *Peaceable Kingdom*,
Edward Hicks (National Gallery)

Faces. Clip magazine pages that have faces on them. Talk about facial features and put out mirrors for the children. Invite children to tear or cut out eyes, noses, and mouths and make faces with them on construction paper. When they are done, have children sit in a circle and share their faces. Talk about places where crowds of people are seen, such as at a sporting event, at a show, or in a class. Then have children take turns gluing the faces to the mural. (NOTE: see chapter 7 on introducing magazine collage to toddlers.)

Connections. LITERATURE: Share the book *Faces* (Brenner, 1970), which shows photographs of all kinds of eyes, noses, mouths, and so on.

SCIENCE: Make a pictograph of the children's eye color, hair color, and/or number of teeth.

MATH: Count the number of eyes, noses, mouths, etc.

KINESTHETICS: Pair children. Have one child imitate the expression on the other's face.

ART AWARENESS: Look at artworks that show different faces: *Gypsy Woman with Baby*, Amedeo Modigliani (National Gallery); *Artist's Daughter with Parakeet*, Berthe Morisot (National Gallery); *Portrait of Artist's Son*, Rembrandt, Mask Prints (Crystal).

Texture collage. Ask children to find examples of a specific texture in the room or use a sensory game from chapter 8. Put out objects that have similar textures. For a higher level activity, have children select items from range of textures. Invite children to glue objects to a background.

Connections. LITERATURE: Share the beautiful poems in *Fingers Are Always Bringing Me News* (O'Neill, 1969), which describe different people and how they sense the world with their fingers.

SCIENCE: When the collage is done, blindfold the children and ask them to try to identify the objects on the collage using just the tips of their fingers.

MATH: Count and classify the textured materials used in the collage. Make a pictograph.

ART AWARENESS: Depending on the specific texture, put out a related artifact such as a basket (rough), or a brass sculpture (smooth).

Shape mural. Offer precut paper in one basic shape (circle, square, etc.) or an assortment of shapes, or let children cut out shapes for the mural. The children can glue the shapes directly on the mural; more experienced children may create a piece of artwork on their shapes using drawing materials, painting, collage, or printing. For printing, offer items that create prints in the same shape as the paper. After children have made their shapes, sit in a circle and ask children to talk about what they have made. Then discuss where it should go on the mural paper. Invite children to come up and glue their pieces on the mural. With each addition, discuss how it looks with the other shapes already there.

Connections. LITERATURE: *The Greedy Triangle* (Burns, 1994) is a rollicking story to share when working with shapes.

MATH: Use the mural to find shapes that are larger, smaller, over, under, high/low, top/bottom, and so on.

ART AWARENESS: Use the following artworks to illustrate specific shapes.

RECTANGLES: *Fall Euphony*, Hans Hofmann, *Composition*, Piet Mondrian.
SQUARES: *Alter Kiang*, Piet Mondrian
CIRCLES: *Wedding Ensemble,* China
TRIANGLES: *Navajo Blanket*, Native American
MIXED SHAPES: *Esquisse for Ode to Kinshasha*, Lois Mailou Jones
(All available from Take 5 Print Sets)

Colored light quilt. Give children colored cellophane and tissue paper. Have children arrange the materials in small plastic bags. Use clear packing tape to tape the bags together. Hang the "light quilt" in a window. For a variation, place lightweight nature objects, such as twigs, leaves, and shells in bags, with or without the colored papers.

Connections. LITERATURE: Read the following books about blended colors: *A Rainbow of My Own* (Freeman, 1966), *The Earth and I* (Asch, 1994), and *Water* (Asch, 1995).

SCIENCE: If the quilt is in a sunny window, watch how the pattern of colored light moves throughout the day. Ask the children what they think causes that. Compare the movement to shadows. Relate it to the sun.

MATH: Count the plastic bags individually and by rows.

ART AWARENESS: Present artwork with blended colors such as *Cosmic Eye*, Merida (Take 5) or *Improvisation* Wassily Kandinsky (National Gallery).

Pebble mosaic. Take a walk and collect rounded or flat pebbles or stones. Toddlers should collect larger stones two to three inches in diameter; older children may find smaller ones, about one-half inch to one inch. Have students glue the stones on a heavy cardboard or wood base. For a variation, have students paint or color the stones first, or use small blocks of wood, bottle caps, or seashells, instead of stones.

Connections. LITERATURE: Read the wonderful book, *On My Beach Are Many Pebbles* (Lionni, 1961), which features pencil drawings of some amazing pebbles.

SCIENCE: Before gluing pebbles to the mural, weigh them using a balance scale.

MATH: Sort the pebbles by size.

ART AWARENESS: Show reproductions of Byzantine or Roman mosaics.

My box, our boxes. To introduce this mural, collect a series of boxes in a range of sizes. Put a tiny treasure in the smallest box, and then nest all the boxes together. Have children take turns opening the boxes until they reach the treasure. Talk about the different ways boxes are used. Explain that each child will be making a special box that will then be joined with the others to create a wall of treasures. Ahead of time, prepare a collection of small boxes such as jewelry boxes, shoe boxes, and cereal boxes that are similar in size. Cut them open on one of the larger sides. Tape other sides closed if necessary. If the box is gray inside, have the children paint the insides. When the boxes are dry, children can insert the "treasures"—natural or other small objects that are special to them. They can also create small, two-dimensional or three-dimensional pieces of artwork. Glue together the boxes, open side facing out, to create a wall or a tower.

Connections. LITERATURE: The simple story *The Gift* (Prater, 1985) is a perfect companion to this activity.

SCIENCE: Use boxes to display nature items collected on walks.

MATH: Count boxes individually and by rows. Sort, count, and graph the objects in the boxes.

ART AWARENESS: Look for examples of "boxlike" constructions such as Nevelson's *Case with Five Balusters* (Take 5) or the work of Marcel Duchamp.

The Shared Space Mural

In this type of mural, the children work directly on the same piece of background paper. Depending on the experience of the children and the location available, the children may take turns or work in larger groups. A long, narrow paper hung on a wall, with open space around it, can have more children working on it than can a wide piece of paper laid out on a table or the floor. If a table is used, a good guideline is to work with no more than the number who usually would fit at that table. Make sure there is ample space for children to move their arms and reach the supplies as they work.

Two broad categories of shared space murals are the printed mural and the painted mural. Printmaking particularly lends itself to a shared surface. All of the printmaking activities presented in chapter 8 can be used to create a mural. More specific ideas are presented in this section.

Painting murals gives the children the opportunity to use large muscular motions that are in sharp contrast to the movements made in the more constrained areas where they usually paint. Be sure to provide plenty of space for children to extend their arms out to full range. Painted murals are best done with the paper affixed to a wall, but can also be done on a table or the floor. Position the paper so the children have to extend their arms full length to paint near the top. Tape up newspaper extending beyond all the edges to catch the inevitable stray strokes.

There is a wonderful element of spontaneity to this type of mural and they are very popular in early childhood programs. They work best when they grow directly out of the interests and activities of the children, and time is spent planning with the children what part each child will do. Most of the following murals use very basic art supplies that are usually on hand and can, therefore, be set up quickly.

Snowflakes. Do this mural on a snowy day. Have the children play outside in the snow and then come in and share how it felt. Invite them to recreate the feeling of snow in a mural. Put out sponge balls or other objects to print with, along with white paint in trays. Invite children to make snowflake prints. Have each child decide where to put their snowflake print in relation to the others. (Note: Snow activities should only be done in regions where it snows. They have no meaning for children who have never experienced snow. See rain mural [Paint Drops] below for warmer climates.)

Connections. LITERATURE: Three wonderful books to share about snow are *Snow on Snow on Snow* (Chapman, 1994), *The Snowy Day* (Keats, 1962), and *Snowballs* (Ehlert, 1995).

SCIENCE: Make two snowballs. Put one in a pan on a table and one in a freezer. Ask children to predict which will melt first. How long will it take? Will they melt before the mural is dry?

MATH: Count the snowflakes on the mural.

KINESTHETIC: Mime a snowflake falling to the ground, then make snowflake print.

ART AWARENESS: Look at how other artists have depicted snow, such as *First Snow at Veneux-Nadon*, by Alfred Sisley or *Winter Harmony*, John Twachtman (both: National Gallery).

Bubbles. Blow bubbles with the children. Talk about their colors, sizes, and shapes. If possible, use a giant bubble wand. Ask the children to think about ways bubbles could be shown in paint. Combine soap, water, and some tempera paint for color. Mix it to make it frothy. Use sponges to print with the bubbly paint or paint bubble shapes on the mural. (Remember, not all bubbles are round.)

Connections. LITERATURE: The perfect book to team up with any bubble activity is *Soap Bubble Magic* (Simon, 1985). Share the story before and after blowing bubbles.

KINESTHETIC: Mime a bubble floating in the air. Talk about different ways to make the painted bubbles look like they are floating.

ART AWARENESS: The painting *Boy Blowing Bubbles* by Chardin shows a boy enjoying bubble making (National Gallery or Take 5).

Shoe prints. Collect some old shoes in different sizes, from baby shoes to high heels. On a day when a child arrives in brand new sneakers and the conversation naturally turns to comparing shoes, make a shoe-print mural. Bring out the paper and shoes, put colorful paint in several trays, and take the shoes for a walk across the paper.

Connections. LITERATURE: There are many books about shoes. Try the delightful cumulative text, *Shoes From Grandpa* (Fox, 1989), which is illustrated with torn-paper collages.

MATH/SCIENCE: Put out the assortment of shoes and have children match pairs, arrange them in size order, or sort into groups by shape, color, or style, before printing with them.

KINESTHETIC: Do an air-foot dance: Lie on backs. Hold shod feet up in the air and make them dance to some favorite music. Talk about ways to make the shoe prints look like they are dancing.

ART AWARENESS: Display a variety of handmade sandals from different parts of the world.

Handprints. Use this activity to build camaraderie and acceptance of people's differences. Compare the size and color of everyone's hands. Help children mix up paint to match their skin tone (see Teacher Tip Guide to Mixing Colors in chapter 5). Then have the children paint their hands and make handprints across a long sheet of kraft paper. Parents and visitors can be invited to add their handprints to the mural as well. Label the handprints with the child's name.

Suggestions:

- Add liquid detergent to the paint to simplify cleanup.
- Paint can be applied by placing a small amount in a shallow pan and then pressing the hand in it.
- Paint can also be applied with a brush. The feel of the brush on the sensitive nerves of the palm is an indescribable sensory experience that every young child and adult should experience.
- Provide a dishpan of warm soapy water for cleanup.

Connections. LITERATURE: Read books that celebrate skin color, such as *Black is Brown is Tan* (Adoff, 1973) and *All the Colors We Are* (Kissinger, 1994).

MATH: Count how many hands and how many fingers are on the mural.

ART AWARENESS: *Li'l Sis and Uncle Willie* (Everett, 1991) presents the art of African-American William H. Johnson. Point out all the different colors of paint Johnson used for skin tones. Display prints of his work, available from William Johnson Print Collection (Sax).

Footprints. This mural can follow activities such as dancing barefoot, studying body parts, or talking about animal tracks. It works best if there are two adults, one to supervise the children putting on the paint and walking across the mural, and the other to help the children wash and dry their feet. This is a great outdoor, warm weather activity.

Suggestions:

- Have children remove shoes and socks and sit on a low chair placed at one end of a long piece of kraft paper.
- Fill a shallow baking pan with a small amount of paint and have children press both feet in the paint.
- Help children stand and walk across the paper to the other end. Wet paint is slippery so supervise closely. Encourage children to make an original track. Play some music to accompany gentle dancing or try some tiptoe prints.
- Have a bucket of warm soapy water and towels at the other end of the mural and help the children clean the paint off their feet.

Connections. LITERATURE: Read *Whose Footprints?* (Yabuuchi, 1985), and look for tracks made by animals or people.

MATH: Make a single print of each child's foot. Graph the prints by size. Put it near the mural and have children match the graphed prints with those on the mural.

SCIENCE: Compare the feet of different animals.

KINESTHETICS: Mime walking barefoot on different surfaces.

Wheels. Relate to children's interest in wheeled vehicles by organizing a wheel mural. Place a large sheet of paper on table or floor. Make sure each child has plenty of room as this is a very active project. Fill several shallow trays with a small amount of paint. Place a variety of vehicles with different types of tire treads in the trays. Children will love driving their vehicles and leaving colorful tracks behind. When the mural is dry, let the children try to match the vehicles with their tracks. For variations, use small plastic animals instead of vehicles to make tracks, or draw roads first and then drive the cars on them.

Connections. LITERATURE: Share the book *Wheel Away* (Dodds, 1989), which reinforces the concepts of up and down, over and around.

MATH: Use pieces of string to measure the different "tracks" on the mural. Make a graph by taping strings to a piece of paper.

KINESTHETIC: Mime rolling like a wheel or moving like different kinds of vehicles.

SENSORY: Fill a stuff bin with wheels from broken toys.

ART AWARENESS: *California Crosswalk*, by John Outerbridge (Take 5) is a good accompaniment.

Paint drops. Rain is running down the window panes. It is a perfect day for drip painting! Add water to tempera paint so that it drips slowly. (Try it out first.) Hang a long sheet of paper on a wall and be sure to put plenty of newspaper on the floor. Show the children how the paint drips and encourage them to make many drips of their own.

Connections. LITERATURE: Read: *Rain* (Kalan, 1978) or *Umbrella* (Yashima, 1967), in which a child watches rain running down a window and which illustrates rain falling everywhere.

MATH/SCIENCE: Time how long it takes for the paint to run down.

SENSORY: Mime a raindrop falling, running down a window, and splashing in a puddle.

ART AWARENESS: Display reproductions of Jackson Pollock's action paintings (Crystal 20th-century art prints).

Thematic Murals

Murals can provide a way for children to express what they have experienced and learned in a thematic unit. A thematic mural starts with the common experience of the children. It

FIGURE 10–3 In mural making, children contribute in their own unique ways to create a marvelous whole.

provides an opportunity for children to talk with each other about what they know about the subject and then work together to produce a unified presentation of the theme.

- Sitting with the whole group, create a list of all items related to the theme. For example, if the theme is water and the children have visited a pond, read books about pond life, and observed fresh water creatures, the children might suggest fish, turtles, cattails, algae, pebbles, and so on.
- Ask the children what colors they saw in the pond water and list these as well. To expand the color ideas, present pieces of art on the same theme, such as Monet's *Waterlilies*. Explain that first they will paint the background using these colors.
- Provide small cups and have children mix their own paint color by taking about two tablespoons of a base color and then adding several drops of a supplementary one. The base color should be the predominant color of the subject. Some sample subjects and colors are listed here:

SUBJECT	BASE COLOR	SUPPLEMENTARY COLORS
Water	blue	White, green, purple, brown
Grass, forest or garden	green	White, yellow, brown
Sky	blue	White, lavender
Snow	white	Gray, blue, purple
Fall	orange	Red, yellow, brown
Beach	beige	Yellow, white, tan, brown

- Have children select the places on a large sheet of mural paper where their color would look best, and then in small groups paint the paper with their colors. Children should be encouraged to blend their colors into each other so that the whole paper is covered. This activity provides opportunities for children to interact with each other by sharing paint and location. Emphasize that it is important to respect each other's work and not to paint over someone else's color.
- While the paint is drying, the children should return to the original list and select an item they would like to include in the mural. Younger children can be given paper on which to draw or paint their selection. When it is done it should be cut out. Older children can be asked to sketch their idea.
- Call the group together and share the artwork or sketches. Discuss where each item would best be placed on the mural. For example, a turtle might be at the bottom of the pond and a fish swimming in the middle.
- Have the children glue the cutout artwork in the chosen location. Older children can redraw their sketch directly on the mural surface and then paint it.
- Both cutout pieces and painted artwork can be enhanced with glued-on collage materials. Natural materials can be added as well. For example, real shells collected on a field trip could be glued to a beach theme mural. Display the finished mural with other theme-related projects such as children's writing, books, and sculptures.

HOW CAN YOUNG CHILDREN USE THE COMPUTER TO CREATE ART?

The computer provides another medium for imaginative play.

JANE ILENE DAVIDSON (1989, P. 6)

This very sophisticated conversation about art is not happening at the art table, but between two three-year-olds working at the classroom computer. Computers have found their way into the hands of the very young, and are providing an interactive medium that is unlike any other art form. Like collage, computer graphics provide an avenue of art exploration that challenges both child and teacher to accept new ways of thinking and working with the elements of art. This section will look at how the use of computers can enhance the art program offered to children.

Young Artists at Work

Marc and Terry, deep in conversation, huddle together in the corner of the room, ignoring the active play of the other children.

"Put a yellow line there."

"Make it go that way."

"Cover it all up with green."

"Wow, look at that; those lines are thick."

"Should we make rainbow lines, again?"

"Oh, look the line just got thinner."

"Now I will make a circle."

The Computer As Art Medium

When the computer is viewed as an art medium rather than a teaching tool, the logic of its inclusion in any art program involving children becomes apparent. A computer loaded with a simple graphic "paint" program is another way to create lines and shapes. The monitor screen is the "paper" and the mouse is the tool for applying the lines and shapes and colors. The child manipulates colored light rather than pieces of paper, paintbrushes, or glue, but the artistic decisions are the same.

Using the Computer for Art Activities

In this technologically sophisticated society, even very young children are often familiar with computers. The similarity of the computer monitor to the ever present television makes children feel quite comfortable with a medium that sometimes intimidates adults. Being able to create their own "television" picture makes children feel independent and powerful. With the increasing number of computers in the home, home-based child care programs may be even more likely than more formal programs to have a computer available for children to use. Properly selected and set up, computer art software provides a wonderful way to introduce children to the computer, beginning a pattern of comfort and success with this technology that will play such a large role in children's futures.

The computer can be viewed as another component of the art program, just like easels and collage centers. It is neither more nor less important than any of the other art activities offered to children. Like the other activities, the computer allows children to play with the art elements in a creative way. Opportunities to work at the computer can be offered as one of the children's daily play choices.

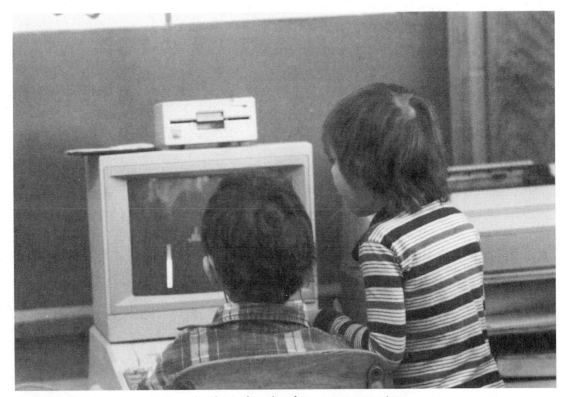

FIGURE 10–4 The computer provides the perfect place for an art conversation.

Selecting Art Software

The computer software being discussed in this section is of one type only. These are often called "paint," "graphic," or "drawing" programs and may come as part of the initial software booted on the computer, may be the graphic part of "works" programs that combine word processing, spreadsheets, and data processing, or may be purchased in special versions designed just for children. Because specific software programs that are available change rapidly, use the following general guidelines for making sure that the one selected will work well for young artists. (See Appendix A for some specific examples of excellent computer art programs.)

1. The program should be mouse-driven or use a joystick, not key-driven.
2. There should be a large open work space of white or black on which to draw.
3. The cursor should be large and easy to see.
4. The menu of color, shape, and line choices should be visible at all times, either at the side or top of the screen.
5. Menu choice boxes should be large, with logical symbols for line types, shape, and fill options.
6. Select a program that has a limited number of menu options. Children do not need such things as multiple pages, graduated colors, and inversions.
7. Programs that boot up quickly and directly are most convenient. If the only one available requires a complicated loading procedure, be sure to load the program before the children arrive. Turn the monitor off until it is time for the children to work.
8. The ability to save and print the children's pictures allows the children to review what they have done, or put on a computer art show. Some programs save groups of pictures with a "slide show" feature.
9. Most important—the program should be open-ended. It should not have pre-drawn coloring-book-style pictures to color, nor should it involve the manipulation of shapes or pictures on an already drawn background. Just because the words "draw," "paint," "picture," or "art" are in the title of a program does not mean it is a true art program. Always preview a program before offering it to the children.

Locating the Computer

The computer should be located away from heavy traffic and in a "clean hands" location. There must be an electric outlet capable of handling the necessary power, preferably with surge protectors. Make sure the computer area will be visible from all parts of the room so that assistance can be offered when needed.

Choosing Equipment

Consider the following when setting up a computer art program:

Computers. Any computer that runs the appropriate software can be used. Many child-appropriate art programs can be used on older, lower-powered machines. If the right combination of a program and older machine can be found, one computer can be dedicated just to art exploration.

Printers. A black and white or color printer is a nice addition as it provides a way to capture the children's work, but it is not essential. For young computer artists, just as in

FIGURE 10–5 "I like the computer. The lines 'round the screen. Look I made a blue line turn green." Nicholas, age 3

all the other art forms, process is more important than product, and the printed versions of their art are often pale imitations of the glowing images on the screen anyway. For many children, part of the fun seems to be making their pictures disappear when they are done.

Input devices. A mouse is the best way for young children to draw on the computer. Joysticks can also be used. Key-driven programs should be avoided as they do not provide the same flow of line across the screen and detract from the artistic decisions of the child.

Try to put the keyboard out of the way so that the child can focus on the mouse and the screen. On some computers, the keyboard can be placed on top of the monitor, or it can be removed and the mouse plugged in directly. If the keyboard is not removable, it is essential to cover the keys with a protective skin (see Appendix A). This will keep sand and other deleterious items out of the keyboard. The keyboard can also be covered with a cardboard box when children are using the mouse to draw.

SUMMARY: COOPERATIVE ART BINDS PEOPLE TOGETHER

In this society, art is all too often seen as something a person does alone. Yet some of the most joyful art experiences children can have are those in which they work in a group to create something massive—a mural, a box robot, or a wall of boxes. Working together for a common purpose forges children into a group. It becomes "our mural," "our robot," or "our wall." It is not surprising that so many of the "class-building activities" of cooperative learning programs are art-based. It is easy to incorporate the ideas and skill levels of each individual into an art activity. Using themes and providing opportunities for projects are other ways to increase group bonding.

Peers Model Skills

Imitation is one way that children learn new skills. Slightly more advanced peers provide better models for young children than adults, whose skills may be far greater than children need or are capable of imitating. Working together on a mural or at the computer provides the perfect opportunity for children to learn from one another.

Coming Together

Educators also benefit from working alongside their peers. Teaching, like art, is often seen as an individual affair. Teachers need to meet often with peers to share ideas and frustrations. Thematic units are easier to plan when there are two or three minds brainstorming. Teachers need to involve parents as partners in their programs. Foot painting and nature collages are easier to manage when there are extra hands. Everyone needs to come together in order to grow together. The program will be richer and the young artists will show more growth.

FIGURE 10–6 "I figured out how to make this circle shape, but spray paint is my favorite. It has a little spray-bottle picture you touch." Katelyn, age 4

FURTHER READING

> The computer should function like... other resources in the classroom, being no more or less important than other activities.
>
> SUE HAUGLAND (1993, P. 30)

To learn more about introducing the computer to young children:

Davidson, J. I. (1989). *Children and computers together in the early childhood classroom*. Albany, New York: Delmar.
  This book provides many excellent ways to introduce young children to the computer.

Hohmann, C. (1990). *Young children & computers*. Ypsilanti, MI: Highscope Press.
  Presenting computer activities in many curriculum areas, Hohmann shows how such activities help children develop cognitively, socially, and creatively.

For ways to help young children cooperate:

Crary, E. (1984). *Kids can cooperate: A practical guide to problem solving*. Seattle, WA: Parenting Press.
  Using real life examples, Crary provides a step-by-step approach to helping children work together to solve disagreements.

Janke, R. A., and Peterson, J. P. (1995). *Peacemaker's A,B,Cs for young children*. Marine on St. Croix, MN: Growing Communities for Peace.
  This book presents a well-organized, thoughtful program for teaching children to take an active role in getting along peacefully with others.

Kagan, S. (1994). *Cooperative Learning*. San Juan Capistrano, CA: Resources for Teachers.
  A systematic program for developing cooperative group behavior is presented in this comprehensive manual. There are special suggestions for introducing cooperative skills to children five and up.

Stone, J. G. (1969). *A guide to discipline*. Washington, DC: National Association for Young Children.
  Using simple clear language, teachers are shown how to deal in a firm, caring way with the everyday behaviors of young children.

Art Focus

COMPUTERS, CHILDREN, AND ART

> Children working together at one computer will spend a great deal of time engaged in problem-solving, peer tutoring, and cooperation.
>
> DANIEL D. SHADE (1991, p. 45)

Children approaching the computer for the first time explore in the same way that they explore crayons or markers or paint. Unlike adults, who often have difficulty knowing which direction to move the mouse, children quickly learn, sometimes in as little as one or two moves, how to control the direction of their lines as they watch the screen. Control over the computer image develops in the same way in both young children and adults encountering a free-drawing software program for the first time.

1. There is an initial fascination with how the rhythmic movement of the hand and mouse create lines of colored light on the screen. Toddlers and adults alike fill the screen with linear designs reminiscent of the first scribbles of childhood.
2. Next the computer artist becomes fascinated with the choices of colors, line types, and shapes that are available. One colored line or shape is placed over another, again and again.
3. When the user, child or adult, is familiar with the options, deliberation sets in. Lines are carefully placed, shapes positioned, and symbols created. Because there is no preset notion of how computer art must look, just as with collage, all artists can find their own ways of creating with the computer medium.

Children Grow through Creating Art on the Computer

Children will develop:

1. Physically, by exercising the small muscles of the wrist and fingers to manipulate the mouse, and by using hand-eye coordination to follow the lines and shapes created on the screen by their hand movements (Bodily-Kinesthetic)
2. Socially, by interacting verbally with a partner while creating computer art, and by sharing time on the computer with others (Interpersonal)
3. Emotionally, by feeling independent and powerful in being allowed to use a complex and valuable machine (Intrapersonal)
4. Visual perception skills, by associating the movement of the hand with the placement of shapes within a boundary (Spatial)
5. Cognitively:
   - By learning a computer-based vocabulary and by learning to "read" symbols on the menu (Linguistic)
   - By solving problems as they occur in the operation of the program (Logical-Mathematical)

Group composition. Computer art can be created by children of all ages. Very young toddlers, sitting on an adult's lap, enjoy moving the mouse and seeing what happens. Three-year-olds and older children like to work in pairs with a buddy of the same age or older. The computer seems to

FIGURE 10–7 Provide a large mouse pad and move the keyboard out of the way to make space for exuberant computer artists.

elicit more verbalization about the art elements than other art forms. Children often converse, help each other, or work together on the same screen image. Watching the visual images appear on the screen is intriguing enough to hold the attention of one child while the other one operates the mouse.

Setup. The computer should be placed on a low table at which two children can comfortably sit or stand. One computer can service about ten children working in pairs on a daily basis. If only one computer is available for a larger number of children, the children may have to take turns. It is important to make sure that girls have equal

Art Words

A Guide to the Computer

Clicking

Pressing the button on the mouse to select an item on the menu.

Cursor

A blinking line or shape that indicates where the first mark will appear on the screen. It is controlled by the mouse.

Disk

Contains the program.

Disk Drive

Reads information from the disk.

Hardware

The physical equipment used—computer, mouse, printer.

Icon

The symbol representing a menu option.

Joystick

A hand-held device that has a stick which is moved in different directions to control the cursor.

Mouse

A hand-held device, rolled along a surface, that sends instructions to the computer when pointed at options on the screen.

Mouse Pad

A soft foam pad used under the mouse to protect it.

Menu

A listing of choices available with the program. Items are selected by placing the cursor on the icon and clicking the mouse.

Printer

Produces a paper copy in black and white or in color of what is visible on the screen.

Software (or Programs)

Sets of instructions that tell a computer how to perform a particular task.

access to the computer. Research shows that when computer access is limited, boys often get more opportunities at the computer than girls (Davidson, 1989, p. 23).

Set up a system so that the children know that they will each get a turn to work for as long as they wish.

Have the program loaded and the computer on, but the screen off. Preset the program to draw with a thick straight line in a bright color, rather than the thin black line of the initial setup.

Materials. Besides the computer, mouse, and software program, a mouse pad is required. Purchase the largest size available to allow for the larger arm movements of young children.

Optional, but highly recommended, is a cover for the keyboard.

Transition in. Children are naturally fascinated by a computer. When introducing it, the many operations needed to create a picture need to be explained. Several children can be instructed one-on-one and then they can be paired with novices as "teachers."

What to do. Children are far more accepting of the computer as an art medium than adults. They quickly learn how to move the mouse. Depending on their age and fine-motor control, some will need more monitoring.

- If the child is having difficulty holding the button down continuously, check hand position. Some young children do better if they use two fingers (index and middle finger) on the button.
- If the child is constantly hitting the menu bars and losing the line setting, reset the menu and remind him or her gently to keep the cursor on the white or black screen part. Children usually self-correct for this after a few times, because it is no fun waiting for an adult to come and reset the machine.
- Accidentally hitting menu choices may also be the way children discover other menu options independently.
- In the beginning some children will need help changing the color. When they ask, slowly demonstrate how to do it, or pair the child with another who already knows how to do it.

What to say. It is important to use the correct computer terminology. This early experience with the computer will set the stage for later computer literacy. Words to introduce include: screen, mouse, menu, and cursor. Computer art, by its very nature, engages children in a discussion of art elements; line qualities, geometric shapes, and basic colors must be chosen from the menu. Verbalize these choices: "You are making wide yellow lines, now" or "What shape will you choose to use now?"

Transition out. When children finish, take a moment to describe what they did, such as "You covered the screen with so many straight lines!" or "Look at all the colors you used!"

If the work will be saved, consider having one work disk for each child. This makes it easier to find the work when reloading. If this is cost prohibitive, then have one work disk for every four or five children. Label the disks with colorful stickers, covered with clear package-sealing tape, to make it easier for the child to find hers.

Extending the learning. Printing out a picture is exciting. The children love to watch the picture slowly appear. It is possible to teach four- and five-year-olds how to save and then print out their own work. However, when the computer is printing, no one else can draw on it. If there are many children who are waiting a turn, it is better to print most of the pictures after the children have left.

SPECIAL NEEDS

Peripherals

There are many peripheral devices available that allow children who cannot use their hands to work on the computer. In some cases a joystick will work better than a mouse. There are also touch screens and tablets (see Appendix A for sources).

OBSERVATION: CHILDREN WORKING TOGETHER

Observe two groups of two or three children playing together or working on a common project. Group A should be children under three years old. Group B should be children four and up.

Group A Composition:

Child A: Age: Sex:

Child B: Age: Sex:

Child C: Age: Sex:

Group A Observation:

1. In what activity were they involved? _____

2. How long did they work together? _____

3. What did they say to each other? (Tape recording can be used.) _____

4. Which child/children imitated the other actions of another? _____

5. Which child/children initiated group actions? _____

6. How often did an adult intervene, if at all? _____

Group B Composition:

Child A: Age: Sex:

Child B: Age: Sex:

Child C: Age: Sex:

Group B Observation:

1. In what activity were they involved? _____

2. How long did they work together? _____

3. What did they say to each other? (Tape recording can be used.) _____

4. Which child/children imitated the other actions of another? _____

5. Which child/children initiated group actions? _____

6. How often did an adult intervene, if at all? _____

Studio Page **60**

ANALYSIS: POST-OBSERVATION

Based on your observations defend or oppose the following statement:

> When working in the same room or at the same table, each child speaks for himself, even though he thinks he is listening to and understands the others. This kind of 'collective monologue' is really a mutual excitation to action rather than a real exchange of ideas.
>
> JEAN PIAGET (1967, P. 29)

_____

_____

_____

_____

_____

_____

_____

_____

_____

_____

_____

_____

_____

_____

_____

_____

_____

_____

_____

_____

_____

_____

_____

Caring and Sharing

*Dealing with Physical
and Cultural Differences
Through Art*

> ❝ *Art enlarges
> experience by
> admitting us to
> the inner life
> of others.* ❞
>
> •
>
> WALTER LIPPMANN
> ("THE GOLDEN RULE AND AFTER,"
> *A PREFACE TO POLITICS,* 1914)

Questions addressed in this chapter:

How can teachers create a climate in which art can flourish?

How can art be used in anti-bias activities?

How are children with special needs integrated into the art program?

What is the role of holidays in an art program for young children?

What is art therapy?

SUMMARY: Caring for Each Other

FURTHER READING

ART FOCUS: Puppets, Masks, and Other Art Forms for Dramatic Play

---

Young Artists at Work

Timothy: The man in that painting is ugly.

Teacher: Why do you say that?

Timothy: His face is painted all black.

Teacher: It is unfair and hurtful to say someone is ugly because of his skin color. In our classroom we respect how everyone looks. Why do you think the artist used black paint for the skin tone of this man?

Timothy: Some people have black skin.

Teacher: What color paint would an artist use to show your skin? Let's go mix some paint to match your skin color.

HOW CAN TEACHERS CREATE A CLIMATE IN WHICH ART CAN FLOURISH?

> Anti-bias is not a subject you can teach and be done with; it's a way of life. You teach anti-bias by living it...
>
> LOUISE DERMAN-SPARKS AND THE A.B.C. TASK FORCE (1989, P. 118)

In offering art to young children, teachers need to be sure that the choice of activities creates an environment in which children from all backgrounds feel comfortable and can be creative in their artwork. Children differ in their racial, religious, cultural, and ethnic backgrounds. Research shows that children begin to be aware of these individual differences by two years of age, and that between the ages of three and five they develop a sense of who they are and how they differ from others (cited in Derman-Sparks, 1989, p. 1). Before children can feel free to relax and express themselves in creative art activities, they need to feel valued for who they are, not for how they look, talk, and behave. They need to be treated fairly and have their differences seen as strengths that enrich the learning of all the children.

The visual and tactile nature of art allows children, regardless of their differences, to explore and learn together. Children who speak different languages can learn by observing each other as they create with the art materials. Because art is common to all cultures, it can be a vehicle through which cultural differences can be explored.

Creating an Art Environment That Celebrates Differences

> It is not differences in themselves that cause the problems, but how people respond to differences.
>
> LOUISE DERMAN-SPARKS, ET AL. (1989, P. 6)

Teachers must take action to encourage the development of an anti-bias atmosphere among children. They need to consider the materials they choose to supply and the

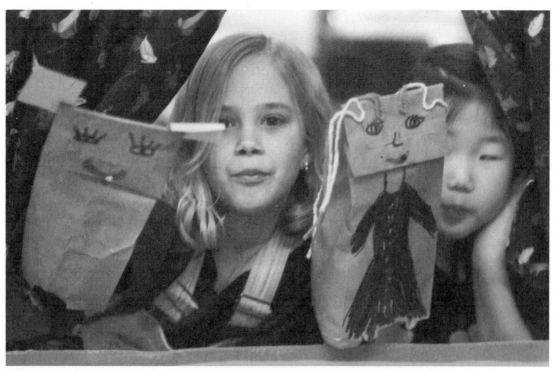

FIGURE 11–1 Children need to feel comfortable in order to express themselves through art.

pictures they display. Activities should be provided that foster discussion and the elimination of the misconceptions that are the basis of many prejudicial beliefs held by young children. There are a variety of ways that art can be used to support an anti-bias curriculum.

1. Provide art materials that reflect the wide range of natural skin tones. Paints, papers, play doughs, and crayons in the entire range of skin colors need to be regularly available, along with the other colors.
2. Mirrors should be available at all times for children to study themselves.
3. Images of people who represent the racial and ethnic groups found in the community and in the larger society need to be displayed. There should be a balance in the images so that there is no token group. It is recommended that about half the images should represent the background of the predominant group of children in the class. The remainder of the images should represent the rest of the diversity found in society. (Derman-Sparks et al., 1989.)
4. When selecting artworks, look for pieces that show a range of people of different ages, sexes, sizes, colors, and abilities, who are involved in activities that reflect current life. Many prints are available that reflect this diversity, including prints depicting art from Haitian, African, African-American, Native American, Mexican, and Asian sources. (See chapter 9 for suggestions and Appendix A for sources.)
5. Artworks should also represent artists of diverse backgrounds and time periods, including the present. This is particularly important for Native Americans.
6. Illustrations in the books read to the children and available for them to use should also reflect society's diversity.
7. Stereotyped and inaccurate images should be removed from display in the room and be used only in discussions of unfair representations of groups of people. Avoid so called "multicultural" materials such as bulletin-board kits and patterns

which depict people from around the world wearing traditional clothing from the past. These materials leave children with the impression that, for example, all Native Americans wear leather and feathers, all Japanese wear kimonos, and all Africans wear dashikis.

Talking To Children About Differences

When art materials that reflect skin differences and images of a variety of people are introduced to young children, occasions will arise in which biased or unkind remarks will be made and a response will be required on the part of the teacher. A child may not want to handle black play dough because it is "ugly," or another may say, "My skin-color paint is prettier than yours." Whether it is during an art activity, or at any other time of the day, children's discriminating behavior must be addressed. Such comments, even by very young children, must not be ignored or excused, nor is the teacher's personal discomfort in dealing with difficult subjects a reason to not act. The following suggestions may help.

1. Immediately address the child's negative response. A response to the statements above might be: "All colors are beautiful. Why do you say that?" If the comment is directed to another child: "That is a hurtful thing to say. Why do you say that?"
2. Help children figure out why they are uncomfortable.
3. Explain what remarks are hurtful and give examples of things the child might say or do instead.

HOW CAN ART BE USED IN ANTI-BIAS ACTIVITIES?

A torn jacket is soon mended; but hard words bruise the heart of a child
HENRY WADSWORTH LONGFELLOW (TRIPP, 1970, P. 79)

Art activities can be used to help children express their feelings about individual differences. They provide an opportunity for teachers to initiate a dialogue to correct mistaken beliefs and model respect for others.

Sample Activities.

The following examples provide models of these kinds of activities. These activities are suitable for children two and up. They use a variety of materials and approaches. Most are designed for small groups or for one-on-one.

Mixing my special color. Help children mix paint that matches the color of their skin. Place the paint in a labeled container that closes tightly. Give the color a beautiful name. Explain that whenever children want to paint a picture of themselves they may use their own special color of paint.

Extending the learning. Read any of these books about skin color: *All the Colors We Are* (Kissinger, 1994), *Black Is Brown Is Tan* (Adolf, 1975), *Colors around Me* (Church, 1971), *Bright Eyes, Brown Skin* (Hudson, 1990).

Valuing children's unique colors. Make sure that there are skin-color paints available at the easel. Then when children use the paint color that is closest to their skin color, hair color, or eye color, make a comment about the beauty of that color and express

FIGURE 11–2 "Friends." Crayon—Laurel, age 4

its relationship to the children's coloring, such as: "You are painting with a beautiful almond brown (rich peach, soft beige, deep brown, etc.). It is the same color as your skin (hair, eyes)."

Extending the learning. Read the book, *We Are All Alike...We Are All Different* (Cheltenham Elementary School Kindergarten, 1994). Collect a variety of paint-chip samples from a paint store. Have children sort them into groups. Then have them find the ones that match their hair, skin, and eye color. Make a graph or chart of the different range of colors in the group.

Washing up. This interaction can occur following any messy activity in which the children's hands get covered with an art material, such as finger painting, printing, clay work, or painting.

When the child or children are washing up at the sink say: "What do you think might happen to the color of our skin when we wash the paint off? Look, it stays the same color. Our skin color doesn't come off, only the paint."

Extending the learning. Provide opportunities for children to wash dirt off dolls that have different skin colors as well.

It's me. Create life-size renderings of each child.

1. Invite child to lie down on a sheet of kraft paper cut to the length of the child and trace around child. (Do not force a child to participate. This activity makes some children feel uncomfortable.)
2. Cut out the tracing for toddlers and preschoolers with beginning cutting skills. More adept cutters can cut their own.
3. Help children select the color of paint or crayons that best matches their skin, hair, eyes, and clothing, so they may color in their "Me Persons."

Extending the learning. Read: *Bodies* (Brenner, 1973). Develop awareness of body parts and names by calling out a body part and a way to move it, such as: "Shake your arm up and down. Wiggle your toes. Put your hands on your head." Develop a rhythmic pattern and repeat the actions several times. Another way to develop awareness is to encourage the children to touch the different body parts on their finished silhouettes.

Color awareness collages. Transition in by reading *Black is Beautiful* (McGovern, 1969). Have children find or make a list of all the beautiful black or brown things that they know. Put out the collage items, exclaiming over the beautiful color of each material.

Extending the learning. On a neighborhood or nature walk, look for brown or black things.

HOW ARE CHILDREN WITH SPECIAL NEEDS INTEGRATED INTO THE ART PROGRAM?

> Most important to remember is that they are children first, and they can learn.
> LINDA MCCORMICK AND STEPHANIE FEENEY (1995, P. 16)

Because of the open-ended nature of well-designed art activities, children with special needs can participate fully in most art programs, often without many modifications. If necessary, changes can be made in the tools and environment to allow active participation. The other children also need to be encouraged to accept and support those with special needs.

FIGURE 11–3 Open-ended art activities are suitable for all children.

General Modifications for Art

All children with special needs are individually unique in terms of how they cope with art materials. The following list provides some general ideas. Specific suggestions are also found in the Art Focus sections throughout the book.

Meeting needs for muscular control.

1. Put trays across wheelchairs.
2. Provide wheelchair-height table.
3 Use pillows to position child to better manipulate the materials.
4. Art tools such as crayons, markers, pencils, brushes, and pens can be wrapped in foam hair curlers to improve grip. Velcro pieces can be attached to a cotton glove and on the art tool.
5. Attach drawing tool or paintbrush to arm, prosthesis, foot, or headgear. Some children without use of their arms use their mouths. Drawing tools can be taped into cigarette holders or a special holder can be made or purchased. Remember, children do not draw with their hands, but with their minds.
6. If necessary, provide a rotary cutting wheel and a cutting mat instead of scissors.
7. Use no-spill paint containers and thickened paint. Choose brushes in a size that best matches the child's muscle control. Short, stubby brushes may work better than long-handled easel brushes. Foam brushes may make the paint easier to control.

Meeting visual needs.

1. Place a screen or textured surface under the paper, to add texture to drawn lines.
2. Use a fabric tracing or marking wheel to create a raised line. Place pads of newspaper or rubber mats beneath lightweight paper.
3. Use scented crayons and markers; add scents to paint and glue (see chapter 7).
4. Provide many tactile materials.
5. Place supplies in the same locations every time and attach tactile, identifying symbols on supply containers. For example, attach an actual piece of each collage material to collage storage bins. This will allow children to develop independence in obtaining their own supplies.
6. If the child has some vision, find out which colors are easiest to see and provide many materials in those colors. For example, fluorescent colors and reflective safety tapes may appeal to some children.

Other assistance.

1. Some children who have visual or motor difficulties may need hand-over-hand assistance. Place a hand over the student's to assist such skills as dipping the paintbrush in the container and then on the paper, or dipping a finger in paste and then applying it to the object to be glued.
2. Some children may need their base paper taped to the table to keep it from moving or wrinkling when they work.

Behavioral and emotional needs.

1. Select activities that have few steps and instant results, such as modeling, painting, and printmaking. Expect lots of exploration and physical expression of feelings.
2. For children who are easily distracted, provide work areas that allow plenty of space and seem separate from the rest of the room.
3. Select and arrange art supplies carefully to help limit distractions as well.

Helping Other Children Accept Those with Special Needs

1. Do not criticize children for expressing curiosity. When children notice and ask questions about disabilities and special equipment, answer matter-of-factly with a simple and accurate reply. It is important to be honest when answering. Use correct terminology whenever possible.

> Child: Why does Jared need a special holder for his crayons?
> Teacher: Jared uses a holder because he has trouble holding small objects tightly. Jared likes to draw like you do, but he has muscular dystrophy, so we figured out a way that he could do it.

2. Do not deny differences, but help children see their shared similarities.

> Child: Maya just messes with the paints.
> Teacher: Maya likes to paint just like you do. She has learned how to do many things. Now she is learning how to hold the brush.

3. Children need to become familiar with special equipment and devices, but also learn to respect the equipment of a child with special needs. If possible, rent or borrow a variety of equipment for children to explore, but make it clear that they must respect the personal equipment of the child who must use it.
4. If a children are comfortable doing so, have them explain how their special equipment helps them create art and why it is important to take care of it. If they cannot do this on their own, have them demonstrate how the equipment is used while an adult explains.
5. Invite artists with disabilities to share their art. Make sure they are prepared for the sometimes bold questions of children.

WHAT IS THE ROLE OF HOLIDAYS IN AN ART PROGRAM FOR YOUNG CHILDREN?

The possibilities for doing are limited only if we limit our vision of what is possible.
BARBARA THOMSON (1993, P. 23)

In many early childhood programs, holidays have become a major focus for the creation of art. Art activity books abound that purport to deliver exciting new ways to create holiday art and decorations. We all like to celebrate, but we need to take a deeper look at the effect this focus has on the child's view of the purpose of art. Holidays are fun; they create rituals which build a sense of solidarity; they are part of a society's cultural life; but there are dangers in relating art creation so closely to holidays.

Fairness

First of all, how do teachers select which holidays to celebrate and what symbols the children will make? Not all holidays are celebrated in the same way by everyone. The holidays of all children in the group must be presented with equal emphasis. One holiday should not receive more time and attention than another. Holiday activities are

FIGURE 11–4 "Mr. Snowman." Crayon—Melody, age 4½

often seen as one way to teach children about other cultures. However, for young children, they are best set in the context of the daily life and culture of specific children and their families in order to avoid creating stereotypes.

Presenting Multicultural Art Beyond the Holiday

Presenting artwork that relates to that culture throughout the year rather than just in the context of the holiday helps prevent children from associating the art and culture with only the holiday. For example, Native American art and culture should be displayed and discussed in many art contexts—when making masks, working with beads, creating with clay, learning to spin and weave, and examining baskets—not just at Thanksgiving.

Avoiding Stereotyped Symbols

> The overuse of holiday units interferes with a developmental approach to curriculum as too many "canned" activities take the place of activities tailored to the needs of specific groups of children.
>
> LOUISE DERMAN-SPARKS, ET AL. (1989, P. 86)

One of the hardest things to avoid when dealing with holiday-related art activities is the stereotyped images that relate to the holidays. These images limit children's creativity, visual imaginations, and often undermine their artistic self-confidence as they quickly learn they cannot replicate the commercial perfection of a holiday symbol.

The perfect Christmas-tree shape, for example, is impossible for young children to make successfully without resorting to patterns or step-by-step copying, and the image becomes so ingrained that many upper-level art teachers find they have to take their students on nature walks just to prove that all pine trees are not symmetrical and that they can be represented in many other ways in their art. Hearts, egg shapes, bunnies, turkeys, and pumpkins all become bland, perfect symbols instead of reflecting the infinite variety of their actual forms.

It is hard to avoid these symbols as they permeate the markets and media of this society. However, guiding adults need to consider carefully what images they want to surround the children in their care. Teachers can take the following actions to expand children's artistic imaginations and fight the prevailing stereotypes.

1. Avoid all holiday-related shapes in art activities. Do not give children cutouts of Christmas trees, turkeys, pumpkins, hearts, or other holiday shapes, or holiday coloring pages or stickers for the children to paint, draw, or make into collages.
2. Do not give children holiday-shaped cookie cutters to print with or to use with play dough. Instead use simple geometric shapes from which they can build their own versions of these symbols if they wish.
3. Do not limit color choices of materials to only those of the prevailing holiday.
4. Instead of displaying stereotyped holiday images, provide aesthetic experiences by making a collection of pumpkins, piles of pine boughs, a display of turkey feathers, a basket of eggs, or a cage of real rabbits, so that the children can see and touch them and discover similarities and differences on their own.

WHAT IS ART THERAPY?

> The idea that self-expression through art is good for people, and especially unhappy people, has been widely accepted.
>
> EDITH KRAMER (1971, p. 1)

The art therapist functions as an educator who modifies art activities to meet the emotional needs of troubled children. All children find emotional release through the expressive nature of art activities, and some children may use art to work through traumatic experiences. For example, a child who has experienced a natural disaster may draw pictures of houses and trees which are then scribbled over or "destroyed" as happened in the disaster. Gradually such pictures decrease as the child comes to terms with the occurrence.

For some children, however, art can be used to release otherwise unexpressed feelings and thoughts which they may need adult help to understand. A child whose pet was killed in an accident may draw increasingly bloody pictures indicating that the incident is still very disturbing to him and may need to work through these deep feelings.

Qualified art therapists work with a team of professionals to interpret the child's art, based on many samples. They then provide healing art activities. Art therapy is a distinct field of study that requires expertise in both art and psychology.

It is dangerous for untrained observers to make judgments about a child's emotional state based on just one or a few pieces of artwork. The constant use of one color of paint may simply reflect what color was available or in the position closest to the child. Research indicates that many young children often use paint colors in the order they are arranged at the easel (Winner, 1982, p. 151). Pictures of family members may reflect attempts by the child to control his world. The parents may be shown small and the

FIGURE 11–5 "Whirly lines." Tempera paint—Tyler, age 5

child huge, a new baby may be left out, or divorce and remarriage may not be reflected at all in the child's "family" portrait. On the other hand, the arrangement of images may just indicate how well the child controls the art medium.

The educator's role should be to allow children to use art as a personal way to express their thoughts and emotions—a safe place to show their feelings, and incidentally give adults a peek inside an often otherwise private world.

SUMMARY: CARING FOR EACH OTHER

> Art is an outlet that lets children convey what they might not be able to say in words.
> DIANE DODGE AND LAURA COLKER (1992, P. 161)

The graphic symbols of art can often be used to express thoughts and feelings that are hard to put into words. Teachers need to be sensitive to the personal needs and beliefs of ther children. Children can and should talk about the differences among them, but actually painting with different skin tones and working on the same art projects with those who are different from them, helps to form tangible links. The art activities teachers choose can help children broaden their perspective in ways that will make them more successful participants in the future.

In this chapter, ideas have been offered that challenge the educator to address sometimes controversial issues. Overheard comments could be ignored. Black and

FIGURE II–6 Dramatic play using artwork of their own creation draws all children closer together.

brown play dough could be avoided, because it makes some children uncomfortable or act silly. Teachers could focus on the more readily available "old masters" instead of looking for the harder-to-locate artwork of African-Americans and Latinos and those of other cultures. Teachers could give into the pressure to make commercialized holiday "art." Or teachers can make the other choice, the one that takes a little more effort. Teachers must make a commitment to do what is best for the children, knowing that change happens not all at once but a little bit every day.

FURTHER READING

These references will help guide the development of an anti-bias program:

Derman-Sparks, L., and the A.B.C. Task Force (1989). *Anti-bias curriculum: Tools for empowering young children*. Washington, DC: National Association for the Education of Young Children.
Using realistic examples, this book provides many positive ways teachers can address bias in the classroom.

Gonzalez-Mena, J. (1993). *Multicultural issues in child care*. Mountain View, CA: Mayfield.
Often teachers do not realize that common practices and beliefs about child care are culturally determined. Gonzalez-Mena helps educators analyze their own behavior from a cultural viewpoint.

Thomson, B. J. (1993). *Words can hurt you.* Menlo Park, CA: Addison-Wesley.
Many activities suitable for children under eight are presented in this program designed to help children accept individual and cultural differences.

For detailed information on modifying activities for children with special needs:

Art Educators of New Jersey. (1976, 1995). *Insights: Art in special education.* Cherry Hill, NJ: Art Educators of New Jersey.
This comprehensive book on art for children with special needs, preschool to grade 12, represents the combined experience of many teachers. It is full of detailed suggestions that are invaluable.

Rodriquez, S. (1984). *The special artist's handbook.* Palo Alto, CA: Dale Seymour.
This book is directed more toward children over the age of five, but it still has many usable ideas for the early childhood classroom.

To learn more about art therapy:

Kramer, E. (1971). *Art as therapy with children.* New York: Schocken Books.
This book explains what art therapy is and gives examples of how it is used with children.

Dalley, T., & Case, C. (1992). *Handbook of art therapy.* New York: Routledge.
A comprehensive review of the practice of art therapy.

Art Focus

MASKS, PUPPETS, AND OTHER ART FORMS FOR DRAMATIC PLAY

> Puppets speak a universal language of their own which qualifies them as one of the few international arts. They are capable of conveying feelings, values, emotions, and drama without spoken language. They represent the essence of human experience in a symbolic way...
>
> JEAN REGES BURN (1989, P. 29)

Masks, puppets, and a variety of other three-dimensional art forms provide children with an opportunity and an impetus to actively engage in social interactions. Of all art forms, these call forth dramatic imaginative play. Putting on a mask allows children to transform themselves into new creatures. Speaking through a puppet, they invent a new persona. Wearing a special hat changes the way a child walks. Shy children become bold. Loud children speak in tiny voices. These are truly magical creations.

Selecting Open-Ended Activities

In this section, activities are presented which allow children to create original artwork with

which they can play. Most of these activities provide a simple base upon which the children work their own magic. Unfortunately, there have been many puppet, mask making, and other related projects suggested for children which provide detailed patterns or elaborate precut pieces. These do not allow the children to express themselves or solve construction problems on their own. Often this is due to an attempt to have young children make projects that are too complex for their skill level, such as paper-bag puppets with talking mouths, or masks in sophisticated shapes.

In selecting activities, teachers must make sure that they are open-ended and allow the children to make most of the artistic decisions. They should build on the child's experiences and thematic curriculum ideas, but they must not limit the child's expression. The activities that follow may seem very simple. There are no tricky moving parts or multiple steps. It is the children who will add the magic—their own imaginations.

How Children Grow through Puppetry and Mask Making

Children will develop:

1. Fine motor skills, through the manipulation of a wide variety of materials to create three-dimensional art (Bodily-Kinesthetic)
2. Socially, by using masks and puppets to interact with other children through dramatic play (Interpersonal)
3. Emotionally, by being able to express feelings through the puppet or mask art form (Intrapersonal)
4. Visual perception skills, by using a wide variety of materials in new combinations, and by solving a variety of three-dimensional construction problems.
5. Cognitively:
   - By using vocabulary to describe three-dimensional forms, and by developing literacy skills through the use of the puppets and masks to tell oral stories (Linguistic)

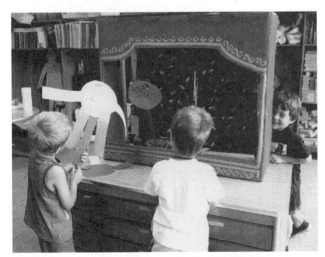

FIGURE 11–7 Puppets come to life in children's minds.

- By observing cause and effect as their actions effect motion and reaction from peers (Logical-Mathematical)
6. Art awareness, by gaining familiarity with masks and puppets from many times and places

Group Composition

Puppet and mask making activities can be done with small groups working on individual projects at a table, or by individual children who need to create a puppet or mask to meet some particular requirement of their own self-selected play activities. These art forms are also ideal for the project approach, in which pairs or very small groups of older children plan a dramatic activity based on an experience and then create the needed props.

Puppets

A puppet is really any inanimate object brought to life through the active manipulation of a child's hand. The addition of art materials fleshes out the child's conception. Most young children do not truly see the actual puppet, but rather the imaginary being that it becomes through the child's play.

The transition into puppet activities is very important. Making a puppet should not be a one-time activity, but something the child will return to again and again in order to create a character or persona with which to face the world. Introduce children to the world of puppets by including purchased or adult-made puppets as regular visitors to the program. Puppets can share secrets, read stories, and play with the children. They allow the adult to enter the child's world. Many of the most successful early childhood television programs, such as *Mr. Roger's Neighborhood* and *Sesame Street*, depend heavily on the use of puppets.

After introducing the puppet-making supplies, they should be available on a regular basis for whenever a child wants or needs to create a puppet. This is another reason to keep the design of the puppets very simple, and within the ability of children to create independently, without step-by-step instruction.

Once made, puppets can be played with anywhere, but the addition of a simple puppet theater can lead to hours of performances. There are

1. Select a very large box that is wider than it is deep. A box 12 by 24 by 36 inches makes a theater big enough for three or four children to play in at once.

2. Cut off flaps.

3. Cut opening in bottom of box.

4. Cut up corners.

5. Poke holes in corner joints. Fasten with wire or chenille stems.

6. Make a curtain from filmy material and put it on a dowel. Attach the curtained dowel to the inside of the stage opening. Affix with chenille stems through holes in the cardboard.

7. Paint front of theater if desired.

8. To use: place on a table with the back edge even with the edge of the table. For string puppets, place it on the floor and children can stand behind it with their puppets suspended below.

FIGURE 11–8 Folding puppet theater

many wonderful commercial puppet theaters. Some come as part of play houses or fit across a doorway. More inexpensively, a theater can be made from a large box (see figure 11–8).

Stick puppets

A stick puppet consists of a shape mounted on a sturdy stick. It can be as simple as a face drawn on a circle or as elaborate as an animal complete with moving legs operated with supplementary sticks. Make several simple stick puppets ahead of time. These should simply be different shapes glued to the end of the cardboard strip or tube. Make up a story to tell with them, such as "Where is the missing triangle?"or use them as part of a shape activity. Show children where the puppet supplies are and invite them to make their own stick puppets any time they want. Suggest ways of using the collage materials. Children may want to make puppets to interact with the sample ones. Leave the samples out for them to play with.

Be open to all the children's versions of this activity. Even if it is just a scribble drawing attached to the end of the tube, in the child's mind it is a persona. Interact with the children and their puppets to find out their intent.

Group Size. Independent or table group.

Materials.
- Strips of corrugated cardboard (1- by 12-inches) and/or paper towel tubes
- Precut construction paper in geometric shapes: circles, squares, triangles (Do not provide patterns or elaborate precut shapes that predetermine what the puppet will be.)
- Drawing materials: crayons, markers
- Collage materials: fabric, yarn, Styrofoam packing material, etc.
- White glue
- Scissors (optional)

What to do.

1. Select a large shape.
2. Glue stick or tube to back of shape.
3. Add details: draw on features, glue on other shapes for "limbs," attach collage materials for hair, clothing, etc.

A problem sometimes occurs when the stick is attached so low down on the construction paper shape that it bends, especially if loaded down with collage materials and heavy glue. Encourage the children to find their own solutions to the problem. Ask: "How could you make the stick hold better so that the paper doesn't bend?"

If necessary, give a hint: "How could you move or add on to the stick or the tube to make it hold the paper up?" Cardboard strips can be doubled up over each other to make them extend to the top.

Which are better, sticks or tubes? Cardboard sticks have the advantage of being easily obtained by cutting up cardboard boxes. They bend with active use, but can be reinforced by gluing a new stick to the old bent one. If a child glues the stick too low, a second one can be attached that extends the cardboard to the top of the shape.

Tubes have to be collected, but are very sturdy and take a lot of active play. However, if glued too low it is hard to extend them. Cardboard strips can be used to provide more reinforcement in this case.

Extending the learning.

1. Children with well-developed fine-motor skills can make smaller stick puppets using craft sticks as the support.
2. Stick puppets can be used as shadow puppets. For toddlers and young preschoolers who prefer to see the effect they are creating, use an overhead projector or unshaded lamp to cast a light on a wall, in front of which they can play.

FIGURE 11–9 Stick puppets can be made independently by young children.

3. Older children who understand that they can create an effect for others to see, can use a shadow theater. Place a piece of white paper over the puppet theater opening. Use an overhead projector or lamp to cast a light from the back.
4. Moving parts can be made by using paper fasteners. Because most preschoolers will need an adult to help use them, offer them as an option, not a requirement.

Connections. SENSORY: Make colored shadows by projecting colored light.

ART AWARENESS: Introduce older children to Balinese Shadow puppets (see Appendix A: Sources).

String puppets

Children are enthralled by anything on a string. It seems almost magical the way the object responds to their pulls and tugs. String puppets can be made as part of a thematic unit on flying things during which the children have observed the different ways familiar things fly, such as a bee, fly, butterfly, kite, plane, and so on. They can also relate to themes concerning weather (wind), seasons (falling leaves, snowflakes), birds, vehicles, fish, and insects. Another way the idea could be initiated is through carefully placed questions: "What do you think might happen if you put a string on what you made? Would you like to find out?" String puppets may also be a child-initiated activity; many times if the string and hole punch are available, children will come up with the idea of putting a string on their artwork all by themselves.

Group size. Individual or table group.

Materials.

- Construction paper
- Scissors
- Paste or glue
- String or yarn
- Hole punch
- Optional: collage materials, drawing materials, paint

What to do.
1. Children cut out a large shape of their own design. Depending on the initiating activity, this may either be in response to the idea of

creating something that can fly or it can be a cutting activity being done for its own sake.
2. They may paste on other shapes or collage materials. The shapes may also be folded or bent.
3. Children can punch their own holes in the shapes, but may need help attaching the string. (Hint: A quick and easy way to attach the string is to put it through the hole, double it up, and tie an overhand knot at the end.)
4. Children can then experiment with making their art form fly in different ways. If the weather is pleasant, this is fun to do outside.

Extending the learning. Mobiles: Particularly in response to themes concerning flying subjects, artwork on strings can be suspended from the ceiling to float on the air currents.

Vehicles: Strings can be attached to "vehicles" made from shoe, cereal, and gift boxes, which can then be pulled along the floor. Even older children who may have "outgrown" pull toys enjoy playing with ones they have made themselves.

Connections. SCIENCE: Observe how the different shapes fly. For older children create a chart of the different motions, such as spinning, low flying, dipping, etc.) Ask questions that make the children think about the relationship between the size of the shape and its weight and the resulting motion. For pulled-box projects, have the children pull them over different surfaces, such as a smooth tile or wood floor and various rugs and mats. Compare how differently the vehicle moves. Differently weighed objects can be put in the boxes and children can compare the difference in how much effort is needed to pull them.

KINESTHETICS: Play music such as *The Flight of the Bumblebee* (Rimsky-Korsakov) and have children move with their puppets in relationship to the sounds they hear. A tape of vehicle sounds could accompany a parade of pulled-box vehicles. Allow plenty of space for these activities.

ART AWARENESS: Introduce the work of Alexander Calder, the inventor of the mobile. Children enjoy hearing about the miniature circus he made and then used to put on performances for his friends, and about how he made the world's largest mobiles by painting jet planes with original artwork. (Print available: *Fish Tail and Lobster Trap* [Take 5].)

Hand puppets

It does not take much to spark children's interest in hand puppets. Slipping a hand in a box or putting a tube over our fingers and saying, "Can you make me into someone to play with?" can inspire great feats of imagination. Creating hand puppets for a show of their own creation also makes an excellent small group project for children.

Group size. Individual or table group.

Materials.

- Hand covering: sock, lunch bag, short tube, cereal box, or juice can. (The item should be able to fit over the child's hand or several fingers.)
- Paste or glue
- Scissors
- Construction paper
- Optional: collage materials, drawing materials, paint

What to do.

1. Have child figure out how the object best fits the hand or fingers and what will be the front and back.
2. Place the object front-side up on the table.
3. Add cut-paper shapes, collage items, drawings and/or paint to create the character.

FIGURE 11–10 A paper bag can quickly be turned into a new creation using a child's imagination.

4. Let dry before doing other side (optional) or before using it. Waiting is the hard part for children. Fast-drying glue is a help.

Extending the learning. Finger Puppets: Fold three-inch-wide strips of felt in half lengthwise and sew up along outer edge. Cut resulting tube into three-inch sections. Children can slip these on their fingers. Use marker, small assorted felt shapes, or small collage items (yarn, buttons, etc.) to create the puppets. Cut an opening out of the bottom of a shoe box and glue on fabric curtains to make a mini-theater.

Connections. LITERATURE: Invite children to use their puppets to retell a favorite story in a new way. Encourage them to be inventive with the characters.

KINESTHETICS: Have children move their puppets to the rhythm of a variety of musical pieces.

ART AWARENESS: Invite a puppeteer to visit and put on a show.

Mask Making

Mask making activities can be initiated in several ways. Interest can be aroused by studying masks from other cultures, putting mask prints or handmade masks on display, or reading a book such as *Who's in Rabbit's House* (Aardema, 1967). This Masai tale from Africa is illustrated with pictures of people wearing masks, representing the characters in the story. Masks fit into thematic units on the face, senses, and body. If the precut mask bases are available, children will also self-initiate mask making as part of collage-making, painting, or drawing activities.

Like puppets, masks allow children to express themselves in ways that they might not otherwise. Behind a mask, children feel like they are someone else; they may try acting in a new way or attempt things that might be too frightening barefaced. Like puppets, mask making should be available at all times for children to create as they feel the need, such as when dramatic play activities inspire children to turn themselves into particular characters or when a child has a deep emotion to express but needs to do so from behind a mask. Again, simple masks that children can do independently make the best mask making activities.

FIGURE 11–11 Paper-bag masks combine imaginative peeking and hiding.

Face masks

Group size. Individual or table group.

Materials.
- Mask bases: construction paper, tagboard, or cardboard face-sized rectangles or circles with eye holes precut.
- Paste or glue
- Scissors
- Colored paper, collage materials, drawing materials, and/or paint

What to do.
1. Glue on paper and collage items, paint, or draw on the mask base. Mask bases can be clipped to an easel for ease in painting.
2. If glue or paint is used, let the mask dry.
3. Masks can be used in several ways. Most simply, they can be held up to the face with hands or they can be attached to a handle made from a tube or cardboard strip. This is the preferred method because most children can attach the handle themselves. It also works best for children who wear glasses or have

TEACHER TIP

Preparing Mask Bases

The requirement for all maskmaking activities is to have available paper, cardboard, or bags in which eye holes have already been cut. Few young children can manage to locate eye holes in a usable place and then poke a scissors into the paper to cut them out. It is also important that the eye holes be large enough to provide safe visibility for the child. Eye holes should be circles, not eye shapes, at least two inches in diameter, separated by half an inch. Make a cardboard template to use on a regular basis.

hairstyles that prevent tying the mask on well. Masks with handles are easy for the child to take on and off. Some children, however, may want their masks tied on. Yarn or string can be used on tagboard or cardboard, but tears paper too easily. For paper masks, cut a strip of paper about 2 inches wide and staple or glue it to the sides of the mask so it fits the child when resting on the top of the ears.

Extending the learning. Half masks: Some children may not want their full faces covered or may want to make goggles. Have available rectangular pieces, about four by nine inches, with precut eye holes. These will need to be worn with a paper strip fastened around the back of the head. Goggles can be made into an aesthetic experience by taping colored cellophane on the inner side of the eye holes.

Dramatic possibilities: Try to encourage the children not to take their masks home right away. That way they will be able to develop richer dramatic play through interacting with the other children. By using their mask ideas, teachers can find related literature and themes to expand their play. For example, if several children have made animal masks, and others have made monsters, an interesting zoo or circus could result. A group of robots could lead into dramatic play about outer space.

Connections. LITERATURE: Read *Dancing Masks of Africa* (Price, 1975) which, in beautiful, simple language, describes how African masks are used.

SCIENCE: Study the different parts of the face and their functions (eyes, nose, mouth, teeth, tongue, ears). Match them to features on masks. Compare how they are similar or different.

KINESTHETICS: Move to music while wearing masks.

ART AWARENESS: Display mask prints from many cultures (see Appendix A).

Paper-bag masks

Children love paper-bag masks because once they are inside they feel completely hidden. They like to have people try to guess who they are as they use funny, made-up voices. A parade of children wearing paper-bag masks is a sight to see. It is easy to interest children in making paper-bag masks. If the bags are precut and ready, just trying on a plain bag and showing the children how it is worn often gets everyone excited about making one. Paper-bag masks can also be used as part of small group, creative dramatic play or as a self-initiated art activity. Masks tie in well with a theme that includes parades.

Group size. Individual or table group.

Materials.

- Brown paper grocery bags with precut eye holes (Before cutting holes, try bag on a child.) The top of the bag should rest on the top of the child's head. The eye holes will need to be higher than one might expect. Cut slits up the sides of the bag so it can extend past the child's shoulders.)
- Drawing, collage, or painting materials
- Scissors and glue (if needed)

What to do.

1. Place bags eye-hole-side up on a table. To paint them, clip the bags to an easel.
2. Children can draw on or attach paper and collage items to bag.
3. Important: Let bags dry before wearing.

Extending the learning. Helmets: Instead of eye holes, cut an face-size oval opening in each bag.

Connections. LITERATURE: Children can compare their parade to the one in the book *Parade* (Crews, 1983)

KINESTHETIC: Have a parade wearing the masks.

ART AWARENESS: Display prints or actual masks from many cultures such as Native American, African, and Asian.

Bodywear

Making hats, jewelry, and other body decorations is another way art and dramatic play interact. Bodily ornament is one of the oldest art forms. Prehistoric people cherished their jewelry so much that intricately wrought pieces were buried with their loved ones only to be found by archeologists today. Wearing hats and jewelry makes the children feel they are acting like grown-ups.

As with puppets and masks, bodywear items should be simple enough for the children to create on their own without adult assistance.

Hats

Wearing a hat is another way children can transform themselves. Creating original hats provides them an opportunity to use a variety of art materials in a three-dimensional form.

Group size. Individual or table group. An interest in hats can be sparked by observing some unusual ones, studying the hats of different workers in the community, or reading a book such as *Hats! Hats! Hats!* (Morris, 1993). Suggest that children make thinking hats, reading hats, or hats for dancing. Hat making also relates to themes that involve parades and circuses. Hats can be used to enrich dramatic play and storytelling.

Keep a collection of hats to wear when reading related stories, such as a sunbonnet for a book about gardens or a ski cap for a winter story.

Materials.

- Premade hat bands: Two-inch-wide strips of tagboard glued into circles large enough to fit over the children's heads and rest on their ears OR
- Paper cones: Bring the two corners of 12-by-18-inch paper rectangles together to form a

conelike shape; glue or tape together. This hat form can be worn in several ways. It may need to be tied on to keep it in place. (Safety Note: Do not use staples. They get caught in the children's hair.)

- Drawing and collage materials
- Scissors
- Paste or glue

What to do.
1. Children attach collage materials or shapes they have cut out and perhaps drawn on to the hat base.
2. Let glue dry before wearing.
3. For cone hats, attach strings to tie under chin, if necessary.

Connections. LITERATURE: Share the charming story, *Jennie's Hat* (Keats, 1966) about a little girl with a fantastic hat.

MATH/SCIENCE: Group hats by related characteristics—color, brim, brimless, etc.

KINESTHETICS: Invent a movement to go with the hat.

ART AWARENESS: Look at and discuss paintings that show people wearing hats, such as: *Sunday in the Park*, Seurat (Modern Learning) or *Hope Street: Church Mothers*, M. Johnson-Calloway (Take 5).

Jewelry

Jewelry can take many forms. Necklaces, bracelets, pins, and badges can all be simple enough for children to make independently. For example, strips of paper can be decorated, glued into circles, and worn as bracelets, armbands, or watches. These activities provide an excellent way to work with the art element or theme of pattern. Arouse children's interest by pointing out someone wearing unusual jewelry or by having a jewelry craftsperson visit the class. Jewelry making may be initiated through dramatic play.

Group size. Individual or table group.

Materials.
- Items to string: cut cardboard tubes (half- to one-inch sections), paper shapes with holes punched in them; small pieces of Styrofoam cut into shapes with punched holes in the center, straight macaroni,* child-made soda-clay beads (see Appendix A: Recipes). (Safety Note: Items for children under age three must pass choke test.)
- Yarn or heavy string. Wrap tape around one end for easy stringing. Tie a large piece of folded paper or a cardboard tube section to the other end to prevent strung items from falling off.

What to do.
1. Assemble items to string in small trays. Prepare many measured pieces of yarn, with taped tips and paper ends. Lay them out on a table or counter so children can help themselves without tangling them.
2. Children string items in a pattern of their own design.
3. When done, remove tied on paper and use an overhand knot to tie ends together.

Extending the learning. Children with more developed fine-motor control can string the larger sizes of pony beads sold commercially (see Appendix A: Supplies). These mix well with the handmade soda beads.

Connections. LITERATURE: Read: *My Painted House/My Friendly Chicken* (Angelou, 1994) or the section on wampum in *The Story of the Dreamcatcher and Other Native American Crafts* (Lord, 1995).

MATH/SCIENCE: Look for patterns created as children string the beads. Ask them to find the patterns.

ART AWARENESS: Look at and discuss patterns in the beadwork of Native American and African people.

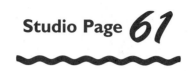

MODIFYING AN ART PROGRAM

Imagine that you have just been told that a four-year-old girl with limited vision will be joining your group of preschoolers.

What modifications would you make in how art activities were offered?

_____

_____

_____

_____

_____

_____

_____

_____

_____

_____

_____

_____

_____

_____

How would you rearrange the environment to accommodate her needs?

_____

_____

_____

_____

_____

_____

_____

_____

_____

_____

_____

_____

_____

Studio Page 62

DEALING WITH DIFFICULT SITUATIONS

Consider each of the following situations and decide what you would say and do.

1. A parent picks up her son's painting and says, "Another painting all in black! Why don't you use some pretty colors when you paint?"

    _____

    _____

    _____

    _____

2. A little girl refuses to touch the brown play dough. "It's yucky!" she declares.

    _____

    _____

    _____

    _____

3. Michael, age five, only draws faces with blood coming out of their mouths.

    _____

    _____

    _____

    _____

4. An aide shows the children how to trace their hands to make turkeys.

    _____

    _____

    _____

    _____

5. A child with muscular dystrophy is having trouble holding her crayon.

    _____

    _____

    _____

    _____

Studio Page 63

OBSERVATION: BIAS IN THE ENVIRONMENT

For this observation, visit a school or child care center when children are not present and observe the following:

1. Are there crayons, paper, plasticine, play dough, or paints available in a wide variety of skin colors?

   _____

   _____

2. Are there child-height mirrors?

   _____

   _____

3 Are there images or artwork that depict people of different racial and ethnic groups?

   _____

   _____

4. Do half the images represent the predominant groups?

   _____

   _____

5. Do the other half represent the diversity of our society?

   _____

   _____

6. Are there books available that reflect the diversity of our society?

   _____

   _____

7. Are there any stereotyped or inaccurate images representing certain groups, such as Native Americans?

   _____

   _____

8. Are there any commercial or stereotyped holiday artworks on display?

   _____

   _____

Studio Page

ANALYSIS: POST-OBSERVATION—ELIMINATING BIAS

Based on what you observed, would you judge this to be a bias-free environment for young children?

_____

_____

_____

_____

If yes—write a letter to the director telling him/her what you especially liked about what the program offers young children. (Optional: This letter may be mailed to the director, if desired.)

_____

_____

_____

_____

_____

_____

_____

_____

_____

_____

If no—make a plan of action that could be used to eliminate bias in the environment. Include cost, time frame, and personnel necessary to accomplish this task. Remember that change occurs bit by bit.

_____

_____

_____

_____

_____

_____

_____

_____

_____

_____

12

Assessing Growth

What Does a Successful Art Program Look Like? Authentic Assessment of Children, Teachers, and Programs

Questions addressed in this chapter:

What is authentic art assessment?

How can children's artistic growth be assessed?

What daily observation methods can be used?

How can portfolios be used for long-term assessment?

What can be learned by looking at a child's art?

How do teachers share with parents?

How do teachers assess themselves?

SUMMARY: A Vision to Grow On

FURTHER READING

ART FOCUS: Displaying Children's Art

Young Artists at Work

"Come see my bear!" my daughter shouted happily. She grabbed my hand and pulled me down the hall. It was the kindergarten open house and the school was crowded with families. She looked carefully at each painting and drawing carefully hung in neat rows on both sides of the hall.

"Is it this one?" I kept asking.

She shook her head no. Finally after several trips up and down the hall she said dejectedly, "It's not here."

"We'll ask your teacher where it is," I said encouragingly.

"Why, it's right here," said the teacher, pointing to a group of brown finger paintings that had been cut into identical teddy-bear shapes, each trimmed with a colorful bow at the neck.

"Here's yours," I said, showing her the one with her name on it.

My daughter studied it carefully. "No, that's not mine. I made a bear."

"This is a bear," said the teacher. "Don't you remember we made finger paintings and then I cut them into bear shapes?"

"That's not mine," my daughter insisted stubbornly.

The teacher rolled her eyes and said, "These little ones never remember what they make."

The teacher turned to talk to another family and my daughter scampered off to greet a friend. I turned back to the finger painting and studied it closely. Yes, although parts were missing, I could see that there had been a bear there, carefully drawn with a little finger—a childish bear, now brutally cut in order to fit the adult image of a pleasing bear shape.

As I turned away to join my daughter, I heard a family behind me exclaiming, "Oh, what cute little bears! The teachers here always have the children make such charming art. The children are fortunate to have such a great kindergarten program!"

WHAT IS AUTHENTIC ART ASSESSMENT?

Nobody sees a flower—really—it is so small it takes time—we haven't time—and to see takes time, like to have a friend takes time.

GEORGIA O'KEEFE (CAMERON 1992, P. 22)

Art, unlike many other pursuits of young children, produces a tangible product. It is easy to fall into the trap of assessing the child, the teacher, and even the total program based on that product. How teachers view a child's artwork, and what they

FIGURE 12–1 "The Artists." Crayon—Laurel, age 4

choose to do with it, will reflect the strength of their philosophy about child art. It takes a strong and dedicated educator to withstand the natural inclination to judge children by the art they produce, and to combat the pressure to dress up the program with parent-pleasing art.

This does not mean that teachers should not assess their art programs, but that they need to do so on the many components that enable the child to produce art. Assessment is evaluating the progress the children and the educators have made toward the goals they have set. Authentic assessment consists of looking at this progress in many different ways, using a variety of assessment tools. Properly done, such an assessment allows teachers to constantly improve the program so that they can provide the richest art experiences to young children.

HOW CAN CHILDREN'S ARTISTIC GROWTH BE ASSESSED?

> Portfolios, collections of the child's work, and written observations are becoming an accepted method of documenting the child's progress. Written observations which are thorough, objective, regular, and done in the natural classroom environment are accurate measures of a child's progress.
>
> BARBARA NILSEN (1997)

Watching children is an essential component of good teaching. Teachers can learn many things from how children behave and react artistically.

Observing the Individual

Individual behavior patterns can give us information about the following growth areas.

1. Physical: The child's physical control of the art media
2. Social: The child's ability to work with others in art activities
3. Emotional: The child's comfort level with art media and the art of others as expressed in art activities
4. Spatial: The child's visual perception skills
5. Symbolic language: The child's skill in relating graphic images and oral language
6. Cognitive understanding: The child's ability to express art concepts graphically and through oral language

Observing Group Dynamics

No child functions alone. Teachers must also place the child in the context of the group. Children learn as much from interacting with their peers as they do from adults. Every group has a unique dynamic, and no two groups react in the same way to the art activities that teachers offer. Observations of the behavior of groups of children can help teachers see each child more broadly. Group behavior patterns can provide the following information.

1. The suitability of the art experience for the particular group
2. The interests of the group
3. The role of the child within the group

WHAT DAILY OBSERVATION METHODS CAN BE USED?

Working with very young children requires that teachers constantly interact with one or more children throughout the day. Every interaction and casual observation becomes stored in teacher's memories, and becomes what is often characterized as their "feeling" about a child or the group. If, day after day, a child builds with blocks, the teacher feels the child must like blocks more than the other activities. If some children refuse to use finger paint, teachers conclude they must not like to get messy and and probably come from a home that stresses cleanliness. Teacher intuition is one of the basic forms of assessment.

Memories are far from perfect, however, and teachers are more likely to remember the unusual occurrences than the everyday behavior that is more reflective of an individual child and group. Past experiences also influence how teachers process their observation.

There is no way to record in memory every single behavior of a child. There will always be only partial images. That is why it is so important to have a system for recording behavioral observations in a systematic way. The crucial factor is always time. Teachers want to spend their time interacting with the children, not writing about them. Systems for recording assessment information must be quick and simple.

Checklists

Checklists strategically placed about the children's environment can provide a convenient way to record behavior. Design a checklist by first creating a brief list of desirable behaviors in each art area. Then develop a simple symbol for each behavior, such as the initial letters or a shape. Choose symbols that directly relate to the behavior. Although it may take a while to learn them, eventually their use will become automatic. Make a list of the children's names and then hang it at the easels, by the blocks, near the collage supplies, and so on. Use Velcro to attach a pencil near each list.

Throughout the day, mark the lists with symbols to indicate that a child is in a particular area and what behavior is being observed. Done on a regular basis, these checklists will provide a better picture of the child's daily behavior and skill development than memory alone. (See figures 12–2 and 12–3).

Anecdotal Record Keeping

Anecdotal records provide an ongoing picture of the child's behavior at set times in specific settings. They can be made at the time of the observation or soon after the event. To be useful the record should document the setting of the event, including the time, the children involved, and any other related information. Anecdotes should be objective, recording only observed behaviors and direct quotes of the child, not the teacher's opinion about the reason for that behavior.

Brief anecdotal records. Simple anecdotal notes can be made in checklist style by adding a space for date and comments. Next to the child's name on a behavioral checklist, simple notations can be recorded at the same time that other behavior is observed (see figure 12–4).

Detailed anecdotal records. More detailed observations may need to be recorded for a variety of purposes. A listing of the steps a child went through to create a piece of art may show how the child was able to solve a problem. A description of the creation of a painting may be used in an art display or to make the child's art more meaningful for the parents. An ongoing record of how a group project evolved may become an integral part of the learning process when it is shared with the children and families (see figure 12–5).

Sample Behaviors and Checklist Symbols

1.	Works independently	I
2.	Asks for help	H
3.	Cleans up after self	Cl
4.	Interacts positively with others	↕
5.	Controls tools	T
6.	Cuts with scissors	Cts
7.	Stays on paper	Sp
8.	Verbalizes about work	V
9.	Identifies art elements	ID
10.	Includes alphabet letters in work	ABC
11.	Includes numerical information	123
12.	Uses materials in a new way	*
13.	Observes cause and effect	C&E
14.	Observes similarities/differences	S/D
15.	Shares materials	→

FIGURE 12–2 Sample behaviors and checklist system

If possible, teachers should try to write one detailed anecdote about a child daily. To make it easier, prepare forms with the children's names and date already on them. Having the names on them prevents children from being missed. Index cards work well as they can be carried in a pocket. Some teachers are more comfortable using clipboards or

AT THE EASEL AREA

Child's Name	Observation
Michelle	I ID Sp
Nick	T I → ↕
Stan	123 V H
Berette	V Cl
Jared	I ID Sp
Lin	H Cl

FIGURE 12–3 Checklist sample

DATE: March 4

Child's Name	Behavior
Rosario	Cts (heavy board)
Henry	↕ (worked on project with Bill)
Marcia	123 (counted squares on collage)
Bill	↕ (initiated collage with H.)
Ronnie	V "Look at my elephant!"

FIGURE 12–4 Sample checklist with anecdotal notes

Mario 2/4
At easel 10:04 to 10:10.
Started by making yellow line.
Then used blue. Touched where made green.
Put finger up to eye. Smiled.
Then took brush and smeared the colors together.
I asked, "What color is that?"
He said, "Green."

Susan 2/4
Drawing/cutting 10:50 to 11:05.
Took markers and went to block area.
Made a sign for building.
Said, "This is a supermarket."
Then drew rectangles and got scissors and cut them out.
Called them food.

FIGURE 12–5 Sample anecdotal records

notebooks with one page divided into sections for each child. Another method is to write on large self-stick labels. They can then be peeled off and attached to the child's portfolio.

Recording project work. Project work can be recorded on a specially designed sheet that allows input from the children. A large sheet of paper can be divided into days. Each day the group can dictate their accomplishments. Children can also be encouraged to record on the sheet in their own way. Alternatively, each day's work can be recorded on separate sheets that are later bound together to create a book about the project.

Process Folios

A process folio is a collection of materials that records how a piece of artwork or series of artworks were accomplished. Process folios might be made for a group project such as the dinosaur described in figure 12–6, or for a group of easel paintings done over a week's time. Folios contain information from the checklists for the particular child or group of children, anecdotal records, related sketches, or notes done by children, and audiotapes, photographs, and/or videotapes of the work in progress. Materials should be placed in the folio on a daily basis.

The process folio becomes an integral part of the artwork and serves to reproduce the multimedia process of creating graphic art. If the artwork is to be shared with parents or displayed in an exhibit, the process folio materials can be used to give meaning to the work.

Depending on the nature of the materials being collected about the artwork, process folios can be as simple as a file folder or large brown envelope, or as complex as a bound looseleaf notebook or child-decorated box.

Our Dinosaur Project C

Day 1: We have decided to build a dinosaur. Michelle is making a head out of a box. Frank is making a big tail.

Day 2: Michelle's mom gave us a big box for the body.

Day 3: We decided to paint our dinosaur purple. We painted the head today.

Day 4: Toma and Mark helped us paint the body and tail. Michelle made neat teeth out of a Styrofoam tray.

Day 5: We tried to put our dinosaur together today. First we tried glue, but it fell off. Then Michelle thought we should use tape. So we taped it, but when Mrs. Denal moved it so we could have reading time the head fell off. Everyone laughed. Frank was upset. He went and played with the blocks.

Day 6: Mrs. Denal showed us how to use wire to attach the parts of our dinosaur together. She made the holes and we pushed the wire through. Now our dinosaur is real strong. His head even moves because of the wire.

Day 7: We named our dinosaur "Purple." Margo wrote the name for us and we hung it on a string around his neck. We measured him and he is four feet high. He is taller than us. We pretended he was wild and Kate, Toma, and Frank built a pen for him out of the big blocks. Then we knocked it down and let him out. He is really friendly and will guard our room when we aren't here.

FIGURE 12–6 Sample project record

CONTENTS OF A SAMPLE PROCESS FOLIO: DINOSAUR PROJECT

Calendar showing days and time project was worked on

Child dictated anecdotal records (figure 12–6)

Teacher's anecdotal records

Photos of dinosaur being built.

Photos of finished dinosaur and everyone who worked on it

Class graph comparing heights of dinosaur and children in class

Michelle's drawings of finished dinosaur

Frank's story about the dinosaur (dictated and illustrated)

Margo's and Toma's story about the dinosaur (recorded on audiotape)

Sheet of comments about dinosaur written by parents and visitors to program

---

FIGURE 12–7 Contents of sample process folio: Dinosaur project

Photography

> Photography provides many opportunities for discovering and developing space-time
> concepts and relationships. A photograph freezes both space and time.
>
> LYDIA A. GERHARDT (1973, p. 165)

Anyone working with children should always have a camera near at hand. It does not
have to be a fancy one, but it should be simple and foolproof to operate. Automatic
focusing, a light sensor, and a built-in flash are essential and generally available on
even lower-priced cameras. If the camera is convenient to use and nearby, it is more
likely to be picked up at opportune moments.

FIGURE 12–8 Children see their surroundings
differently through a camera. (Photo credit: Kenneth
Rozek)

To save costs, consider asking each family to donate a roll of color print film. Explain how the photographs will be used and make sure to distribute the photographs to the parents at the end of the session.

The uses of photos are multitudinous.

1. Photographs of block structures, sculptures, and other three-dimensional projects can be displayed long after the originals are gone.
2. Photo albums of children's art, field trips, and special events can be kept in the book area.
3. Photographs of children working can be saved in process folios and portfolios as a visual way to remember how something was done.
4. Photographs of class members, families, friends, and visitors, as well as the children's homes and family events, can be used in portrait lessons and family studies.
5. Photographs of familiar objects shown from unusual viewpoints can challenge children's visual perception.
6. Photographs can be used to record art activities, setups, and child interactions for teachers to later review their teaching methods.

Photography Tips. In the beginning, children are sometimes silly when photographs are taken. The more photographs are taken, the more accustomed children will become to the process. If necessary, walk around taking pictures with a camera empty of film. This also offers an opportunity to learn the best locations from which to capture activities in the different areas. Other suggestions:

- Try to get down at the children's level when taking photographs so all the pictures do not reflect an adult's point of view.
- If using a flash, check the distance from the subject to avoid washed-out pictures. Consider using high-speed film instead.
- Do not shoot against a bright background, such as a window.
- Consider using an instant camera, if one is available, for situations in which there is not enough time to return developed pictures.

Videotaping

The availability of camcorders has made it possible to truly record the multimedia process of child art production. If a camera is available on a regular basis, it can be used to create a time record of a child's artistic growth. Have each parent donate a videotape for their child's record. Label the tape with the child's name and the dates and then, at regular intervals, videotape the child creating art. At the end of the term, return the tape to the family, who will then have a treasured record of the child's artistic growth.

Videotapes can also be made to record projects, as part of portfolios, and as a way to assess our teaching style.

Videotaping Tips.

- Built-in microphones tend to be very sensitive to background noise. Make sure that there is no banging or moving of furniture while taping. A directional microphone will produce better results.
- Do not film with windows behind the child. The light meter will adjust to the window brightness and the child will be in shadow.
- Before filming, practice using the camcorder. The tape may rewind slightly when it is stopped. Before starting the next taping session, wind it forward slightly.

- It is a good idea to start each taping with a view of a placard on which is written the date and the art experience being filmed. Some camcorders have an automatic data and time display feature as well.

Obtaining releases. Before taking any photographs or making a videotape, it is essential to obtain a signed release from all families. Many institutions have parents fill out such forms upon enrollment. However, if special use is going to made of the pictures, such as a public display in an exhibit or at a workshop presentation, a more specific release should be obtained. If a parent refuses to sign a release, that request must be respected. When taking photographs, be careful to avoid taking pictures of children without releases, except from the back.

HOW CAN PORTFOLIOS BE USED FOR LONG-TERM ASSESSMENT?

A portfolio is a collection of artwork and related materials made over a period of time. It may contain all the same items as a process folio, as well as completed process folios and child-created books about their art. Each child should have an art folder in which completed or unfinished artwork is stored, along with any other art-related materials. The child and parents should know where the folder is kept and be able to look through it at will.

Sample Model Release

The undersigned hereby grants _____ the right to make and have made,
Photographer's name

publish, reproduce, use, and reuse photographs or likenesses of my child _____,
Child's name

in which my child appears, with or without his or her name, and to circulate and use the same for

educational purposes. I further agree to hold _____ harmless from any claim
Photographer's name

action and damages based on a violation or alleged violation of these representations.

All photographs, negatives, prints, transparencies, drawings, reproductions, and sketches made

by_____ shall be the exclusive property of _____.
Photographer's name   *Photographer's name*

_____
Parent's Signature

_____   _____
Witness   *School Official*

_____   _____
Date   *Title*

FIGURE 12–9 Sample model release

Introducing Portfolios

Young children often do not seem to want to part with their artwork. This is partly a function of their wanting something tangible to share with their families at the end of the day, and partly a function of how art programs are run. A "make and take" view of art education encourages children and their parents to feel they must walk out the door clinging to a dripping painting or a gluey, paper-bag puppet. However, if children are introduced to the idea of an art folder or portfolio on the very first day, if they participate in choosing the color of the paper or decorating the folder, and if they see where it will be kept, they will be far more willing to leave their artwork behind. Parents also need to be informed about the portfolio from the beginning and invited to look through it whenever they wish.

Constructing the Portfolio

The portfolio can be simply made from a very large piece of paper folded in half, or from two sheets taped together. If it will be used only for a short time this will suffice. If the folder will be used over a long period such as a year or two, it can be made sturdier by using clear packing tape to protect the edges, or by being made from two corrugated cardboard pieces taped together along one side to form a hinge. The portfolio must be as large as the largest paper used by an individual child.

Small or bulky items such as video- and audiotapes can be stored separately in shallow gift boxes labeled with the child's name. These boxes can be sent home for the family's enjoyment on a regular basis.

Storing the Portfolios

One of the reasons educators hesitate to initiate portfolios is the problem of storing them and still retaining easy access. A pile of large floppy papers is unsightly and heavy. It becomes almost impossible to remove folders on the bottom without handling all the folders above.

One solution is to use the commercially made, vertical, divided storage boxes that are used to store art prints (see Appendix A). Another is to construct a giant drying box (see figure 5–9) with one-inch separations between the shelves, to store one portfolio on each shelf.

Labeling the Portfolios

For easy access to be offered to children and parents, the folders need to be clearly labeled. An index card stapled to the folder provides a sturdy tab. Cards placed at varying locations across the top of each folder allows individual children to locate their folders more easily. Color-code or mark the cards with special symbols as well as names, to make folders quicker to locate.

Selecting Work for the Portfolio

Having a portfolio does not mean that every piece of artwork is put in the folder forever. Once children have been introduced to the portfolio, they should be asked daily if they wish to put their artwork in the folder. If it is three-dimensional, ask if they would like a photograph taken for the portfolio. The teacher can also select pieces for the folder. Children are more willing to part from art if they know why it is being selected such as saying,"This painting shows how you have learned to make orange and brown. Let's put it in your portfolio. Would you like me to write anything about it to go with it?"

Time Line for Collecting Work

The portfolio should represent a natural time line, such as one session, three months, or a half year. The time period should be long enough to show growth, but not so long that the collection becomes unwieldy. Each piece in the portfolio should be labeled with the date. At the end of the time period, the work should be ordered by date, to highlight the child's growth or changing interests. If the program is long-term, extending over a year or more, a few pieces from older portfolios can be selected to begin a new one.

When sending the work home, always send it in the portfolio itself, and create a new one to use for the next time period. This provides the parents with a unified presentation of the artwork, rather than a hodgepodge of papers, and keeps these simply constructed folders from becoming dog-eared. It is also beneficial for the child to reestablish ownership of the portfolio concept through the creation and decoration of a new folder on a regular basis.

Preparing Artwork for the Portfolio

Artwork placed in a portfolio does not have to be mounted, but should not be wrinkled. Each piece should be labeled with name, date, and any comments by the child. A simple preprinted form can be filled in and affixed to the back (see figure 12–10).

Using the Portfolio

The portfolio system allows art experiences to be richer and deeper in many ways.

- The child, teacher, and parent can look through the portfolio individually or together, to review past progress (see figure 12–11).
- The child can decide to store a piece of artwork to be worked on another day.
- The teacher can suggest reworking a piece of artwork, such as using chalk over a painting or painting over a crayon drawing.
- Work can be collected, categorized, and made into work logs, booklets, or series that show growth in skill or knowledge, or variations on a theme (see chapter 2).
- Work for display can be selected from a range of work rather than on the spur of the moment.
- At the end of the session the portfolio can be sent home as a marvelous record of the child's artistic growth.

Portfolio Label

Name: _____

Date completed: _____

Title or comment by child: _____

FIGURE 12–10 Portfolio label

Self-Reflection on Portfolio Contents

1. Which artwork took the longest time to make? The shortest?
2. Which artwork shows something new you learned?
3. Which artwork has the most colors? Lines? Patterns? Shapes?
4. Which art material did you use the most?
5. Is there any work you want to add more to?
6. Is there any work you would like to make into a book?
7. Is there any work you want to make a story about?
8. Which is your favorite piece?

FIGURE 12–11 Self-reflection on portfolio contents

What to Include in an Art Portfolio

Artwork
- In a wide range of media
- Done at different times

Photographs
- Of three-dimensional projects
- Of group projects such as murals
- Of child doing art

Videos
- Of child doing art

Checklist summaries
- Of time spent at different activities
- Of common art activity choices

Anecdotal materials
- Child generated
- Teacher generated
- Parent generated

Dictation
- Child's ideas written down by teacher
- Audiotapes of child talking about art

Interviews
- Record of what child learned and observed about own art

Attitude lists (figure 12–13)
- Favorite art activities
- Favorite art prints and artifacts
- Favorite artists
- Favorite book illustrations
- Home art activities

Process folios
- For projects
- For a series of works

FIGURE 12–12 What to include in an art portfolio

Attitude toward Art

(Conduct at spaced intervals to assess changes in attitude toward art.)

1. What is your favorite art material or activity?
2. What do you like best about doing art?
3. What art print/artifact do you like to look at?
4. Who is your favorite artist?
5. Which book has the best pictures?
6. Do you ever do artwork at home? Tell me about it.

FIGURE 12–13 Attitude toward art

WHAT CAN BE LEARNED BY LOOKING AT A CHILD'S ART?

Once teachers understand how children create art they can also look at the individual artworks themselves, as a means of assessing how a child is learning and thinking. Engel (1995) identifies two approaches to evaluating child art. One is descriptive of the individual piece and what it says about how the child is communicating through art. The other is developmental—looking at the work's commonalities with the work of other children at the same level and using this to place the child's work in perspective. By combining the two evaluative approaches, teachers can create a summary statement of a child's growth in art.

The Descriptive Approach

Engel suggests that starting with basic description of the visual elements in a piece of artwork forces teachers to look carefully before making interpretive statements. She offers a continuum of questions to ask about the piece, from the most to least objective.

1. What is it made from? When and where was it made?
2. What are the basic art elements used? What lines, shapes, colors, patterns, forms, and textures can be seen? What art techniques did the child display (such as using the point or side of a crayon, or varying pressure to make different-sized lines with the same brush)?
3. What, if anything, does the artwork represent? Is it a picture of a face or a house or is it unidentifiable?
4. What is the organization of the picture? Where are different elements placed? What was done first? Last? Is the piece symmetrical or unbalanced?
5. What is its purpose? Was the child experimenting? Does it tell a story?
6. Where did the idea for the piece come from? Is it a response to an experience? Does it reflect the child's interests? Has it been influenced by TV or other cultural factors?

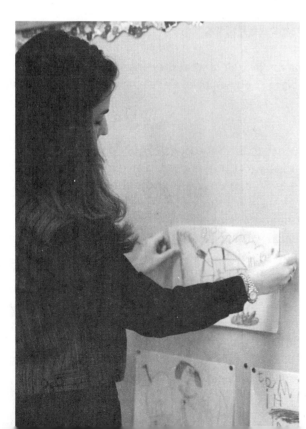

FIGURE 12–14 Children's art tells us many things.

Developmental

Although each piece of child art is unique, it also reflects the graphic mode in which the child is operating. As described in chapter 3, children's art can be characterized as random marks, consciously controlled lines and shapes, action symbols, object symbols reflecting spatial and numerical understandings, and story pictures showing the use of notation. Looking at a particular work and knowing something of the conditions under which it was created, teachers can compare it to these artistic modes in order to place it in the general context of children's art.

1. Are the marks random or controlled?
2. Do they represent an action (such as driving a truck or going to Grandma's)?
3. Do the graphic symbols show spatial understanding?
4. Do the graphic symbols show numerical concepts?
5. Are the graphic symbols understandable to other observers from the same culture?
6. Does the piece use any of the conventions common to art of this culture, such as foreground and background, relative size, realistic shape and detail, shading, and overlap of things in front of others? (NOTE: Most of these would be found only occasionally in self-initiated work by young children.)
7. Does the piece communicate the child's knowledge of the media or subject? Does it express how the child feels about the media or subject?

Composing a Summary Statement

Using the responses to the above questions and, if possible, combining it with anecdotal notes and what the child says about the work, teachers can create a meaningful summary of the piece. Such a summary (see figure 12–15) can be used as part of the portfolio presentation, as part of the display of an artwork, in parent reports, and for the teacher's own records.

HOW DO TEACHERS SHARE WITH PARENTS?

Creating art which reminds children of what they enjoy about school, then displaying the art in a prominent place at home positively reinforces a child's independence.

SIMONE ALTER-MURI (1994, P. 5)

Parents have a very different relationship with their children than do teachers and other caregivers. Children look to their parents for exclusive attention and ultimate acceptance as capable people. When children show their artwork to a parent and say, "Look what I made!" they want more than a tepid "That's nice," or an ordinary "Good work." They definitely do not want criticism from this all-important person whom they wish to please. Children really want to know that their parents have taken the time to acknowledge their efforts and joy.

Unfortunately, parents are far less equipped to give the deep response the child is seeking than are teachers and other trained caregivers. Where the educator sees exploration and creative experimentation, the parents may see only what they think is a visible (and perhaps uncomplimentary) reflection on the quality of their child and their parenting.

Helping Parents Appreciate Their Child's Artwork

It is the teacher's job to educate parents about their child's artwork. Remember that unless teachers make an effort to record the child's process, the parent will only see and make judgments based on the child's product.

Four-year-old Heather's painting of a cat is typical of her work over the last three months. It was done in tempera paint on smooth tag board. She used a stiff bristle brush and three colors of paint—red, yellow, and blue. Heather demonstrated that she has learned how to make green by putting yellow paint over the blue to make the green grass. She controlled the paint well, using the brush to keep the line size uniform throughout the picture.

She began by painting the sky and the grass. Then she made the cat's face. The shape of the head shows her spatial understanding that the ears are part of the cat. The cat is facing toward us and the lack of a body may represent her inability to show it from the front or her attempt to show that the body would be covered up by the head if viewed up close. Heather's number concept is strong. She shows three whiskers on each side, two ears and two eyes. The addition of the second sun represents a need to maintain the strong symmetry of the picture, rather than a lack of knowledge.

We can tell from the picture that Heather is familiar with and likes cats. Her cat and sun symbols are easily recognizable to the viewer. Heather's work is characteristic of early childhood art that uses simple, but recognizable, symbols to tell a story. As she learns to control the size of her painted line, we would expect that she will refine her symbol for a cat, using thinner lines for the whiskers and experimenting with views that would show more of the body. With time she may also add more details to her painting to expand her visual stories.

FIGURE 12–15 Sample Summary Heather's Cat

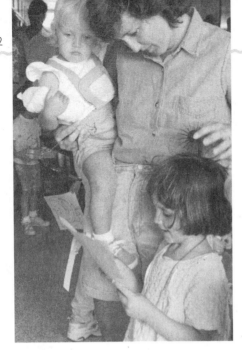

FIGURE 12–16 Parents need to know how to respond to their children's art.

Ways to help parents appreciate their child's art process. These general suggestions are accompanied by specific "Teacher to Parent" samples.

- Provide many opportunities for parents to review process folders and portfolios.
- When talking to parents about the child's art activities, emphasize process and growth rather than the project, and then help the parent see these in the artwork. Checklists and anecdotal records will prove invaluable in remembering specific actions of the children.

TEACHER TO PARENT

Art Note
(Attach to paintings going home)

This painting was done at the easel using tempera paints and a variety of brushes. Painting helps children grow in many ways.

- They learn to use large and small muscles as they reach and stretch to make colorful strokes.
- Their hand-eye coordination improves as they move the brush from the paint container to the paper and back again.
- Their visual perception increases as they see how new colors are made as one color mixes with another.

Take time to enjoy this painting with your child. Some things to say include:

- You made many colorful lines.
- You made some interesting colors with the paint.
- Can you show me a yellow (or other color) line you made?
- Is there a story to go with your picture?

Through sharing this painting you can discover what your child has learned and thought about today.

Your child's teacher,

Instead of saying, "Mary made a painting today," say, "Mary used paint today and learned how to make pink. See the pink spots in her painting."

Instead of saying, "Arturo made a collage today," say, "Arturo cut many shapes from a piece of paper today. He used them in his collage. He made these triangles by cutting the corners off the paper."

- Schedule "Art Happenings" throughout the year at which parents are invited to create art alongside their children. This is a good time for group projects, such as murals, in which everyone can participate (see chapter 10). Watching parents interact with their child also gives teachers a better idea of their attitude toward their child's artwork.
- Attach simple prepared descriptions of art processes to artwork being sent home.
- Send home letters or better yet, institute a regular newsletter that describes the children's art activities along with other class activities, in terms of process and growth.
- Prepare an attractive booklet, illustrated with children's drawings, that briefly explains the goals of the art program, what the children learn through art, and what kinds of art experiences will be offered.
- Send home suggestions for setting up a simple art center in the home. It should not be project based, but rather provide a few basic art supplies that are always available such as crayons, markers, paper, glue, scissors, and a modeling material such as play dough that children can use in their own ways. Help parents by suggesting ways they can contain messes, such as by setting up a small area as an art studio, providing an "art table," or if space is limited, designating a plastic tray as the art spot.
- Use a home art survey to find out the artistic background and experience of individual children.

TEACHER TO PARENT

Checklist: Home Art Experiences

1. What kinds of artwork does your child do at home?

   _____

2. Where in your home does your child do artwork?

   _____

3. Where in your home do you display your child's artwork?

   _____

4. Is there artwork by other people on display in your home?

   _____

5. Has your family recently visited children's museums, craft shows, or other places where art is displayed?

   _____

6. Would you be interested in sharing any artwork that you or family members have done or could you demonstrate an art technique to the children?

   _____

TEACHER TO PARENT

Sample Newsletter

Dear Family,

This week we have been observing water—a perfect activity for such a wet, rainy week. We began by experiencing a variety of water activities. We put ice in the water in the water table and the children had fun seeing how long it took for the ice to melt. We boiled water and observed the steam rising. Then we used the boiling water to make some delicious mint tea. At the easel some children experimented with what happens when water is mixed with the paint. Tuesday we went outside and splashed in the puddles on the playground. We observed the various ways water looked when it moved.

We talked about different ways to remember what we observed. Some children decided to make charts. Others made drawings of what they saw. Several decided to make books and used each page to draw pictures of different kinds of water. The children used creativity in inventing symbols to represent ice, steam, and water. They also had to decide what colors to use to represent water.

Please take time to talk to your child about what he or she learned about water as you enjoy the water projects that are coming home.

Your child's teacher,

Ways to help parents understand artistic development. Parents often do not have other children's artwork with which to compare their child's artwork and so cannot tell if what their child brings home is appropriate or not. Teachers need to help parents understand the process of artistic development and have them come to understand that scribbling and exploring are a natural part of every child's art. It is the teacher's job to assure parents that their children are performing in ways that are to be expected. There are a variety of ways to do this.

- Display many examples of artwork of all kinds, by children at all ages, either in the public areas where parents congregate or through the mechanism of exhibits and open houses.
- Hold parent workshops in which examples of child art and process folios are shared, and concerns about artwork are discussed.
- Send home, on a regular basis, summaries of their child's art detailing what the child has accomplished (see figure 12–15).
- Parents gain a better appreciation for the process of art if they participate in workshops that allow them to draw, paint, use play dough, and other supplies available to their children.

HOW DO TEACHERS ASSESS THEMSELVES?

The people I encounter who are most whole, most alive, and most fulfilled are not those who have mastered only the intellectual work of facts and logic. Rather they are those who have looked inside themselves seeking to know themselves.

ADELAIDE BRY (1978, P. 8)

Probably the most important assessment teachers can do is of themselves. Without self-assessment, teachers cannot grow and improve. Teaching is not a static profession with only one right way to get the job done. The most exciting educators are those who constantly tinker with their programs, who try new methods, and are willing to take risks. Those educators must have methods of assessment to help them know what is working and what is not.

Since program self-assessment is done privately for ourselves, it is tempting for teachers to skip this crucial activity when they are exhausted from a busy day with energetic and challenging youngsters. Preplanned, easy-to-use assessment methods make it more likely that teachers will take the time to assess the programs they deliver. The following methods are suggested as ways to accomplish this task. Each provides a different viewpoint; when used in combination they give an overall view of how teachers are doing.

Checklists

Checklists can be designed to quickly survey almost any area of the program. They provide objective information on frequency of particular behaviors and areas that may require attention. Checklists do not work if they are buried on a desk or in folders. They need to be strategically placed where they will be seen daily and once filled in, acted upon and then filed with program planning materials so that the information will be used in future planning. Checklists can be created for assessing the environment, the activities, and teaching methods (see figures 12–18 to 12–21).

Feedback from the Children

The checklists and anecdotal records that have been suggested for assessing the children can also be used for program assessment. These checklists reveal which

FIGURE 12–17 Teachers need to know how they are doing and how they can improve.

activities attract interest and which are ignored. They document how many children choose to work in certain areas, how long they stay there, how much they interact, and what skills they are exhibiting. They also capture some teacher interaction with the children and provide a picture of what teachers have said.

Personal Art Notebook

Create a notebook in which to keep all of the materials generated in formulating the art aspect of the total program (see Studio Page 37). The notebook serves as a tangible memory of the form and nature of the program. Keep copies of plans, anecdotal records of how the activities went, checklists, and notes on actions taken to deal with

---

Assessing the Physical Art Environment

Area Observed	Organization	Safety	Upkeep	Cleanliness	Aesthetics
Art Print Displays					
Artifact Displays					
Blocks					
Book Displays					
Bookmaking					
Child Art Displays					
Collage					
Computer Area					
Dramatic Art					
Drawing Supplies					
Easel					
Modeling					
Painting					
Printing					
Sand Area					
Sensory Items					
Sink					
Storage Areas					

*Condition: Acceptable/Needs Attention**

*If an area needs attention take action as soon as possible:

- ORGANIZATION: Areas that need major straightening up daily after the children leave require reorganization.
- SAFETY: Places where children were injured or nearly injured need to be checked for hazards.
- UPKEEP: Items that look worn or broken should be removed or fixed.
- CLEANLINESS: Dirty areas need to be looked at for ways to make them easier to clean during use.
- AESTHETICS: Cluttered areas may be distracting. Too many colors may assault the senses. Materials may need to be rearranged to improve appearances.

FIGURE 12–18 Checklist: Assessing the Physical Art Environment

---

Analyzing the Social Art Environment

Category	Observation (Check applicable description)
SPACE :	❏ Children have plenty of space for art activities.
	❏ Children interfere with each other during art activities.
	❏ Furniture constantly has to be moved to make room for art activities.
PRIVACY:	❏ Many children utilize private art spaces.
	❏ Few children utilize private art spaces.
COMFORT:	❏ Children are quiet and calm in art areas.
	❏ Children are noisy and irritable in art areas.
	❏ Children avoid art areas.
SOCIAL INTERACTION:	❏ Many positive interactions take place in art areas.
ADULT USAGE:	❏ Many adult-child interactions take place in art areas.
	❏ Few adult-child interactions take place in art areas.

FIGURE 12–19 Checklist: Analyzing the Social Art Environment

difficult or unusual situations. Keep copies of all letters sent home to parents. Looking back over this material will be invaluable in making better plans the next time.

Reflective Teaching Journal

A reflective journal provides a place for teachers to record their inner feelings about their work. Teachers need to set aside a time once a week, such as when the children are resting, to write a few reflective sentences on how they personally feel about what has been happening in this program of their creation. One way to approach this task is to respond to these sentence starters:

This week I felt competent when…
This week I felt frustrated when…
This week I felt exhilarated when…

"Terrific Me" Folder

Place a file folder labeled TM in a strategic place. Whenever complimentary notes from parents, children, or others are received, place them in this folder. Also include copies of materials from workshops attended or given, extra work done, notes about major accomplishments, and any other positive materials and activities. It is human nature to remember the negatives. Reviewing the materials in this folder every few months will provide not only an uplifting experience, but also a more rounded view of one's accomplishments.

Art Experience Assessment

ART EXPERIENCE: _____

DATE(S): _____

GROUP COMPOSITION: _____

ASSESSMENT AREA	CHECK IF PRESENT
Physical Growth	
• Required the use and control of large muscles	☐
• Required the use and control of small muscles of the hand	☐
• Required hand-eye coordination	☐
• Required the use of more than one sense	☐
Social Growth	
• Allowed children to work alongside others	☐
• Required sharing of supplies	☐
• Fostered positive peer interaction	☐
• Fostered positive child-adult interaction/dialogue	☐
Emotional Growth	
• Allowed children to work independently	☐
• Allowed children to express personal feelings	☐
• Provided time for introspection and concentration	☐
Cognitive Growth	
• Encouraged children to verbalize about their work	☐
• Fostered development of new graphic symbols	☐
• Provided opportunities to use the vocabulary of art	☐
• Enabled children to observe: Change	☐
Cause and effect	☐
Pattern	☐
• Enabled children to make comparisons	☐
• Provided experience with spatial concepts	☐
• Required children to make artistic decisions	☐
• Required children to order the sequence of their actions	☐
Creativity	
• Utilized and challenged existing skills and knowledge	☐
• Children were motivated to try activity	☐
• Provided sufficient time for immersion	☐
• Encouraged children to combine familiar elements in new ways	☐
• Required children to solve challenging problems	☐
Integration	
• Utilized knowledge from other curriculum areas	☐
• Enhanced knowledge of other curriculum areas	☐
• Enabled children to find connections among areas	☐
Art of Others	
• Included opportunities to view art of others	☐
• Included opportunities to discuss art of others	☐
Reflection	
• Allowed children to talk about their own work	☐
• Allowed children to decide what to do with their work	☐
• Allowed children to participate in presenting the work	☐

NOTE: Very few art experiences include all these areas. The more areas checked, however, the better designed and the more worthwhile that art experience is for children.

FIGURE 12–20 Checklist: Art Experience Assessment

Teacher Self-Assessment

ART EXPERIENCE: _____

DATE(S): _____

GROUP COMPOSITION: _____

BEHAVIOR   CHECK IF PRESENT

Personal Behavior
I showed confidence in my art ability. ❑
I avoided terms of self-deprecation. ❑
I expressed enthusiasm for the activity. ❑
I wore art-related clothing. ❑
I participated in the activity by modeling process and/or technique. ❑

Nonverbal Responses
My face mirrored my words. ❑
I lowered myself to the child's level. ❑
I shared my feelings. ❑
I allowed wait time. ❑
I made eye contact before speaking. ❑

Verbal Responses
I used descriptive statements. ❑
I used paraphrasing. ❑
I made interpretive statements. ❑
I initiated artistic dialogue using questions based on:
• Art elements ❑
• Process ❑
• Artistic decisions ❑
• Predictions ❑
• Cause and effect ❑
• Connecting events ❑
• Curriculum extension ❑
I elicited stories. ❑
I took dictation. ❑

Responses to Problems
I gave encouragement when needed. ❑
I provided comfort when needed. ❑
I provided direction when needed. ❑
I fostered children's self-confidence by avoiding patterns and models. ❑

FIGURE 12–21 Checklist: Teacher Self-Assessment

SUMMARY: A VISION TO GROW ON

> We make sure to give children materials that will take any child's imprint and rejoice with the children over the beauty and differences in their creations.
>
> SYDNEY GUREWITZ CLEMENS (1991, P. 5)

Art is a way of learning and communicating about the world that can enrich every aspect of an early childhood program. Teachers must constantly strive to offer a rich and thoughtful art program to young artists. No program is perfect. Although we do our best, we all make mistakes and fall into ruts. We do not always have the leisure or energy to choose our words with care, to clean up the unsightly clutter, to read every beautifully illustrated book, to place each artwork carefully in a portfolio, to snap the perfect picture, or to select the most appropriate art experience for that moment in time. In the midst of a real-life, early childhood program surrounded by paint-covered hands, broken crayons, and too many unpredictable children, teachers need to keep before them a vision of a thoughtful art program as a worthwhile goal toward which to strive.

The Program

A thoughtful art program:
- Provides opportunities for verbal communication
- Is rich in sensory, kinesthetic, and multicultural experiences
- Helps children experience the art of others
- Provides a way to deal with individual and cultural differences
- Allows time for immersion, reflection, and self-assessment

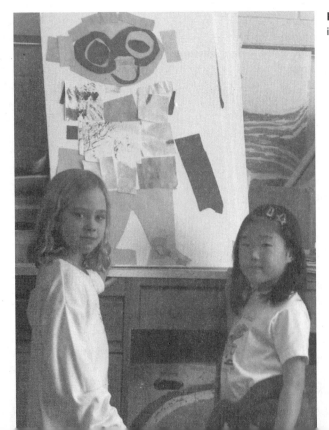

FIGURE 12–22 Children's art can be viewed in many ways. It speaks to us all.

The Teachers

Excellent early childhood teachers:

- Are self-confident and enthusiastic
- Are creative and knowledgeable
- Are willing to take risks and try new approaches
- Choose words and behaviors that foster artistic dialogues with children
- Constantly assess their programs and themselves, and strive for improvement

Step by Step

Change does not occur all at once. Teachers need to set small goals for themselves, working to improve one component of the program at a time. If in our hearts we truly care about the children, if we are amazed by the meaning they create through art, then improvement will follow. We will greet each smiling face and each "Look what I made!" with a heartfelt response, and our program will be as rich we can make it.

FURTHER READING

> Nothing can be rushed. Things must grow, they must grow upward.
> PAUL KLEE (WINKUR 1992, P. 43)

To learn more about assessment methods:

Genishi, C. (1993). Art, portfolios and assessment. *Early Childhood Today*. 8(2): 67.
This article details various assessment methods using art and portfolios.

Nilsen, B. (1997). *Week by week*. Albany, NY: Delmar.
This book provides a comprehensive system of assessment methods, in all growth areas, for the practicing educator.

Paced, M., and Black, J. (1994). *Authentic assessment of the young child: Celebrating development and learning*. New York: Macmillan.
This book provides detailed analysis of and uses for a wide variety of assessment methods.

Art Focus

DISPLAYING CHILDREN'S ART

> It's important to keep in mind that how you handle children's art when it is finished says a lot about how much you value their efforts.
>
> DIANE TRISTER DODGE
> AND JOANNA PHINNEY (1990, P. 175)

No matter how much teachers recognize that process is more important than the finished product, at the end of each day they will be faced with many tangible art products that will require attention. Toddlers, who are immersed in explorations, may care little about what happens to these products and may not even remember making them. Older children will have many different attitudes

to their work depending on their purposes. Some, like toddlers, may care little for exploratory pieces. Others may cherish every piece they have touched. Work that expresses a particular feeling or subject may be highly valued. Art that the child intends as a "gift" will be viewed differently than art that is done just because the materials are there and the mood struck. For many children, of all ages, who use art as an emotional release the artwork is viewed as an extension of themselves. Its treatment is taken personally.

Adults may have a difficult time ascertaining how a child feels about a particular piece of artwork. Often this is not verbalized by the child. It is always best if the adult treats all children's artwork with respect. This models for the children how deeply adults value them and the work they produce.

Showing Respect for Children's Art

1. Strive to put names on the back of all pieces of work. Attach pencils or markers to walls with Velcro so that they are always handy. Develop a shorthand code or use initials if pressed for time. If there are different sessions in the program, consider using a different color of marker for each session. For example, all the green names might belong to the A.M. group and all the orange ones to the P.M. group. Label a shelf, cubby, or floor space with each child's name and teach the children to always put their projects in their spots. Holding up children's artwork and saying, "Whose is this?" tells the children that the teacher did not care enough to notice what art they were making that day.
2. Do not fold artwork. If work is too large to fit in a space, roll it up. Folded artwork can never be mounted properly. If stored for a period of time it will tear at the folds. Art portfolios need to be large enough to hold the largest size of paper that individual children use.
3. Never throw artwork away in front of the children. There will always be a few pieces that remain unidentified, no matter how hard

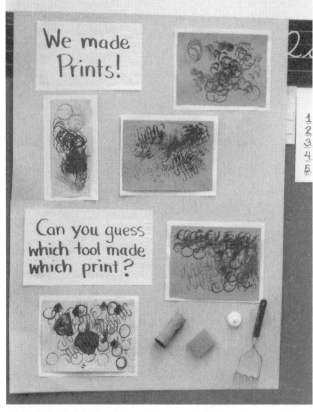

FIGURE 12–23 Displays can have many purposes.

TEACHER TIP

Mounting Two-Dimensional Artwork

SUPPLIES NEEDED:
   Colored construction paper
   scissors
   stapler or white glue

METHOD A: Single Mount
1. Select a piece of construction paper slightly larger than the artwork. If the paper is the same size as the largest piece of construction paper, overlap two sheets to make the mount larger. Artwork can be trimmed for the purpose of making neater edges or so a smaller mount can be used. Trim up to one inch around the edges as long as no part of the artwork is being cut off. Never cut off any major part of the work such as turning rectangular paintings into circles or bear shapes. Standard paper sizes can be mounted on the next size up (8½ by 11 inches on 9 by 12 inches, 12 by 18 inches on 18 by 24 inches, 18 by 24 inches on 24 by 36 inches.)
2. Center the artwork. If desired, the bottom border can be slightly larger than the top.
3. Staple or glue artwork to mount. If gluing, place a small line of white glue around the very edge of the work. Never put glue in the center of the work. It can cause wrinkling or discoloring.
4. Attach child's name to the mount using a self-stick label, or staple on piece of paper.

METHOD 2: Double Mounts
1. Cut a piece of white or black paper so that it is one inch longer and wider than the artwork on all sides.
2. Center artwork and white/black mount on a larger piece of colored construction paper and glue or staple.

OTHER METHODS:
1. Commercial mats are available to fit standard sizes of paper. They give a finished look to the artwork and can be used for exhibits or special works (See Appendix A).
2. Small pieces by the same child or several children can be mounted on one large backing paper.
3. Glue a corrugated cardboard strip or dowel to the back upper edge of the artwork. Punch holes in each end of the cardboard and attach a piece of yarn for hanging. This works well for projects done on cloth.
4. Purchase several glass or plexiglass frames in a size that fits most artwork produced. Tape a selected piece into the frame. Change the framed artwork on a regular basis. This system works well for work displayed in offices and bathrooms.
5. Avoid using trash items, such as Styrofoam trays, which trivialize the art work.

---

teachers strive to label them all. If work must be discarded, do so discreetly. When children see artwork in the trash, they worry that the same thing may happen to theirs. Make sure parents are taught to do the same thing. Many children become disillusioned about creating art because "it will just get thrown away at home."

4. Make sure that all artwork that goes home or is displayed is properly labeled and presented.
5. Never cut off pieces of an artwork, or draw or

work on it to make it "better." This is insulting to the child artist and reflects a lack of self-confidence on the part of the educator.

Sending Artwork Home

Artwork that is not being put in a portfolio will need to be sent home. But how it is sent will often make a difference in how the child and family come to value the art. Ideally each work that goes home should be labeled, accompanied by an explanatory note, and neatly mounted on a backing paper or stapled into a booklet labeled with the child's name and comments. In reality such care for the individual works is impossible unless two things are done.

1. Children need to be encouraged to spend time on their work. Rather than creating six drawings in five minutes, they need to learn how to spend ten minutes on one drawing. Encouraging children to spend more time on their art does not mean forcing them to do so. Toddlers and young preschoolers will usually spend less time on their art then older children because of their shorter concentration spans. However, concentration on an art project can be fostered by:

   • Provide quiet, private spaces for art to eliminate the distraction of other beckoning activities.
   • Instead of putting out piles of paper at the table from which children help themselves with abandon, store paper out of the way so that the child has to get up and select another piece.
   • Ask extending questions: "What other lines (shapes, patterns, flowers) can you add to your drawing?" or "Are you sure you are finished? Have you used all the colors that you wanted to?"
   • Provide reassurance: "There is plenty of time for you to work some more on your picture and then go play in the sand."

2. An area must be set where artwork is prepared to go home or to be put in the portfolio. This area can be a small table or shelf containing a stapler, colored paper in various sizes, markers, and preprinted labels. When children finish a drawing or other dry project, or on the following day for projects that have been left overnight to dry (such as paintings, prints, and collages), the artwork is brought to the table. Ask the child to select a color for the background mount. Staple the artwork on the mount along with the label and any art notes for the parents. The child then takes the work to a designated storage place or portfolio.

If a child does produce a series of artworks on one day or over several days, they can be stapled together between two mounting sheets to form a book of art.

Displaying Artwork in the Classroom

In the classroom itself, teachers need to carefully consider their purpose in displaying the children's artwork. Some teachers do it as a form of self-flattery, rather than a way to educate the children. Hanging up everyone's paintings or collages at the same time creates an overwhelming display—fine for a special occasion but hard to live with day after day. It does not take long for that art to become treated as just some colorful background.

Teachers need to limit the classroom displays to a selection of works that illustrate the theme or learning that is going on, or to acknowledge the artistic accomplishment of one or a few children at a time. Remember that despite this seemingly limiting suggestion, each day the room will still be filled with art—art that is in the process of being made—paintings at the easel, sculptures of play dough on the table, puppets at the stage.

Organization of children's artwork on display. One way to create a purposeful display is to establish an artist of the week or month. With that child, select a piece from the portfolio for display. Accompany the piece with a photograph of the artist, a transcribed interview, and/or dictation about the piece. Take time to introduce the child and the art to the group. Discuss it with a group in the same way a print would be discussed (see chapter 9). Hang the artwork in a place of honor. Because the artist is present, in addition to descriptive questions and statements, questions about technique can be answered:

> "What kind of brush made this line?"
> "What did you do to make this color?"

This same approach can also be used to present a group project.

Another method is to create a display of thematically related art that adds to or creates a unique environment and elicits the creation of more art. For example, for an underwater theme, turn one corner of the room into an aquarium

TEACHER TIP

Mounting Three-Dimensional Artwork

Wall Mounts

— For work that is relatively lightweight, such as papier-mâché or cardboard sculptures, bulky but lightweight collages, small modeled sculptures, and fiber projects.

1. Straight pins: Use to mount bulky or thick items in showcases or on bulletin boards outside classroom areas where art is displayed to the public. If the pins are hammered into the cork, they will remain very secure and should pose no danger to young children.
2. Wire or chenille stems: Use to attach lightweight sculptures to a heavy paper or cardboard base, which can then be stapled to the wall.
3. String or yarn: Tie to sculptures and then suspend from pins, nails, or thumbtacks.
4. Boxes: Staple to small boxes to a wall, or join a group of boxes together with glue, wire, paper fasteners, or chenille stems. Paint the boxes a neutral color such as white or gray. Place small sculptures in each box.

Ceiling Mounts

— For lightweight three-dimensional projects, particularly those made of paper, tagboard, tubes, and fiber, such as mobiles.

1. Depending on the ceiling composition, use straight pins, staples, or hooks. Suspend artworks from strings so that they are just above the children's reach and out of the path of traffic, such as over tables or shelving. If the ceiling is high, consider attaching clips to the ends of suspended strings so work can be quickly hung up without resorting to a ladder.
2. String wires across the room, from which projects can be suspended using clothespins.

Floor Mounts

— For heavy, large, and/or delicate sculptures.

1. Raise work to child's eye level by using cardboard boxes of various sizes, painted neutral colors.
2. Place oversized work on a piece of large paper, a cloth, or a rug, to set it off from the rest of the floor.

with sea creatures hanging from the ceiling. Hang an undersea mural on the wall. Drape fishnets and shells on the shelving and place sea-theme sculptures among them. Place the sand or water table in the center, or use the area to display and read books about the sea.

For Parents and Friends: Public Displays of Children's Artwork

The purpose of public exhibits of children's art is different from home and classroom displays. The public arena is used to present the program to people who have not participated directly in the children's art process. Depending on how they are approached, public exhibits can destroy or benefit an art program.

What is the purpose of the display? Teachers must begin by analyzing why they are creating a public display in the first place. When the sole purpose of presentations of child art is to boost the egos of the children or the educators, they can create pressured situations which are detrimental to the art process. Fearful of being judged by parents or outsiders, educators exhort the children to do their best because their parents are going to see it. Or they select pseudo-art projects for the children to do that they hope will make a good impression. Teachers may display work that they think is most adult-pleasing, and reject work that looks out of control or unpleasant. Some teachers think "I can't show this. Their parents will be so disappointed in them. They'll think I'm not teaching anything."

TEACHER TIP

Guidelines for Classroom Displays

Avoid clutter.
Display only one or a few pieces of art at a time.
Change displayed artwork frequently.

Nor do competitions and judged art shows belong in early art education programs. They also emphasize adult-pleasing products and foster the attitude that certain types of art are better than others. Such events may have a positive effect on the winners, but can cause the losers to give up on art creation entirely.

There are, however, several positive functions that the public presentation of child art can serve, that also enhance an art program. All of them depend on having a portfolio/process folio system in place. Presentations with such carefully considered purposes will ultimately lead to more genuine ego-building than those that have "ego-boosting" as their sole purpose.

Positive presentations. EDUCATIONAL: Carefully designed exhibits can help parents and friends learn more about how and why young children create art. They can also teach about art concepts and techniques, about other curriculum areas, and can help introduce adults to art created by people from other places and cultures.

PROMOTIONAL: A well-put-together public display can introduce a program's best aspects. It can be a multimedia glimpse into the children's daily pursuits.

CELEBRATORY: A public display can be a culminating experience for a theme unit or set of group projects. It is a way of sharing what the children have accomplished and learned.

Locating the display. Depending on their purpose, these kinds of public displays can be located in a variety of places.

Walls outside the children's work space are convenient for educational and promotional displays. Lobbies, hallways, stairwells, doors, offices, bathrooms, and any other space that is visited on a regular basis by the public can be used.

Celebratory presentations will require much more space, as they involve more than a static display of artwork. Auditoriums, cafeterias, hallways, out-of-doors, or if necessary, the whole classroom, cleared of its normal furnishings, can be used.

Educational displays. There are a multitude of ideas for educational displays.

To show artistic growth, display a series of works done by one child over a period of time. Accompany the display with photographs of children's hands illustrating different grips on art tools or anecdotal descriptions of how the works were created.

To illustrate art elements, display a series of works by different children that illustrate the use of line, shape, color, texture, form, or pattern. Accompany the display with bold graphics representing the art element and children's descriptions of the element in their artwork. Photographs of children exploring sensory experiences related to the particular element can be included, as can children's books about the element.

To demonstrate a particular technique, select artworks done using that technique, such as papier-mâché puppets, clay bowls, or dyed-wool collages. Accompany the artworks with step-by-step photographs of how the children made them and their dictated or written explanations.

Learning from other curriculum areas can be displayed by hanging up charts and graphs, sample experiments, child-created comments and stories (experience charts), and photographs accompanied by any illustrative artwork the children created.

Experiences with artwork from other cultures can be shown by displaying artifacts or prints of the featured pieces, accompanied by descriptions of the culture and how they were made, along with children's art that reflects a related concept. For example, combine printed cloth from India with children's prints, or Mexican clay pottery with children's clay forms.

Promotional displays. A promotional display should give a feeling for the art experiences in which the children participate. Select one or more pieces of artwork that show a range of techniques and approaches. Accompany the works with photographs of children creating similar art and/or children's comments or explanations.

Label displays with bold signs that attract attention to them, such as *"Our Artists at Work"* or *"The Wonderful World of Paint."* Examples of the range of promotional presentations include brochures and calendars, showcases and bulletin boards, and badges and T-shirts, all featuring child art.

Celebratory presentations. Celebrations are more than just art exhibits, and as such they involve far more elements and preparation, including any or all of the following:

- Artwork—with descriptions (by children or adults)
- Banners
- Demonstrations—of technique and/or of art forms
- Dramatic performances (children, adults, mixed groups, professional)
- Guest performers—artists, musicians, dancers (children or adults)
- Interactive exhibits (viewers are asked to respond to a question or survey, or decide what tool or method was used to make an artwork)
- Invitations
- Participatory displays (such as a mural to which every guest contributes something)
- Photographs
- Posters
- Process folio materials
- Videotape

Sample Plans for a Celebratory Presentation

Festival of Lines

A Celebration for Toddlers and Their Families
An Introduction to Our Art Program

Location: The playground

Time: 2:00 to 4:00 PM

Welcome Table: Program and map. Painted or paper streamer lines for visitors to follow to the different activities.

Art Display: Children's drawings and paintings with associated dictation.

Photography Display: Photographs of children creating art.

Interactive Art Display: Children's paintings with a set of brushes hung on string. Participants are invited to match the lines in the painting with the brush that created them.

Participatory Art Activity 1: Large sheet of mural paper, baskets of colorful markers, and an invitation to add some original lines.

Participatory Art Activity 2: Partner loom (see figure 9–12) is set up with a basket of colorful yarn and an invitation to weave a line.

Art Element Display: Children's paintings are interspersed with bold graphics showing different kinds of lines. Participants are asked to find the total number of each kind of line visible in the paintings. A box and coupons are provided for the guesses. At end of celebration names will be drawn to receive door prizes.

Puppet Show: Put on by parent volunteers, the show features a simple tale about a magic string, based on the book *Billy and the Magic String,* (Karnovsky, 1995).

Demonstration 1: High school student volunteers demonstrate and teach about string figures from around the world.

Demonstration 2: Professional spinner demonstrates how wool is turned into yarn. She gives pieces of yarn to participants to use on partner loom.

Demonstration 3: Basket weaver creates willow baskets. Surrounded by a display of photographs showing examples of lines in nature.

Demonstration 4: Washtub instrument. Participants can try making different tones by changing length of strings.

Measurement Table: Volunteers measure a length of string the height of each participant and tape them to a chart prelabeled with names.

Musical Entertainment: Harp player and/or string players.

Refreshments: Linelike foods
Pretzel sticks	Carrot sticks and curls
Licorice sticks	Spaghetti
Breadsticks	

FIGURE 12–24 Sample plans for a celebratory presentation

Studio Page **65**

METHODS OF ASSESSMENT

List the possible uses of the following assessment methods for art activities, in a child care program for two- and three-year-olds:

Checklists:

_____

_____

_____

_____

Anecdotal Records:

_____

_____

_____

_____

Photographs:

_____

_____

_____

_____

Process Folio:

_____

_____

_____

_____

Portfolio:

_____

_____

_____

_____

Studio Page 66

ANECDOTAL RECORDS

Based on the following anecdotes, describe the areas of growth being demonstrated by each child as you would explain them to the child's parent.

Lien 10/3 Age 3
Approached easel. Stirred paint in each container.
Dipped brush in green and made a green line. Then dipped brush in red and smeared it over the green line. Exclaimed, "I made brown!"

_____

_____

_____

Salvo 11/9 Age 4
At collage center. Took tray and filled it with buttons. At table began to place buttons in rows. I suggested that he glue the row on a piece of paper. Shook head no. Five minutes later was still playing with the buttons. Cam approached and began to join in sorting. Together they made a row of buttons from one end of the table to the other. Very animated discussion about which button should come next in row. Cam invited me to see their "pattern."

_____

_____

_____

Wendy 3/24 Age 2½
Wendy was standing in front of the African mask print. I asked her what shapes she saw in the print. She pointed to the eyes and said, "Circles."

_____

_____

_____

Loren 4/12 Age 5
Loren sat under the table and worked on her book for all the free time. Used crayon and marker. Worked very slowly and kept hesitating before selecting a color. Didn't want to talk about it when I came by so I left her alone. Later I noticed she was "reading" her book to Valerie in the book nook.

_____

_____

_____

Studio Page

ART NOTES FOR PARENTS

Compose a general art note that could be attached to artwork going home that would explain:

- What the art experience is
- What the child learns by doing it
- What the parent might say about it
- How the parent might display it

For your simple note, choose one of the following art areas: drawing, collage, printmaking, puppet making, box sculpture.

_____

_____

_____

_____

_____

_____

_____

_____

_____

_____

_____

_____

_____

_____

_____

_____

_____

_____

_____

_____

_____

_____

_____

_____

_____

_____

Studio Page

THE HOME-SCHOOL CONNECTION

Compose a letter or brochure that would be sent home to parents describing:

- What children learn from doing art
- What art materials children should have at home
- How to set up a work space for art
- What comments to make about their child's art
- How artwork can be displayed and stored

_____

_____

_____

_____

_____

_____

_____

_____

_____

_____

_____

_____

_____

_____

_____

_____

_____

_____

_____

_____

_____

_____

_____

_____

DISPLAYING CHILDREN'S ART

Sketch a plan for an educational display of children's artwork. Include supplementary graphics (headings, labels, explanations, questions) as well as commentary about the art itself.

LAYOUT:

GRAPHICS:

Heading:

_____

Explanation:

_____

Questions:

_____

_____

Commentary on art:

_____

_____

_____

_____

Studio Page *70*

PLANNING A CELEBRATION OF ART

Select a topic or a theme and plan a celebratory presentation:

Title:

_____

Welcome:

_____
_____

Educational Art Displays:

_____
_____

Dramatic Performances:

_____
_____

Musical Performances:

_____
_____

Interactive Exhibits:

_____
_____

Participatory Displays:

_____
_____

Demonstrations:

_____
_____

Graphic Elements (invitations, brochures, posters, signs, banners):

_____
_____

Teacher Resources

ART SUPPLIES SOURCES

Boxes, for storing large prints, big books, portfolios (chapters 7,12)

> Calloway House (cardboard storage boxes and units)
> 451 Richardson Dr.
> Lancaster PA 17603-4098

Package sealing tape, clear (chapter 5)

> Reliable
> Suite 300 West
> 1501 Woodfield Road
> Schaumberg IL 60173
> 1-800-735-4000

> National Bag, Inc.
> 2233 Old Mill Rd.
> Hudson, OH 44236
> 1-800-247-6000

> Quill Office Products
> 100 Schelter Rd.
> Lincolnshire IL 60069-3621

Paint markers, refillable (chapter 4)

Papier-mâché paste (chapter 5)

Precut mats (chapter 12)

Tempera blocks (chapter 4)

Vertical floor loom (chapter 9)
> These five items are available from many art supply companies including:

> Dick Blick
> P.O. Box 1267
> Galesburg IL 61402-1267
> 1-800-447-8192

> J. L. Hammet Co.
> P.O. Box 9057
> Braintree MA 02184-9057
> 1-800-333-4600

> NASCO
> 901 Janesville Ave.
> Fort Atkinson WI 53538-0901
> 1-800-558-9595

> Sax Arts and Crafts
> P.O. Box 51710
> New Berlin, WI 53151
> 1-800-558-6696

> Triarco
> 14650 28th Ave No.
> Plymouth MN 55447
> 1-800-328-3360

Pony beads, large (chapter 11), are available from the art supply companies above and:

> Kirchen Bros.
> P.O. Box 1016
> Skokie IL 60076
> 1-708-647-6747

Wool (chapter 9)

> Earth Guild
> 33 Hayward St.
> Asheville NC 28801
> 1-800-327-8448

> Jas. Townsend & Son, Inc.
> 133 N. First St.
> Pierceton IN 46562
> 1-800-338-1665

ARTIFACT SOURCES

Art Institute of Chicago
> The Museum Shop
> Michigan Avenue at Adams St.
> Chicago IL 60603
> 1-800-621-9337
> Huichol yarn painting and beadwork
> Guatemalan weaving

Davis Publications
> 50 Portland St.
> Worchester MA 01608
> 1-800-533-2847
> African artifact kit

Global Crafts
Christian Children's Fund
P.O. Box 518
New Windsor MD 21776-0518
1-800-366-5896
Wide assortment of baskets from Africa, Asia, and Caribbean well as other artifacts

Great Alaska Catalog
5750 Glacier Hwy.
Juneau AL 99801
1-800-326-2197
Fossilized ivory carvings and scrimshaw by Eskimo carvers

Jas. Townsend & Son, Inc.
133 N. First St.
Pierceton IN 46562
1-800-338-1665
Colonial American: pierced tinware, large assortment of hats, wool, spinning supplies

Marketplace
1455 Ashland Ave.
Evanston IL 60201-4001
1-800-726-8905
Handprinted and embroidered fabric from India

Mola Lady
Janet Gruver
8500 Creek Side Dr.
Bismark ND 58504
1-800-880-6677
Molas made by the Kuna people of Panama. (Sales go toward providing health care.)

Museum of Modern Art
11 W. 53rd St.
New York NY 10019-5401
1-800-447-6662
Chinese Brush Painting Workstation with book on Chinese brush painting by I. Ching Hsu

Oxfam America
P.O. Box 821
Lewiston ME 04240
Handmade items from India, Africa, Indonesia, South and Central America: weaving, pottery, carvings, masks, shadow puppets, baskets

Pueblo to People
2105 Silber Rd., Suite 101
Houston TX 77055
1-713-956-1172
Baskets, weavings, pottery, beadwork, amate bark paper, and more from Mexico, Guatemala, and Peru

Save the Children
P.O. Box 166
Peru IN 46970
1-800-833-3154
Carvings, masks, and other handmade artifacts from Africa and Asia

SOURCES OF PRINTS AND POSTERS

Art Institute of Chicago
The Museum Shop
Michigan Avenue at Adams St.
Chicago IL 60603
1-800-621-9337
Prints and postcard reproductions from their collection

Art with Heart
Syracuse Cultural Workers
P.O. Box 6367
Syracuse NY 13217
1-315-474-1132
Contemporary posters and postcards, many featuring African American and Native American artists

Cherokee Publications
P.O. Box 430
Cherokee NC 28719
Native American books, posters, kits, and music

Crizmac
P.O. Box 65928
Tucson AR 85728-5928
1-800-913-8555
Individual and sets of prints, including Take 5, of Native American, Haitan, African, and other art from many times and places

Dale Seymour Publications
P.O. Box 10888
Palo Alto CA 94303-0879
1-800-827-1100
Individual posters and sets of art reproductions on many topics, including symmetry, pattern, and multicultural art

Davis Publications
50 Portland St.
Worcester MA 01608
1-800-533-2847
Sets of large laminated reproductions on many topics, including the art elements and multicultural art

Dover Publications
31 E. 2nd St.
Mineola NY 11501
Postcards and inexpensive books that can be cut apart to use as prints: Native American, African, Asian, Central and South American

Knowledge Unlimited
P.O. Box 52
Madison WI 53707-0052
1-800-356-2303
Sets of (Take 5) prints: Native American, African American, women artists, and others

Metropolitan Museum of Art
255 Gracie Station
New York NY 10028-9998
1-800-468-7386
Print and postcard reproductions of artwork
in their collection

Modern Learning Press
P.O. Box 167
Rosemont NJ 08556
1-800-627-5867
Shorewood print sets on many topics

Museum of Fine Arts, Boston
P.O. Box 244
Avon MA 02322-0244
Prints and postcard reproductions from
their collection

Museum of Modern Art
11 W. 53rd St.
New York NY 10019-5401
1-800-447-6662
Prints and postcards from their collection

Nasco Arts and Crafts
901 Janesville Ave.
Fort Atkinson WI 53538-0901
1-800-558-9595
Caraway book series on world art forms, Take 5
and many other print series, and famous artists
postcard sets

National Gallery of Art
2000B South Club Dr.
Landover MD 20785
Postcards and medium-sized prints of works in
their collection

Print Finders
15 Roosevelt Pl.
Scarsdale NY 10583
1-914-725-2332
Print Finders will try to locate a particular print and
its size, cost, and availability, and then order it

Sax Visual Arts Resources
P.O. Box 51710
New Berlin WI 53151
1-800-558-6696
Print sets reproducing African American, African,
Native American art and more

Southwest Indian Foundation
P.O. Box 86
Gallup NM 87302-0001
1-505-863-4037
Native American artifacts from the Southwest
United States

S & S
P.O. Box 513
Colchester CT 06415-0513
1-800-243-9232
Integrated fine arts program on the themes of families, communities, and make-believe, including large
reproductions of fine art

Unicef
P.O. Box 182233
Chattanooga TN 37422
1-800-553-1200
Contemporary cards featuring multinational artists,
silk boxes from Bangladesh, handmade paper from
Nepal

University Prints
P.O. Box 485
Winchester MA 01890
Small, postcard-sized prints, in black-and-white and
color, that require mounting (very inexpensive)

COMPUTER SUPPLIES AND SOFTWARE

Art Software
APL = Apple IIE family of computers (uses 5.25" disks)
IIGS = Designed only for IIGS (uses 3.5" disks)
IBM = IBM PC or compatible. DOS 2.1 or later, 286 or
faster, VGA, and at least 512 RAM. Requires color
monitor, mouse
MAC = Apple Macintosh compatible with MAC Plus
or later. Uses 3.5" disks. Requires color monitor,
mouse, 4mb RAM, hard drive
WIN = IBM 286 or better or a compatible capable of
running Microsoft Windows 3.0 or later. Requires
color VGA monitor, 512 K RAM, mouse, hard drive

Please note:
Some of these programs contain coloring-book types
of activities. These are not creative art. Use only the
free draw sections that allow the child to start with a
blank screen and draw lines and shapes.

AppleWorks 5.0 by Quality Computers: IIGS
(Graphic Program)
Art Explorer by Adobe: MAC (Free draw program
only)
Beagle Draw by Beagle Bros: IIGS
Brushstrokes by Claris: MAC
ClarisWorks by Claris: MAC/Power MAC/WIN
(Graphic Program)
ClarisDraw by Claris: MAC Plus or better
Color Me by SVE: APL/IBM
Color 'n' Canvas by Sunburst: IIGS
Dabbler by Fractal Design: MAC/ Power MAC/WIN
Dazzle Draw: Apple/IIGS
Delta Drawing Today by Power Industries: APL
(Key-driven)
Flying Colors by Davidson: Power MAC/WIN (Free
draw program only)
Kid-Pix 2 by Broderbund: IBM/ MAC/WIN (Free
draw program only)
Kid Works 2 by Davidson: IBM/MAC/WIN (Free
draw program only)
Kindercomp Draw by Spinnaker: IBM/MAC
Koala Paint: Apple/IIGS (Uses a touch pad and stylus
to create drawings)

MacPaint by Claris: MAC
Paintworks Plus: IIGS
Platinum Paint by Quality Computers: IIGS

Suppliers

Educational Resources
1550 Executive Dr.
Elgin IL 60123
1-800-624-2926

Quality Computers
20200 Nine Mile Rd.
St. Clair Shore MI 48080
1-800-777-3642

Sunburst
101 Castleton St.
Pleasantville NY 10570-0100
1-800-321-7511

Input Devices

Art Pad: IBM/MAC/Power MAC
Computer Crayon: APL/ IIGS
   Held and used like a crayon; use on any surface
Koala Touch Tablet: Apple/IIGS
   A pressure-sensitive drawing board that attaches
to computer
Touch Window: APL/MAC
   Attaches to computer screen and allows drawing
with a finger

Keyboard Protective Cover (Safeskins)

Quality Computers (see above under Suppliers)

Reliable
Suite 300 West
1501 Woodfield Rd.
Schaumberg IL 60173

RECIPES

Modeling Doughs

Play dough

INGREDIENTS:

1 cup water
food coloring (optional)
¼ cup of salt
1 tablespoon vegetable oil
1 tablespoon alum
1 cup flour*

DIRECTIONS:

1. Bring water to a boil
2. Add salt and food coloring
3. Remove from heat
4. Add the oil, alum, and flour
5. While it is still hot, mix and knead for five
minutes

MAKES 2 CUPS

Notes:
1. This is a pliant play dough that stays soft for a
long time.
2. It can be stored in a tightly closed container or
plastic bag for several weeks.
3. Add cornmeal, sawdust, coffee grounds, sand, or
other grainy items to change the texture.

Uncooked Baking Dough

INGREDIENTS:

1 cup flour*
½ cup salt
½ cup warm water
food coloring (optional)

DIRECTIONS:

1. Combine all the ingredients in a bowl
2. Mix and then knead until smooth
3. Add more flour if too sticky, more water if too dry

MAKES ONE CUP

Notes:
1. This dough does not keep. Use it in one day.
2. Add 1 teaspoon alum as a preservative if you want
to use it longer.
3. This dough can be baked at 300°F until hard—
approximately 20 to 60 minutes depending on the
thickness of the pieces.

Soda Clay for Beads

Children can make bead shapes from dough made from
the following recipe. They must be made a day or two
before stringing.

INGREDIENTS:

1 cup baking soda
½ cup cornstarch
⅔ cup warm water
food coloring or tempera paint (optional)

DIRECTIONS:

1. Mix ingredients and heat until thick as mashed
potatoes
2. Pour on a cool surface and knead when cool
3. Add coloring if desired during kneading process
4. Store in plastic bag until ready to use
5. Shape beads
6. Use a drinking straw to make holes (Holes made
with toothpicks are too small for young children
to thread)
7. To speed drying, bake 10 minutes at lowest oven
setting or 30 seconds in a microwave set at
medium

MAKES 1 CUP (Suggestion: Make several batches in different colors)

Homemade Pastes

Recommended Homemade Pastes:

Flour paste: Recipe—Add water to flour until it reaches a thick but spreadable consistency.

Advantages: This is a quick and handy recipe. It is easily made from ingredients found in most kitchens in any amount needed. It works very well on most kinds of paper. It is safe and does not stain clothing. The texture is very different from school paste and provides an interesting change for the children. This is one of the few pastes that children can make themselves.

Disadvantage: Flour paste cannot be stored and should be used when it is first made. It wrinkles thinner papers and provides a relatively weak bond so it cannot be used with collage objects. (See chapter 6 for a discussion about using food items for art supplies.) It washes off easily when wet, but requires soaking and scrubbing if allowed to dry on surfaces.

Cornstarch paste: Recipe—Mix one part cornstarch to three parts cold water in a saucepan. Add two tablespoons of sugar and one tablespoon vinegar for each part of cornstarch (¼ cup cornstarch and ¾ cups water will make about half a pint). Stirring constantly, slowly heat the mixture until it clears and thickens. Cool before using. Paste can be stored in the refrigerator several weeks, if kept in a tighly sealed container.

Advantages: Cornstarch paste has a very pleasant texture and is not too sticky. If it safe, almost colorless paste and dries clear and washes out of clothing. It forms a stronger bond than flour paste and can be used for lightweight items such as fabric, yarn, ribbon, rice, and thin cardboard.

Disadvantages: This is probably one of the better homemade paste recipes in terms of strength, but because it must be cooked, it has to be prepared ahead of time. It is also hard to remove from surfaces when dry, requiring soaking and scrubbing.

Children's Literature on Art

There are many excellent annotated bibliographies on children's art books (Dupree and MacKinnon, 1994; Ivy, 1995). In recent years there has been a great increase in children's books written about art and it is hard to keep any bibliography up to date. This list is not intended to be comprehensive; instead the books on this list have been specifically selected for their effectiveness with children eight and under. Where appropriate, those books especially appealing to toddlers have been noted. There is a mix of recent publications and classics, all of which have been child-endorsed. A number in brackets (e.g., [1]) indicates the chapter in which uses for the book have been mentioned. An asterisk highlights Caldecott winners. For each book the main focuses have been indicated under the following headings:

Art Awareness: Books that describe the lives and work of artists, past and present.

Art Elements: Books focusing on the basic elements of art—color, form, line, pattern, shape, space, and texture. If a book features one particular element, that is also listed.

Becoming an Artist: Books expressing the kinds of feelings artist have and the decisions they make when creating art.

Child Art: Books that provide examples of children's art.

Developing Understanding: Books using art to help children learn to appreciate individual differences and the importance of caring about each other.

Media: Books describing how different art media are used, or that are illustrated in a particular art media.

Multicultural: Books featuring the art and cultures of people from all over the world.

Museums: Books that introduce the concept of a museum to young children.

Sensory Perception: Books that increase children's sensitivity to the aesthetic elements in the world around them.

Aardema, V. (1967). *Who's in rabbit's house?* New York: Dial Books. **(Media: masks; Multicultural: Africa) [11]**
The characters in this tale from the Masai of Africa are shown as people wearing masks.

*Aardema, V. (1976). *Why mosquitos buzz in people's ears.* New York: Dial Books. **(Art elements: shape, pattern; Multicultural: Africa)**
A mosquito's teasing leads to a chain of events that leaves a baby owlet dead. In punishment the mosquito is condemned to make its presence known by buzzing. Aardema illustrates this African folktale with subtly colored shapes and patterns.

Aardema, V. (1985). *Bimwilli and the Zimwi.* New York: Dial Books. **(Multicultural: Africa) [8]**
A delightful tale of how a young African boy uses a conch shell to save his garden. Follow a reading of the story by presenting a conch shell as a sensory experience.

Adoff, A. (1973). *Black is brown is tan.* New York: Harper-Collins. **(Art elements: color; Developing understanding) [11]**
A simple, energetic text describes the skin colors in an interracial family.

Agee, J. (1988). *The incredible painting of Felix Clousseau.* New York: Farrar, Straus & Giroux. **(Media: painting)**
Children love this humorous story of an artist's paintings that come alive at inopportune moments.

Alexander, M. (1995). *You're a genius BLACKBOARD BEAR.* Cambridge, MA: Candlewick Press. **(Art elements: line; Media: chalk drawing) [8]**
A chalk-drawn bear comes to life and draws the parts of a spaceship. Together he and a little boy build the ship, but then they chicken out of traveling to outer space.

Allen, C. (1991). *The Rug Makers.* Austin, TX: Steck-Vaughn. **(Media: weaving; Multicultural: India)**
A young boy from India explains how Oriental carpets are made in his village. Illustrated with many photographs.

Allington, R. (1979). *Colors.* Milwaukee, WI: Raintree Press. **(Art elements: color)**
Twelve base colors and how to mix them are illustrated.

Angelou, M. (1994). *My painted house My friendly chicken.* New York: Clarkson-Potter. **(Art awareness: architecture; Media: bodywear; Multicultural: Africa) [11]**

In a child's voice, the painted houses of the Ndebele of Africa are described. Photographs illustrate the beautiful costumes and jewelry of the women.

Anholt, L. (1994). *Camille and the sunflowers.* Hauppage, NY: Barron's Educational Series. **(Art awareness) [9]** This simply told story presents the art of Vincent Van Gogh through the eyes of Camille, a young boy in one of his paintings. Richly illustrated with actual paintings and scenes based on his paintings.

Anno, M. (1989). *Anno's faces.* New York: Philomel Books. **(Art awareness: portraits; Media: mask making)** Transparent plastic pages turn pictures of fruits and vegetables into faces that smile and frown.

Asch, F. (1978). *Sand cake.* New York: Parents Magazine Press. **(Art elements: texture; Media: sand)** Asch's lovable bear character makes a cake out of sand after receiving much advice from his friends. After reading this book, place different containers for molding the sand at the sand table or in the sandbox.

Asch, F. (1981). *Bread and honey.* New York: Parents Magazine Press. **(Becoming an artist; Media: painting)** Ben paints a picture of his mother in school. On the way home he shows his picture to his friends, each of whom make a suggestion on how he can "improve" his artwork. By the time he arrives home the painting no longer resembles his mother, but she "likes it just the way it is."

Asch, F. (1985) *Bear shadow.* New York: Simon & Schuster. **(Sensory perception)** A little bear tries to get away from his shadow. This is a good book to use with toddlers and younger preschoolers to accompany shadow activities.

Asch, F. (1994) *The Earth and I.* New York: Harcourt Brace.

Asch, F. (1995). *Water.* New York: Harcourt Brace **(Media: watercolor; Sensory perception) [10]** In these two books, soft rainbow-hued watercolors illustrate simple texts about our world. Following the reading of either of these books, provide the opportunity for the children to paint on wet paper and create their own blended rainbows.

Ata, T., & Moroney, L. (1989). *Baby rattlesnake.* San Francisco: Children's Book Press. **(Art elements: pattern, shape; Multicultural: Native American)** This Native American folktale features traditional symbols and patterns in the borders around each painted illustration.

Baker, A. (1994). *Brown rabbit's shape book.* New York: Larouse Kingfisher. **(Art elements: form) [4]** A large package arrives, containing smaller parcels of various forms, such as a cylinder and a cube, inside of which are balloons. The rabbit blows up the balloons and describes their forms. Follow up reading this book with a surprise package of forms inside forms or blow up balloons of different sizes and forms.

Baker, A. (1994) *White rabbit's color book.* New York: Larouse Kingfisher. **(Art elements: color; Media: paint) [8, 10]**

Through simple text and charming illustrations a white rabbit dips himself in different paint pots with predictable results. On his last dip into green and red, he turns into a brown rabbit. A good book for toddlers and preschoolers to lead into a discussion of browns.

Baker, J. (1987). *Where the forest meets the sea.* New York: Greenwillow Books. **(Art elements: texture, Media: mixed collage) [7]** A visit to the Australian rainforest is illustrated with three-dimensional, found-object collages. This is a perfect book to use in conjunction with a nature walk to find materials for collages. Also available as a Big Book from Scholastic.

Baker, J. (1991). *Window.* New York: Puffin Books. **(Art elements: texture; Media: mixed collage) [7]** Three-dimensional collages of windows show an increasingly urban environment. Children enjoy identifying the different materials used in the pictures.

Barrett, P., and Barrett, S. (1972). *The line Sophie drew.* New York: Scroll Press. **(Art elements: line; Media: drawing) [3]** Using a black line, Sophie draws pictures that take her on all kinds of adventures. This book can be used when introducing children to the element of line.

Bartalos, M. (1995). *Shadow Willie.* New York: Viking Press **(Sensory perception)** Bold, black shadow shapes illustrate a story about a boy playing with his shadow. Use this book as part of a kinesthetic activity involving shadow play.

Blizzard, G. S. (1992). *Come look with me: Exploring landscape art with children.* Charlottesville, VA: Thomasson-Grant. **(Art awareness)** Twelve landscape paintings are presented, with information on the artists and thought-provoking questions suitable for preschoolers. Part of a series that also includes: *World of Play, Animals in Art,* and *Enjoying Art with Children.*

Blood, C. L., and Link, M. (1980). *The goat in the rug.* New York: Four Winds Press. **(Media: fiber art; Multicultural: Native American) [9]** An angora goat tells how her hair is processed into a blanket. A fun way to introduce the steps of fiber preparation, including spinning, dyeing, and weaving, to children.

Blos, J. W. (1984). *Martin's hats.* New York: Morrow. **(Media: hats)** A boy has imaginary adventures while wearing different hats. This is an excellent book to tie into hat-making activities.

Bouchard, D. (1993). *The elders are watching.* Golden, CO: Fulcrum Publishing. **(Art awareness; Multicultural: Native American)** An ecological message is interwoven with artwork by Northwestern Indian artist Roy Henry Vickers. Various sections can be used to relate to nature walks and art activities.

Brenner, B. (1970). *Faces.* New York: Dutton. **(Art awareness: portraits; Media: mask making) [10]**

Photographs show eyes, noses, mouths, and ears reacting to pleasant and unpleasant sensations.

Brenner, B. (1973). *Bodies*. New York: Dutton **(Sensory perception) [11]**
Photographs show different body parts in action. Relate this book to kinesthetic activities of all kinds.

Brown, L. K., and Brown, M. (1996). *Visiting the art museum*. New York: E. P. Dutton. **(Art awareness; museums) [9]**
This cartoon-like book depicts a humorous family outing to the art museum. Includes photos of actual paintings. Younger children will not understand all the humorous parts. Read selected sections that will enhance their understanding of a museum visit.

Brown, M. (1979). *Listen to a shape*. New York: F. Watts **(Art elements: shape)**
The basic shapes of the square, the circle, and more are introduced using simple poetry and examples from nature. A good introductory book for toddlers and preschoolers who are just learning shapes.

*Brown, M. (1982). *Shadow*. New York: Macmillan. **(Media: masks; Multicultural: Africa; Sensory perception)**
A mystical view of shadows, set in Africa and featuring African dance and masks. A perfect book to accompany children's mask-making activities. When their masks are done, turn off the overhead lights, set up a spot light, and let the children create their own shadow dance.

Brown, M. (1984). *There's no place like home*. New York: Parents Magazine Press. **(Art awareness: architecture; Media: construction)**
Simple rhymes describe the many varieties of places where people and animals live. A good introduction for toddlers and preschoolers, to the different kinds of buildings in which people live.

*Bunting, E. (1994). *Smoky night*. New York: Harcourt Brace. **(Art elements: texture; Media: collage) [8]**
A fire in the night drives a young African American boy from his apartment during the 1992 Los Angeles riots. He overcomes cultural differences to help his Asian neighbors. Illustrated with paintings framed with textured collages that give a feeling for the chaos and scariness of the riot. This Caldecott winning book will give children ideas for ways they can "frame" their artwork.

Burke-Weiner, K. (1992). *The maybe garden*. New York: Beyond Words Publicatons. **(Becoming an artist)**
A boy plants a garden of fantastic colors and shapes while his mother plants a real one. Use this book to show how artists can imagine the real world in their own fantastic way.

Burns, M. (1994). *The greedy triangle*. New York: Scholastic. **(Art elements: shape) [10]**
A rollicking story finds shapes in many places. This book features complex shapes and a detailed text, suitable for older children who already know basic shapes.

Bush, T. (1995). *Grunt, the primitive cave boy*. New York: Crown. **(Art awareness; Media: drawing)**
A tongue-in-cheek story about a prehistoric boy who loves to draw animals. Somehow his pictures always seem to attract the animal he draws, making him very popular with the hunters of his clan. Explains, on a simple level, the idea that the prehistoric artists might have believed that drawing had magical powers.

Carle, E. (1972). *The secret birthday message*. New York: Harper Trophy. **(Art elements: shape) [8]**
A message, made from shapes, follow cutout pages that repeat the shapes. An excellent book for older preschoolers who are beginning to use graphic symbols.

Carle, E. (1974). *My very first book of shapes*. New York: Harper & Row. **(Art elements: shape) [8]**
The presentation of differently sized and shaped objects helps children become aware of the shapes found in the environment. Use this book to introduce the basic shapes to toddlers and younger preschoolers.

Carle, E. (1977). *The grouchy ladybug*. New York: Harper Collins. **(Media: cut-paper collage) [7]**
An aggressive ladybug challenges other creatures, regardless of their size. A clever book design shows the different sizes of the animals who are illustrated with cut-paper collage. After reading this book provide many different sizes and textures of paper in the collage area.

Carle, E. (1984). *The mixed-up chameleon*. New York: Crowell. **(Art elements: shape; Media: collage) [7]**
A chameleon wishes he could be other animals. Shapes are put together to make new creatures. Different shapes also form the borders of the pages. This book will inspire children to create their own creatures by combining cut-paper shapes.

Carle, E. (1987). *The tiny seed*. Natich, MA: Picture Book Studio. **(Media: cut-paper collage, printmaking)**
Collages of paint-splattered papers illustrate how a seed grows. Follow this book with kinesthetic activities that involve growing plants. Invite the children to make painted and printed paper to use in their collages. Also available as a Big Book from Scholastic.

Carle, E. (1992). *Draw me a star*. New York: Philomel. **(Becoming an artist; Media: drawing) [9]**
Painted-paper collages illustrate the story of how the author learned to draw a star. This book is most suitable for older children as drawing a star can be a very frustrating experience for many younger children. Emphasize that there are many ways to draw a star. Shift the focus of the book to how (and from whom) we learn to do different things. Invite the children to invent their own ways to draw a star, and then to "teach" a friend their original method.

Carlstrom, N. W. (1992). *Northern lullaby*. New York: Philomel Books. **(Art elements: pattern; Media: drawing; Multicultural: Native American) [3]**
A simple text about sleep draws on Native American symbols and patterns. A perfect read-aloud for a quiet time.

Castaneda, O. S. (1993). *Abuela's weave*. New York: Lee & Low. **(Media: fiber art; Multicultural: Central America) [9]**
A young Guatemalan girl and her grandmother grow closer as they weave beautiful cloth to sell at the market. This book helps children understand why some artists sell their work.

Cazet, D. (1993). *Born in the gravy*. New York: Orchard Books. **(Developing understanding; Media: drawing)**
A child tells about a day in kindergarten, using both Spanish and English. It includes drawing a dead bug and making a picture about the school day.

Chapman, C. (1994). *Snow on snow on snow*. New York: Dial Books. **(Media: painting) [5]**
Flat paintings that show the brush strokes illustrate a story of an African American boy who loses and then finds his dog in the snow.

Charles, O. (1988). *How is a crayon made?* New York: Simon & Schuster. **(Media: drawing) [3, 8]**
Colorful, sharp photographs show the complete process of making crayons. Children love learning how those mysterious and ever present crayons are really made, and may be inspired to reinvestigate their artistic possibilities.

Chase, E. N., and Chase, B. (1984). *The new baby calf*. New York: Scholastic. **(Art elements: texture; Media: modeling clay) [6]**
A simple story about a baby calf is made special by the textured illustrations made from modeling clay. This book will inspire young children to create picture stories from their modeling clay.

Cheltenham Elementary School Kindergarten (1994). *We are all alike...We are all different*. New York: Scholastic. **(Art awareness: portraits; Child art; Developing understanding) [11]**
Children's drawings illustrate this book about how people are the same and different. Also available as a Big Book from Scholastic.

Chocolate, D. M. N. (1994). *Imani in the belly*. New York: Bridgewater Books. **(Media: cut-paper collage; Multicultural: Africa)**
A West African folktale is boldly illustrated with cut-paper collages made of bright solid colors. This is an excellent book to accompany children's collage activities.

Christiana, D. (1990). *Drawer in a drawer*. New York: Farrar, Straus & Giroux. **(Art elements: line; Media: drawing) [3]**
This beautifully illustrated book uses simple rhyme to tell the fanciful story of a little boy who sleeps in a drawer. The boy uses a pencil to draw a line that becomes a box full of adventures. A perfect book to share with toddlers and preschoolers when focusing on the element of line.

Church, V. (1971). *All the colors around me*. Chicago: Afro-American Press. **(Developing understanding; Media: color) [11]**
A walk through the neighborhood comparing different skin colors emphasizes how, regardless of skin tone, African Americans all belong to one family.

Clark, A. N. (1955). *The little Indian pottery maker*. Chicago: Melmont. **(Media: firing clay; Multicultural: Native American) [6]**
The pottery making of the Pueblo tribe is described through the eyes of a young girl. It provides a detailed step-by-step description of how the clay is collected and prepared, how the pot is shaped, and how it is baked in an open fire.

Clark, A. N. (1957). *The little Indian basket maker*. Chicago: Melmont. **(Media: basketry; Multicultural: Native American)**
The basket weaving of the Papago tribe of the Southwest is described in simple text. The use of desert plants for basket making is clearly explained. Use this book to accompany the display of a basket.

Cohen, M. (1979). *Lost in the museum*. New York: Greenwillow Books. **(Museums)**
Although this book describes a trip to a museum of natural history, the message "stay together" is an important one for any field trip. Share this book before taking children on any art-related trip.

Cohen, M. (1980). *No good in art*. New York: Greenwillow Books. **(Becoming an artist; Media: painting)**
Inappropriate comments by the kindergarten art teacher make a child afraid to paint. The first grade art teacher encourages him with positive comments. A must-read for anyone teaching art to young children.

Cohn, J. (1995) *Why did it happen?* New York: William Morrow. **(Developing understanding; Media: drawing)**
A young boy uses drawing to work out his feelings of anger and fear after his friend, the neighborhood grocer, is killed during a robbery. It includes information for parents and teachers on ways to help children cope with violence.

Collins, P. L. (1992). *I am an artist*. Brookfield, CT: Millbrook Press. **(Sensory perception; Media: painting)**
In simple poetic language, this book shows children that responding aesthetically to beautiful things is part of being an artist. A good read-aloud for a quiet time.

Crews, D. (1978). *Freight train*. New York: Greenwillow Books

Crews, D. (1983). *Parade*. New York: William Morrow. [11]

Crews, D. (1986). *Flying*. New York: William Morrow.

Crews, D. (1995). *Sail away*. New York: Greenwillow Books. **(Art elements: color, pattern, shape) [9]**
Crews' illustration style of airbrushed shapes provides a perfect way to introduce the concept of pattern as repeated shapes. All of these books feature repeated images of objects, creating visual patterns. Help the children see the different repetitions in each book and point out how the repetition makes the objects seem like they are moving. These books can also be used in related thematic units.

Crimi, C. (1995). *Outside inside*. New York: Simon & Schuster. **(Art elements: space; Media: cut-paper collage; Sensory perception) [10]**
Cut-paper collages show opposing pictures of what a young girl is doing inside compared to what is happening outside.

Crosbie, M. J., and Rosenthal, S. (1993). *Architecture COLORS*. Washington, DC: Preservation Press. **(Art awareness: architecture; Art elements: color, form) [4]**
This board book illustrates each color with a photograph of an architectural feature on a home or building, opposite the word for the color and the feature. This is a good read-aloud for toddlers and a read-it-myself book for preschoolers. Follow up reading this book with a walk through the neighborhood, looking for the colors and architectural features mentioned in the book. One of a series published by the National Trust for Historic Preservation that also includes *Architecture SHAPES* and *Architecture COUNTS*.

Day, N. R. (1995). *The lion's whiskers: An Ethiopian folktale*. New York: Scholastic. **(Media: mixed collage; Multicultural: Africa) [7]**
Beautiful textured-paper collages illustrate a story about how a stepmother won the love of her stepson. Ideal for sharing when children are involved in collage activities.

Demarest, C. L. (1995). *My blue boat*. New York: Harcourt Brace. **(Art elements: color)**
Using her imagination, a little girl sits in her little boat and pictures a sea voyage. Beautifully illustrated with watercolors, use this book when studying the color blue or to relate to a thematic unit on the sea.

Demi (1980). *Liang and the magic paintbrush*. New York: Henry Holt. **(Media: painting; Multicultural: China)**
A Chinese boy is given a magic paintbrush that can make his pictures come alive.

dePaola, T. (1973). *Charlie needs a cloak*. Englewood Cliffs, NJ: Prentice-Hall. **(Media: fiber art) [9]**
Charlie is a shepherd who needs a new cape to wear in the winter. In simple language, the story describes the basic processes of turning wool into a finished garment. At each step, the sheep "help" Charlie. This book is an excellent introduction to fiber processing for all children, who particularly love the antics of the delightfully illustrated sheep.

dePaola, T. (1988). *The legend of the Indian paintbrush*. New York: G. P. Putnam's Sons. **(Media: painting; Multicultural: Native American)**
This retelling of a Plains Indian tale of the origin of the flower called "Indian paintbrush" explains the role of painting in the life of the Plains tribes. This book relates well to painting activities involving different types of paintbrushes or using natural materials such as twigs and grasses to apply paint. Also available as a Big Book from Scholastic.

dePaola, T. (1989). *The art lesson*. New York: Trumpet Club. **(Becoming an artist; Media: drawing)**
This book tells the autobiographical story of how young Tomie was frustrated by an overly directive art teacher and how he finally reached an unsettling compromise with her. It provides a model of poor art teaching in the school setting, as well as a model of good parenting, and should be read by all adults who work with young children.

Desimini, L. (1994). *My house*. New York: Henry Holt **(Art elements: texture; Media: mixed collage) [7]**
Wonderful collages using all kinds of materials show a simple house in changing weather, providing children an opportunity to see the same subject done in a variety of media.

Dewey, A. (1995). *The sky*. New York: Green Tiger Press. **(Art elements: shape, texture; Media: chalk; Sensory awareness)**
A simple, subtle text and soft pastel-colored chalk drawings show different views of the sky.

Dillon, L., and Dillon, D. (1994). *What am I? Looking through shapes at apples and grapes*. New York: Blue Sky Press. **(Sensory perception: space; Developing understanding) [9]**
Cut out windows highlight luscious photographs of fruit and vegetables. The book ends with a rainbow of hands in many shades. Looking through the windows helps children focus on the details of these everyday objects. Precede or follow up a reading of this book by putting out view tubes or viewfinders or alternatively tie the book into a sensory experience with fruits or vegetables.

Dixon, A. (1990). *Clay*. New York: Garrett Educational Company. **(Media: firing clay) [6]**
This book shows how clay is dug from the ground and then used to make many useful objects including drainpipes, dishes, and china figurines. Use this book with older preschoolers and primary children when introducing firing clay to them.

Dixon, A. (1994) *The sleeping lady*. Anchorage, AK: Alaska Northwest Books. **(Art elements: shape, pattern; Multicultural: Native American)**
Beautiful paintings with borders illustrate a Native American folktale about the origin of the mountains.

Dobrin, A. (1973). *Josephine's imagination*. New York: Scholastic **(Media: collage, construction, puppets; Multicultural: Haiti) [11]**
A Haitian girl uses her imagination to create a doll from one of her mother's broken brooms. The text is overly long for very young children but can be read in sections or retold. The story can be related to using collage or construction materials in a new way or in puppetry.

Dodds, D. A. (1989). *Wheel away*. New York: Harper & Row. **(Media: painted paper collage, murals; Kinesthetics) [10]**
Cut-paper collages with splatter-paint designs illustrate a wheel as it goes over, under, and around. This is a perfect book to accompany printmaking, paintings, and murals done using toy trucks and cars. Follow reading of the book with kinesthetic activities in which children can also "wheel" over, under, and around. Also available as a Big Book from Scholastic.

Dorros, A. (1992). *This is my house*. New York. Scholastic. **(Art awareness: architecture; Media: three-dimensional construction) [4]**
Drawings and a rhymthic text present different houses from around the world. A good introduction to the different ways homes are built. Also available as a Big Book from Scholastic.

Druscher, H. (1983). *Simon's book*. New York: Lothrop, Lee & Shepard. **(Media: bookmaking, drawing)**
A boy starts a drawing of a monster and then goes to bed. During the night, the pen, the ink, and the monster come alive and finish the drawing, with surprising results. The simple animated text enchants children of all ages and can be used to lead into a discussion of how a book is made.

Dunrea, O. (1995). *The painter who loved chickens*. New York: Farrar Straus Giroux. **(Becoming an artist; Media: painting)**
A painter who only wants to paint pictures of chickens struggles to paint what other people want, but finally becomes a success with his chicken paintings. Children enjoy finding all the different ways he paints chickens—big ones, little ones, brown ones, white ones and so on—in the realistic illustrations.

Ehlert, L. (1988). *Painting a rainbow*. Orlando, FL: Harcourt Brace Jovanovich. **(Art elements: color; Media: cut-paper collage) [7, 9]**
A simple text with boldly colored cut-paper illustrations present the planting of bulbs in a garden. The plants that grow are grouped by colors. Pages are cut so that a rainbow is formed. An excellent book to use in conjunction with a sensory display of forced spring bulbs. Also available as a Big Book from Scholastic.

Ehlert, L. (1989). *Color zoo*. New York: HarperCollins, **(Sensory perception: space) [8, 9]**
Layered openings in the book form abstract animals that change shape as the page is turned. The wordless book appeals to children of all ages and inspires them to create their own book of "holes."

Ehlert, L. (1991). *Red leaf yellow leaf*. New York: Harcourt & Brace. **(Art elements: texture; Media: mixed collage) [9]**
Collages of paper and objects illustrate autumn and the seasonal cycle of a tree.

Ehlert, L. (1994). *Mole's hill*. New York: Harcourt & Brace. **(Art elements: pattern; Media: paper collage; Multicultural: Native American) [7, 9]**
Based on a Native American folktale, the story is illustrated with paper collages inspired by Woodland tribe beadwork and ribbon appliqué.

Ehlert, L. (1995). *Snowballs*. New York: Harcourt Brace. **(Art elements: texture; Media: mixed collage) [8]**
Collages of corn, raisins, cloth, and buttons are used to decorate cut-paper snowmen of different shapes. From page to page, a cut-paper bird "snacks" on the goodies.

*Emberly, B. (1968). *Drummer Hoff*. New York: Prentice-Hall. **(Art elements: pattern)**
Bright colors and patterns make this Caldecott winner attractive to young children. The repetitive rhyme is easy for beginning readers to follow. Use this book to transition into pattern activities.

Emberly, E. (1961). *A wing on a flea: A book about shapes*. Boston: Little, Brown and Co. **(Art elements: shape) [8]**
Shapes are found in parts of everyday objects.

Emberly, E. (1992). *Go away big green monster*. New York: Little, Brown and Co. **(Art elements: shape, space; Sensory perception) [8]**
In this delightful book, holes are cut out of each page. As the pages turn, the holes form pictures that end up as part of a monster's face. Use it as a model for a "book of holes" of your own design or to inspire children to look at their own art through holes of different shapes.

Ernst, L. (1983). *Sam Johnson and the blue ribbon quilt*. New York: Lothrop, Lee & Shepard. **(Developing understanding; Media: quilting)**
A farmer becomes fascinated with making quilts, and much to everyone's astonishment, he joins his wife's quilting club. This book combats the stereotype that only women like to sew and make quilts.

Everett, G. (1991). *Li'l sis and Uncle Willie*. New York: Hyperion. **(Multicultural: African American) [5, 10]**
The art of African-American artist William H. Johnson is used to create the story of his life.

Falk, A. (1964). *Matthew blows bubbles*. New York: McGraw-Hill. **(Sensory perception) [10]**
A simple story about bubbles to read when involved in bubbly art activities such as whipped-soap finger paint or when creating a bubble mural.

Fanelli, S. (1995) *My map book*. New York: HarperCollins. **(Child art; Media: drawing) [3]**
Maps drawn by a young child, who has lived in Italy and England, show her room, home, face, and more. These will inspire children to draw their own maps of special places.

Feelings, M. (1974). *Jambo means hello: Swahili alphabet book*. New York: Dial Books. **(Media: clay, wood; Multicultural: Africa)**
Using the alphabet, Feelings illustrates many things from life in Africa including the art forms of pottery and woodcarving.

Felix, M. (1992) *Opposites*. Mankato, MN: Creative Editions. **(Sensory perception: space) [8]**
A mouse chews out differently shaped windows in blank white pages. As the windows open, different opposing pictures appear, such as a rainy day and a sunny day. Use with activities that involve looking through openings. Wordless.

Felix, M. (1993). *Colors*. Mankato. MN: Creative Editions. **(Art elements: color) [5]**
This small wordless book features beautifully detailed drawings of a mouse who opens tubes of red, yellow, and blue paint and then creates green, orange, purple, and black.

Felix, M. (1993). *House*. Mankato, MN: Creative Editions. **(Art awareness: architecture; Sensory perception)**

The same little mouse begins by chewing a heart shape out of the page. It then gnaws out a paper shape, underneath which a detailed drawing of grass and plants appears. At the end the paper is shown folded into a house. The heart shape becomes a window for the mouse to peek through. Wordless.

Fine, J. (1979). *I carve stone*. New York: Thomas Y. Crowell. **(Art elements: form; Becoming an artist)**
Excellent photographs and a sensitive text explain how a woman sculptor carves stone sculptures.

Fisher, A. (1971). *Feathered ones and furry*. New York: Thomas Y. Crowell. **(Media: printmaking)**
Charming poems about a variety of animals are illustrated with simple linoleum cuts by Eric Carle. Use Styrofoam print making to get a similar effect.

Fisher, L. E. (1984). *Boxes! Boxes!* New York: Viking Press. **(Art elements: form; Media: box construction) [4]**
Differently sized and shaped boxes are used to hold a variety of items in a child's room.

Fleming, D. (1993). *In the small, small pond*. New York: Henry Holt. **(Art elements: texture; Media: painting) [5, 10]**
Bright paintings of nature and animals show a variety of textures. An excellent choice to accompany texture walks.

Florian, D. (1993). *The painter*. New York: Greenwillow Books. **(Becoming an artist)**
Using simple text, who a painter is and what a painter does and feels is explained. Use this book with young children before introducing a piece of adult art.

Fox, M. (1989). *Shoes from grandpa*. New York: Orchard Books. **(Art elements: texture; Media: mixed collage) [10]**
Torn tissue and other paper are combined with real buttons, lace, and more, illustrating a cumulative story of a little girl who receives a pair of shoes from her grandfather, and then gets too many pieces of clothing to go with them.

Frasier, D. (1991). *On the day you were born*. Orlando, FL: Harcourt Brace. **(Art elements: shape; Media: cut-paper collages)**
Cut-paper collages are used to illustrate people's place in the universe. The bold, bright colors and shapes are appealing to young children and the heartwarming text makes everyone feel special. An ideal book to share on birthdays and other special days.

Freeman, D. (1959). *Norman the doorman*. New York: Viking Press. **(Becoming an artist; Museums)**
This is a wonderful book for introducing the idea of a museum to young children. A little mouse lives in a suit of armor in a museum and enjoys giving tours to art-loving creatures. Using the wire from mousetraps he makes a sculpture and enters it in an art contest with great success.

Freeman, D. (1966). *A rainbow of my own*. New York: Puffin Books. **(Art elements: color; Sensory perception) [10]**
A little boy imagines a rainbow is his friend.

Freeman, D. (1976). *The chalk box story*. New York: J. B. Lippincott. **(Art elements: line; Media: chalk) [3]**
Pieces of colored chalk draw a story about a boy who is stranded on an island and then rescued by a turtle.

Garza, C. L. (1990). *Family pictures/Cuadros de familia*. Chicago: Children's Book Press. **(Art awareness; Multicultural: Mexican-American)**
Paintings by Mexican-American artists tell the story of a child growing up in a Hispanic community in Texas.

Gerstein, M. (1984). *The room*. New York: Harper & Row. **(Media: mural; Sensory perception)**
Detailed drawings and a simple text show how an apartment is successively lived in by several different people including some artists who paint the walls with bold colors. Have children compare how the appearance of the room changes when the walls are decorated differently.

Gilman, P. (1992) *Something from nothing*. New York: Scholastic. **(Media: collage, construction)**
A story of a little boy, who as a baby is given blanket made by his grandfather. As the years go by, the blanket wears out and the grandfather makes it into something new. When that item wears out, the clever grandfather again makes something else from it. An excellent story to tie in with reusing items for art activities. Also available as a Big Book from Scholastic.

Gomi, T. (1989). *Spring is here!* San Francisco, CA: Chronicle Books. **(Art elements: pattern)**
Simple pictures and text illustrates spring with many close-ups of patterns.

Grifalconi, A. (1986). *The village of round and square houses*. New York: Little, Brown and Company. **(Art awareness: architecture; Multicultural: Africa)**
A story about why the villages in Cameron have round and square houses. This book can be used to lead into a discussion of why buildings are certain shapes.

*Hall, D. (1980) *The ox-cart man*. New York: Viking. **(Art awareness; Art elements: pattern; Media: fiber art)**
Folk art style paintings illustrate how in the past a subsistence farm family's chores changed with the seasons. Use this book to teach children how food and fiber are part of the cycle of life.

Hanna, J. (1992). *The petting zoo*. Garden City, NY: Doubleday. **(Art elements: texture; Media: collage) [8]**
In this book, designed for toddlers, pieces of differently textured cloth are used to illustrate how different wild animals might feel.

Haskins, J. (1989) *Count your way through Mexico*. Minneapolis, MN: Carolrhoda Book. **(Media: papier mâché; Multicultural: Mexico)**
Mexican life is presented using the numbers from one to ten in Spanish. Presents the use of papier mâché masks on the Day of Three Kings.

Hausmann, G. (1992). *Turtle island ABC*. New York: St. Martin's press. **(Media: chalk drawing; Multicultural: Native American)**
Each letter of the alphabet is illustrated with a Native American symbol, such as an arrow for "A" and a

buffalo for "B". The meaning and importance of each symbol is beautifully explained. The illustrations are rendered in monochromatic chalks.

Hawkinson, J. (1974). *A ball of clay*. Chicago: Albert Whitman. **(Media: firing clay) [6]**

A book about clay—what it is, where to find it, how to prepare it and use it. Select relevant parts to share with older preschoolers and primary children who want to know more about clay.

Heide, F. P. (1970). *Sound of sunshine, sound of rain*. New York: Parent's Magazine Press. **(Developing understanding; Art elements: texture)**

A blind African-American boy describes his daily life through touch, smell, and sound. Shorten the long text by selecting just one part of the boy's day to share with young children.

Heller, R. (1995). *Color! Color! Color!* New York: Grosset & Dunlap. **(Art elements: color) [8]**

With rhythmic language, Ruth Heller presents a multitude of concepts about color. The book includes color acetates that overlap to show color mixing. A good book to share with one or two children so they can investigate the complex illustrations.

Hoban, R. (1989). *Monsters*. New York: Scholastic. **(Media: drawing) [3]**

John loves to draw monsters, but his parents worry that there is something wrong with him. They take him first to his art teacher who sees his creativity and is not bothered by his monsters. Next they take him to a doctor who most certainly is bothered, especially when the monster drawing comes alive. Illustrated by Quentin Blake, the pictures are extraordinarily reflective of young children's artwork. Older children love the surprise ending.

Hoban, T. (1971). *Look again!* New York: Macmillan. **(Sensory perception; Art elements: space) [8]**

This book uses differently shaped windows to focus on interesting parts of photographs.

Hoban, T. (1974). *Round! Round! Round!* New York: Macmillan.

Hoban, T. (1978). *Is it red? Is it yellow? Is it blue?* New York: William Morrow.

Hoban, T. (1979). *Circles triangles squares*. New York: Macmillan.

Hoban, T. (1986). *Shapes shapes shapes*. New York: Greenwillow Books.

Hoban, T. (1987). *Dots, spots, speckles, and stripes*. New York: Greenwillow Books.

Hoban, T. (1988). *Look look look*. New York: Greenwillow Books.

Hoban T. (1989). *Of colors and things*. New York: Greenwillow Books.

Hoban, T. (1995). *Colors everywhere*. New York: Greenwillow Books. **(Art elements: color, form, shape, pattern, texture) [4, 8]**

Hoban's wordless books of magnificent photographs entice children's eyes to see the details of color, shape, form, and pattern in everyday objects. These are excellent books for toddlers and preschoolers to study on their own. They can also be used to intro-duce sensory activities involving the art elements. *Of colors and things* and *Look Look Look* are also available as Big Books from Scholastic.

Hoyt-Goldsmith, D. (1990). *Totem pole*. New York: Scholastic. **(Art awareness; Media: wood carving; Multicultural: Native American) [9]**

Photographs illustrate the contemporary life of a boy whose father is a totem pole carver of the Tsimshian tribe of the Pacific Northwest. The text may need to be simplified for younger children, but the pictures are excellent for discussion.

Hudson, C. W., and Ford, B. G. (1990). *Bright eyes, brown skin*. Littleton, MA: Sundance. **(Developing understanding) [11]**

Illustrated with pictures of four African-American children enjoying typical preschool activities (including drawing), this rhyming poem celebrates physical appearance. A perfect book for toddlers and young preschoolers.

Hughes, L. (1994). *The sweet and sour animal book*. New York: Oxford University Press. **(Child art; Media: modeling)**

Lively two- and three-dimensional artwork by children illustrates Langston Hughes' alphabet book of poetry. Very suitable to share with children of all ages.

Hughes, L. (1995). *The block*. New York: Metropolitan Museum of Art. **(Art awareness: collage)**

The cut-paper collages and photomontages of African-American artist Romare Beardon illustrate selected poems of Langston Hughes in this beautiful book.

Hughes, S. (1986). *All shapes and sizes*. New York: Lothrop, Lee & Shepard. **(Art elements: shape)**

A rhythmic text describes the shape and size of familiar objects.

Humphrey, H. (1969). *What is it for?* New York: Simon & Schuster. **(Art elements: pattern, shape)**

Black-and-white photographs of objects found in the city provide many examples of patterns. The accompanying text explains what the objects are and how they are used. Use the book before or after a walk in the neighborhood looking for patterns.

Hutchins, P. (1972). *Changes changes*. New York: Macmillan. **(Art elements: form; Media: blocks) [4]**

A wordless story (appealing to toddlers) is told using brightly colored blocks and two wooden figures. Children wil enjoy making up their own "block" stories after reading this book.

Isadora, R. (1985). *I touch*. New York: Greenwillow Books. **(Art elements: texture) [5]**

This board book for toddlers features a simple text describing different textures such as a sticky lollipop.

James, B. (1994). *The mud family*. New York: Putnam's. **(Art elements: texture; Media: painting; Multicultural: Native American) [5]**

A young Native American girl of the prehistoric past makes a family from mud (clay) to help bring rain to the parched Southwest. Wonderfully illustrated with paintings done on textured fabric.

Jenkins, S. (1995). *Looking down*. New York: Houghton Mifflin. **(Media: collage; Sensory perception)**

Starting with a view of the earth, each collage illustration moves in closer and closer, ending with close-up of a ladybug. Use this book to introduce the concept of enlargement. Follow up by displaying a poster size print and a postcard size reproduction of the same artwork.

Johnson, C. (1955). *Harold and the purple crayon*. New York: Harper & Row. **(Media: bookmaking, crayon drawing) [3]**

Using a purple crayon, Harold draws himself an adventure. This classic remains a child-pleaser. A good book to introduce the idea of drawing a story that continues from one page to the next for when children begin "writing" their own books.

Johnston, T., and dePaola, T. (1985). *The quilt story*. New York: G. P. Putnam's Son's. **(Media: quilting)**

A treasured quilt provides comfort to two little girls from different times. Also available as a Big Book from Scholastic.

Jonas, A. (1985). *The trek*. New York: Greenwillow Books. **(Sensory perception)**

Using her imagination, a girl turns her walk to school into a jungle adventure. The illustrations are perfect introductory optical illusions for young children.

Jonas, A. (1987). *Reflections*. New York: Greenwillow Books. **(Sensory perception)**

Slightly more sophisticated than *The Trek,* this book features paintings that when turned upside down become different pictures. This book can inspire activities using mirrors, and is a good companion to walks on which children study reflections in puddles and ponds.

Jonas, A. (1989). *Color dance*. New York: Greenwillow Books. **(Art elements: color; Sensory perception)**

Three children dance with transparent cloth that overlaps to create new colors. Follow up by giving children transparent or translucent materials, such as cellophane, sheer cloth, or tissue in a variety of colors to explore in sensory activities.

Kalan, R. (1978). *Rain*. New York: Greenwillow Books. **(Sensory perception)**

This book focuses on the sensory elements of rain as it falls on people everywhere.

Karnovsky, S. (1995). *Billy and the magic string*. New York: Troll. **(Art elements: line) [5, 12]**

This book features a little boy and his adventures with a magic string that can become anything he chooses. Following this book, give each child a piece of yarn and let them make their own "magic" string pictures on the floor or table.

*Keats, E. J. (1962). *The snowy day*. New York: Viking Press. **(Media: painted paper collages) [7]**

In this Caldecott winner, painted cut-paper collages illustrate the experiences of an African-American boy as he explores the snow. Also available as a Big Book from Scholastic.

Keats, E. J. (1966). *Jennie's hat*. New York: Harper & Row. **(Media: mixed collage, hats) [11]**

Jennie does not like her new hat. Delightful collages show her "improving" the hat.

Keats, E. J. (1978). *The trip*. New York: Mulberry Books. **(Media: box construction) [4]**

In this story a lonely boy makes a simple diarama in a shoe box and then imagines himself inside. The story ends with the boy making friends with children dressed in costumes for Halloween.

Keats, E. J. (1981). *Regards to the man in the moon*. New York: Macmillan. **(Media: construction, murals)**

Children paint a space mural, build spaceships out of junk, and then take an imaginary trip through space.

Kent, J. (1975). *The Christmas piñata*. New York: Parent's Magazine Press. **(Media: papier mâché; Multicultural: Mexico)**

Told from a view of a broken clay pot, this book details how a piñata is made and used in a Mexican village for Los Posadas.

Kesselman, W. (1980). *Emma*. New York: Doubleday Books for Young Readers. **(Becoming an artist)**

An elderly woman takes up painting in order to surround herself with the joyful memories of her life. A wonderful way to introduce children to the idea that art brings personal joy and can be created by artists of any age.

Kissinger, K. (1994). *All the colors we are*. St. Paul, MN: Redleaf Press. **(Developing understanding) [11]**

Beautiful photographs illustrate this book that explains simply why people have different color skin. Use this book to accompany mixing skin-toned paints. (Bilingual: Spanish)

Klamath County YMCA Preschool (1993). *The land of many colors*. New York: Scholastic. **(Art elements: color; Developing understanding) [9]**

A small child settles a conflict between the purple, blue, and green people. This book was written by preschoolers and speaks to them in their own language.

Knutson, K. (1992). *Muddigush*. New York: Macmillan. **(Media: painted paper collage) [4, 7]**

Children love the descriptive words and patterned and marbled paper collages that show a child's joy in playing in the mud.

Krauss, R. (1953). *A very special house*. New York: Harper & Row. **(Media: drawing)**

In joyful rhyme, a small boy draws and imagines a house full of excitement and fun. This classic book, illustrated by Maurice Sendak, celebrates the ability of imagination to create new worlds, on a level appropriate for toddlers and preschoolers.

Krensky, S. (1991). *Children of the earth and sky*. New York: Scholastic.

Krensky, S. (1994). *Children of wind and water*. New York: Scholastic. **(Media: firing clay, weaving, wood; Multicultural: Native American) [9]**

These two books consist of short stories about a Hopi painter and a Navajo weaver. The second introduces a Tlingit carver.

Kroll, V. (1992). *Wood-Hoopoe Willie*. Watertown, MA: Charlesbridge. **(Art elements: pattern; Media: fiber art; Multicultural: Africa)**

A young African-American boy saves a Kwanza celebration by playing the drums when the adult drummer is incapacitated in a car accident. The book describes and illustrates many African instruments. Richly patterned African cloth is featured throughout the book.

Kurtz, S. (1991). *The boy and the quilt*. Intercourse, PA: Good Books. **(Media: quilting) [9]**
A little boy collects fabric squares of many colors and sews his own crazy quilt. It shows, step by step, how the quilt is made and combats the stereotype that only girls make quilts.

Kuskin, K. (1965). *Sand and snow*. New York: Harper & Row. **(Art elements: texture; Media: sand; Sensory perception)**
This book uses poetry to compare the beach in the heat of summer and the snow in the cold of winter. Accompany this book with modeling doughs to which sand has been added or provide sensory bins of sand and snow. In winter have a "Beach Day" complete with towels, pails, sunbonnets, and, of course, sand art activities.

Kusken, K. (1994). *Patchwork island*. New York: Harper-Collins, **(Art elements: pattern, texture; Media: quilting)**
A mother makes an "island" quilt for her son. There are many patterns in this book for children to find.

La Coccinella. (Eds.). (1994). *Shadow magic*. New York: Universe. **(Sensory perception)**
This board book features cut-out pages that are designed to be placed in front of a light source in order to create interesting shadows. Children enjoy working in pairs to create the shadows using a flashlight.

Lawson, J. (1992). *Kate's castle*. New York: Oxford University Press. **(Art elements: texture; Media: sand)**
This cumulative text follows the construction of a mighty sand castle, and is illustrated with softly colored pictures. A good read-aloud for kindergarten and primary children who may want to write a cumulative book about their own sand constructions.

Leaf, M. (1987). *Eyes of the dragon*. New York: Lothrop, Lee & Shepard. **(Media: painting; Multicultural: China)**
An artist paints eyeless dragons on the city wall. When the artist is ordered by an official to put eyes on them, the dragons come alive and break loose from the wall. Use this book to make children think about why artists include some things and leave other things out of their artwork.

Lee, H. V. (1994). *At the beach*. New York: Henry Holt. **(Media: cut paper collage; Multicultural: China) [8]**
In this story, children learn to write Chinese characters in the sand on the beach. The pictures are made of intricate cut-paper collages. Following a reading of this story, children may want to "write" in sand or sensory bins.

Le Ford, B. (1995). *A blue butterfly: A story about Claude Monet*. New York: Doubleday. **(Art awareness) [5]**
A simple text and soft impressionistic watercolors present the life of one of the great Impressionists. A good read-aloud for all ages.

Leigh, N. K. (1993) *Learning to swim in Swaziland*. New York: Scholastic. **(Media: drawing; Multicultural: Africa)**
A child's view of the South African country of Swaziland illustrated with photographs and the child's crayon drawings.

Lepschy, I. (1992). *Pablo Picasso*. Hauppage, NY: Baron's Educational Series. **(Art awareness; Becoming and artist)**
This biography of Picasso focuses on his difficulties as a young child, both at home and at school. It demonstrates how artistic creativity in young children is often hard to recognize. This is a must-read for both teacher and parents. The text may need to be shortened and simplified for preschoolers. This book is part of a series called Children of Genius. Another book in the series is *Leonardo daVinci* (1984).

Lessac, F. (1987). *My little island*. New York: Harper Trophy.

Lessac, F. (1989). *Caribbean alphabet*. New York: Tambourine Books. **(Art awareness; Multicultural: Haiti)**
Brilliantly colored folk art paintings illustrate the life and culture on a Caribbean Island.

Lewis, S. (1991). *African American art for young people*. Worcester, MA: Davis. **(Multicultural: African-American)**
Twelve African-American artists are discussed on a simple level and an example of their artwork is reproduced. The work of Powers (quilting), Barthe and Lewis (sculpture), Tanner, Hunter, Hayden, Johnson, Jones, Bearden, Lawrence, and Catlett (painting), and Butler (found art constructions) are presented.

Lionni, L. (1959). *little blue and little yellow*. New York: Mulberry Books. **(Art elements: color; Media: torn-paper collage) [5]**
A delightful tale about color mixing, illustrated with torn-paper circles and other simple shapes. A classic to be shared with children.

Lionni, L. (1961). *On my beach there are many pebbles*. New York: Mulberry Books. **(Sensory perception; Media: drawing)**
Beautiful pencil drawings of pebbles, both real and amazing, show children how to look at a simple things and see beauty. A quiet time read-aloud to accompany sensory art activities involving collecting, observing, and using pebbles and stones.

Lionni, L. (1963). *Swimmy*. New York: Alfred A. Knopf. **(Developing understanding; Media: printmaking) [8]**
A fish learns how to cooperate with others in this book illustrated with simple prints. Also available as a Big Book from Scholastic.

Lionni, L. (1975). *A color of his own*. New York: Alfred A. Knopf. **(Art elements: color, pattern; Media: printmaking)**
A lizard tries out many colors until he finds the one just right for him. A favorite read-aloud. Also available as a Big Book from Scholastic.

Lionni, L. (1982). *Let's make rabbits*. New York: Alfred A. Knopf. **(Media: collage, drawing) [7]**

Two rabbits, one drawn and one cut out of paper, get a taste of real life. Use this book to help children see the difference between two-dimensional drawings and collages, and three-dimensional forms.

Lionni, L. (1991). *Matthew's dream*. New York: Alfred Knopf. **(Becoming an artist; Museums) [9]**

A visit to an art museum inspires a young mouse to become a painter, against the wishes of his family.

Littlechild, G. (1993). *This land is my land*. Emeryville, CA: Children's Book Press. **(Art awareness; Media: painting; Multicultural: Native American)**

The Native American artist George Littlechild discusses each of his paintings in terms children can understand. In doing so he also explains a lot about Native American history, culture, and the people's hopes and dreams. Choose a selection that relates to what the children already know about Native American life and read only one section at a sitting.

Locker, T. (1994). *Miranda's smile*. New York: Dial Books for Young Readers. **(Art awareness: portrait; Becoming an artist; Media: painting)**

An artist tries to paint his daughter's portrait with her special smile. Illustrated with several different portraits of the girl, this book is a wonderful way to introduce portraits to children aged three and up.

Lopez, A. (1972). *Celebration*. Garden City, NY: Doubleday. **(Art awareness; Media: drawing, painting; Multicultural: Native American)**

Native American dances and games are presented through a simple text illustrated with reproductions of fine art drawings and paintings of many different tribes. An excellent book to help introduce toddlers and preschoolers to Native American culture. Also available as a Big Book from Sundance.

Lord, S. (1995). *The story of the dreamcatcher and other Native American crafts*. New York: Scholastic. **(Media: beadwork, masks; Multicultural: Native American) [11]**

This book tells, in simple language, a little bit about several Native American crafts, including the dreamcatcher, beadwork, and mask making. It is illustrated with color photographs of examples of these art forms.

MacDonald, S. (1994). *Sea shapes*. New York: Harcourt Brace. **(Art elements: shape; Media: cut-paper collage) [7]**

Opposite each intricate cut-paper seascape are three shapes for the children to find in the picture. Share with one or two children, or let one child explore it independently.

*McCloskey, R. (1942). *Make way for ducklings*. New York: Viking.

Some city-born ducklings get some help along the way to the park in this Caldecott winner.

McDermott, G. (1993). *Raven: A trickster tale from the Pacific Northwest*. New York: Harcourt Brace. **(Art elements: shape, pattern; Multicultural: Native American)**

This Native American story is illustrated with pictures based on the traditional art forms and patterns of the Northwest coastal tribes.

McGovern, A. (1969). *Black is beautiful*. New York: Scholastic. **(Art elements: color; Developing understanding) [11]**

This book celebrates the color black. Use it to help children become more comfortable using black art materials.

McLerran, A. (1991). *Roxaboxen*. New York: Lothrop, Lee & Shepard. **(Art awareness: architecture; Media: construction) [4]**

On the edge of the desert, a group of neighborhool children build "houses" out of stones, sticks, old pottery, and crates. Using their imaginations, a town is created.

Micklethwait, L. (1994). *I spy a lion: Animals in art*. New York: Greenwillow Books. **(Art awareness; Sensory perception)**

Readers are asked to find animals and other details in a variety of famous artworks. A good book to share with one or two children or for older children to investigate on their own. One of an extensive series.

Moncure, J. (1982). *The touch book*. Chicago: Children's Book Press. **(Art elements: texture)**

A wide variety of textures is presented in this rhyming text.

Moon, N. (1994). *Lucy's picture*. New York: Dial Books for Young Readers. **(Becoming an artist; Media: mixed collage) [7]**

Lucy wants to make a gift for her grandfather, but a painting is just not right. She decides to make a collage of things she collects inside and outside the schoolroom. A perfect read-aloud for young children. It emphasizes that the element of artistic choice as an important part of the art process.

Moore, R. (1993). *Native artists of Africa*. Santa Fe, NM: John Muir Publications. **(Multicultural: Africa) [9]**

Interviews with contemporary African artists provide information about their work. Readers are introduced to a Berber rug weaver, a painter, and a basket weaver. Text will need to be simplified for young children. Photographs show the artists at work.

Moore, R. (1993). *Native artists of North America*. Santa Fe, NM: John Muir Publications. **(Multicultural: Native American) [9]**

In the same format, contemporary Native American artists provide information on how and why they create their art. Artists introduced include Valdez (Huichol yarn painting), Teters (painter), and Rahr (beadwork and cornhusk dolls).

Morris, A. (1992). *Houses and homes*. New York: Mulberry. **(Art awareness: architecture; Media: construction) [4]**

Photographs show homes from many different places in the world.

Morris, A. (1993). *Hats hats hats*. New York: Mulberry Books. **(Media: hats) [11]**

All kinds of headgear from around the world are shown in vividly colored photographs. A perfect book to accompany hat-making activities.

Moss, S. (1995). *Peter's painting*. Greenvale, NY: MONDO Publishing. **(Becoming an artist; Media: painting) [5]**

This book expresses the multi-media nature of child art in a beautifully expressed story of a little boy whose simple "scribble" paintings transport him into the world of his imagination. It is illustrated with richly colored paintings of Peter painting in his bedroom which with each page has more and more paintings hanging on the walls. A perfect book to share with toddlers and preschoolers who love to paint. Have them find each painting he makes on the walls on the next page.

Munsch, R. (1992). *Purple, green and yellow*. Toronto, Canada: Annick Press. **(Media: drawing) [3]**

In this delightfully illustrated book, a little girl gets bored with using washable markers. She then uses permanent markers to color herself and her dad. The splendid drawings do not wash off, but after applying a special marker they both look good as new—as long as it does not rain. Although the book is obviously fantastic, some children may be tempted to write on themselves after reading the book. It is most suitable for older children and should be accompanied by a discussion of safe ways to use markers.

Myers, W. D. (1995). *The story of the three kings*. New York: HarperCollins. **(Art elements: pattern; Multicultural: Africa)**

A folktale, set in African setting, features jewellike paintings with intricate patterns. A good companion to pattern activities for primary age children.

Myrus, D., and Squillance, A. (1963). *Story in the sand*. New York: Macmillan. **(Art elements: texture; Media: sand) [8]**

A visit to the beach is illustrated with photographs of patterns and textures made with footprints, and drawings in the sand detailed with shells and beach finds.

Neitzel, S. (1989). *The jacket I wear in the snow*. New York: Greenwillow Books. **(Media: fiber art)**

Pictures show the different articles of clothing a little girl wears to go out in the snow. This book is a good introduction to a thematic unit on clothing. Also available as a Big Book from Scholastic.

Olabye, I. (1994). *Bitter bananas*. Honesdale, PA: Boyds Mill Press. **(Media: chalk, collage; Multicultural: Africa) [9]**

Cut-paper and chalk collages illustrate a simple tale of an African boy who figures out a way to save the bananas from the baboons. This book can be used to introduce the idea of combining collage and drawing materials.

O'Neill, M. (1961). *Hailstones and halibut bones: Adventures in color*. Garden City, NY: Doubleday. **(Art elements: color) [8, 10]**

Beautiful poems describe each color in terms of the things that come in that color. Includes purple, gold, black, brown, blue, gray, white, orange, red, pink, green, and yellow.

O'Neill, M. (1969). *Fingers are always bringing me news*. Garden City, NY: Doubleday **(Developing understanding; Art elements: texture) [10]**

Each poem in this book describes different people's fingers and what they touch and feel. Use these poems to relate to activities involving the sense of touch.

Osofsky, D. (1992). *Dreamcatcher*. New York: Orchard Books. **(Media: chalk drawing; Multicultural: Native American)**

Soft pastel drawings and a simple text tell the tale of a poor child and a special patchwork coat. A wonderful book to read aloud when sharing a dreamcatcher as an artifact.

Parton, D. (1994). *The coat of many colors*. New York: HarperCollins. **(Media: quilting)**

Based on the song of the same name, this book tells the tale of a poor child and a special patchwork coat.

Paterson, B. (1990). *My first animals*. New York: Thomas Y. Crowell. **(Art elements: shape; Media: torn-paper collage)**

Familiar animals are illustrated with torn-paper shapes in this simply written book, suitable for toddlers.

Paul, A. W. (1991). *Eight hands round*. New York: HarperCollins. **(Art elements: pattern; Media: quilting) [9]**

Traditional American quilt patterns are presented along with actual or fanciful explanations for their origins. Can be read in short sections.

Peek, M. (1985). *Mary wore her red dress*. New York: Houghton Mifflin. **(Art elements: color)**

Traditional children's song about colors of clothing help teach colors using movement.

Pfister, M. (1992). *The rainbow fish*. New York: North-South Books. **(Developing understanding) [1, 5]**

The most beautiful fish in the ocean discovers that by giving of himself he can find friendship and happiness. The scales on the rainbow fish which he shares with the other fish in the sea are made with real reflective foil. A powerful book to use to teach children the values of cooperation and sharing.

Phillip, N. (Ed.). (1995). *Songs are sung*. New York: Orchard Books. **(Art element: texture; Media: painting; Multicultural: Native American)**

Inuit poetry is illustrated with paintings rendered with bold strokes of paint on a textured canvas background.

Pinkwater, D. M. (1977). *The big orange splot*. New York: Scholastic. **(Becoming an artist; Developing understanding)**

An exuberant story about a man who paints his house in his own unique way, much to the initial distress of his neighbors. Children love the colorful language and exaggerated happenings in this book, which extols creativity. Follow up the story by encouraging the children to paint a box or picture in their own way.

Polacco, P. (1988). *The keeping quilt*. New York: Simon & Schuster. **(Media: quilting)**

Four generations of a Jewish family are linked together by a handmade quilt. Each generation treasures the quilt but uses it in different ways. This book can be used with children to start them thinking about why people keep artworks instead of discarding them.

Polacco, P. (1988). *Rechenko's eggs*. New York: Philomel Books. **(Art elements: pattern; Multicultural: Ukranian) [8]**
Patterns are everywhere in this engaging story of a magic goose and some beautifully decorated Pysanky eggs. An excellent book to encourage children to find patterns in the illustrations.

Polacco, P. (1990). *Thunder cake*. New York: Putnam & Grosset. **(Art elements: pattern) [8]**
Clothing and quilts are covered with patterns in this simple story of a grandmother who helps her granddaughter learn to be brave during a thunderstorm. After reading the book, have children find patterns on their clothing as well.

Porte, B. A. (1995). *Chickens chickens*. New York: Orchard Books. **(Becoming an artist; Media: painting) [5]**
A painter who only wants to paint chickens finds happiness on a chicken farm. Brightly colored illustrations done in poster paint give the children lots of chickens to compare, count, and enjoy.

Prater, J. (1985). *The gift*. New York: Viking Press. **(Media: box construction) [4, 10]**
In this wordless book, a gift arrives in a big box. Children in the book then use the box to transport themselves on an imaginary trip.

Price, C. (1975). *Dancing masks of Africa*. New York: Charles Scribners Sons. **(Media: maskmaking; Multicultural: Africa) [11]**
An enthusiastic text and bold illustrations present a variety of African masks, in the context in which they are used. Information on the sources of the different masks is provided at the back of the book. This is an excellent introduction to African masks for children aged three and up. Enrich the images of the book with large reproductions of similar masks or actual masks if possible.

Reed, G. (1968). *The sand lady*. New York: Lothrop, Lee & Shepard. **(Art elements: texture; Media: sand) [8]**
A young girl makes a mermaid from her beach combings. The mermaid comes to life and gives her a special message.

Reed, M. (1990). *The button box*. New York: Dutton. **(Art elements: pattern)**
A young boy plays with the family's button collection, sorting and making patterns. Use this book to accompany sensory activities using buttons or when using buttons in collages.

Reid, B. (1987). *Sing a song of six pence*. New York: Scholastic. **(Art elements: texture; Media: modeling clay) [9]**
Traditional Mother Goose Rhymes are illustrated with dimensional modeling clay pictures. Also available as a Big Book from Scholastic.

Ringgold, F. (1991). *Tar beach*. New York: Random House. **(Multicultural: African American; Media: quilting) [8]**
This autobiographical story about growing up in Harlem incorporates many African-American traditions. Faith Ringgold is an artist who works in painted and quilted fabrics. The book is illustrated with paintings done on textured canvas and based on her "Woman on the Bridge" series. The quilted border is from the actual quilt and the quilt is shown at the end of the book. Also available as a Big Book from Scholastic.

Roalf, P. (1993). *Looking at painting: Children*. New York: Hyperion. **(Art awareness)**
Each double-page spread shows a reproduction of a painting featuring children, followed by a brief discussion about the artist and the painting. One of an extensive series by this author that includes the subject of cats, the circus, dancers, landscapes, families, and seascapes.

Robbins, K. (1984). *Building a house*. New York: Four Winds Press. **(Art awareness: architecture) [4]**
Using clear black-and-white photos, this book details the complete construction of a house. It includes not only putting up the foundation and walls, but also installation of electricity and water, and more. Children will be fascinated by these pictures. If possible, visit a house being built and compare it to the information in the book.

Robenberg, L. (1991) *The scrap doll*. New York: HarperCollins. **(Becoming an artist; Media: puppets)**
A little girl transforms a plain rag doll into a beautiful one by painting on a face and making new clothes for it. Use this book to show children how plain or ordinary things can be converted into special ones, such as turning a bag into a puppet, through the use of imagination.

Roessel, M. (1995). *Songs from the loom*. Minneapolis, MN: Lerner Publications. **(Art awareness; Media: fiber art; Multicultural: Native American) [9]**
Ruth Roessel, a Navajo weaver, teaches her granddaughter how to spin, dye, and weave. The text is too complicated for younger children but the story and activities can be retold while showing the excellent photographs.

Rosetti, C. (1992). *Color*. New York: HarperCollins. **(Art elements: color)**
Poetry introduces colors to very young children.

Ross, D. (1993). *The serpent shell*. Hauppauge, NY: Barron's Educational Series. **(Sensory perception)**
Pastel watercolors combined with crayon illustrate a fanciful tale of how a sea serpent is saved by a young boy and a marvelous conch shell. Following this story put a conch on the sensory table.

Schick, E. (1987). *Art lessons*. New York: Greenwillow Books. **(Becoming an artist; Media: drawing)**
An eight-year-old boy takes drawing lessons from a neighbor who provides a model of positive art teaching and teaches him how to observe beauty. It is a must-read for all adults who teach art to young children.

Schwartz, A. (1983). *Begin at the beginning*. New York: Harper & Row. **(Becoming an artist; Media: painting)**
A young girl who is making a painting for the second grade art show does not know where to begin. This book helps children think like artists.

*Sendak, M. (1964). *Where the wild things are.* New York: Harper & Row. **(Art elements: line) [9]**
This children's classic about a little boy who does not want to eat his supper provides the perfect transition into making "wild things" whether drawn, painted, or modeled. Have the children notice how Sendak has used lines to add detail to his drawings.

Serfozo, M. (1988). *Who said red?* New York: Macmillan Company. **(Art elements: color; Media: water-color painting)**
A simple text about colors is illustrated with softly toned watercolor paintings.

Shalom, V. (1995). *The color of things.* New York: Rizzoli International. **(Art elements: color; Sensory perception)**
Colors are drained from a town and children paint them back again. This thought-provoking book helps children see how important color is to our world.

Shaw, C. G. (1988). *It looked like spilt milk.* New York: Harper Trophy. **(Shape)**
Free-form shapes turn into ordinary objects. A fun book for all young children. Also available as a Big Book from Scholastic.

Showers, P. (1991). *The listening walk.* New York: Harper-Collins. **(Sensory perception: sound)**
This simple text describes a "listening" walk as a child walking outside hears different sounds in his environment. Use this book to accompany activities focusing on the sense of hearing.

Siberell, A. (1982). *Whale in the sky.* New York: Dutton Children's Books. **(Media: printmaking; Multicultural: Native American) [7]**
Woodcut prints are used to illustrate this retelling of a traditional Northwest Coast myth. The book also explains in a simple way how and why totem poles were made, and describes the tools and paints that were used.

Simon, S. (1985) *Soap bubble magic.* New York: Lothrop, Lee & Shepard. **(Sensory perception) [10]**
This science book for children presents the fun and excitement of bubble making while explaining why bubbles do the things they do.

Skofield, J. (1984). *All wet! All wet!* New York: Harper & Row. **(Sensory perception) [5]**
A boy and the animals of the woods enjoy the sights, smells, and sounds of a rainy day in the summer. A perfect book to accompany a walk in the rain.

Testa, F. (1982) *If you take a paintbrush.* New York: Dial Books. **(Art elements: color)**
This book compares the colors of a variety of objects.

Thompson, B. (1995) *The magic quilt.* Littleton, MA: Sundance. **(Art elements: color; Media: chalk drawing)**
Beautiful chalk drawings illustrate a simple story of a young African-American girl who is afraid to sleep at night while her mother is away. Together she and her grandmother make a quilt of many colors, using her mother's clothing, which helps her feel her mother is near. The simple text is perfect for toddlers and preschoolers. The colors yellow, gold, pink, green, and purple are integrated into the story.

Tompert, A. (1984). *Nothing sticks like a shadow.* New York: Houghton Mifflin. **(Sensory perception)**
In this lighthearted story a misguided woodchuck tries to get rid of his shadow. Children enjoy the humorous story and become more aware of the nature of their own shadows. Follow the reading with shadow activities.

Tripp, V. (1987). *The penguins' paint.* Chicago: Children's Book Press. **(Art elements: color; Media: painting)**
Penguins find some buckets of paint and have fun painting everything in new colors. A lighthearted approach to color mixing for toddlers and young preschoolers.

Venezia, M. (1991). *Paul Klee.* Chicago: Children's Book Press. **(Art awareness)**
This child-appealing biography of Klee tells the story of his life, starting in childhood, and is illustrated with reproductions of his artwork and with Venezia's humorous cartoons. The text is simply worded, but is rather long and contains difficult concepts for preschoolers. Read selected passages and retell other parts. This book is one of a series by this author called *Getting to Know the World's Greatest Artists.* Other books in the series include *Rembrandt* (1988), *daVinci* (1989), *Hopper* (1989), *Monet* (1989), *Cassatt* (1990), *Michelangelo* (1991), *Botticelli* (1992), *Bruegel* (1992), *Pollock* (1992), *Goya* (1993), and *O'Keefe* (1993).

Waber, B. (1996). *"You look ridiculous," said the rhinoceros to the hippopotamus.* Boston: Houghton-Mifflin. **(Media: printmaking)**
Bold prints illustrate this humorous tale making it an excellent accompaniment to printmaking activities.

Waber, B. (1975). *I was all thumbs.* New York: Houghton Mifflin. **(Media: printmaking) [8]**
A laboratory octopus escapes and has to learn how to live in the dangerous but beautiful freedom of the ocean. Use this book to accompany printmaking activities especially with sea related thematic activities and murals.

Walsh, E. S. (1989). *Mouse paint.* New York: Trumpet Club. **(Art elements: color; Media: painting) [5]**
A delightful story, with a simple text about mice who play in some paint and discover color mixing. It is an excellent read-aloud for toddlers. Also available as a Big Book.

Walter, M. P. (1995). *Darkness.* New York: Simon & Schuster. **(Art awareness; Art elements: color)**
Bold, sweeping paintings by an African-American artist illustrate the beauty of dark colors through pictures of eruptions, night, and more. Sharing this book is a wonderful way to focus on the often ignored deep, rich, dark colors of our world.

Ward, L. (1978). *I am eyes * Ni macho.* New York: Greenwillow Books. **(Art elements: pattern; Multicultural: Africa) [9]**
In simple text and patterned pictures an African boy observes his world. A good companion for pattern activities. Also available as a Big Book from Scholastic.

Waters, K. (1990). *Lion Dancer*. New York: Scholastic. **(Multicultural: China)**
This book follows a young boy from Chinatown as he gets ready to celebrate the Chinese New Year. Also available as a Big Book from Scholastic.

Wegen, R. (1977). *Sandcastle*. New York: Greenwillow Books. **(Media: sand)**
In this delightful book, sea creatures join together to build a sand castle. Have children work together to build a sandcastle out of dampened sand or blocks.

Williams, K. L. (1990). *Galimoto*. New York: Lothrop, Lee & Shepard. **(Becoming an artist; Media: construction; Multicultural: Africa) [5]**
An African boy collects a variety of discarded materials to build a toy car. This is an excellent book to use with children to inspire them to be "inventors."

Williams, L. E. (1995). *The long silk strand*. Honesdale, PA: Boyds Mills Press. **(Media: mixed collage; Multicultural: China)**
Real silk thread and cut-paper collages illlustrate this Chinese folktale. Ask children to think of ways they could use a thread in their collages.

Wilson, F. (1969, 1988). *What it feels like to be a building*. Washington, DC: The Preservation Press. **(Art awareness: architecture) [4]**
Simple people shapes illustrate an analogy of how buildings are constructed. Beside each simple drawing of an architectural feature, such as a column or arch, are illustrations that show how the stress and strains would feel if the structure were built out of people. Very sophisticated ideas are made easy to understand, and children of all ages will learn more about building from this book. Follow up with a walk to find examples of these forms in the neighborhood, and try some kinesthetic activities inspired by the book.

Winters, J. (1991) *Diego*. New York: Random House. **(Art awareness: murals; Multicultural: Mexico)**
This Spanish/English biography of Mexican muralist Diego Rivera focuses on his childhood and youth.

Winthrop, E. (1988). *Shoes*. New York: Harper & Row. **(Media: murals, printmaking)**
This book illustrates shoes from around the world, and then, delightfully concludes that bare feet are the best. A perfect book to accompany a shoe or foot print mural.

Witte, E. and P. (1992). *Touch me book*. Racine, WA: Western Publishing. **(Art elements: texture)**
Pieces of real wood, cloth, and other textured materials illustrate this board book about textures. A fun book for toddlers to explore on their own.

Wolff, R. J. (1968). *Feeling blue*. New York: Charles Scribner's Sons.

Wolff, R. J. (1968). *Hello yellow*. New York: Charles Scribner's Sons.

Wolff, R. J. (1968). *Seeing red*. New York: Charles Scribner's Sons.
(Art awareness: color; Sensory perception) [10]
These outwardly simple books present sophisticated concepts of color that help children see more than basic red, yellow, and blue.

Wolkstein, D. (1992). *Little mouse's painting*. New York: Morrow Junior Books. **(Becoming an artist; Media: painting; Sensory perception)**
A little mouse creates a painting that looks different depending on the viewer's distance. This book introduces the idea that the appearance of a piece of art can change depending on how one views it. Follow up the story by having the children stand at different distances from a selected print or piece of art and then describe what they can see.

Xiong, B. (1989). *Nine-in-one, grrr, grrr*. Emeryville, CA: Children's Book Press. **(Media: embroidery; Multicultural: Southeast Asia)**
A simple folktale from the Hmong people of Southeast Asia is illustrated with traditional embroided storycloths.

Yabuuchi, M. (1985). *Whose footprints?* New York: Philomel Books. **(Media: murals, printmaking) [10]**
Footprints are matched with the animal that made them. Use this book to initiate or accompany murals that feature foot painting. Also available as a Big Book from Macmillan.

Yashima, T. (1967). *Umbrella*. New York: Viking. **(Sensory perception)**
A young girl uses her new umbrella to walk to nursery school. Along the way she listens to the different sounds of the falling rain.

Yenawine, P., and the Museum of Modern Art (1991). *Colors*. New York: Delacorte. **(Art awareness; Art elements)**
Artwork from the Museum of Modern Art illustrates this simple art concept book suitable for toddlers and young preschoolers. One of a series including *Lines, Shapes,* and *Stories*.

*Yolen, J. (1988). *Owl moon*. New York: Philomel **(Art elements: color; Media: painting)**
Beautiful prose poetry describes how a young boy and his father go for a walk on a snowy moonlit night. The illustrations can be used to help children see that artists do not only use white when painting snow.

Young, E. (1991). *Seven blind mice*. New York: Philomel. **(Sensory perception)**
Based on the tale of the blind men and the elephant, seven blind mice use their senses to investigate an elephant. Also available as a Big Book from Scholastic.

Ziebel, P. (1989). *Look closer!* New York: Clarion. **(Sensory perception)**
Close-ups of objects are followed by a full view of each object in use. A favorite for increasing the visual awareness of toddlers. After reading the book provide magifying glasses of various types with which the children may explore.

Ziefert, H. (1986). *A new coat for Anna*. New York: Alfred A. Knopf. **(Media: fiber art) [9]**
During World War II, a mother trades a watch for wool and makes her daughter a coat from scratch. The process of spinning, dyeing, weaving, and tailoring requires many people to cooperate to produce Anna's new coat.

Teacher References

BOOKS

These books will help teachers learn more about the world of visual art.

Baird, B. (1965). *The art of the puppet.* New York: Macmillan.
Puppets from ancient to modern times and from around the world are shown in beautiful illustrations.
Batterberry, A. (1975). *The Pantheon story of art for young children.* New York: Pantheon Books.
Overview of art history presented in simple language.
Baumann, H. (1954). *The caves of the great hunters.* New York: Pantheon Books.
This book tells the story of the discovery of the cave paintings of Lascaux, France. Use it to create a retelling of the story that will fascinate young children.
Caraway, C. (1981). *The mola design book.* Ownings Mill, MD: Stemmer House.
This book tells the history of molas as made by the women of the San Blas Islands off the coast of Panama. It includes many black-and-white drawings of mola designs.
Chan, A. (1990). *Hmong textile designs.* Owings Mills, MD: Stemmer House.
This book provides a brief history of the Hmong people of Southeast Asia, the role of textile needle art in their culture, and current directions of the art form as practiced by recent Hmong immigrants in America. Black line drawings illustrate many Hmong pieces.
D'Alleva, A. (1993). *Native American arts and cultures.* Worcester, MA: Davis.
Native American art from the past and the present are organized by region and tribe. Art is clearly described in the text accompanied by black-and-white and color photographs.
Depree, H., and MacKinnon, L. (1994). *Art, books and children.* Bothell, WA: Lands End.
This beautifully illustrated book provides many ideas for relating poetry and stories to children's art activities. It contains lists of children's books organized by topic.
Glubok, S. (1964). *The art of the American Indian.* New York: Harper & Row.

Glubok, S. (1964). *The art of the Eskimo.* New York: Harper & Row.
Glubok, S. (1965). *The art of Africa.* New York: Harper & Row.
Glubok, S. (1966). *The art of ancient Peru.* New York: Harper & Row.
Glubok, S. (1973). *The art of China.* New York: Macmillan.
These are beautifully illustrated books with simple, clear descriptions.
Greenfeld, H. (1990). *First impressions: Marc Chagall.* New York: Harry N. Abrams.
The story of Chagall's childhood and development as an artist illustrates the kinds of choices artists make in their lives.
Ivy, B. (1995). *Children's books about art.* Palo Alto, CA: Dale Seymour.
This annotated bibliography of children's books about art also provides a range of activities utilizing these books.
Janson, H. W., and Janson, A. F. (1987). *The history of art for young people.* New York: Harry E. Abrams.
This overview of art from prehistoric times to the present will provide a source of background information on changing art styles and practices.
Lyons, M. E. (1993). *Stitching stars: The story quilts of Harriet Powers.* New York: Charles Scribner's Sons.
This beautifully written book tells the story of how former slave Harriet Powers created her two unique "story quilts." Illustrated with beautiful photographs and set against the background of the history and beliefs of African-Americans, this book provides information that will enrich any discussion of American quilt making. (Part of a series titled African American Artists and Artisans.)
Rodari, F. (1991). *A weekend with Picasso.* New York: Rizzoli.
Intended for older children, this book uses facts from Picasso's life to create a fictional weekend spent with the artist. Illustrated with photographs and Picasso's artwork, it provides a rich source of information to share with young children.
Schuman, J. M. (1981). *Art from many hands.* Worcester, MA: Davis.

Although most of the art projects presented in this book are too advanced for children under eight, the information about the different folk-art forms is invaluable and can be used to create simple books about multicultural artwork. The bibliography is excellent.

Stewart, H. (1979). *Looking at Indian art of the Northwest Coast*. Toronto, Canada: Douglas & McIntyre.
An excellent guide to both past and contemporary art of the Northwest Coast tribes. This book discusses meanings of the different symbols and forms, with many illustrations of totems, carvings, garments, and paintings.

Turner, R. M. (1993). *Faith Ringgold*. New York: Little, Brown.
A beautifully illustrated biography of African American quiltmaker Faith Ringgold, this book provides background information to share with Ringgold's children's book *Tar Beach*.

Ventura, P. (1984). *Great painters*. New York: G. P. Putnam's Sons.
A cleverly illustrated overview of European painting from the Renaissance to Picasso, this book provides a general overview of the milestones of art history.

CD-ROM

The following CD-ROM can be used as a source of information about art of many kinds. Some of the reproductions of artwork can be shared with young children.

Sources include Crystal Publications: 1-800-913-8555, Sax Arts and Crafts: 1-800-522-4278, and Quality Computers: 1-800-777-3642.

Electronic Library of Art (Sony)
Exploring Modern Art : Tate Gallery (Microsoft)
History through Art Series
History and Cultures of Africa (Queue)
Microsoft Art Gallery (Microsoft)
The Ultimate Frank Lloyd Wright: America's Architect (Microsoft)

With Open Eyes: Art Works from the Chicago Institute of Art (Chicago Institute)

VIDEODISCS

Videodiscs allow access to individual pieces of information and pictures. Selected pieces of artwork can be shared with children as an occasional alternative to prints, especially in cases where a print is unavailable.

All of the following are available from Crystal Publications: 1-800-913-8555. Other sources include Sax Arts and Crafts: 1-800-522-4278, and Quality Computers: 1-800-777-3642.

American Art from the National Gallery
Ancient Egypt
Art of the Western World Series
Great Artist Series
In a Brilliant Light: Van Gogh at Arles
The National Gallery of Art
Van Gogh Revisited
With Open Eyes: Art Works fron the Chicago Institute of Art

WORLD WIDE WEB

With access to an online service or the Internet, information on art can be obtained directly from museums around the world. In some cases it is possible to tour parts of the museum or see examples from current exhibits. To share some of this with children, download the material beforehand. It takes a long time to receive graphic images and young children often lose patience. A few examples of places to "visit" include:

The Exploratorium, San Francisco
The Louvre, Paris
The Metropolitan Museum, New York City

References

Alter-Muri, S. (1994). Art eases the process of attachment and separation. *Day Care and Early Education, 22* (1), 4–11.

Amabile, T. (1983). *The social psychology of creativity.* New York: Springer-Verlag.

Arieti, S. (1976). *Creativity: The magic synthesis.* New York: Basic Books.

Arnheim, R. (1969). *Visual thinking.* Berkeley, CA: University of California Press.

Ayres, W. (1995). Teaching is an act of hope. *Teaching Tolerance, 4* (2), 22–25

Bender, S. (1989). *Plain and simple: A woman's journey to the Amish.* San Francisco: HarperCollins.

Becker, J., Reed, K., Steinhaus, P., and Week, P. (1994). *Themestorming.* Beltsville, MD: Gryphon.

Biber, B. (1984). *Early education and psychology development.* New Haven, CT: Yale University Press.

Boden, M. A. (1990). *The creative mind.* New York: Basic Books.

Bos, B. (1978). *Don't move the muffin pans.* Roseville, CA: Turn-the-Page Press.

Brandt, R. (1995). Punished by rewards?: A conversation with Alfie Kohn. *Educational Leadership, 53* (1), 13–16.

Bredekamp, S. (Ed.). (1987). *Developmentally appropriate practice in early childhood programs serving children from birth through age 8.* Washington, DC: National Association for the Education of Young Children.

Brooks, S. W., and Sentori, S. M. (1988). *See the paintings!* Rosemount, NJ: Modern Learning Press.

Bruner, J.(1979). *On knowing: essays for the left hand.* Cambridge, MA: Harvard University Press.

Bry, A. (1978). *Visualization: Directing the movies of your mind.* New York: Harper & Row.

Burn, J. R. (1989). Express it with puppetry—an international language. In S. Hoffman and L. L. Lamme (Eds.), *Learning from the inside out* (pp. 29–34). Wheaton, MD: Association for Childhood Education International.

Caine, R. N., and Caine, G. (1974). *Making connections: Teaching and the human brain.* New York: Addison-Wesley.

Cameron, J. (1992). *The artist's way: A spiritual path to higher creativity.* New York: G. P. Putnam's Sons.

Catlin, C. (1994). *Toddlers together.* Beltsville, Maryland: Gryphon.

Cecil, N. L., and Lauritzen, P. (1995). *Literacy and the arts for the integrated classroom: Alternative ways of knowing.* White Plains, NY: Longman.

Chapman, L. (1978). *Approaches to art in education.* New York: Harcourt Brace Jovanovich.

Cherry, C., Godwin, D., and Staples, J. (1989). *Is the left brain always right?* Belmont, CA: David S. Lake.

Cherry, C. (1990). *Creative art for the developing child.* Carthage, IL: Fearon Teacher Aids.

Church, E. B., and Miller, K. (1990). *Learning through play: Blocks.* New York: Scholastic.

Clemens, S. G. (1991). Art in the classroom: Making every day special. *Young Children, 46* (1), 4–11.

Cohen, E. P., and Gainer, R. S. (1976, 1995). *Art: Another language for learning.* Portsmouth, NH: Heinemann.

Colbert, C., and Taunton, M. (1992). *An NAEA briefing paper: Developmentally appropriate practices for the visual arts education of young children.* Reston, VA: National Art Education Association.

Costello, R. (Ed.). (1995). *Webster's College Dictionary.* New York: Random House.

Crary, E. (1984). *Kids can cooperate.* Seattle, WA: Parenting Press.

Davidson, J. I. (1989). *Children and computers together in the early childhood classroom.* Albany, NY: Delmar.

Dennis, W. (1966). Goodenough scores, art experience, and modernization. *Journal of Social Psychology, 68,* 213–215.

Depree, H., and Mackinnon, L. (1994). *Art, books and children.* Bothwell, WA: Lands End.

Derman-Sparks, L., and the A.B.C. Task Force. (1989). *Anti-bias curriculum: Tools for empowering young children.* Washington, DC: National Association for the Education of Young Children.

Dewey, J. (1958) *Art as experience.* New York: Capricorn Books.

Di Leo, J. H. (1970). *Young children and their drawings.* NY: Brunner/Mazel.

Dodge, D. T., and Colker, L. J. (1992). *The creative curriculum.* Washington, DC: Teaching Strategies.

Dodge, D. T., and Phinney, J. (1990). *A parent's guide to early childhood education*. Beltsville, MD: Gryphon.

Edwards, B. (1979). *Drawing on the right side of the brain*. Los Angeles: J. P. Tarcher.

Edwards, B. (1986). *Drawing on the artist within*. New York: Simon & Schuster.

Edwards, C., Gandini, L., and Forman, G. (1992). *The hundred languages of children: The Reggio Emilia approach to early childhood education*. Norwood, NJ: Ablex.

Edwards, L. C. (1990). *Affective development and the creative arts*. New York: Macmillan.

Edwards, L. C. (1993). The creative arts process: What it is and what it is not. *Young Children, 48* (3), 77–81.

Einon, D. (1985). *Play with a purpose*. New York: Pantheon.

Eisner, E. (1972). *Educating artistic vision*. New York: Macmillan.

Eisner, E. (1976). *The arts, human development and education*. Berkeley, CA: McCutchen.

Eisner, E. (1983). *Beyond creating*. Los Angeles: Getty Center for Education in Art.

Elkind, D. (1974). *Children and adolescents*. New York: Oxford University Press.

Engel, B. S. (1995). *Considering children's art: Why and how to value their works*. Washington, DC: National Association for the Education of Young Children.

Engel, B. S. (1996). Learning to look: Appreciating children's art. *Young Children. 51*, 2: 74–79

Feldman, E. B. (1970). *Becoming human through art*. Englewood Cliffs, NJ: Prentice-Hall.

Fein, S. (1976). *Heidi's horse*. Pleasant Hill, CA: Exelrod Press.

Fein, S. (1993). *First drawings: Genesis of visual thinking*. Pleasant Hill, CA: Exelrod Press.

Gardner, H. (1973). *The arts and human development*. New York: John Wiley & Sons.

Gardner, H. (1980). *Artful scribbles*. New York: Basic Books.

Gardner, H. (1982). *Art, mind and brain*. New York: Basic Books.

Gardner, H. (1983). *Frames of mind*. New York: Basic Books.

Gardner, H. (1990a). *Art education*. An invitational address at the Conference for the National Art Education Association, Kansas City, MO.

Gardner, H. (1990b). *To open minds*. New York: Basic Books.

Gardner, H. (1991). *The unschooled mind*. New York: Basic Books.

Gardner, H. (1993). *Multiple intelligences: The theory in practice*. New York: Basic Books.

Gardner, H. (1995). Reflections on multiple intelligences: Myths and messages. *Phi Delta Kappan, 77* (1), 200–209.

Gardner, H., Winter, E., and Kircher, M. (1975). Children's conceptions of the arts. *Journal of Aesthetic Education, 9* (3), 60–77.

Gelfer, J. (1990). Discovering and learning art through blocks. *Day Care and Early Education, 17* (4), 21–24.

Genishi, C. (1993). Art, portfolios and assessment, *Early Childhood Today, 8* (2), 67.

Gerhardt, Lydia A. (1973). *Moving and knowing: The young child orients himself in space*. Englewood, Cliffs, NJ: Prentice-Hall.

Goleman, D., Kaufman, P., and Ray, M. (1992). *The creative spirit*. New York: Dutton.

Golomb, C. (1981). Representation and reality. *Review of Visual Arts Education, 14*, 36–48.

Goodenough, F. L. (1926). *Children's drawings as measures of intellectual maturity*. New York: Harcourt Brace Jovanovich.

Gratz, R., and Boulton, P. (1993). Taking care of kids: A director's concerns about environmental hazards. *Day Care and Early Education, 21* (2), 29–31.

Greenberg, P. (Ed.). (1972). *Art education: Elementary*. Washington, DC: National Art Education Association.

Greenberg, P. (1992). Teaching about Native Americans? Or teaching about people including Native Americans? *Young Child, 47* (6), 27–30.

Greenfeld, H. (1990). *First impressions: Marc Chagall*. New York: Abrams.

Greenman, J. (1988). *Caring Spaces, learning places: Children's environments that work*. Redmond, WA: Exchange Press.

Harris, D., and Goodenough, F. L. (1963). *Children's drawings as measures of intellectual maturity*. New York: Harcourt, Brace & World.

Hart, K. (1994). *I can paint!* Portsmouth, NH: Heinemann.

Haugland, S. W. (1993). Are computers an important learning resource? *Day Care and Early Education, 20* (3), 30–31.

Haugland, S. W., and Shade, D. S. (1990). *Developmental evaluations of software for young children*. Albany, NY: Delmar.

Hendricks, G. (1981). *The centered teacher*. Englewood Cliffs, NJ: Prentice-Hall.

Herefore, N., and Schall, J. (Eds.). (1991) *Learning through play: Art*. New York: Scholastic.

Herman, G. N., and Hollingworth, P. (1992). *Kinetic kaleidoscope*. Tucson, AZ: Zephyr Press.

Hirsch, E. S. (Ed.). (1974). *The block book*. Washington, DC: National Association for the Education of Young Children.

Hohmann, C. (1990). *Young children and computers*. Ypsilanti, MI: High/Scope.

Hymes, J. L. (1989). *Teaching the child under six*. West Greenwich, RI: Consortium Press.

Ivy, B. (1995). *Children's books about art*. Palo Alto, CA: Dale Seymour.

Janke, R. A., and Peterson, J. P. (1995). *Peacemaker's A,B,Cs for young children*. St. Croix, MN: Growing Communities for Peace.

Jansen, H. W. (1962). *History of art*. New York: Harry N. Abrams.

Kantner, L. (1989). Beginnings: Children and their art. In S. Hoffman and L. L. Lamme (Eds.), *Learning from the inside out* (pp. 44–51). Wheaton, MD: Association for Childhood Education International.

Katz, L. G., and Chard, S. C. (1991). *Engaging children's minds: The project approach*. Norwood, NJ: Albex.

Kellogg, R. (1969). *Analyzing children's art*. Palo Alto, CA: National Press Books.

Kellogg, R. (1979). *Children's drawings/children's minds*. New York: Avon Books.

Kindler, A., and Darras, B. (1994). Artistic development in context: Emergence and development of pictorial imagery in the early childhood years. *Visual Art Research, 20,* 1–3.

Kohl, M. F. (1985). *Scribble cookies.* Bellingham, WA: Bright Ring.

Kohl, M. F. (1989). *Mudworks: Creative clay, dough, and modeling experiences.* Bellingham, WA: Bright Ring.

Kramer, E. (1971). *Art as therapy with children.* New York: Schocken Books.

Laskey, L., and Mukerji, R. (1980). *Art: Basic for young children.* Washington, DC: National Association for the Education of Young Children.

Lay-Dopyera, M., and Dopyera, J. E. (1992). Strategies for teaching. In C. Seefeldt (Ed.), *The early childhood curriculum* (pp. 16–41). New York: Teacher's College Press.

LeeKeenan, D., and Nimmo, J. (1992). Connections: Using the project approach with 2- and 3-year-olds in a university lab school. In C. Edwards, et al. (Eds.), *The hundred languages of children.* Norwood, NJ: Ablex.

Leeper, S. H., Dales, R. J., Skipper, D. S., and Witherspoon, R. L. (1974). *Good schools for young children.* New York: Macmillan.

London, P. (1991). *No more second hand art.* Boston, MA: Shambhala Press.

Lowenfeld, V., and Brittain, W. L. (1987). *Creative and mental growth.* New York: Macmillan.

Luvmour, J., and Luvmour, S. (1993). *Natural learning rhythms.* Berkeley, CA: Celestial Arts.

Marshall, H. H. (1995). Beyond "I like the way..." *Young Children, 50,* 25–28.

Mayesky, M., Neuman, D., and Wlodkowski, R. (1975). *Creative activities for young children.* Albany, NY: Delmar.

McCann, M. (1985). *Health hazards manual for artists.* New York: Nick Lyons Books.

McCormick, L., and Feeney, S. (1995). Modifying and expanding activities for children with handicaps. *Young Children, 50,* 10–16.

McFee, J. (1961). *Preparation for art.* San Francisco: Wadsworth.

McFee, J. (1978). *Visual literacy and art education.* Invitational address at the Conference for the National Art Education Association. Kansas City, MO.

McFee, J., and Deggae, R. M. (1981). *Art culture and environment: A catalyst for teaching.* Dubuque, IA: Kendall/Hunt.

McWinnie, H. J. (1992). Art in early childhood education. In C. Seefeldt (Ed.). *The early childhool curriculum* (pp. 264–285). New York: Teachers College Press.

Merryman, R. (1991). *First impressions: Andrew Wyeth.* New York: Harry N. Abrams.

Mesrobian, J. (1992). Rediscovering the Ninja Turtles' namesakes. *Day Care and Early Education, 20* (1), 18–19.

Miller, S. A. (1994). *Learning through play: Sand, water, clay & wood.* New York: Scholastic.

Mogelon, A. (1969). *One hundred ways to have fun with an alligator.* Blauvelt, NY: Art Education.

Montessori, M. (1967). *The absorbent mind.* New York: Holt, Rinehart & Winston.

Nachmanovitch, S. (1990). *Free play.* Los Angeles: Jeremy P. Tarcher.

National Association for the Education of Young Children. (1986). Position statement on developmentally appropriate practice in early childhood programs serving children from birth through age 8. *Young Children, 41* (6), 3–9.

New, R. S. (1990). Excellent early education: A city in Italy has it. *Young Children, 45* (6), 4–10.

Nilsen, B. (1996). *Week by week.* Albany, NY: Delmar.

Noyce, R. M., and Christie, J. F. (1989). *Integrating reading and writing instruction.* New York: Allyn & Bacon.

Olson, J. L. (1992). *Envisioning writing.* Portsmouth, NH: Heinemann.

Parsons, M. (1987). *How we understand art.* New York: Cambridge University Press.

Parsons, M. (1994). Can children do aesthetics? A developmental account. *Journal of Aesthetic Education, 28* (1), 33–45.

Paced, M., and Black, J. (1994). *Authentic assessment of the young child: Celebrating development and learning.* New York: Macmillan.

Paulsen, G. (1991). *The monument.* NY: Dell.

Piaget, J. (1959). *The child's conception of the world.* (J. Tomlinson and A. Tomlinson, Trans.). Savage, MD: Rowman & Littlefield. (Original work published 1929)

Piaget, J. (1967). *Six psychological studies.* (A. Tenzer, Trans.). New York: Random House. (Original work published 1964)

Pinkerton, S. (1989). Concoctions: Creative mixtures to make and enjoy. *Day Care and Early Education, 17* (2), 25–29.

Prescott, E. (1978). Is day care as good as a home? *Young Children, 33,* 13–19.

Qualley, C. A. (1986). *Safety in the art room.* New York: Davis.

Read, H. (1956). *Education through art.* New York: Pantheon Books.

Redleaf, R. (1983). *Open the door: Let's explore: Neighborhood field trips for young children.* Mt. Rainer, MD: Gryphon.

Rodriguez, S. (1984). *The special artist's handbook.* Palo Alto, CA: Dale Seymour.

Rogers, F. (1982). *Talking with families about creativity.* Pittsburg, PA: Family Communications.

Rowe, G. (1987). *Guiding young artists.* South Melbourne, Australia: Oxford University Press Australia.

Rubin, W. S. (1968). *Dada and surrealism and their heritage.* New York: Museum of Modern Art.

Saracho, O. N., and Spodek, B. (Eds.). (1983). *Understanding the multicultural experience in early childhood education.* Washington, DC: National Association for the Education of Young Children.

Schiller, M. (1995). An emergent art curriculum that fosters understanding. *Young Children, 50* (3), 33–38.

Schirrmacher, R. (1986). Talking with young children about their art. *Young Children, 41* (5), 3–7.

Schirrmacher, R. (1993). *Art and creative development for young children.* Albany, NY: Delmar.

Sciarra, D. J., and Dorsey, A. G. (1995). *Developing and administering a child care center*. Albany, NY: Delmar.

Schuman, J. M. (1981). *Art from many hands*. Worcester, MA: Davis.

Seefeldt, C. (Ed.). (1992) *The early childhood curriculum*. New York: Teachers College Press.

Seefeldt, C. (1995). A—a serious work. *Young Children. 50* (3), 39–45.

Shade, D. D. (1991). Integrating computers into the curriculum. *Day Care and Early Education, 19* (1), 45–47.

Shectman, A. E. (Ed.). (1995). *Insights: Art in special education*. Cherry Hill, NJ: Art Educators of New Jersey.

Shuman, J. M. (1981). *Art from many hands*. Worcester, MA: Davis.

Smith, N. R. (1979). How a picture means. *New Directions in Child Development. 1979* (3), 59–72.

Solomon, K. (1989). Bringing the outside in: Craftspeople share. *Day Care and Early Education, 16* (4), 26–27.

Stallings, J. (1975). Implementation and child effects of teaching practices in follow-through classrooms. *Monographs of the Society for Research in Child Development, 40* (Serial No. 163).

Stoddard, A. (1988). *Living a beautiful life*. New York: Avon Books.

Stone, J. G. (1969). *A guide to discipline*. Washington, DC: National Association for the Education of Children.

Szekely, G. (1991). *Play to art*. Portsmouth, NH: Heinemann.

Thomson, B. J. (1993). *Words can hurt you: Beginning a program of anti-bias education*. New York: Addison-Wesley.

Torrance, E. P. (1970). *Encouraging creativity in the classroom*. Dubuque, IA: William C. Brown.

Turner, T. (1990). *Whole language planning*. Transitions: SDE Sourcebook. Peterborough, NH: The Society for Developmental Education.

Tzu, Lao (1963). *Tao Te Ching*. (D.C. Lau, Trans.). New York: Viking Penquin.

United States Department of Education. (1986). *What works: Research about teaching and learning*. Washington, DC.

Vygotsky, L. S. (1978). *Mind in society*. Cambridge, MA: Harvard University Press.

Whitehead, A. N. (1929). *The aims of education*. New York: Macmillan.

Willard, C. (1972). *Frank Lloyd Wright*. New York: Macmillan.

Williams, R. A., Rockwell, R. E., and Sherwood, E. A. (1987). *Mudpies to magnets*. Mt. Rainer, MD: Gryphon.

Whitehead, A. N. (1929). *The aims of education*. New York: Macmillan.

Winkur, J. (1992). *Friendly advice*. New York: Penguin Books.

Winner, E. (1982). *Invented worlds: The psychology of the arts*. Cambridge, MA: Harvard University Press.

Winner, E. (1989). Children's perceptions of aesthetic properties in art. *British Journal of Developmental Psychology, 4*, 149–160.

Winner, E., Blank, P., Massey, C., and Gardner, H. (1983). Children's sensitivity to aesthetic properties in line drawings. In D. R. Rogers and J. A. Sloboda (Eds.), *The acquisition of symbolic skills*. London: Plenuum.

Wolf, A. D. (1984). *Mommy, it's a Renoir!* Altoona, PA: Parent Child Press.

Wolf, D. (1979). *Early symbolization*. San Francisco CA: New Directions for Child Development.

Wolf, D., and Perry, M. D. (1989). From endpoints to repertories. *Journal of Aesthetic Education, 22*, 17–34.

Zavitkovsky, D. (1994). *Docia's stories*. Redmond, WA: Child Care Information Exchange.

Index

washing up, 335
Smell, activities, 243–244
Smocks, **147**
Snacks
  as sensory activity, 245, 313
  use of artifacts for, 274
  use of pottery for, 185
Sniffing, as a risk factor, 166
Snips
  all-purpose, **220**
  for special needs, 222
Snowflake mural, 316
Social growth
  assessment through art, 359
  through cooperative art activities, 309–312
  developmentally appropriate practice and, 3
  role of art in, 7
Soda clay
  recipe for, **397**
  using for beads, 351
Software
  for art activities, 321
  defined, **327**
  selection of, 322
  sources of, **396–397**
Solvents, substitutions for, 169–170
Songs
  "The Body Shape Song," **248**
  "Colors," **233**
  "Modeling Chants," **185**
  "My Lines," **90**
  "Pasting," **213**
  "Printing Chant," **253**
  "Scissors Passing Song," **219**
  "Touch-it Song," **234**
Space
  element of, 236
  kinesthetic activities for, 248
Spatial development. *See* Visual perceptual development
Spatial Intelligence, definition of, 12
Special needs
  behavioral and emotional
    selection and placement of activities, 337
  boxes, explanation of, x
  integration into art program, 336–338
  physical
    computer use, **328**
    cutting, **222**
    hand-over-hand assistance, 337
    modifying position, tools, and materials, 337
    painting, **148**
    pasting, **214**
  planning for, 61
  visual
    color-blindness, **232**
    modeling materials, **184**
    modifying set-up, tools, and materials, 337
    use of scented materials, 244
Spindle whorl, 294
Spinning yarn, 294–295, **295**
Sponge printing, 254
Sponges
  for bubble painting, 316
  as painting tool, 152
  for printmaking, **254**
Squeeze bottles, as painting tool, 152

Stereotypes
  in artwork selection, 271
  avoidance of, 112, 333
  in holiday art, 339–340
Stick sculptures, 187
Still life, subject of, defined, **267**
Stitching, 296
Stone, J. G., 325
Stones
  as drawing surface, 91–92
  use in mosaic mural, 315
Storage areas, 112
Storycloths, Hmong, 297
Straws, drinking
  as beadmaking tool, **397**
  unsafe use of, 169
  use in play dough sculptures, 187
Studio pages, explanation of, x
Stuff bins, items for, **242**, 294
Style, defined, 229
Styrofoam
  collage, **216**
  form activity, 235
  in stuff bins, **242**
  use in stitching activities, 297
  ways to join, 171
Subject matter
  of artworks**267**, 369
  questions about, 276
  for thematic murals, 319
Supplies. *See* Materials
Surrealism, style of, 229, **266**
Symbolic play, 182
Symbolic shapes, defined, 234
Symmetrical shapes, defined, 234
Symmetry, in children's artwork, 369
Szekely, G., 5

Tacky craft glue, use of, 173
Tactile sense, 240–243
Tag board, **94**
Talc-free clay, see Firing clay
Tape, use of, **216**
Taste, activities using, 245
Teacher Tips, explanation of, x
Teacher, role of
  activity delivery and, 10
  aesthetic growth and, 230, 249–250
  anti-bias education and, 333, 334, 338, 341–342
  apprentice-master relationship, 12
  art therapy and, 340–341
  assessment and, 351
  cooperative art activities and, 312
  creativity and, 35, 37, 208–209
  extending working time, 384
  as facilitator, 56–57, **57**
  factors affecting, 35–38
  as guiding adult, defined, xii
  hand-over-hand assistance, 337
  nurturing art development, 54, 55, 57, 83
  open-ended activities, 37, 56–57
  painting activities and, 152
  as participant, 40
  personal appearance, 40
  presenting adult artwork, 272, 276–**278**, 289
  respecting children's artwork, 382
  safety and, 164, 173
  selecting work for public display, 385
  self-assessment, **379**
  sensory activities and, 238

Teacher-parent communication
  art happening, 373
  art notes, 372, **373**
  child health survey, **172**
  explanation of, x
  about guest artists, **286**
  home art
    center, **373**
    survey, **373**
  letter,
    how to respond to child's art, **53**
    about painting, **146**
  program booklet, 373
  newsletter
    use of, 373
    sample, **374**
  sample request for supplies, **217**
  summary statements, 370
  ways to talk about child's art, 373
  workshops, 374
Television, effect on child art, 38
Tempera blocks, 151
Tempera paint
  as basic art supply, 27
  to paint firing clay, 170
  to paint plaster, 171
Tempera painting. *See* Painting
Texture. *See also* Tactile sense, Sensory activities
  activities for, 233
  in appliqué, 297
  books about, 233
  description words for, **47**
  kinesthetic activities for, 248
  modeling, 187
  related science and math activities, 233
  song for, 233
Texture collage mural, 314
Texture hunt, 248
Thematic collage, 200
Thematic murals, 318–320
Thematic teaching
  combined with project approach, 143
  displaying artwork produced, 384–385
  example of, **18–22**
  fiber art focus, 292
  initiating a unit, 138
  organization of unit, 134–140
  planning a unit, 137–138
  purpose of, 14
  relating color to theme, 149
  selection of activities, 136–137
  selection of theme, 134–136
  topic web, 155–156
  unit plan format, 158–159
  using masks in, 348
  using string puppets, 347
Thomson, B. J., 338, 343
Three-dimensional activities. *See also* Architecture; Blocks; Boxes; Modeling; Puppets
  using form, 235–236
  using photography with, 364, 366
Three-dimensional art, mounting methods, **385**
Three-dimensional forms, description of, **118**, 235
Three-year-olds
  characteristics of, 4
  cognitive growth of, 79
  drawing skill development, 74–75, 76
  promoting cooperative behaviors in, 309–311

Index of Artists and Artwork